EXTINCTION AND
RELIGION

RELIGION AND THE HUMAN
Winnifred Sullivan and Lisa Sideris

EXTINCTION AND RELIGION

EDITED BY
Jeremy H. Kidwell
AND
Stefan Skrimshire

INDIANA UNIVERSITY PRESS

This book is a publication of

Indiana University Press
Office of Scholarly Publishing
Herman B Wells Library 350
1320 East 10th Street
Bloomington, Indiana 47405 USA

https://iupress.org

© 2024 by Trustees of Indiana University

All rights reserved

No part of this book may be reproduced or utilized in any form or by any means, electronic or mechanical, including photocopying and recording, or by any information storage and retrieval system, without permission in writing from the publisher. The paper used in this publication meets the minimum requirements of the American National Standard for Information Sciences—Permanence of Paper for Printed Library Materials, ANSI Z39.48–1992.

Manufactured in the United States of America

First printing 2024

Cataloging information is available from the Library of Congress.

ISBN 978-0-253-06846-0 (hdbk.)
ISBN 978-0-253-06847-7 (pbk.)
ISBN 978-0-253-06849-1 (web PDF)

*This book is dedicated to the memory of
Deborah Bird Rose.*

CONTENTS

Foreword / Catherine Keller   ix

Acknowledgments   xiii

Introduction: Questioning Extinction, Questioning Religion / *Jeremy H. Kidwell and Stefan Skrimshire*   1

1. Loving Swarms: Religious Ethics amid Mass Extinction / *Willis Jenkins*   16
2. Absence and (Unexpected) Presences: Reflecting on Cosmopolitical Entanglements across Time / *Jeremy H. Kidwell*   60
3. Sacred Waters, Sacred Earth: Contemporary Paganism inside Extinction Rebellion; A Relational Analysis of Protest Death Rituals / *Maria Nita*   98
4. Replanting a Tree of Peace: Naturalizing Relations in an Age of Extinction / *Timothy B. Leduc*   139
5. A World in Exile? Extinction, Migration, and Eschatology / *Stefan Skrimshire*   178
6. Oceanic Extinctions and the Dread of the Deep / *Kate Rigby*   213
7. Praising Salmon: Creaturely Discernment in a Time of Species Metacide / *James Hatley*   247
8. Resisting De-extinction: The Uses and Misuses of Wonder / *Lisa H. Sideris*   293

Bibliography   333

Index   365

FOREWORD
Catherine Keller

EXTINCTION AND RELIGION? WHAT DOES this distinctive pairing, an anthological first, portend? Your initial reaction to the title might be *Well, yes, the mass extinctions now underway do bear a certain analogy to the state of religion.* But no, these essays do not belabor the precarious future of religion. They face the greater question—at once more primal and more final—of the death of countless species, just possibly including our own. This is not a question I want, or even quite know how, to face. When writing about ecological degradation through these decades of its intensification, I far more frequently specify climate change than extinction. In this, I am typical of environmental thought in religion or theology. Yet anthropogenic climate crisis comes enfolded in the same period's extinction spasm. Does the discourse of global warming veil with a certain abstraction the tragic creaturely particularity of extinction? After all, it is *extinction*, at once so singular and so multiple, that names the embodied effects, the life-or-death stakes, of planetary warming, melting, degrading—hence the unique and manifold importance of this volume.

Extinction and Religion interrogates the meaning of *extinction*, its epochal particularities, its multiplicities, its worlds. In each essay, "religion" is revealed—differently—as entangled in the human framing and practice of those worlds. It is read variously as driver, prophecy, warning, sanctification, repression, and interpretation of extinction. It has served to justify human causes of extinction or to resist them. Therefore, critical attention to religion's relation to the interdependent life of all of us terrestrial species pervades the startling richness of these essays. The volume exudes a shadowy beauty: as you read, a saltmarsh sparrow flickers by, a run of salmon swarms along, a melting glacier is mourned. The essays never retreat into tones of scientific neutrality or devolve into a fanfare of the freaky facts. And they have no recourse to a preachy ecomoralism, let alone a promise of providential rescue. Nor do they rehash the familiar denunciations of the Genesis dominion or of Christian habits of otherworldliness. They probe with nuance the sanctifications of a civilization's deadening use of its own materiality. And they attend also to "the emergence of novel forms of life" (Kidwell, chap. 2). In their varying postsecularity, these essays probe the depths, the grounds, and the collective lives of a process of irreducibly complex materializations. The prehuman history of prior extinctions echoes in the present spasm, where the entwined lives of endangered species, including that of the prime endangerer, signal not just threat but vibrancy. Therefore, the present writhes with widely divergent possible futures—futures that refuse to abstract themselves from wildly different species, inseparable from each other in their fatality and indeterminacy.

Just to raise the question of religion and extinction, however, triggers the signifier of the greatest fatality: Isn't the apocalypse the ultimate story of extinction? The Christian Bible, that most influential of books, runs from the alpha of creation to the omega of apocalypse. If its prophecy of the collapse of Earth life—a mass dis-creation—is not predictive of our moment, does it function as a self-fulfilling prophecy of doom? I have long queried the apocalypse habit of Western civilization, with its normalization of any level of systemic violence, and for almost as long have recognized the symbolism of imperial power and economic greed that foments revolutionary struggles and leaps toward ecosocial justice. Any apocalyptic signal emitted by the present volume carries the original meaning of *apocalypsis* as unveiling disclosure, more interesting than mere closure. As another timely text puts it: "The Anthropocene is the Apocalypse, in both the etymological and the eschatological senses. Interesting times, indeed."[1] Indeed, the Book of Revelation ends neither in The End, mere extinction, nor in a return to Eden, but in a radical urban renewal of the Earth, specific in its multinational polity, its ecology of urban orchard and fresh water "free for all to drink." There is no total extinction, no utopian guarantee, but a voice of the ancient thirst for a just and sustainable world.[2] While the present volume does not get tangled in the apocalypse, Stefan Skrimshire has elsewhere brilliantly captured its conflicting deployments, its resonance with ecological disaster, indeed its capacity to inspire a nonviolent militance as "activism for end-times."[3]

Extinction and Religion steers us away from the totalizing question of The End, indeed of The World. Reflections on specific crises and contexts of extinction keep bringing us back to specific bodies buzzing and blurring into each other and so into their specific worlds—into *our* specific worlds. Perhaps it is this creepy concreteness that makes reflection on extinction now crucial, neither to be boxed under climate change nor to compete with it for attention. The two or three degrees of warming, the quantifiable economic causes, are set to deliver terrifyingly concrete effects on bodies assembled within and across species. And the inverse is also true: the great loss of species life, botanic and zoomorphic, oceanic and terrestrial, alters the atmosphere, affecting its ability to absorb excess carbon and depriving it of the oxygen we breathe. But as this book makes clear, a discourse of extinction can also lock into a numbing abstraction. Our lack of proximity, or of awareness thereof, to threatened species can trap them into codes of fetish or distance.

This volume's strategy for relating religion to creaturely vulnerability works to undermine that distance—to give flesh to the abstraction-prone data of environmental catastrophe. It sensitively fosters mourning what has already gone extinct. It warns of what may and what will yet go. And it unveils a mysterious persistence and an irrepressible creativity within and on behalf of Earth's collective of species. Indeed, the dark and disarming eloquence of this anthology invites what it performs: a renewed and renewing attention to our creaturely cohabitation of each other—both human and vastly otherwise.

NOTES

1. Déborah Danowski and Eduardo Viveiros Castro, *The Ends of the World* (Cambridge, UK: Polity Press, 2017), 22.
2. See Catherine Keller, *Facing Apocalypse: Climate, Democracy and Other Last Chances* (Maryknoll: Orbis, 2021).
3. Stefan Skrimshire, "Activism for End Times: Millenarian Belief in an Age of Climate Emergency," *Political Theology* 20, no. 6 (2019): 518–536.

ACKNOWLEDGMENTS

MOST OF THE CHAPTERS IN this book are the fruit of a series of workshops that were held at the University of Birmingham and University College, Cork, between 2018 and 2019. The editors would like to thank David Farrier and Michelle Bastian—our invited "critical friends"—for their generous conversations and astute observations and Anne-Marie Culhane, our resident artist and facilitator. Thanks also to the conveners of the Society for the Study of Religion, Nature and Culture annual conference at Cork, Ireland, where aspects of the book were presented and debated. We are grateful to the Arts and Humanities Research Council, which funded these workshops and conference participation.

EXTINCTION AND RELIGION

INTRODUCTION

Questioning Extinction, Questioning Religion

JEREMY H. KIDWELL AND STEFAN SKRIMSHIRE

HAS THERE EVER BEEN a piece of news as harrowing and disorienting as the claim that human activities have precipitated a time of *mass extinction* and that this process of destruction may prove to be equal in magnitude to the catastrophes that wiped out the dinosaurs many millions of years ago? The idea proposed by biologists of a "sixth mass extinction" has been around for a long time, of course. It is already a regular feature of media reporting, nature documentaries, and scholarly discussions. And yet, in spite of this steady drip of information, it seems—at least to the authors of this volume—as if scholars have only just begun to take full measure of the impacts that the extinction crisis has had and continues to have on human cultures and the beliefs, values, and doctrines that underpin them. This book is a first step toward addressing a double lacuna: the paucity of explicit engagement with religion in extinction research and the paucity of explicit engagement with mass extinction in religious studies research. A range of questions and ambiguities present themselves: What does living in a "time of extinctions" mean to us? How is that meaning framed by religion? And how is religion—in its doctrines, practices, identities, and legacies to secular cultures—impacted by it?

In pursuit of such questions, we began the research project that produced this volume by *questioning extinction*, not just in scholarly fora but also in everyday spaces and grassroots contexts. This questioning orientation arose from fieldwork with Extinction Rebellion (XR) activists, artists, faith leaders, and scholarly research seminars and public-facing workshops hosted between 2018 and 2020. Across all these contexts, we found that the word *extinction* often referred to quite sharply different things to different people. In some cases, the key concern related to the extinction of the human species. For others, it referred to quite specific regional creatures and habitats. There were also cases where the concept was left unspecified—an undefined horizon of anxieties and concerns about the future of life on our planet. We concluded that not only conceptually but also in its emotional registers, extinction is grasped, understood, and communicated in ways that sometimes appear paradoxical if not merely vague. In spite of this, we often also found an unusual level of solidarity around the demands of the extinction crisis and an implicit sensibility that everyone is working off the same script. So while a quite lively plural sense of extinction may be lurking in the background, people are being galvanized into action due to a shared and somewhat straightforward concern that is perhaps centered on the value of life.

Of course, as a number of other projects and studies have highlighted, there *are* many different faces to extinction. One might choose to begin with the technical criteria provided by the International Union for Conservation of Nature and Natural Resources, particularly those many species now marked "extinct" on their regularly updated Red List of Threatened Species, such as the splendid poison frog (*Oophaga speciosa*) or the dodo (*Raphus cucullatus*). Interestingly, none of our authors focus on iconic endangered species, though there is a discussion of the desire to *revive* some of them (Sideris, chap. 8), a focus on those lesser mourned because they are lesser known (Jenkins, chap. 1), and a plea to consider in a different light those of the mysterious "oceanic deep" (Rigby, chap. 6). In conservation studies, there are overlapping categories of *extinct in the wild* and *regionally extinct*, making the boundaries of extinction even more fuzzy. Many endangered species, including those now referred to as "ghost species"—such as the last two remaining and same-sex white rhinos—rely on habitats and microclimates that are irrevocably lost so that their eventual extinction is inevitable. The meaning of extinction does not stop at the level of species. There are now landscapes and landforms such as glaciers facing extinction (Kidwell, chap. 2). Furthermore, the death of languages, cultures, and other forms of memory are recognized to be inseparable—as both cause and effect—from those losses of so many life relations (Leduc, chap. 4). As we move further along this continuum toward imagined extinctions and extinction-as-metaphor, we find an increasingly wide range of losses (Hatley, chap. 7), culminating in what is for many activists and scholars the ultimate concern: the loss of human life, or, more ambiguously, the collapse of civilization (Nita, chap. 3).

There are a range of possible reactions to this inherently pluralistic approach to extinction. On the one hand, it might be tempting to form a working group and develop the one true definition, excluding all others as reflecting a different *kind* of concern. There is, justifiably, strong criticism of such attempts. Some scholars, including authors in this volume, would argue precisely that the search for a universal definition partakes in those tendencies that are connected to the extinction crisis itself—an internal loss of diversity that spreads outward. Another option might be to develop a relativistic account of extinction that is so generic that it includes all phenomena labeled as such. Steering between such extremes, another prior research project, the Extinction Studies Working Group, which has some overlapping membership with our project team, argued that "there is no singular phenomenon of extinction; rather, extinction is experienced, resisted, measured, enunciated, performed, and narrated in a variety of ways to which we must attend."¹ Their response to this complexity was to focus on stories as a nexus containing "detailed case studies of complex processes of loss, exploring the 'entangled significance' of extinction" in "specific sites of loss."² Key to their approach was paying attention to particular human-nonhuman (moral and material) entanglements in specific locations where particular creatures have disappeared or are facing extinction. Reflecting in a similar way, another working group surmised that extinction is a resolutely anthropological affair. Extinction stories, they suggest, are also about the loss of "indigenous languages, vehicles of entire cosmologies."³ Both of these volumes also highlight the ways extinction can carry forward in a number of registers. This includes the sort of mourning that is driven by a reckoning with loss but also an awareness that extinction, as Charles Darwin himself believed, was a phenomenon that can be "generative, as well as degenerative," as "the coterminous extinctions of biotic species, indigenous cultures, and specific cultural formations ... create voids that direct attention to certain paths forward and are filled by emergent forms of life."⁴ So, it is possible to swing from the register of lament toward something more positive: "The destructiveness of extinction to social group cohesion, livelihoods, and ecosystems can simultaneously be productive, insofar as it may yield new thoughts about temporality and existence, inspire creativity, propel technological advancement, and mobilize social movements."⁵ Our authors also engage their writing with a wide spectrum of responses to extinction, from gut-wrenching lament (Hatley, chap. 7) to gleeful excitement (Sideris, chap. 8). And in the midst of this potentially confusing array of responses, it becomes all the more important to articulate, as many of our authors do, the ethical and political dimensions of extinction—for instance, the need to consider the global extinction crisis not as a tragic inevitability but as an act of ecocide made possible by global systems of injustice and exploitation.

What is interesting across these and many other subsequent explorations of extinction is the near-universal lack of references to religion. Authors may implicitly include religion and spirituality among other features of *culture*. They might reference culturally specific rituals of death and mourning, for instance, or ceremonial practices of indigenous cultures. But religious ways of knowing and critical framings of religiosity are rarely explicitly in view in scholarly treatments of extinction. Given all this plurality and ambiguity, it might be reasonable to question the wisdom of bringing a potentially contested concept like religion into what is already such a chaotic space. Yet, as we explored this question in our research, we were consistently struck by how religion often appears implicitly in the cracks of extinction studies, where one finds ghosts, resurrections, rituals of lament, and questions of affective self-transcendence. Often, what might be called religious frames appear to tacitly consolidate or organize concern about extinction and lurk just behind scholarly framings but are never explicitly addressed.

This lurking of religion among extinctions is true not just of scholarly discourse but also in public. In a similar way, extinction itself has implicitly provoked the formation of what might also be called, without disparagement, new religious movements. To take one example, the manifesto for the Dark Mountain Project, written by Paul Kingsnorth and Dougald Hine in 2009, highlights the way that "religion . . . that bag of myths and mysteries . . . was straightened out into a framework of universal laws and moral account-keeping."[6] The authors have gone on to highlight the ways that ecological crisis and extinction in particular are a result of a great failure of imagination and call for new forms of ritual and mythmaking in response, including "religious stories that used to be at the heart of our culture."[7] Such a response has been witnessed more recently in the appetite for ceremony, ritual, and liturgical forms of protests within XR—the international activist movement that began in the United Kingdom in 2016.[8]

Perhaps more than any other ecologically focused social movement, extinction activism seems to have revitalized a desire for performative engagements with death and mourning, as publics seek both intelligible and visceral responses to the extinction crisis (Nita, chap. 3). Some of these engage liturgies of "established" religious institutions, whereas others are more syncretistic and performatively fluid.

A more prominent though less overtly religious example can be found in the Deep Adaptation movement sparked by a 2018 paper written by Cumbria University Professor of Sustainability Leadership Jem Bendell. After summarizing recent climate change and extinction research, Bendell surmises that it is "sobering that humanity has arrived . . . where we now debate the strength of analyses of our near-term extinction."[9] The piece is noteworthy for its attention to "emotional and psychological responses" to environmental crises and recourse to spirituality as a resource.[10] In confronting the hopelessness that environmental crises can precipitate, Bendell points to the potential for adaptation and the pursuit of new culturally generated "alternative hopes" alongside the acceptance of unpredictable futures and of death and a redirection of spiritual energies toward clear-eyed reflection on the end times.[11] In a way, so-called post-denial attitudes toward "Inevitable Near Term Human Extinction" serve as the successor to late-modern philosophical conceptions of the sublime.[12] That is, extinction has come to signify not just one ecological crisis among others but the horizon of all our concerns, a catalyst for reflection on matters of ultimate importance. As Bendell suggests, it can "lead me to focus on truth, love and joy in the now" or "it can also make me lose interest in planning for the future."[13]

These examples reflect a broad sympathy for religious or spiritual orientations to crisis, often in response to what they perceive as the secular roots of Western crisis response. In today's context, such secularism might refer to the persistent belief that technological ingenuity, some Green version of neoliberalism, genetic de-extinction (as Sideris addresses, chap. 8), or the colonization of other planets will save us. In this sense, we are seeing an emerging extinction awareness that is arguably already postsecular and very consciously seeking discursive and imaginative frameworks that lie outside of secular reason. For scholars of religion in the public sphere, this is interesting in its own right. For religious insiders and particularly those already committed to taking some sort of action on the ecological crisis, it clearly looks like religion is being *mobilized* in response to the extinction crisis. This can be seen as an extension of what sociologists Conrad L. Kanagy and Fern K. Willits first called the "greening of religion."[14] But there is another side to the phenomenon we are describing. For many people, including those who consider themselves to be located outside religion (personally or academically), the extinction crisis pushes the meanings of religion and its interaction with publics in new directions. It is arguably the latter concern that has most motivated this book.

If it is true that religion is becoming increasingly visible as a public, performative, or discursive mode of responding to extinction, an important preliminary question arises: Whose religion is this? As several of our authors acknowledge, contemporary movements of extinction protest are not globally representative or even, some argue, diverse. The demographic of the leadership and membership of groups can often be overwhelmingly white and higher-income. This provokes a deeper question as to the connection of extinction and *religions*. Is extinction everybody's concern, or does the very framing of the problem in the language of possible "human extinction" belie a certain white, Global North conceptualization of otherwise intersectional protests that go under other names?

A recent attempt to describe extinction activism as a "global" movement can illustrate this point. XR's debut in the United Kingdom was linked by some in the print media with a very different mobilization on the other side of the Atlantic in the same year: the Indigenous uprising against the Dakota Access Pipeline running through ancestral land in the Standing Rock Sioux reservation. Journalists were evidently delighted by what this comparison offered to a global extinction narrative. Indigenous peoples have themselves faced extinction, and extinction of their cultures, knowledge, and practices will also spell threats to ecosystems to which such knowledge is bound.[15] But Indigenous scholars themselves have cast suspicion over the categories of both extinction and religion, precisely because the implied ghettoization of religious belief on the one hand and the hard scientific facts of the extinction crisis on the other are problematic. XR's relationship with religion, while in many ways novel (see Nita, chap. 3), follows a familiar pattern in European environmental activism whereby religious rituals serve to draw attention to or accompany telling the (scientific) truth about climate change. On the other hand, Standing Rock was described *first and foremost* as a prayer camp, enacting the ancestral right to practice defense of life on sacred land. Its participants called themselves not activists but Water Protectors, and their actions were in defense of land, water, custom, and belief.[16] So while activists in Global North cultures (such as XR) might be accustomed to conceptually distinguishing religious practice from environmental action, this appears like something of a category mistake for many other cultures around the world. What this comparison reveals, therefore, is that we need to explore not only how extinction might relate to religion (and vice versa) but also how the moment we are in challenges the very way in which we think about the relation between those words. As Timothy B. Leduc argues in chapter 4, our understanding of religion as a way of life is bound up with the historic colonial roots of our understandings of nature and place and the resulting conceptions of extinction that follow.

Where does religion exist? Is it in what certain people do (its public performances) or what they believe (the privacy of faith)?

How could one test whether a given phenomenon is a distinctively religious (and not merely cultural) thing? And how is our judgment of what counts as religion framed by a certain cultural experience of dominant religions? In light of the unexpected (to sociologists of the Global North) resurgence of religion in the twentieth and twenty-first century globally,[17] these are not idle questions. Furthermore, the legacy of modern ways of thinking about religion sketched earlier—that is, the legacy of secularism (e.g., as easily identifiable, measurable, and separable from other phenomena)—weighs heavily on the kinds of questions that have so far addressed species extinction and religion. For sociologists of religion and those identifying more broadly with the study of religion, the practices and behaviors of people who identify as "religious" really matter. It matters a great deal what counts as religious if we want to find out, for instance, to what extent religious practitioners change their behavior in light of the specter of a planetary extinction crisis or whether their holy scripture speaks to the challenge of the crisis and offers guidance. Such scholars want to know what identifiably religious people and institutions are doing about or how they are impacted by anthropogenic extinctions. This would necessarily open a vast field of research. In *The Routledge Handbook of Religion and Ecology*, the editors impressively capture the particularities of ecological thought, not only of specific traditions with their doctrines but also of specific place-based and problem-based approaches. What is fascinating in such a survey approach is that it parallels the very way that the category of religion is increasingly seen to defy simplistic binary definitions. Especially when explored in relation to specific ecological contexts and problems, the traditional divisions of religion as private versus public and belief versus practice and references to the transcendent versus the material really start to break down. It is notable that in similar ways, it has increasingly become the case that the environmental sciences have acknowledged that the concept of extinction is at work in multiple and overlapping contexts rather than constituting an easily identified and specific ecological problem.

In light of such challenges, we have become skilled at knowing what sort of study we are *not* engaged in with this volume. We have not sought to represent specific faith traditions' teachings about a phenomenon that is, as we have argued, only just beginning to register at the level of public discourse. One cannot interrogate what scriptures, doctrines, or ritual practices have to say about the extinction crisis in the same way that one interrogates what they have to say about animal cruelty, deforestation, or pollution. Extinction is also different from a number of other issues in environmental ethics. On the other hand, the extinction crisis is implicated in so many of these adjacent issues both as cause and effect. Perhaps extinction can mean multiple things to people in different contexts precisely because it is implicated in pretty much all of our lives, even if it is not conceived or discussed as such. We might consider extinction as something like one of Timothy Morton's "hyperobjects"—an entity that both defines our existence and is too big to theorize independently of ourselves. This ambiguity does not drive one away from religious or theological forms of thought. However, appreciating this requires some reflection on the relationship between *certainty* and the lived complexity of these traditions. The status of extinction as an elusive meta concept relates to specific affective responses. We can fear hyperobjects for their hegemony and for the introduction of persistent forms of uncertainty and ambiguity, as Morton suggests. Alternatively, as Catherine Keller asserts, we can find the pursuit of "some practice of mindful unknowing" to be a salutary exercise.[18] And this turn need not imply an anti- or postreligious formulation. Extinction, in its all-encompassing nature, does not *necessarily* press us toward a more postreligious space. Rather, it unexpectedly implicates religion in a way that forces the latter back to some of its most fundamental principles—the study of "ultimate things" or a questioning of the very building blocks of religious explanation—which are more familiar to theological and philosophical study: creation, time, life, death, the human, God, the apocalypse.

There have been some prior attempts in theological scholarship to address a theology of (species) extinctions alongside discussions of evolution and suffering.[19] A theology of mass extinction would be a very different endeavor from the one we have undertaken in this project. While the essays in this volume do not seek to provide this, neither do our inquiries rule out the possibility of such a thing. A number of chapters contribute something to a kind of theologically attuned debate. Some of our authors discuss what the reality of mass extinction does to beliefs in the goodness of creation (Hatley, chap. 7; Skrimshire, chap. 5), while others directly comment on the relevance of theological ethics (Jenkins, chap. 1) and theological notions of the creaturely (Sideris, chap. 8). And some discuss whether the prospect of human extinction tallies already with eschatological and apocalyptic narratives or simply mobilizes it in new imaginative and activist ways (Nita, chap. 3; Skrimshire, chap. 5). These approaches are also reversible. We can ask whether and how a certain theological framing of the world affects the ways that we perceive the extinction crisis itself. There are arguably presentiments of apocalyptic, eschatology, wonder, mystery, faith, or hope lurking inside some of the more secular responses to extinction, from the search for solutions to the predictions of the future.

Any mention of theology in this context reminds us that belief comes from particular (albeit dynamic and fluid) traditions and that any attempt to speak to the question of faith, belief, or religion *in general* is bound to sneak in the prejudices of a particular tradition as representative of the whole. This is one of the reasons we have not attempted to represent distinctive faith traditions in the project. We also struggled with our use of *religion* in the title, since we were so clearly not providing a comprehensive representation of a diversity of religious traditions.

Many of these chapters comment directly or indirectly on Jewish and Christian traditions, and all the authors are residents of the Global North whose conceptualization of religion is steeped in a Christian-centrism. As scholars working within certain cultural and religious contexts, such biases must come to the fore and be interrogated for what they are. We quite consciously want to interrogate what the category *religion* has come to mean and by what means it is now being co-opted through the European dominance of that discourse. Neither does our volume attempt to tackle head-on a crucial dimension of this broader topic: the entanglement of religion with contemporary nationalisms, right-wing political movements, and white supremacists, all of which play a continuing role in current drivers of extinction.

Nevertheless, *questioning religion* in the context of mass extinction means, for the authors of this volume, examining what legacies of the term *religion* are radically undermined, challenged by, reaffirmed, or call for reinterpretation. This means questioning not only the mostly Christian-centric language of religion that inhabits such discussions but also the historical and continuing legacy of colonial religion and theologically underwritten racism as themselves drivers of global extinction. Religion might well signify for some people an expression of those death-dealing forces upon the Earth that are the very focus of extinction studies—that is, as inextricable from colonial practices in virtually every continent that led directly and indirectly to the extinction of life forms, including Indigenous human cultures and populations. For us, as white, European, and American scholars researching a topic that is explicitly linked to a history of capitalism, extractivism, and environmental injustice, it is imperative to acknowledge the ongoing role in such injustices of ideologies that frequently go under the name, if not the legacy, of religion. The questions raised by such persistence are complex and not easily resolved or resolvable. Even though they are all specialists in these subjects in various ways, the authors of this volume share a sentiment that the task of thinking about religion and extinction proved more intellectually and emotionally challenging than was first expected. The careful labor needed to unpack those questions is reflected in the length of some of the chapters, they are longer than some edited volumes, to be sure, but richly rewarding.

It is also fair to say that each chapter in this volume is testimony to the *persistence* of the power of religion—via a critical consideration of the doctrines, practices, identities, and legacies of which we have experience—in shaping how publics are facing the extinction crisis. And for many of us, the task is also to identify, where we can, those elements of religious life that, in responding to them, point away from, not toward, the death-dealing cultures that give rise to it.

—☙—

A thinker whose scholarly influence and personal friendship looms large for several authors of this book is that pioneer of extinction studies, the late Deborah Bird Rose. She passed away at the same time that we first met as a group, and that news reached us even as her insights were being shared around the table. In the construction of this book, we have often pondered a connection that she makes, in *Wild Dog Dreaming: Love in a Time of Extinctions* (2011), between extinction and religion. Rose wonders whether—if it is true (as conservation biologist Michael Soulé puts it) that we "save what we love"—humans might be capable of loving the very creatures and ecosystems that they are also destroying. For "love," she says, is "complex and full of problems as well as possibilities." But then, in a following paragraph, writing of her constant fascination with religion as a source of ethics, she says her approach has always been "seeking meeting points between what I value in religion and what I love in the world."[20] Perhaps the intention of this book is to extend the connection that is latent if not explicit in the way Rose makes it. For religion, too, is "complex and full of problems as well as possibilities."

Perhaps our task is to begin discerning where religion leads us in our engagements with extinction and where extinction leads us in our engagements with religion—and to discern, in both directions, where the dangers lurk.

NOTES

1. Deborah Bird Rose, Thom van Dooren, and Matthew Chrulew, "Introduction," in *Extinction Studies: Stories of Time, Death, and Generations*, ed. Rose, van Dooren, and Chrulew (New York: Columbia University Press, 2017), 2–3.
2. Rose et al., "Introduction," 3.
3. Genese Marie Sodikoff, "Introduction," in *The Anthropology of Extinction*, ed. Sodikoff (Bloomington: Indiana University Press, 2012), 1.
4. Cited in Sodikoff, "Introduction," 3.
5. Sodikoff, "Introduction," 3.
6. Paul Kingsnorth and Dougald Hine, "Uncivilisation: The Dark Mountain Manifesto," Dark Mountain Project, accessed May 24, 2022, https://dark-mountain.net/about/manifesto/.
7. "The Myth of Progress: An Interview with Paul Kingsnorth," *Emergence Magazine*, August 22, 2018, https://emergencemagazine.org/interview/the-myth-of-progress/.
8. Stefan Skrimshire, "Extinction Rebellion and the New Visibility of Religious Protest," Open Democracy, May 12, 2019, https://www.opendemocracy.net/en/transformation/extinction-rebellion-and-new-visibility-religious-protest/.
9. Jim Bendell, "Deep Adaptation: A Map for Navigating Climate Tragedy," rev. 2nd ed. Initiative for Leadership and Sustainability paper, July 27, 2020, https://www.lifeworth.com/deepadaptation.pdf.
10. Bendell, "Deep Adaptation."
11. Bendell, "Deep Adaptation."
12. Bendell, "Deep Adaptation."
13. Bendell, "Deep Adaptation."
14. Kanagy, C. L., and F. K. Willits. "A 'Greening' of Religion? Some Evidence from a Pennsylvania Sample," *Social Science Quarterly* 74, no. 3 (1993): 674–683.
15. Gene Ray, "Resisting Extinction: Standing Rock, Eco-Genocide, and Survival," accessed May 24, 2022, https://www.documenta14.de/en

/south/25218_resisting_extinction_standing_rock_eco_genocide_and_survival.

16. See Nick Estes and Jaskiran Dhillon, eds., *Standing with Standing Rock* (Minneapolis: University of Minnesota Press, 2019).

17. Scott M. Thomas, *The Global Resurgence of Religion and the Transformation of International Relations* (London: Palgrave Macmillan, 2005).

18. Catherine Keller, *Cloud of the Impossible: Negative Theology and Planetary Entanglement* (New York: Columbia University Press, 2015), 276.

19. See Christopher Southgate, *The Groaning of Creation: God, Evolution, and the Problem of Evil* (Louisville, KY: Westminster John Knox, 2008).

20. Rose, *Wild Dog Dreaming: Love and Extinction* (Charlottesville: University of Virginia Press, 2013), 16.

ONE

LOVING SWARMS

Religious Ethics amid Mass Extinction

WILLIS JENKINS

MASS EXTINCTION BEARS A CULTURAL depth that might be described as religious. Involving eons of time and stories about ends of life, mass extinction is an epic knot of evolutionary and cultural histories. Indeed, in popular culture, extinctions and the responses they elicit are often described using religious vocabularies (e.g., *apocalypse, lament, atonement, resurrection*). In the field of religion and ecology, however, scholars seldom develop sustained interpretive engagement with extinctions. Our work often invokes anthropogenic mass extinction as an indicator of deep trouble with humanity, standing with climate change as a leading example of some rupture in relationships that calls for religious response. Yet whereas climate change has stimulated diverse forms of religious creativity and attracted detailed analyses from religious ethics, less attention is paid to extinctions. Why?

I initially pursue that question in this chapter by discussing a particular imperiled species, Saltmarsh Sparrow, and a particular religious tradition, the North Atlantic form of Christianity that currently inhabits Saltmarsh Sparrow territory. In part II, I counterpoint that way of framing the inquiry by turning to indistinct swarms—of insects and of religion. Global insect decline deepens the challenge to conceptualizing extinctions, while the range of cultural response to it points to alternative notions of religion within which scholars may find new convocations of practice and politics.

This essay proceeds in two parts in order to query the conceptions of extinction and of religion at work in making the connection between them. Working first with a tradition-based version of religion and a species-death case of extinction, I develop a line of inquiry with familiar conceptions: What does Christian ethics have to say about the imminent loss of Saltmarsh Sparrow? In the second part, I reconsider the lead concepts by developing a more complex meshwork of extinction and an affect-oriented account of religion as murmuration. Here I consider the swarm as a form of life whose diminishments may be felt in dread and as a metaphor for spontaneous associations of cosmological meaning-making.

Understanding the relation of religion and extinctions matters because, as Ursula Heise writes in *Imagining Extinction*, accounts of extinction "gain sociocultural traction to the extent that they become part of the stories that human communities tell about themselves: stories about their origins, their development, their identity, and their future horizons."[1] Although Heise has little to say about religion, many of the stories that human communities tell about their origins and identity involve religion in some form. How religious inheritances shape imaginations of extinction and what possibilities may be opened from traditions of moral thought should bear expansive significance. If the reason for neglecting religion is that there is little to find, perhaps because communities are not incorporating contemporary extinctions into their central stories of meaning and purpose, then that indifference or incompetence is its own significant biocultural production. Insofar as mass extinction is "entangled with human ways of being in the world," it is also entangled with all the ways religion animates, influences, or haunts humans' ways of being.[2]

PART I: "HIS EYE IS ON THE SPARROW": CHRISTIAN ETHICS AND SALTMARSH SPARROW

Consider the sparrow—specifically, Saltmarsh Sparrow, which lives along the East Coast of North America. Named after its habitat, this creature's unique and only home is the salt-marsh meadows of the Atlantic littoral zone. Once an extensive and resilient feature of the Atlantic coast, those meadows are now pinched between rapid sea-level rise and hardened shoreline developments. Diminished in size and altered in function by centuries of coastal engineering, remaining salt-marsh habitats are threatened by rising seas. As its home is inundated, Saltmarsh Sparrow faces likely extinction within a couple decades.

Declining by about 9 percent per year, their population has probably collapsed by more than 75 percent since 1990, meriting escalation from Vulnerable to Endangered on the International Union for the Conservation of Nature Red List.[3] While there might be fifty thousand individuals still singing their song, because they are tied to a disappearing habitat, ornithologists see little chance of Saltmarsh Sparrow surviving beyond the middle of this century.[4] The vulnerability of this creature lies in its reproductive connection with spartina marsh grasses and the expected rhythm of flood tides. It nests midway up the grass column, just above mean tide lines and just below predator sight lines. And it nests between lunar flood tides, with the period from laying and incubating eggs to nursing fledglings capable of climbing out of flooded nests (twenty-three to twenty-seven days) timed to fit just inside the twenty-eight-day span between flood tides.[5]

With the growing frequency of unusually high tides, storm tides, and inland flooding events accelerated by hardened shorelines, their nests fail at increasing rates. Saltmarsh Sparrow has developed adaptive responses, including, remarkably, adding a canopy over its nests to keep eggs from floating out. But its adaptations cannot keep pace with the increasing frequency of floods and with rising seas: "As sea level rises, there will be a point where the neap and spring tides will flood most or all nests. When this happens, these species will have limited or no annual fecundity."⁶ In other words, incremental sea level rise does not incrementally reduce the number of Saltmarsh Sparrow; when daily high tides reach nest height, nests will fail along the entirety of the East Coast, and extinction will happen suddenly.⁷

Why does this extinction seem inexorable? While some of the causes are indirect, the main drivers are unquestionably anthropogenic. Settler people, broadly Christian and post-Christian in inheritance, have pushed Saltmarsh Sparrow to the brink of non-existence by first halving the bird's homeland and then causing it to flood. This extinction happens at the hands of humans who are living around the sparrow's habitat and watching it happen in real time. Expert observers document Saltmarsh Sparrow's decline, analyzing drivers of its demise and creating predictive models. Saltmarsh Sparrow's death is foreseen, its causes known and still perhaps avoidable. In the short term, tidal flooding barriers could be constructed to protect nesting sites and sediment deposition projects undertaken to build marsh elevation. In the longer term, societies could allow marshes to migrate upland, away from the rising sea, and stop the greenhouse gas emissions driving the rapid sea-level rise.

How does the plight of Saltmarsh Sparrow matter for religious ethics? Is there something in the stories that North American coastal people tell themselves about their origin or identity that inhibits the formation of responsibility for Saltmarsh Sparrows or justifies their extinction? Beginning from a major religion in the bird's habitat, we could ask how this creature's imminent extinction matters to Christian ethics.

Christian theology has had little to say about the life and death of particular species. Concern for the general phenomenon of extinctions regularly appears within Christian environmental ethics, but even there, it is usually treated as a symptom of something more troubling to the ethicist—industrialism, modernity, colonialism. In other domains of Christian thought, the presence of nonhuman lives barely registers, much less their deaths. Of course, the phenomenon of anthropogenic extinctions is sometimes lamented, but seldom does responsibility for the survival of another species appear as a meaningful part of the relations described by political theologians. "Humanity," or maybe modern industrial peoples, may be endangering "biodiversity," but that general relation seems to remain external from imaginations of biopolitical membership. While there are many Christian churches along the salt-marsh corridor of the Atlantic coast, including some taking principled action on environmental matters, few could imagine Saltmarsh Sparrow as a member of their assembly or the dying of this species as a significant theological event for their community.

How can this be so? It cannot be that extinctions are so novel to North American attention that religious thought has yet to catch up. Anthropogenic extinctions have been widely known and worried over for more than a century.[8] Climate change is a newer ecological idea yet has attracted much more robust theological engagement. If extinctions still form no serious part of North American theological ethics, there must be some other explanation. I briefly sketch two ways that the Christian imagination of the sparrow contributes to its endangerment; I then show how a minority strain of theological ethics could recenter the sparrow's plight and raise critical questions in part II about this entire approach to the problem.

The Sparrow as Disposable Life

One of the few instances in which sparrows appear in the Bible exhibits precisely why the death of Saltmarsh Sparrow might not register in the Christian imagination. In the gospels of Luke and Matthew, Jesus is recorded as offering assurances to anxious listeners by comparing their value to that of sparrows. "Are not two sparrows sold for a penny? Yet not one of them will fall to the ground without your Father's care. . . . So do not be afraid; you are worth more than many sparrows" (Matt. 10:29–31). Jesus seems to say that if God attends to even a sparrow, who is worth so little, how much more valuable must humans be in God's sight?

Now, context would suggest that the moral point of that verse is not human supremacy over other species but God's care for a people under imperial occupation. As Howard Thurman pointedly observed in 1949 for a Jim Crow–era readership, Jesus spoke to "a member of a minority group in the midst of a larger dominant and controlling group."[9] People who were demeaned, abjectified, and exposed to unaccountable violence would take comfort in the sparrow verse. Roman soldiers could take the life of a Jewish person as if her life were worth less than a sparrow's, just as armed authorities might (still) kill Black people in white supremacist America as if their lives were disposable. In Thurman's reading, Jesus's exhortation *Do not be afraid* tells those up against the wall that they possess a dignity that cannot be taken or alienated. That assurance, writes Thurman, was part of "a technique of survival for the oppressed," for it refused to accept the politics of dehumanization as any indication of one's worth in God's eyes, one's actual human dignity.[10]

The sparrow thus plays a representative role in a major twentieth-century project of North American Christian theology: vindicating the equal humanity of all persons over against the manifold forms of white supremacy. The sparrow here is a symbolic foil to equality in God's special regard for humans. Making good on human exceptionalism perhaps seemed to require staying silent as Passenger Pigeon, Ivory-billed Woodpecker, and California Condor fluttered at death's door. While theologians and church people must have read the popular accounts of disappearing Bald Eagle and American Bison, there is little record that nonnative North American Christians made much meaning of them. Many coastal-dwelling clergy and theologians in the 1920s would have followed the press-covered updates on Heath Hen's dwindling fate (see Barrow 2009), yet there is scant evidence that they incorporated its dying into their accounts of grace or salvation.

Of course, the white theologians who thought settler colonialism providential would have perceived the extinctions as sadly inevitable signs of progress, just as they regarded the displacement and genocide of Indigenous peoples as sadly inevitable. Yet anti-racist theologians like Thurman who denounced white supremacy may have been silent for another reason: worry that theological concern for birds might weaken the ground of universal human dignity. If so, they would have seen their fear realized in the public alliance of eugenic white nationalism with early twentieth-century wildlife conservation, in which certain endangered animals, like American Bison, gained symbolic value for their association with European encounter and settlement.[11] In fact, the convergence of species-preservation ideals with white colonialist nostalgia provoked the dean of Black liberation theology, James Cone, to disparage white ecotheologians with more concern for Spotted Owl than for Black lives. Cone's main point was that if ecotheology continued to embrace conservationist ideas from colonial culture, it would never reach the entangled roots of white supremacy and of ecological destruction. "They are fighting the same enemy—human beings' domination of each other and nature."[12] The sting of his conclusion—"if it is important to save the habitats of birds and other species, it is at least equally important to save black lives in the ghettos and prisons of America"—depends on the gospels' passerine premise that if even birds matter, oppressed humans matter that much more.[13]

As an icon of God's solidarity with people who find their lives devalued or rendered disposable, the sparrow guarantees human exceptionalism. That also seems to be the prevailing sense of the (less liberationist, more anodyne) hymn "His Eye Is on the Sparrow," written at the turn of the twentieth century and still widely popular across North America. "I sing because I'm happy, I sing because I'm free / His eye is on the sparrow, so I know he watches me." If God's eye is on the lowly sparrow, people can find assurance that however forgotten they may feel, God surely cares for them. The *so* tellingly shades the sparrow to reassure the human.

In both liberationist and anodyne receptions, the premise of comfort to humans rests on the assumed disposability of the sparrow. In precisely that indifference, the sparrow represents all nonhuman life in a theological cosmology: neither of disvalue nor of special value but indifferently standing outside the exceptional relationship of God with the human creature. God elected to incarnate Godself as a human, after all, not some other kind of creature—not Spotted Owl, Heath Hen, or Passenger Pigeon, and certainly not as a sparrow. It is rather a sign of the abundance of God's love that it overflows the human, extending even to the lowly, disposable sparrow. As Psalm 84 puts it, "*Even* the sparrow finds a home near your altar."

Fantastic Hegemonic Ignorance

A second way that Christian theology may endanger Saltmarsh Sparrow shows up in theological attempts to *counter* such narrow anthropocentrism. Ecotheologies often treat extinctions as symptomatic of some more fundamental relation. For example, Michael Northcott, one of the few Christian political theologians to seriously engage extinctions, characteristically treats them as signs of the corruption of the modern industrial social order.[14] That tracks with a pattern in environmental thought more broadly. As Heise observes, "The endangerment of a particular species comes to function as a synecdoche for the broader environmentalist idea of nature's decline as well as for the stories that communities and societies tell about their own modernization."[15]

Now, it may be quite correct that Saltmarsh Sparrow's peril cannot be understood apart from colonialism and capitalism or, as Northcott has it, the ontological and epistemological foundations of modern liberalism. The liability to being treated as synecdoche, however, is that the particular lifeway of Saltmarsh Sparrow begins to slip out of focus. For its life and death are not really the object of theological attention but rather the fate of a broader biocultural complex with which the theologian supposes the fate of humans also lies. The particular bird can easily be replaced by some other species, which the writer will be motivated to do if the sparrow's conservation situation appears complex or ambiguous.

Indeed, it turns out that not every aspect of Saltmarsh Sparrow's predicament aligns with an antimodernization narrative. While infrastructural tidal barriers (e.g., marsh-crossing roads) impede flows of sediment deposition important to long-term marsh mobility, they are sometimes also critical short-term protection from irregular flood events.[16] Meanwhile, wetland restoration programs, which might seem to recover ecological territory from industrial modernity, have not, for a variety of discrete reasons, helped Saltmarsh Sparrow populations recover.[17] If the bird does not reliably play its assigned role in a story about industrial violence and the ethicist therefore turns to a different species or (more likely) remains content with referring to extinctions in general, then moral concern does not really extend to Saltmarsh Sparrow. In either case, attentiveness to the Saltmarsh Sparrow as a particular lifeway is not required; no capacity to know its song is needed for its dying to fit the assigned role in a religious critique.

Some theological narratives that bring Saltmarsh Sparrow to attention may thus simultaneously encourage ignorance, as the bird is overwhelmed by the role it is made to play in a broader narrative. Adapting the concept of "fantastic hegemonic imagination" from Emilie Townes, we might call that *fantastic hegemonic ignorance*.[18] Townes develops her concept to investigate the cultural production of white supremacy in everyday material life. For example, Townes shows how the Aunt Jemima commercial product materially reproduces a Mammy figure—a stout

Black woman cheerfully provisioning white tables. It was first invented to offer a soft memory of plantation life, then reproduced in blackface minstrelsy of Jim Crow parodies of Black experience, then transferred to the label of a consumer product from a white-owned corporation. Aunt Jemima pancake syrup appeared on supermarket shelves for a century and was finally discontinued in summer 2020 in acknowledgment of the Black Lives Matter movement. One might develop an analogous line of inquiry into the way that some charismatic endangered species show up in material life—as cartoon Polar Bear in soda ads, as Snow Leopard plush toys, as Pink Dolphin in children's books. Consumer products represent these animals in ways that make them seem happily present in everyday life, thus softening the reality that they have been pushed to the edge of survival by the very processes that at the same time capitalize the additional cultural value they carry by virtue of being endangered.

Yet those examples actually mislead, for few endangered species exercise such influence over the cultural imagination. Most are unknown. Saltmarsh Sparrow is scarcely known to cultural meaning-making until it is identified as threatened and appears on a Red List and in newspaper headlines—at which point its vulnerability is engulfed and overdetermined by imaginations of mass extinction. So the imaginative issue here is not one of grotesque surplus but rather of hegemonic ignorance reinforced, even and especially in discourses of concern.

The connection with Townes's critique runs deeper than analogy because white supremacy plays a role in theological coproduction of this ignorance. In his pivotal book, *The Christian Imagination*, Willie Jennings traces the way that modern notions of race arose amid colonial displacements of identity from land. In the contexts of settler colonialism and associated missionary practices, Jennings illustrates European Christians learning to imagine humans as separate from nature and masters over it by simultaneously learning to imagine themselves as white. By investing whiteness with a divine mandate to realize their notion of "humanity," settler Christians could moralize violent displacements of Indigenous and African peoples as tutelage in the ways of mastery. "With the emergence of whiteness, identity was calibrated through possession of, not possession by, specific land," writes Jennings, thus rendering "unintelligible and unpersuasive any narratives of the collective self that bound identity to geography, to earth, to water, to trees and animals."[19] As colonial settlers became white, their political processes of land seizure and property ownership reinforced white supremacist understandings of divine providence, which in turn authorized further violence toward humans that whiteness racialized differently and moralized the exploitation of lands that whiteness imagined in terms of "resources." White settler self-understanding was constructed from a theological commitment to ignorance of any moral claims from the peoples and lands they encountered. Ignorance of Saltmarsh Sparrow's song, on this account, is not an accident of inattentiveness but a theological production of identities henceforth carried on bodies rather than articulated through kinship with particular lands.

Most theological accounts of "humanity," argues Jennings, have not yet reckoned with that fundamental displacement of personhood from creaturely kinship. Even in emancipatory, liberationist, and postcolonial versions, much of North Atlantic political theology remains in thrall to a settler notion of humanity in which identity floats above the land, indifferent to other creatures. Jennings writes: "Thus our lives, even if one day freed from racial calculations, suffer right now from a less helpful freedom, freedom from the ground, the dirt, landscapes, and animals, from life collaborative with the rhythms of God's other creatures."[20] Theological projects attempting to repair the inheritances of white supremacy have often advanced equality in a notion of humanity that was made in settler colonialism, where the process of making identities remains committed to ignorance of the ecological relations within which one lives.

Extinction discourse is never only about the loss of nonhumans, observes Audra Mitchell; it also produces certain kinds of human subjects.[21] Jennings's critique shows how theological discourse about nonhuman extinctions can unintentionally reproduce settler subjectivities and thereby continue to authorize violence against Indigenous peoples. When treated as symbol of trouble in "humanity's" relationship with Earth, extinction discourse can assume the settler's elective, abstract relationship with ecological concerns, thus perpetuating the ignorance that at once conceals and abets Indigenous genocide. "Extinction is not a metaphor," protests Mitchell; "it is a very real expression of violence that systematically destroys particular beings, worlds, life forms and the relations that enable them to flourish."[22] Insofar as extinctions discourse maintains ignorance that excludes the particular relations of a place from having a claim on their identity or their politics, then it also maintains the erasure of Indigenous governance institutions that have historically convened the relations of a place.[23]

Theology from the Marshes

A different line of interpretation takes the sparrow's marginality as its theological significance. If Thurman's *Jesus and the Disinherited* interprets the religion of Jesus from the perspective of one "up against the wall," then, in a time of mass extinctions, a theologian might imagine Saltmarsh Sparrow as up against the wall in a sense and therefore as occupying the place of creaturely peril assumed in the incarnation of God. Mark Wallace, meditating on the extinction of the Passenger Pigeon, argues that the saying of Jesus about sparrows should be heard as overturning the presumption of worthlessness. "Jesus knew that this is the attitude of many of us, in his time and ours, but counters that what we find to be useless rubbish in nature God embraces as worthy of care and compassion."[24] Thus, Wallace applies the idea in the sparrow pericope—that God loves those rendered lowly or made marginal—to the birds themselves.

Theology undertaken from the margins, from the marshes where Saltmarsh Sparrow is up against a wall of hardened coastline on one side and rising seas on the other, may thus find God's eye on the sparrow more intently than the majority reading understands. There are in fact some precedents with which to develop this direction. While scarcely a regular topos of theological reflection, anthropogenic extinctions have occasionally haunted the edges of North Atlantic Christian theology. Writing a few generations after Charles Darwin and responding to growing evidence that humans had the power to alter the course of life's evolution, Liberty Hyde Bailey and Paul Tillich both began to contest the (settler) commonsense view that extinctions might be the work of providence by suggesting that God may be allied with life beyond humanity.[25]

Perhaps the first nonnative North American theologian to significantly attend to anthropogenic extinctions was Jim Nash, whose *Loving Nature* develops a theological argument for the rights of all species to exist and to fulfill their evolutionary potential.[26] While biblical notions of justice did not include the rest of the living world, asserts Nash, the contemporary ethicist could extend the moral logic of the sparrow pericope to draw the whole living world into its sphere of protection. Nash is not claiming, as Wallace does, that Jesus's sparrow saying aims to counter anthropocentrism; on the contrary, "the divine valuation of the rest of nature ... sneaks in through a crack in the analogy."[27] Christian ethics works toward "a logical extension of love to its horizons, embracing all life forms in accord with Christian experiences of and testimonies to the unbounded love of God."[28] While there are destabilizing questions to ask about imagining extinctions as Nash did, which I explain in the next section, his work offers the rare example of a response to extinctions driving the interpretation of ideas basic to the Christian tradition.

Toward the end of the twentieth century, concerns about extinction animated a popular Christian movement to protect the US Endangered Species Act. Led by Evangelicals, an alliance of Christians appealed to the Genesis story of Noah rescuing other species from devastation, claiming that the Endangered Species Act was "the Noah's ark of our day."[29] While Nash and a few others had previously referred to the promise of the Noah story for supporting biodiversity,[30] their intervention was surprising to many because, despite its diverse menagerie known to every child, the ark story has long functioned as an allegory of human salvation. Centuries of Christian art and exegesis displaced other animals from the ark. When this popular movement recovered it as an image of God's concern to save endangered species, the moment revealed how exceptionalist theological imagination had become.

Some theologians, such as Christopher Southgate and Denis Edwards, have begun regathering species into the ark of salvation by arguing that efforts to stop extinctions participate in God's work of rescue and redemption.[31] "The Spirit does not abandon the sparrow that falls to the ground," writes Edwards, "but gathers it up, inscribing it eternally in the life of the Trinity."[32] Referring to a particular sparrow on a branch outside his window, Edwards writes: "This sparrow is known and loved by God ... this sparrow participates in redemption in Christ, and ... is eternally treasured and celebrated in ... the Communion of Saints."[33] Although Saltmarsh Sparrow is threatened with extinction, God draws it into eternal life. The sparrow cannot then be ignored but rather must be cherished and protected as a unique participant in divine life. In fact, for Southgate and Edwards, God draws humans into God's life by inviting them to love and protect other creatures.

Indeed, God may be incarnate in Saltmarsh Sparrow. Considering the exposure of all creatures to death and suffering and the ancient soteriological maxim that only that which is assumed may be saved, Niels Gregerson develops a deeper form of incarnation, "according to which God has not only assumed human nature in general, but also a scorned social being and a human-animal body."[34] The implication of deep incarnation, writes Elizabeth Johnson, is that "in Christ, the living God who creates and empowers the evolutionary world also enters the fray, personally drinking the cup of suffering and going down into the nothingness of death, to transform it from within."[35] On this account, Christ is present in the marshes, exposed to the flood tides. "Hope springs from this divine presence."[36] In fact, both Gregersen and Johnson invoke sparrows to make the point that in Christ, God shares the fate and suffering of all creatures.[37] Incarnation may be, when interpreted from the marshes, about God becoming Saltmarsh Sparrow, assuming its vulnerability, perhaps to the point of undergoing death by drowning.

Yet deep incarnation discourse rarely touches on particular jeopardies and only glancingly on anthropogenic extinctions. It is typically preoccupied with "natural evils," wondering why extinctions occur in evolution generally and how God relates to them. So when deep incarnation scholarship explicitly addresses extinctions, it decontextualizes them, shifting attention away from actual biopolitical relations in which writer and reader are enfleshed. Saltmarsh Sparrow and its marshes—and indeed this entire mass extinction, now just one in a series—slide out of focus in the question of what God is doing in evolution.

Moreover, by treating extinction within the decontextualized questions of inherited "religion and science" discourse, deep incarnation theologies miss the ways that human exceptionalism has historically functioned as white exceptionalism.[38] Recalling Jennings, if the colonial production of whiteness created the notion of nonplaced human relations to other creatures, then understanding contemporary extinctions cannot be found by deepening theologies of incarnation. For it is not exclusive humanism that devalues the sparrow but rather production of racialized humans, including white settler subjects, Blackened subjects, criminalized subjects, and absent subjects.[39] To the colonial imagination with its redemption-oriented perception of space, Charles Mills writes, "The nonwhite body is a moving bubble of wilderness in white political space."[40] Expanding the scope of redemption through deep incarnation while adding a partnership role for (white) humanity to transform evolutionary processes would therefore actually exceed the worst fears in antiracist criticism of the Anthropocene idea.[41]

Redemption narratives, observes Native American theologian Tink Tinker, have long been overemphasized by settler forms of Christianity.[42] Soteriology undergirded the doctrine of discovery that justified the taking and transformation of Indigenous lands. American Indian theologies prioritize instead the doctrine of creation, writes Tinker, which they understand through particularized relations of a place, with all the relatives of a land. The theological repair of the relations that push Saltmarsh Sparrow up against the wall of extinction may then need to begin where Jennings finds that the settler Christian doctrine of creation went awry: in the colonial origins of race. For it was there, Jennings holds, that identity formation was sundered from multispecies geography, from "the fine webs that held together memory, language, and place to moral action and ethical judgement."[43] Trying to value sparrows apart from those identity-making relations abstracts from the context in which they are specific relatives. Tinker's doctrine of creation assumes Indigenous sovereignty as a condition of possibility for the creatures of a land to be known as relatives. Theology for Saltmarsh Sparrow would begin from the margins of settler culture, with those ancestral caretakers of coastal territories who continue to convene the relations of the marshlands: the Nanticoke, Shinnecock, Wampanoag, Lenape,

Piscataway, Pequot, and Mohegan, among others. Restored sovereignty, for Tinker, is a condition of possibility for knowing the creatures of the land as relatives and thus for repairing relations with Saltmarsh Sparrow. Indigenous sovereignty would also be, says Tinker, a liberative gift "to share with our colonizer-settler relatives," because it would disavow the settler imperative to redeem land that keeps in fact alienating them from it, replacing it with a creation-centered politics of kinship that would open the possibilities of belonging to land.[44]

In this third approach, the basic point is that attempts to extend sparrow logic to the birds themselves show extinctions shifting Christianity's self-interpretation. While less radical, the shift can be seen in Pope Francis's *Laudato Si'*, which mentions biodiversity and extinctions even more frequently than it does climate change, describes nonhuman creatures as kin, and states that humans have no right to drive other species to extinction.[45] Each species gives glory to God in its own way and has intrinsic value of its own, says Francis, although he hesitates to prioritize the voices of the Indigenous in theology and of nonhumans in politics.[46]

Although most Christian political theologies still exclude the rest of the living Earth, the existence of these marginal strategies suggests that extinctions have the potential to unsettle premises of human exceptionalism and perhaps the connection of those premises to settler colonialism. If coastal Christian stories of self-understanding held that the life and death of Saltmarsh Sparrow are important to the life and death of God—may indeed *be* the life and death of God in some sense—then indifference or ignorance toward Saltmarsh Sparrows would be escalated from the regrettable norm to religious crisis. If Christian ethics hears meaningful questions from Saltmarsh Sparrow, it might come to see that theology from the margins has come to require theology from the marshes—which would suggest that extinctions are wending their way into religious stories told about identity.

PART II: SWARMS AND MURMURATIONS

I have so far covered religion and extinction in a conventional way in terms of a particular imperiled species, Saltmarsh Sparrow, and a recognized tradition of thought, Christian theology. Proceeding that way, however, may cloud our understandings of extinction while also obscuring important dimensions of religion. In this section, I will discuss worldwide insect decline to expand the moral imagination of extinction while also shifting the frame of religion from a historic tradition to unnamed affiliations of affect and spirituality. After addressing insect swarms, I turn to religious swarms.

Reimagining Extinction

Until 1995, Saltmarsh Sparrow was known as Sharp-tailed Sparrow and was considered conspecific with what is now known as Nelson's Sparrow. The birds look very similar, are both marsh specialists, and sometimes interbreed to produce fertile hybrids. The key difference is that Saltmarsh Sparrow is obligate to saltwater tidal marshes, whereas Nelson's Sparrow is less exclusive in its nesting requirements, breeding also in inland freshwater marshes. Because of that difference, Saltmarsh Sparrow is endangered while Nelson's Sparrow is not.

If the clan of Sharp-tailed Sparrow that insists on nesting exclusively in tidal marshes disappears while another clan continues to animate the marshes with wing and song indistinguishably different to all but ornithologists, has an extinction happened? Perhaps, but with those interbreeding kin in mind, one might wonder how much protection is owed the clan that has such particular nesting preferences. Is extinction a concept that necessarily goes with the classification of species?

How the question is answered can mean the difference between the allocation of public funds for significant interventions and watching a population dwindle out of existence. In the 1980s, the endangered Dusky Seaside Sparrow was reclassified as one of several subspecies of Seaside Sparrow, which is not endangered. Federal recovery efforts, which had included habitat purchase programs, were consequently suspended, and the last Dusky Seaside Sparrow died on June 16, 1987. Meanwhile, Seaside Sparrow, which specializes in coastal tidal marshes mostly to the south of Saltmarsh Sparrow's range, sustains an overall healthy population.[47] Officially, an extinction did not happen, yet birders of the southern US coasts continue to memorialize a distinct loss.

What is the subject of extinction, the form of life that can disappear or whose disappearing matters? Here, we begin to see the limitations of approaches that connect a particular religious tradition to a particular endangered species. When Nash extended Christian love to establish existence rights for other species, he took species as being a natural kind with a natural lifespan. But species may not be reliable objects of moral regard, and loving them may occlude moral perception from recognizing all that matters in extinction. Attention to extinctions would move differently with a keener appreciation of the dynamism and mutability of lines of life, of the species ideas as a classificatory construct with its own history, and of mutual constitution of human and nonhuman worlds.[48] "By positing 'species' as bounded units," writes Mitchell, "dominant discourses on extinction efface not only the profound entanglement of life forms, but also their synchronic and diachronic plasticity."[49] The ethics of extinction should thus seek out the beings and processes excluded from the species concept.

The recourse to love might actually impede that kind of attention, argues Mitchell, for love's imagination seeks known beings with whom one can relate.[50] One might, perhaps, learn to love sparrows, but the tiny insects on whom they feed seem less relatable and knowable and the spartina grass in which they nest are barely considered. Saltmarsh Sparrow exists as a web of relations involving innumerable beings, some of whom confound or recoil human minds and all of whom are constantly changing over time. Insofar as love seeks a knowable individual, it may obscure those relations.

Thom van Dooren's avian-inspired concept of "flight ways" helps with dynamism and openness: "Extinction is the loss not of a single fixed 'kind,'" he writes, "but of a potentially limitless set of emergent and branching flight ways from the present into the diversity of the future. Each species is ultimately a flight way beyond itself."[51] In this conception, extinction is not best imagined as losing a singular something or as a subtraction from an original endowment but rather as an extinguishment of the lines of possibility. What counts as a flight way? For van Dooren, it may well be a life-form recognized as a species but perhaps also a multispecies kinship or a subspecies population. Flight ways are not natural kinds simpliciter, given for humans to protect or not, but are interpretations arising from mutually involved, coevolutionary forms of life. The programmatic introduction to *Extinction Studies* that van Dooren writes with Deborah Bird Rose and Matthew Chrulew thus calls for "understanding and responding to processes of collective death, where not just individual organisms, but entire ways and forms of life, are at stake."[52]

For different reasons, some environmental scientists agree that thinking of extinction as species loss may be a mistake. The concept of "ecological extinction" points to ecological interactions that are lost at much higher rates than species.[53] The landmark 2019 Global Assessment Report from the Intergovernmental Science-Policy Platform on Biodiversity and Ecosystem Services, while certainly retaining the terminology of species extinctions, places them in an overall context of deteriorating life-support systems in a way that points to an understanding of the deathliness of extinction through relations and processes, communities and migrations, ecosystems and symbioses.[54] Extinction here includes not only the vanishing of discrete species but also more collective, distributed, and therefore vague deteriorations.

A study of decline of North American avifauna argues that "the overwhelming focus on species extinctions . . . has underestimated the extent and consequences of biotic change, by ignoring the loss of abundance within still-common species and in aggregate across large species assemblages."[55] The researchers estimate a net loss of 2.9 billion birds across biomes, a reduction of about 30 percent since 1970. There are untold implications for environmental health stemming from not only the loss of rare and threatened species, they observe, but also and perhaps especially from declines among the common habitat generalists.[56]

Whether a species persists somewhere as a few living individuals matters less for environmental health and biocultural futures than do declines in local populations, missing community links, and fragmented trophic relations. Feedback between defaunation and changing planetary systems thins migrations and empties forests.[57] Phenological mismatch, where synchronized intersections of species come apart as they respond differently to climate change, sends a cascade of missed connections through a trophic web, and its implications are yet unknown.[58] Mistimed migrations fray multispecies knots.[59] "Relationships unravel, mutualities falter, dependence becomes a peril rather than a blessing, and whole words of knowledge and practice falter."[60] Meshwork comes undone, flight ways narrow. Separate from the mass extinction of individual species, even while related to and often driven by it, those diminishments are harder to describe—a threadiness to Earth's pulses of life, a spreading weedy sameness that crowds out seedbeds of creativity, an unevenness in the atmosphere's breathing, a narrowing of evolutionary futures.

Those broader understandings of death worlds and lifeworlds can be lost when the extinctions discourse focuses on endangered species and especially on the survival tales of a particular animal. Thus, we have the brinksmanship tales of saving Golden Lion Tamarin and Whooping Crane, of intrepid humans inventing ways for other animals to stave off death. Yet as Chrulew, van

Dooren, and Heise have argued, those heroic tales are riven with ambivalence and trade-offs.[61] They often depend on unprecedented methods of cross-species collaboration, like teaching cranes to migrate with aircraft or preserving endangered amphibians in engineered and sealed microhabitats. Moreover, by focusing on survivals and perhaps on de-extinction efforts at resurrection, life support for particular species turns attention to the spectacular rather than to fraying knots, thready pulses, or narrowing flight ways. The rescue stories often focus on preserving the species instead of the continuity and complexity of their distinctive worlds.[62]

Salt marshes themselves are threatened by sea-level rise, and with them all the relations, processes, knots, and migrations supported by this meeting zone of oceanic and terrestrial lifeworlds. As a being obligate to those tidal marshes, committed to them in a way that Nelson's Sparrow is not, Saltmarsh Sparrow depicts the vulnerability of a world made possible by the thin, absorptive, and mobile corridor between firm land and open ocean, between fresh and salt. Along this dynamic edge, the marshes live by moving. They migrate with barrier islands, pushing ahead of their lee side in the island's slow-motion wave toward shore. Or, fed by sediment deposition from rivers, they migrate upland when the seas rise and seaward when they recede. If the marshes are trapped by an inflexibly engineered shore, and if they are starved of sediment, they will die for lack of mobility. There will be a littoral zone, of course, but no longer a distinct lifeworld. Insofar as Saltmarsh Sparrow's dying, which is easier to comprehend and quantify, compels attention to these forms of morbidity more difficult to perceive, then perhaps focusing on the endangered bird can expand how we understand extinction.

Swarms of Judgment

During its breeding period, Saltmarsh Sparrow forages almost exclusively on invertebrate animals, including amphipods, larval flies, marsh grasshoppers, lycosid spiders, moths, beetles, and other insects.[63] The bird's future lies with those insects. So how are they faring?

Tracking insect extinctions is a difficult task because taxonomies remain incomplete, archives of long-range tracking are scarce, and (unlike with birds) few citizen scientists have the requisite identification skills. Insects seem less relatable, less lovable, less knowable. However, a recent review of available research on insect decline finds that of those being tracked, "almost half of the species are declining and a third are being threatened with extinction."[64] With insects especially, diminishment is more important than disappearance from the biological register. The proportion of insect species in decline is twice as high as that of vertebrates, and annual biomass decline is estimated at 2.5 percent. That rate, scientists note, would be hardly noticed in year-to-year observation; it takes a long-term record to show up, at which point it looks devastating. One study from Germany found a 76 percent decline in flying insect biomass over twenty-seven years, a rate of about 2.8 percent.[65] "The repercussions this will have for the planet's ecosystems are catastrophic, as insects are the structural and functional base of many of the world's ecosystems since their rise at the end of the Devonian period, almost 400 million years ago."[66] Many worlds, including Saltmarsh Sparrow's, are sustained by insects; in their decline are ominous signs of worlds ending.

Again, extinction here encompasses a type of dying that differs from the dying-out of a species; diminishment of numbers becomes a vector of deathliness. Only in large numbers are insects functionally alive to a food web and a landscape. Their form of life is the swarm.

In the beginning of the Hebrew Bible, swarms are called forth from the waters, blessed, and charged to multiply and fill the Earth (Gen. 1:20–1:22). The flood story also refers to "all the swarming creatures that swarm on Earth" (Gen. 7:21). Though they are a blessed form of life at the opening of Genesis, throughout the rest of the Hebrew Bible, swarms are associated with devastation. Appearing as a sudden cloud that could cast cities and whole populations into famine, they were apparently experienced as divine judgment for some wrong a people had committed or as a plague visited upon one's enemies. Prophets struck fear in their listeners by threatening a cloud of insects. In other traditions, too, swarms of insects appear as a trope of calamity. The Qur'an names locusts as a plague sent by Allah to punish sin (7:133). An ancient Jain text lists swarms of locusts as one of twelve divine calamities for which the specialist should know the appropriate ritual propitiation.[67] Some Zoroastrian texts regard insects as material agents of evil, their swarming becoming the literal undoing of creation.[68] Across traditions, a swarm has often conveyed disaster; its religious affect was doom.

Now it is a lack of swarms that evokes that affect of looming disaster, of judgment for wrongdoing, of famine, and maybe even of the undoing of creation. "Insect Apocalypse" was the title of a widely read article in the *New York Times,* and news reports on the surprising absence of insects generally convey fear, alarm, or a sense of doom. Where prophets once struck fear with a forecast of swarms, they do so now by forecasting their absence.

One need not identify oneself with one of the recognized religions in order to share those feelings. Reports of insect decline may be received as omens of disaster or a foreboding of trouble. They may feel something like judgment on the ways of life causing this diminishment, a curse that demands propitiation, an incurment of existential debt, or a summons to conversion away from the ways of death.

Does it make sense to describe those feelings as religious, even when they appear in people who do not believe in divine judges or karmic debt and who would otherwise disavow the systems from which the names of those feelings and responses are derived? Donovan Schaefer argues that religion is not only about identities and beliefs but also "about *the way things feel*, the things we want, the way our bodies are guided through thickly textured, magnetized worlds."[69] On that view, religion has to do with affect—"the flow of forces through bodies outside of, prior to, or underneath language"—as much as it does beliefs, texts, or identities.[70] With affect theory, Schaefer seeks to recover the animality of religious experience as something that happens before and beyond linguistic cognition in the responsiveness of embodied organisms to their world. His opening example is the ecstatic responses of chimpanzees to a waterfall, which might be seen as religious or at least as exemplifying the way environments can evoke affective response that may be considered protoreligious. The recognized religions are made possible by those feelings, argues Schaeffer, and usually develop bodily technologies to work with them.

In the case of insect decline, the environment evokes negative feelings, as the absence of vitality elicits dismal affects: a slumping anxiety, solastalgia, or sense of foreboding; it is the affective opposite of a waterfall. It is more likely to cause deflationary rather than ecstatic response, and the difficulty of noticing insect decline and the uncertainty about its consequences may deepen the troubling affect. Whereas an absence of insects might ordinarily be welcome, especially by those allergic to bee stings or in communities that still rightly fear destructive locust swarms, now, once people notice the absence, they are more likely to connect it to reports of the overall declines. The pleasing lack of flying nuisances may then produce a cloud of worry. Similar to the combination of concern and enjoyment one feels on an unseasonably warm December day in a northern latitude region, it may be experienced as what is sometimes called "blissonance" or perhaps as an uncanny sense that the insect apocalypse is the first sign of some broader cataclysm.

Now we are pointed toward a sense of religion not as discrete traditions but as affective experiences of dying lifeworlds. James Hatley suggests that extinction rightly evokes a sense of being interrogated and that *failing to feel that way*, or to at least pay attention, may be a problem that is religious in depth. The people responsible for this dying probably should feel judged or condemned. Then he turns to a traditional religious figure. Meditating on a depiction of the Buddha as a fierce combatant against desire, Hatley writes, "We of the global first world are in need of a warrior Buddha with the strength and ferocity to confront our spectacular inattentiveness."[71] Hatley is not arguing that one must be Buddhist in order to feel the world well but that a sense of being judged and of being compelled to pay attention to the diminishment of the living world is a fitting affective experience of living in worlds undergoing extinction.

Calling that experience "religious" may help connect it with practices for naming and responding to it. The diminishment of life's swarming *feels* like the kind of event from which religious formations arose. Indeed, in the few political movements to directly address mass extinction, scholars observe religious behaviors from old traditions and new practices coming together in a shared space.[72] Religion, it seems, helps them give expression to what is happening.

This claim does not imply that any of the recognized traditions are well suited to interpret extinction or that current practices of recognized communities offer fitting responses. It does, however, indicate that understandings of mass extinction that discount its religious significance may miss something important. In an essay for *Conservation Biology* entitled "Three Ways to Think About the Sixth Mass Extinction," Philip Cafaro argues that considerations of character are another way of framing extinction, in addition to resource loss or criminal injustice.[73] This is a familiar third option from virtue theorists, who often argue that moral understanding is impoverished by a perceived choice between framing in terms of consequentialism (e.g., resource loss) or of deontology (e.g., duties not to violate another's dignity). But if religious narratives were also admitted, then many more ways to think and feel about mass extinction would appear; for example, it could be thought of in terms of eschatological anticipation, nonattachment to mutable worlds, compassionate identification with nonhuman life, the incitement of ghosts, the annihilation of nonhuman peoples, a lamentation for wrongdoing, an atonement for sin, alienation from the sacred, the flouting of original instructions, hope in resurrection, Mother Earth's anger, the Creator's punishment, desecration, the withdrawal of relatives, and more. Opened to religion, extinction evokes worlds of affect.

Why entertain such blooming emotional confusion? Religious experiences of extinction do not seem reducible to a common feeling, let alone a common ethic. Yet that profusion of religiosity can diversify understandings of extinction and perhaps help illuminate and prevent the extinction of biocultural worlds. Cafaro seems correct that, from the available logics of mainstream modernity, moral interpretation of extinction can seem limited to either financializing losses of nonhuman life or somehow overcoming the exclusion of nonhumans from reciprocal obligations of justice. Religious expressions may have the irruptive effect of invoking alternative moral worlds and subjecting the forms of life driving extinction to scrutiny by alternative cosmovisions; they may, as Eduardo Gudynas writes, surface conflicts that create "ontological openings."[74]

When Indigenous cosmovisions generate decolonial or nonmodern interpretations of extinction, they may also create conflicts that reveal how settler notions of extinctions reproduce settler worlds. The cosmovisions provincialize settler notions of extinction, thus making it possible to imagine the extinction of settler notions of humanity and sustain the flourishing of many alternatives.[75] Whereas mainstream ideas of extinction sometimes justify conservation measures that displace Indigenous people or further erode their territorial sovereignty, Indigenous interpretations of extinction may be critical to the survivance of Indigenous worlds. Insofar that those worlds are ontologically diverse and perhaps include animacies, cosmopolitics, and many forms of nonhuman or suprahuman kin, then "religion" may aptly name some of the imperiled or excluded relations.[76] As Rosyln R. Lapier documents, the settler assault on bison was an attack not only on kin of the Blackfeet but also on the religious world in which kinship with bison is possible.[77] Zoe Todd makes analogous observations about fish as kin in a Métis world faced with petro-based water violations.[78] Such worlds are the basis for Kyle Powys Whyte's observation that Indigenous environmental governance is often organized as reciprocal responsibilities among relatives.[79]

Insofar as religious interpretations generate alternative or nonmodern interpretations of extinction, their proliferation may produce affect; in relations so odd that they might be called religious, settler modernity is confronted and called to account by other possibilities. From the absence of swarms, there may arise an uncanny sense of being interrogated, judged, or condemned.

Murmurations: Rethinking Religion in a Time of Extinction

When birds swarm together in a collective patterning flock, it is called a murmuration. Swarms develop through emergent behavior that results from many individuals following simple rules of interaction. In flocks of birds, those may be: move with neighbors, remain close to them, avoid collisions. Although there is no central authority, as each individual follows spacing patterns, the result can sometimes take the appearance of a shape-shifting body, a superorganism dancing with light and sky.

Murmuration is an instance of allelomimesis, which is when one organism performing a behavior induces other nearby organisms to perform the same behavior. As birds begin to aggregate and move together, others seem attracted to join. Swarming is a form of contagious biological intelligence, an adaptive interaction with changing environments. Starling and swift swarms may respond to the presence of raptors or to light conditions that favor their attacks. Locust swarms seem to arise from a response to drought by desert grasshoppers. The small, usually solitary grasshoppers respond to the environmental stress by growing larger, becoming gregarious, sprouting wings, and moving collectively in search of food. The dramatic phenotypic change seems stimulated by the behavior and grouping of other desert grasshoppers. Formerly dispersed individuals become a world-altering cloud.

Murmuration can also refer to the low sound of troubled human voices. In a social form of allelomimesis, dissenting murmurs may also become contagious, feeding rapid shifts in social pattern or political collectivity. A regime fears no threat more than murmurs.

A central predicament of mass extinction, as with other Anthropocene plagues, is the apparent asymmetry between moral agency and planetary stress.[80] Without competent forms of planetary governance, is there any meaningful way to bear responsibility for mass extinction? Without a coordinating authority, how can the distributed feelings evoked by extinction connect with political possibility? In *Facing the Planetary*, political theorist William Connolly appeals to what he calls a "politics of swarming." Perhaps the actions available to individuals and collectives need not carry scalable solutions to an entire adaptive challenge. Rather, let them experiment with fitting patterns of interaction knowing that "each role experiment—and all in aggregate—is radically insufficient to the scope of the problems."[81] The wager of the swarm is that the accumulation of individual role experiments, buoyed by a "spirituality of freedom," may be gathered into "militant pluralist assemblage," the results of which relay across scales and registers to give rise to a new political event.[82]

Like the murmuration of birds, this political swarm emerges as individual agents follow a few basic patterns of interaction, "both intensifying diverse attachments to life on this rare planet and pursuing militant cross-regional citizen actions."[83] The simple rules are: care and connect. This shared "spirituality," some kind of faith in the possibility of attending to life and connecting with others, may give rise to emergent patterns of action.

There is the beginning of a suggestion here that in the experiments and attachments, the connecting and assembling—an alternative form of religion may emerge. Connolly appeals to Bruno Latour's Gaian collectivities. Supposing that the Anthropocene casts doubt on the inherited religious traditions as much as on the modern notion that one may elect to be irreligious, Latour redefines religion as "what one protects carefully, what one thus is careful not to neglect."[84] Latour asks people to identify their cosmological collective by acknowledging the organizing respect by which it is convoked. In that view, the deepest and most important conflicts are not between "world religions" but rather run through them and all cultural formations, moving across the identifying boundaries to convoke collectivities characterized by patterns of care and negligence.

For readers who understand themselves as secular, Connolly's spiritual freedom may be pleasingly vague, just as Latour's cosmological collectives are attractively obscurant. By neglecting to specify how one might meaningfully participate in a membership, Latour effaces the actual and ongoing work of collectives who survive colonization and enslavement by generating exactly this sort of cosmopolitical conflict. In his more recent book on climate politics, when Latour recognizes resistance and survival from the colonized, he makes it seem as if they just now have the opportunity to enter cosmological politics—as if they have not been "protecting carefully" a cosmological collective all along.[85] For example, it is as if the "climate politics" of the Standing Rock Sioux protest against the Dakota Access Pipeline were not a continuation of two centuries of Indigenous resistance to settler colonialism along the Mni Sose.[86] Similarly, Connolly's "spiritual freedom" can resonate all too well with the ephemeral commitments of liberal American political theologies, where *spiritual but not religious* functions as an individualist talisman against the claims of any sodality. In contrast, consider the pipeline contests at Standing Rock or Union Hill, which convene "militant pluralist assemblages" from various religious and political backgrounds through prayer or ceremony.[87] The emergence of the swarm in these instances, and the sustenance of its militant and pluralist commitments, seems to require a sacralizing assembly. Participation in the specific assembly draws people into its alternative social imagination and may dramatically increase their sense of agency. As a certain sense of the sacred becomes "highly contagious," formerly dispersed individuals become a world-altering cloud.[88]

With that emendation in place, Connolly's metaphor of the swarm helps illuminate a cosmopolitical spirituality that emerges from the caring and connecting that happens amid responses to extinction. Scholarship on North American nature-based spiritualities suggests that they take form in ways that differ from conventional religions.[89] They often move across cultural space through rhizomatic networks, occasionally appearing within conventional religious groups and more frequently in alternative affinities of spirituality, sometimes without any explicit reference to religion or spirituality. What nature-based spiritualities share, argues Bron Taylor, is a sense that nature is sacred and should be revered and that humans intimately belong to it.[90] Taylor elevates those manifestations of "dark green religion" that offer adherents a way to break with religious imaginations of the transcendent—especially Christianity. However, the spiritual currents that Taylor identifies seem to move through, beyond, and beneath many cultural streams, including religions with relations of transcendence (even Christianity). The identifying marker of a current that one might find flowing through a range of religious and secular contexts, suggests Douglas E. Christie, is a contemplative ecological consciousness shaped by "a deepening of awareness of oneself as existing within and responsible for the larger whole of the living world."[91] These scholars describe a posthumanist sense of spirituality that is attuned to an ecological sense of the sacred to which humans belong among others in a multispecies collective and by which their personhood is shaped.

Those shifts in the basic relations by which people understand themselves as persons do not seem aptly described by notions of religion that correspond to identity formations, formal beliefs, or systematized worldviews. They seem rather protoreligious, marking shifts in what Charles Taylor calls the underlying "imaginary" of the kinds of relations involved in personhood.[92] As imaginaries shift, perhaps in response to environmental conditions that portend deadly threats, so do the possibilities for how people interact and flock together. That is one reason why *religious* and *secular* function ever less reliably as antonymous terms of description; while they retain the institutional and intellectual referents of a relatively settled modern North Atlantic imaginary, pressure from rapidly shifting biosocial conditions and cosmological alternatives may trigger fissures or shifts in the underlying imaginary that are best described in the lexicon of religious studies.

Scholars in environmental humanities exhibit troubled ambivalence toward the apparent fittingness of religious language to interpret the situation. Thinking beyond modern premises, with more-than-human lifeworlds and suprahuman agencies, scholars invoke religion-adjacent terms like *new animism* to gesture toward the depth of rupture in received imaginaries, yet they rarely engage religious thought as they do.[93] "Everybody wants to rethink animacy, but almost no one wants to be an animist," observes anthropologist Kath Weston.[94] The anxiety is vividly displayed in Timothy Morton's call for "not a return to animism as such, but rather ~~animism~~."[95] Thus by performed disavowal a term that was made for nineteenth-century inquiries into "primitive" religions becomes at once acceptable and indispensable. Observing the prevalence of religious language under erasure in the environmental humanities, Oriol Poveda suggests that pressure to understand liveliness on a rapidly transforming planet presses scholars to articulate postsecular forms of enchantment.[96] Because enchanted and animate vocabularies are indebted to worlds that they regard skeptically as "religious," scholars enact their secularity by employing religious terms in self-conscious irony or troubled unease.[97]

Such ambivalence makes sense in unsettled cultural conditions, where rapid environmental changes may seem to outstrip authorized tools of interpretation, compelling scholars to reach for ideas and practices hitherto marginalized by the set of knowledge-authorizing rules known as secularism. However, insofar as their anxiety keeps religion-invoking scholars aloof from constructive religious thought and critical religious studies, the ambivalence can leave their descriptions impoverished. Despite its attraction to religion-like interpretive ideas, Anthropocene discourse, notes Bronislaw Szerszynski, tends to retain Holocene notions of the secular that prevent it from recognizing and thinking with the new orderings of the sacred emerging from rapid planetary changes.[98] Szerszynski's "geo-spiritual formations" and his speculative geo-fictions for a second Axial Age seek to enhance the descriptive capacity of Anthropocene discourse so that it can better articulate the multinatural senses of spirit circulating in response to extinction.

Imagine religions as "lines of flight," suggests Whitney A. Bauman, as a way to refocus on the dynamic trajectories of meaning-making that emerge from shifting planetary relations and attempt to "move life into ever new and creative ways of becoming."[99] Those many lines of flight interact with the flight ways of van Dooren's interpretation of extinction. Now imagine lines of flight attracting, influencing, and imitating one another. Imagine religion as murmuration.

Experiences of and responses to the diminishment of multispecies swarms, I am claiming, can be helpfully understood in terms of religion. Simultaneously, the religiosity of distributed responses to mass extinction might be understood on the model of swarming. As people experiment with ways to intensify attachments to life amid deathliness and gather in pluralist cross-regional polities—Connolly's *care and connect rules*—especially when doing so within multispecies assemblies convened by caretakers of specific territories and through sacralizing practice, the forms of life may become contagious, expressed as a shape-shifting superorganismal intelligence.

Loving Swarms

Consider the experimental forms of attachment and devotion that humans of many different identities undertake in response to dwindling migrations. On the southern tip of the Eastern Shore of Virginia, where a peninsular narrowing of the coast forces southward migratory birds to converge, hawk counters gather every fall to track the migration. One person, who has agreed to serve as the official counter, commits to being present every day, from dawn to dusk, for the extent of the migration—about six weeks. Attended and supported by a changing group of people who devote a day or a week to the vigil, the counter holds her attention over an arc of sky between the Chesapeake Bay and the Atlantic Ocean. Without asking about her beliefs or identity or even worldview, I came to understand that she is attached to the birds that she can identify at staggering distances, that she takes herself to belong to this thinning pulse of migration, and that she find special meaning in her vigil, knowing that it is joined by others up and down migratory flyways and across generations.

The birds themselves obviously help make this biannual vigil, and the participants not only focus on them as objects to count but also seem enchanted and animated by them; certainly the vigil honors their presence as special. Yet a sense of thinning and dwindling haunts that enchantment. As the time between sightings grows, birders may murmur to one another about diminishments, about what they hear from other places; the elder may tell the younger what migrations were like forty years ago. The comparisons are relayed as quantitative information but expressed in tight-lipped grimaces implying senses of loss and fear. The murmured recognition of the overall context of absence alters and intensifies the experience of sighting a bird.[100] When three American Kestrels, whose population has declined by 50 percent during the lifetime of some people there, shoot low over the conversation in rapid-winged, stiff-tailed determination, it can feel as if they are harried south by some deathly pursuer. The vigil cultivates a spirituality (although no one uses that word) in which members learn to understand themselves as existing within this migration and in some way responsible for it. With their skills of perception trained on and honed for these birds, their year organized to this calendar, and their sense of themselves caught up in a broader flock, their attachment should be recognized as love.

Still, this handful of reserved twitchers waiting on silent migrators seem to be unlikely candidates for a "militant pluralist assemblage," unless, by allelomimesis, some surprising shift happens. Not long ago, settlers would have gathered at that same place in the same season to shoot migrating raptors—part of an assault on avian predators that one early twentieth-century clergyman moralized as a "holy war."[101] Hawk Mountain, along a migratory flyway to the west, was a regular scene of seasonal slaughter before a people's movement transformed it into the sanctuary it is now. The bird hunt that used to happen across North America as part of celebrations for the feast day of the birth of Jesus has become the Christmas Bird Count.

It may be incorrect to say, then, as I did earlier, that settler religion has not noticed extinctions. Perhaps religious response to North American extinctions has been happening in unusual formations, hitherto unthematized as *religious*. Consider religion theorist Thomas A. Tweed's summary definition: "Religions are confluences of organic-cultural flows that intensify joy and confront suffering by drawing on human and suprahuman forces to make homes and cross boundaries."[102] The hawk watcher's vigil convokes with the attention of the amateur entomologists who first noticed the diminishing insect swarms, with those who curate cultural memories of extinct creatures, with all those restoring relations and resisting extinctions, because, in some way, it is how they confront suffering and find joy, how they intensify attachments to lifeworlds and connect with multispecies collectives.

Religiosity in this model helps imagine transformations of love for a time of extinction. Whereas Mitchell worries that facing extinction with an ethics of care or love may prevent attention from moving beyond the relatable and knowable, extinction may possibly tutor people into new capacities of love. Lisa H. Sideris argues that, when open to bearing extinction's grief, love may become more capable of entering difficulty.[103] "Love in a time of extinctions," writes Rose, "calls forth another set of questions. Who are we, as a species? How do we fit into the Earth system?"[104] For Rose particularly, how might love for wild dogs reshape one's understanding of humanity in multispecies relations? If one follows love into extinction—love for the insect swarms that we also experience as nettlesome and destructive; love for the not-fully-knowable meshwork of spartina grasses, mudflats, ocean storms, human infrastructure, amphipods, and untold others we could collectively invoke as Saltmarsh Sparrow's world; love for parasites of the human microbiome, at once maligned, feared, and necessary to human beings[105]—the questions that are raised may transform what love does. Following the extinction may make it possible to imagine extensions of care to entire kingdoms of life hitherto poorly understood.[106]

Naming the quality of this love and especially of its convocations as religious can help illuminate the depth of cultural stress created by extinction. If the various forms of care, attentiveness, grief, and fear convene in what van Dooren and his multispecies studies colleagues call "arts of attentiveness" and "techniques of cosmopolitical care," the experiments of attachment to life may have the potential for cascading change within an imaginary.[107] They may be thought of as anticipated murmuration.

The question, unanswerable in advance, is whether, by allelomimesis, other humans will imitate the love and some assembly will sacralize it, perhaps setting in motion the cascade of events that give rise to swarming. If those practices spark a "militant pluralist assemblage," possibly new collectivities emerge, a murmurating cosmological rebellion, a contagious biological intelligence making sudden swerves in the dusk sky.

Loving the dwindling, swarming lives with whom we are entangled implies faith in murmuration. Yet whether swarms of love actually emerge or a rebellion succeeds, the practices of faith seem fitting anyway. According to Rose, "In this time of extinctions, we are going to be asked again and again to take a stand for life, and this means taking a stand for faith in life's meaningfulness. We are called to live within faith that there are patterns beyond our known patterns. . . . And we are called into recognition: of the shimmer of life's pulses and the great patterns within which the power of life expresses itself."[108] Practices of faith in this world here take the form of vigils, of attentiveness to particular flight ways, in the hope that lines of flight take wing.

WILLIS JENKINS lives in the Rivanna River watershed, which is unceded Monacan territory, where he works at the University of Virginia as the Hollingsworth Professor of Ethics and Chair of the Department of Religious Studies.

NOTES

1. Ursula K. Heise, *Imagining Extinction: The Cultural Meanings of Endangered Species* (Chicago: University of Chicago Press, 2016), 5.
2. Willis Jenkins, "Whose Religion? Which Ecology? Religious Studies in the Environmental Humanities," in *Routledge Handbook of Religion*

and Ecology, ed. Willis Jenkins, Mary Evelyn Tucker, and John Grim (New York: Routledge, 2016), 22, citing Deborah Bird Rose, Thom van Dooren, Matthew Chrulew, Stuart Cooke, Matthew Kearnes, and Emily O'Gorman, "Thinking Through the Environment, Unsettling the Humanities," *Environmental Humanities* 1, no. 1 (May 2012): 1.

3. Maureen D. Correll et al., "Predictors of Specialist Avifaunal Decline in Coastal Marshes," *Conservation Biology* 31, no. 1 (February 2017): 172–182.

4. Christopher R. Field et al., "High-Resolution Tide Projections Reveal Extinction Threshold in Response to Sea-Level Rise," *Global Change Biology* 23, no. 5 (May 2017): 2058–2070; Jon S. Greenlaw et al., "Saltmarsh Sparrow (*Ammospiza caudacuta*), Version 2.1," in *Birds of North America*, ed. Paul G. Rodewald (Ithaca, NY: Cornell Lab of Ornithology, 2018).

5. Trina S. Bayard and Chris S. Elphick, "Planning for Sea-Level Rise: Quantifying Patterns of Saltmarsh Sparrow (*Ammodramus Caudacutus*) Nest Flooding Under Current Sea-Level Conditions," *The Auk* 128, no. 2 (April 2011): 393–403; Greenlaw et al., "Saltmarsh Sparrow."

6. W. Gregory Shriver et al., "Population Abundance and Trends of Saltmarsh (Ammodramus caudacutus) and Nelson's (A. nelsoni) Sparrows: Influence of Sea Levels and Precipitation," *Journal of Ornithology* 157, no. 1 (January 2016): 198.

7. Field et al., "High-Resolution Tide Projections."

8. Mark V. Barrow, *Nature's Ghosts: Confronting Extinction from the Age of Jefferson to the Age of Ecology* (Chicago: University of Chicago Press, 2009).

9. Howard Thurman, *Jesus and the Disinherited* (1949; repr., Boston: Beacon, 1976), 18.

10. Thurman, *Jesus and the Disinherited*, 29.

11. Miles A. Powell, *Vanishing America* (Cambridge, MA: Harvard University Press, 2016); John Levi Barnard, "The Bison and the Cow: Food, Empire, Extinction," *American Quarterly* 72, no. 2 (June 2020): 377–401.

12. James H. Cone, "Whose Earth Is It Anyway?," *CrossCurrents* 50, no. 1/2 (Spring/Summer 2000): 37.

13. Cone, "Whose Earth Is It Anyway?," 44.

14. Michael S. Northcott, *Place, Ecology and the Sacred: the Moral Geography of Sustainable Communities* (New York: Bloomsbury, 2015).

15. Heise, *Imagining Extinction*, 32.

16. Correll et al., "Predictors of Specialist Avifaunal Decline."

17. Chris S. Elphick, Susan Meiman, and Margaret A. Rubega, "Tidal-Flow Restoration Provides Little Nesting Habitat for a Globally Vulnerable Saltmarsh Bird," *Restoration Ecology* 23, no. 4 (July 2015): 439–446.

18. Emilie M. Townes, *Womanist Ethics and the Cultural Production of Evil* (New York: Springer, 2006).

19. Willie James Jennings, *The Christian Imagination: Theology and the Origins of Race* (New Haven, CT: Yale University Press, 2010), 59.

20. Jennings, *The Christian Imagination*, 290.

21. Audra Mitchell, "Beyond Biodiversity and Species: Problematizing Extinction," *Theory, Culture & Society* 33, no. 5 (September 2016): 23–42.

22. Audra Mitchell, "Decolonizing Against Extinction Part II: Extinction Is Not a Metaphor—It Is Literally Genocide," *Worldly*, September 27, 2017, https://worldlyir.wordpress.com/category/extinction/.

23. Zoe Todd, "Fish Pluralities: Human-Animal Relations and Sites of Engagement in Paulatuuq, Arctic Canada," *Études/Inuit/Studies* 38, no. 1–2 (2014): 217–238; Kyle Powys Whyte, "Indigenous Environmental Movements and the Function of Governance Institutions," in *Oxford Handbook of Environmental Political Theory*, ed. Teena Gabrielson et al., 563–580 (Oxford: Oxford University Press, 2016).

24. Mark I. Wallace, *When God Was a Bird: Christianity, Animism, and the Re-enchantment of the World* (New York: Fordham University Press, 2018), 93.

25. Panu Pihkala, *Early Ecotheology and Joseph Sittler* (Berlin: LIT Verlag Münster, 2017).

26. James A. Nash, *Loving Nature: Ecological Integrity and Christian Responsibility* (Nashville: Abingdon, 1991).

27. Nash, "The Bible vs. Biodiversity: The Case Against Moral Argument from Scripture," *Journal for the Study of Religion, Nature & Culture* 3, no. 2 (2009): 224.

28. Nash, "The Bible vs. Biodiversity," 235.

29. Laurel Kearns, "Noah's Ark Goes to Washington: A Profile of Evangelical Environmentalism," *Social Compass* 44, no. 3 (September 1997): 349–366.

30. See Kevin J. O'Brien, *An Ethics of Biodiversity: Christianity, Ecology, and the Variety of Life* (Washington, DC: Georgetown University Press, 2010), 137–140.

31. Christopher Southgate, *The Groaning of Creation: God, Evolution, and the Problem of Evil* (Louisville, KY: Westminster John Knox, 2008).

32. Denis Edwards, "Every Sparrow that Falls to the Ground: The Cost of Evolution and the Christ-Event," *Ecotheology: Journal of Religion, Nature & the Environment* 11, no. 1 (March 2006): 118.

33. Edwards, "Every Sparrow that Falls to the Ground," 120.
34. Niels Henrik Gregersen, "The Cross of Christ in an Evolutionary World," *Dialog* 40, no. 3 (Fall 2001): 193.
35. Elizabeth A. Johnson, *Ask the Beasts. Darwin and the God of Love* (New York: Bloomsbury, 2014), 192.
36. Johnson, *Ask the Beasts*, 192.
37. Johnson, *Ask the Beasts*, 196; Gregersen, "The Extended Body of Christ: Three Dimensions of Deep Incarnation," in *Incarnation: On the Scope and Depth of Christology*, ed. Gregersen (Minneapolis: Fortress, 2015), 225.
38. Charles W. Mills, *The Racial Contract* (Ithaca, NY: Cornell University Press, 1997).
39. Mitchell, "Beyond Biodiversity and Species"; Zakiyyah Iman Jackson, *Becoming Human: Matter and Meaning in an Antiblack World* (New York: New York University Press, 2020).
40. Mills, *The Racial Contract*, 53.
41. Nicholas Mirzoeff, "It's Not the Anthropocene, It's the White Supremacy Scene; or, the Geological Color Line," in *After Extinction*, ed. Richard Grusin, 123–149 (Minneapolis: University of Minnesota Press, 2018).
42. George E. "Tink" Tinker, *American Indian Liberation: A Theology of Sovereignty* (New York: Orbis, 2008).
43. Jennings, *The Christian Imagination*, 58.
44. Tinker, *American Indian Liberation*, 49
45. Francis I, *Laudato Si': On Care for Our Common Home* (Vatican City: Vatican Publications, 2015).
46. Jenkins, *The Christian Imagination*; Gaston Kibiten, "Laudato Si's Call for Dialogue with Indigenous Peoples: A Cultural Insider's Response from the Christianized Indigenous Communities of the Philippines," *Solidarity: The Journal of Catholic Social Thought and Secular Ethics* 8, no. 1 (2019), https://researchonline.nd.edu.au/solidarity/vol8/iss1/4.
47. Greenlaw et al., "Saltmarsh Sparrow."
48. John S. Wilkins, *Species: A History of the Idea*, The Species and Systematics series, vol. 1 (Oakland: University of California Press, 2009).
49. Mitchell, "Beyond Biodiversity and Species," 34.
50. Mitchell, "Beyond Biodiversity and Species," 37.
51. Van Dooren, *Flight Ways: Life and Loss at the Edge of Extinction* (New York: Columbia University Press, 2014), 38.
52. Rose, van Dooren, and Chrulew, *Extinction Studies: Stories of Time, Death, and Generations* (New York: Columbia University Press, 2017), 5.

53. Alfonso Valiente-Banuet et al., "Beyond Species Loss: the Extinction of Ecological Interactions in a Changing World," *Functional Ecology* 29, no. 3 (March 2015): 299–307.

54. Intergovernmental Science-Policy Platform on Biodiversity and Ecosystem Services, *Global Assessment Report on Biodiversity and Ecosystem Services of the Intergovernmental Science-Policy Platform on Biodiversity and Ecosystem Services* (Bonn: IPBES Secretariat, 2019).

55. Rosenberg et al., "Decline of the North American Avifauna," *Science* 366, no. 6461 (October 2019): 120.

56. Rosenberg et al., "Decline of the North American Avifauna," 121.

57. Dirzo et al., "Defaunation in the Anthropocene," *Science* 345, no. 6195 (July 2014): 401–406.

58. Susanne S. Renner and Constantin M. Zohner, "Climate Change and Phenological Mismatch in Trophic Interactions Among Plants, Insects, and Vertebrates," *Annual Review of Ecology, Evolution, and Systematics* 49 (November 2018): 165–182.

59. Michelle Bastian, "Encountering Leatherbacks in Multispecies Knots of Time," in *Extinction Studies*, ed. Rose, van Dooren, and Chrulew, 149–185 (New York: Columbia University Press, 2017).

60. Rose, "Shimmer: When All You Love Is Being Trashed," in *Arts of Living on Damaged Planet: Ghosts and Monsters of the Anthropocene*, ed. Anna Tsing, 51–63 (Minneapolis: University of Minnesota Press, 2017), 52.

61. Chrulew, "Saving the Golden Lion Tamarin," in *Extinction Studies*, ed. Rose, van Dooren, and Chrulew, 49–88 (New York: Columbia University Press, 2017); van Dooren, *Flight Ways*; and Heise, *Imagining Extinction*.

62. Mitchell, "Beyond Biodiversity and Species," 35.

63. Greenlaw et al., "Saltmarsh Sparrow."

64. Francisco Sánchez-Bayo and Kris A. G. Wyckhuys, "Worldwide Decline of the Entomofauna: A Review of Its Drivers," *Biological Conservation* 232 (April 2019): 232.

65. Caspar A. Hallman et al., "More Than 75 Percent Decline Over 27 Years in Total Flying Insect Biomass in Protected Areas," *PLOS One* 12, no. 10 (October 2017), https://doi.org/10.1371/journal.pone.0185809.

66. Sánchez-Bayor and Wyckhuys, "Worldwide Decline of the Entomofauna," 232.

67. See Pandurang Vaman Kane, *History of Dharmasastra: Ancient and Mediaeval Religious and Civil Law in India*, vol. I (1930; repr., Pune: Bhandarkar Oriental Research Institute, 2016), 160.

68. I am indebted to Sonam Kachru for this observation and to Michael Allen for the Kane citation.

69. Donovan Schaefer, *Religious Affects: Animality, Evolution, and Power* (Durham, NC: Duke University Press, 2015), 4.

70. Schaefer, *Religious Affects*, 4.

71. James Hatley, "Walking with Ōkami, the Large-Mouthed Pure God," in *Extinction Studies*, ed. Rose, van Dooren, and Chrulew, 19–48 (New York: Columbia University Press, 2017) 2017, 41.

72. Stefan Skrimshire, "Extinction Rebellion and the New Visibility of Religious Protest," Open Democracy, May 12, 2019.

73. Philip Cafaro, "Three Ways to Think About the Sixth Mass Extinction," *Biological Conservation* 192 (December 2015): 387–393.

74. Eduardo Gudynas, "Religion and Cosmovisions Within Environmental Conflicts and the Challenge of Ontological Openings," in *Church, Cosmovision and the Environment*, ed. Evan Berry and Robert Albro, 225–247 (New York: Routledge, 2018).

75. Mitchell, "Beyond Biodiversity and Species."

76. Whether the category of religion, a colonial invention, can accommodate Indigenous lifeways is a fraught disciplinary question. For an affirmative answer from a Blackfeet perspective, see Rosalyn R. LaPier, *Invisible Reality: Storytellers, Storytakers, and the Supernatural World of the Blackfeet* (Lincoln: University of Nebraska Press, 2017).

77. Lapier, *Invisible Reality*.

78. Todd, "Fish, Kin and Hope: Tending to Water Violations in Amiskwaciwâskahikan and Treaty Six Territory," *Afterall: A Journal of Art, Context and Enquiry* 43, no. 1 (Spring/Summer 2017): 102–107.

79. Whyte, "Indigenous Environmental Movements."

80. Bruno Latour, "Agency at the Time of the Anthropocene," *New Literary History* 45, no.1 (Winter 2014): 1–18.

81. William E. Connolly, *Facing the Planetary: Entangled Humanism and the Politics of Swarming* (Durham, NC: Duke University Press, 2017), 127.

82. Connolly, *Facing the Planetary*, 128.

83. Connolly, *Facing the Planetary*, 130.

84. Latour, *Facing Gaia: Eight Lectures on the New Climatic Regime* (Hoboken: John Wiley & Sons, 2017), 152.

85. Latour, *Down to Earth: Politics in the New Climatic Regime* (Hoboken: John Wiley and Sons, 2018). I owe the observation and this specific phrase to an unpublished essay by Matthew Elia.

86. Nick Estes, "Fighting for Our Lives:# NoDAPL in Historical Context." *Wicazo Sa Review* 32, no. 2 (2017): 115–122.

87. Whyte, "The Dakota Access Pipeline, Environmental Injustice, and US Colonialism," *Red Ink: An International Journal of Indigenous Literature,*

Arts, & Humanities 19, no. 1 (Spring 2017); Estes, *Our History Is the Future: Standing Rock Versus the Dakota Access Pipeline, and the Long Tradition of Indigenous Resistance* (New York: Verso, 2019); Jenkins, "'Enemies of Humanity': Political Theology from the Pipelines," *Political Theology Network*, June 11, 2020, https://politicaltheology.com/enemies-of-humanity-political-theology-from-the-pipelines/.

88. Emile Durkheim, *The Elementary Forms of the Religious Life*, trans. Karen Fields (New York: Simon & Schuster, 1995), 224.

89. Catherine L. Albanese, *Nature Religion in America: From the Algonkian Indians to the New Age* (Chicago: University of Chicago Press, 1991); Sarah M. Pike, *For the Wild: Ritual and Commitment in Radical Eco-Activism* (Oakland: University of California Press, 2017).

90. Bron Raymond Taylor, *Dark Green Religion: Nature Spirituality and the Planetary Future* (Oakland: University of California Press, 2010).

91. Douglas E. Christie, *The Blue Sapphire of the Mind: Notes for a Contemplative Ecology* (Oxford: Oxford University Press, 2013), 20.

92. Charles Taylor, *A Secular Age* (Cambridge, MA: Harvard University Press, 2009).

93. Important exceptions include Graham Harvey (2006), who has done more than anyone to redefine and redeploy the term; Deborah Bird Rose (2013), who compares Indigenous and materialist forms of animism to explain her own use; and Robin Wall Kimmerer (2013), whose "grammars of animacy" are carefully derived.

94. Kath Weston, *Animate Planet: Making Visceral Sense of Living in a High-Tech Ecologically Damaged World* (Durham, NC: Duke University Press, 2017), 26.

95. Timothy Morton, "Guest Column: Queer Ecology," *Proceedings of the Modern Language Association* 125, no. 2 (2010), 172.

96. Oriol Poveda, "Religion in the Anthropocene: Nonhuman Agencies, (Re)enchantment and the Emergence of a New Sensibility," in *Routledge International Handbook of Religion in Global Society*, ed. Jayeel Cornelio, François Guathier, Tuomas Martikainen, and Linda Woodhead, 469–477 (New York: Routledge, 2020); See also Jeremy H. Kidwell, "Re-enchanting Political Theology," *Religions* 10, no. 10 (September 2019): 550–564.

97. Weston, *Animate Planet*; Poveda, "Religion in the Anthropocene."

98. Bronislaw Szerszynski, "Gods of the Anthropocene: Geo-Spiritual Formations in the Earth's New Epoch," *Theory, Culture & Society* 34, no. 2–3 (Spring 2017): 253–275.

99. Whitney A. Bauman, *Religion and Ecology: Developing a Planetary Ethic* (New York: Columbia University Press, 2014), 10.

100. Helen Whale and Franklin Ginn, "In the Absence of Sparrows," in *Mourning Nature: Hope at the Heart of Ecological Loss and Grief,* ed. Ashlee Cunsulo Willox and Karen Landman, 92–116 (Montreal: McGill–Queen's University Press, 2017).

101. Barrow, *Nature's Ghosts,* 240.

102. Thomas A. Tweed, *Crossing and Dwelling: A Theory of Religion* (Cambridge, MA: Harvard University Press, 2009), 54.

103. Lisa Sideris, "Grave Reminders: Grief and Vulnerability in the Anthropocene," *Religions* 11, no.6 (June 2020): 293–309.

104. Rose, *Wild Dog Dreaming: Love and Extinction* (Charlottesville: University of Virginia Press, 2011), 2.

105. Jamie Lorimer, "Hookworms Make Us Human: The Microbiome, Eco-immunology, and a Probiotic Turn in Western Health Care," *Medical Anthropology Quarterly* 33, no. 1 (March 2019): 60–79.

106. Claire Régnier et al., "Mass Extinction in Poorly Known Taxa," *Proceedings of the National Academy of Sciences* 112, no. 25 (June 2015): 7761–7766; Colin J. Carlson et al., "Parasite Biodiversity Faces Extinction and Redistribution in a Changing Climate," *Science Advances* 3, no. 9 (September 2017), https://doi.org/10.1126/sciadv.1602422.

107. Thom van Dooren, Eben Kirksey, and Ursula Münster, "Multispecies Studies: Cultivating Arts of Attentiveness," *Environmental Humanities* 8, no.1 (May 2016): 1–23.

108. Rose, "Shimmer," 61.

TWO

ABSENCE AND (UNEXPECTED) PRESENCES

Reflecting on Cosmopolitical Entanglements across Time

JEREMY H. KIDWELL

INTRODUCTION

I spent my teenage years escaping from Seattle with a small group of friends as we backpacked alpine lakes at altitudes above two kilometers in the North Cascade mountain range. The range, which includes several volcanic mountains, covers a 270-mile extent about ten miles east of Seattle, stretching from Southern Canada across the state of Washington. One of the highlights of scrambling around on loose rock in thin atmosphere was the opportunity to meet with glaciers; a kind of living geology, met in massive ice formations had taken shape for millennia and continued to actively etch away at these mountains. On warm days, we could sit on the edge of the ice, which was soft and mushy—a strange counterpoint to the massive ancient power these living, moving forms expressed on the hard and unmoving mountains we sat on. Glaciers, at least in my experience, carry a weirdly active presence: utterly silent, pressing away sound, muting the landscape. From our reading in textbooks, we expect them to be static and silent formations, but the more intimate experience of their presence is that of (an albeit paradoxical) dynamism and noise. In the decades since those early alpine adventures, I have moved to Europe and developed relationships with different mountains, such as Nan Shepherd's Cairngorms in Scotland. I dream of bringing my two sons back to the North Cascades so that we can all sit together and absorb the sound of glacial silence. However, it is increasingly likely that by the time we make a pilgrimage back there, those glaciers will no longer exist. The North Cascades have long been known to have a particular level of temperature sensitivity and thus act as a kind of climate barometer. At least four glaciers have disappeared in the past century, with dozens more retreating rapidly. So it happens that these icy paragons of persistence suddenly begin to melt away, and a scramble by humans to understand and memorialize their significance ensues.

In August of 2019, a group of Icelanders gathered to mourn the departure of Okjökull, a glacier on their island. A century ago, this glacier was fifty meters thick and covered fifteen square kilometers. The terminal decline of this glacier became evident about a decade ago. By 2014, the ice of Okjökull had become too thin to move, and so, in 2019, a group gathered to commemorate one of the first glaciers to officially vanish as a result of anthropogenic climate change. They affixed a plaque with a letter to the future, dated August 19, 2019, etched in Icelandic and English:

> Ok is the first Icelandic glacier to lose its status as a glacier.
> In the next 200 years all our glaciers are expected to follow the same path.
> This monument is to acknowledge that we know
> what is happening and what needs to be done.
> Only you know if we did it.
> 19th August 2019
> 415ppm CO_2

A casual observer might be tempted to dismiss this act as more publicity stunt than ritual. The plaque offered a certain level of formality, but in the midst of what the organizers called an Un-glacier Tour, there were few connections to so-called organized religions or easily recognizable ritual, such as the more overtly ritualized requiem services for extinctions that have begun to emerge.[1] The organizers use terms such as *commemoration* and *memorial*, but given my own relationship with glaciers, I would argue that this act of memorial carried the celebrants into *novel* forms of ritual action, interfacing a range of fields that do not straightforwardly cohere in the modern world: the presence of politicians and other public figures, rituals of mourning, and scientifically measured extinction. There are incursions here of seemingly private rituals into a public sphere and a strange blending of phenomena understood through cold, hard empirical science with more affective sensibilities and forms of knowing. In this way, glaciers also seem to provoke unconventional religious and social hybridities. We might like to have things stay in their bins, but this simply is not the case—nature and culture often intertwine, and public and private life overlap in practice. There are, however, certain examples of intertwining that stand out to us, not because we don't accept the messy world as it is, but because they challenge more deeply held and perhaps less often questioned stereotypes, and thus these examples stand out with a particular sharpness. As many of my coauthors and I have discovered over the course of this project, *religion* and *extinction* are two categories that even experienced practitioners can find unexpectedly challenging to integrate. To return to this Icelandic glacier and the novel ceremony observing its passage, one may be tempted to ask whether this memorial is a moment that one can even call religious. In this essay, I respond by challenging modern expectations of "purity" and instead deploy a postsecular frame that allows us to anticipate how religion is messy, hybrid, and full of lively entanglements. The same is true of extinction. Just as we expect glaciers to be something that closer examination reveals they are not (static, dead chunks of ice), so too can extinction bring an expectation of a pure absence. I consider how the opposite might be true; we might experience uneasy relationships with persistent but fading life, haunted by departed forms of life and surprised by unexpected newcomers. In essence, I argue that the fabric of creaturely coexistence is woven of complex presences—far more than we might expect it to be—and that this close look at extinction and religion forces us to grapple with this reality. In particular, I will explore whether ecological decline and death actually tend to generate novelty and presence. This onset of novelty is paradoxical and the target of contestation. To be fair, given that extinction is most straightforwardly concerned with disappearance, one of the last things that a person might expect to do is engage in a discussion about its opposite: appearances. Yet, this theme is surprisingly pervasive, noted also in chapters by Maria Nita and James Hatley, and it is this relation to novelty and religious reactions to novelty in the face of extinction that I explore in this chapter.

One of the reasons this discussion is so important is because the impulse to separate private religion from other broader publics has proven so persistent and has dogged professional environmental conservation and activism, which are often described as a resolutely secular affair. It is important to appreciate how these glaciers, like so many other forms of life that have the specter of extinction hanging over them, exist in a liminal space, not yet gone and yet not fully present to us any longer. The status of religion also remains liminal, resurging in ways and places that have confounded the theorists of secularization of the early twentieth century. There are exciting counterexamples, such as the attention given to sacred places in work by the Intergovernmental Science-Policy Platform on Biodiversity and Ecosystem Services and the "Faith Bridge" as a recurring feature of Extinction Rebellion demonstrations (explored in more depth in Nita's chapter in this volume). Yet, in spite of these examples, religion also maintains a kind of persistent fragility in public, not fully present and not fully erased. It is an uneasy persistence, sticking to many more things than we might expect but also fragile and fleeting.

Bearing this in mind, in this chapter, I explore how this present extinction crisis comes at us as both a living presence and lively absence that are often ambiguous, unexpected, and entangled in forms of religion. This presses at a key question that pervades the essays in this volume—namely, what sort of "thing" is extinction? And what sort of thing is religion? While, as we note in our introduction, the questioning of extinction has been an increasingly regular and fruitful line of scholarship, the questioning of religion, especially in the context of thinking in an ecological way, has been far less common, though it is no less necessary.

Like extinction, religion does not sit so easily in the places where we try to enclose it. We may be happy to marshal speech on the Christian response to extinction or mobilize specific religious communities, so long as their mobilization remains stereotypically religious (e.g., they bring an evangelical Christian form of action to climate change or a stereotypically Islamic presence to a demonstration). But as this Icelandic ritual suggests, there are aspects of this supposedly secular discourse around extinction that are already religious, sometimes in surprisingly overt ways. What might we gain from the recognition that our public and professional response to the suffering biosphere is postsecular, even while resolutely insisting that it is secular? Is the nature of religion just as unstable as these glaciers—seemingly immovable, then suddenly shifting?

I am aware that some background may be in order so that the reader can appreciate my recharacterization of religion, so I will begin by providing some context on postsecular critical theory. Then I will examine a particular space where religion and extinction seem to meet with special force—the space of mourning. As I will suggest, the act of mourning losses (whether ecological or cultural) is unexpectedly ambiguous and fraught, particularly because the object of mourning does not always offer us a stable sense of absence or loss. This is especially the case in relation to contemporary environmental crises where one finds oneself in mourning for things that are in the process of passing away but have not yet died. In this way, mourning can form the basis for what scholars like Mark Fisher and Jacques Derrida have described as *hauntology*, where loss is never complete. I turn to hauntology later in this chapter but want to stay with the challenges facing our characterization of religion for the time being. This is important preliminary work because the privatization of religion can underwrite a reticence to engage in close analysis or critique of "religious" phenomena. Yet, if we are to try thinking about extinction in the postsecular ways that it demands of us, I suggest that we are pressed beyond the (very important) affirmation of affective response to crisis (such as the one that Willis Jenkins offers in the previous chapter) toward precisely these acts of analysis and critique. I argue that the tools with which we grapple with loss are inextricably religious and accepting them as such opens up the potential for more holistic accounting for this process of reckoning. Undergirding all of this, however, is also a reconsideration of the nature of religion. In particular, I argue that a model of "folk" religion might give coherence to the kinds of *ad hoc* responses that are being mobilized in reaction to the extinction crisis.

TWENTY-FIRST-CENTURY RELIGION

A statement by Peter Berger, in the middle of the twentieth century, captures a commonplace and confident assertion of the ascendancy of secularism. Writing in the *New York Times*, Berger argued, "By the 21st century, religious believers are likely to be found only in small sects, huddled together to resist a worldwide secular culture."[2] Most notable about Berger's position is his dramatic reversal several decades later: "Far from being in decline in the modern world, religion is actually experiencing a resurgence ... the assumption we live in a secularized world is false.... The world today is as furiously religious as it ever was."³ Another notable reversal was that of Jürgen Habermas, who concluded in 2005 that the United States is a postsecular society and has subsequently devoted significant attention to theorizing this new social phenomenon.⁴ The reasons for this are various, with one classic turning point being the Iranian Revolution. As political philosopher Michael Walzer recently observed, "Today, every major world religion is experiencing a significant revival, and revived religion isn't an opiate as we once thought, but a very strong stimulant."⁵ Postsecular societies are not merely marked by the resurgence of personal religious belief—what Paul Lichterman calls the "Beliefs-Driven Actor"—but also by a persistent, often increased presence of religious reasoning of some kind in public life. Postsecularism has been unpacked in a wide range of ways by scholars such as Talal Asad, Wendy Brown, Judith Butler, William Connolly, and José Casanova.

At the same time, a range of scholars in religious studies, aided by postcolonial critical theorists, have called into question the very definition of *religion*. Jonathan Z. Smith points to the appendix of James H. Leuba's *Psychological Study of Religion* (1912), "which lists more than fifty definitions of religion." The point of this plurality for Smith is not to show that religion is *unreal*. Instead, he asserts that *religion* "is not a native term; it is a term created by scholars for their intellectual purposes and therefore is theirs to define. It is a second order generic concept that plays the same role in establishing a disciplinary horizon that a concept such as 'language' plays in linguistics or 'culture' plays in anthropology."⁶ Brent Nongbri suggests that "religion is a modern innovation" characterized by a kind of intuitive reasoning, building up an inductively derived definition from anecdotal evidence.⁷ For many modern scholars of religion, the closest archetype at hand is Christianity, often implicitly Protestant Christianity. This becomes particularly problematic in the colonial encounter: "Most of the debates about whether this or that '-ism'

(Confucianism, Marxism, etc.) is 'really a religion' boil down to the question of whether or not they are sufficiently similar to modern Protestant Christianity."[8] The structure of this mode of definition becomes one where religion is "to refer to a genus that contains a variety of species ... individual religions are generally presumed to be different 'manifestations' of some sort of unitary 'Ultimate Concern.'"[9] A key problem with this sort of view is that each "religion" must be enclosed, its concerns sufficiently circumscribed so that it may be differentiated from other concerns, disentangled from politics and culture and kept in its box. Such a view, as Nongbri argues, is anachronistic and misleading. This is underlined by the way that, prior to the early-modern period, Christians themselves used the word *religious* to refer to certain kinds of monastic practice that involved being "set apart" and held them to be in contrast to "secular" people, such as priests who were not any less religious but were noteworthy only inasmuch as they brought their religion *into* the public sphere. In those contexts where environmental management and the efforts of secular environmental campaigning organizations have opened to the salience of religion for their work, this narrow and frequently stereotypical definition is often functionally the one that organizations gravitate toward as they craft messaging and outreach to target various world religions.[10] To give one example of this at work in practice, we can look to a call by the executive secretary of the United Nations (UN) Framework Convention on Climate Change from 2010 to 2016, Christiana Figueres, to "faith groups and religious institutions to find their voice and set their moral compass on one of the great humanitarian issues of our time."[11] On one hand, this direct address by a UN leader to religious groups marked a significant shift in the desecularization of climate policy. However, on the other hand, in that address Figueres focuses exclusively on the forms of religion cultivated in "churches and mosques to synagogues and temples" and upheld by "leaders of faith groups, from Christians and Muslims to Hindus, Jews and Buddhists."[12]

I would argue that this impulse to develop an anecdotal definition of religion is not in itself problematic. The trouble comes when scholars work with a set of anecdotal data that consists of a sample size of n=1. In many ways, I think that an intuitive, bottom-up theorization is precisely the right way to go about defining religion. The challenge is to find a way of theorizing religion that is adequately plural without becoming incoherent. This should be done in a manner that is, as Nongbri suggests, more playful. He notes that in seeking to abandon the quest for essentialist definitions of religion, we might take up a nonessentialist posture where we provisionally deploy religion for the purpose of analysis. As he suggests, this means that we would no longer ask the question "Is phenomenon X a religion?" Rather, we would ask something like, "Can we see anything new and interesting about phenomenon X by considering it, for the purpose of study, as a religion?"[13]

If religion does not reside (at least not exclusively) in institutions, then where? The answer to this question about the "presence" of religion is a bit messy, and there are far too many options for me to review here. However, in seeking to take this kind of provisional, bottom-up approach a bit further, I would like to commend one program that has sought out a similar approach through an emphasis on lived and everyday religion. Part of the appeal of engaging with everyday religion is that it can wrest the study of religion of individual persons from what was a nearly exclusive focus on religious *institutions* like churches in the early part of the twentieth century. Quite early on in 1967, one apologist for this approach, Thomas Luckmann, argued in a now influential volume, *The Invisible Religion,* that the locus of authority had shifted to the *self.* What we find in practice now are forms of religion that draw from a range of belief systems in what Robert Wuthnow calls "patchwork" and Danièle Hervieu-Léger describes as religious "bricolage."[14] So an individual may now feel (and perhaps has always felt) free to construct forms of belief in more eclectic ways. There has been a welcome increase in scholarly attention toward new religions and neopaganism and the ways that creativity and production can come to play in religious belonging and experience there. But to describe this as a shift *toward* more dynamic expressions may potentially mislead as well. Organized forms of religion, such as Christianity, are not always as static as one might expect. In responding to the critique of Pentecostal Christianity that it lacks a "distinctive religious character," Wolfgang Vondey argues convincingly that it is "held together by an enigmatic theological method: the mode of play."[15] Work by scholars such as Robert Orsi and Sarah McFarland Taylor indicate, in a similar way, that the lived religious experience of Roman Catholics can have very little to do with institutional hierarchy and that many individual Catholics have little clarity regarding official church teaching (e.g., through papal encyclicals) on various social issues. My fieldwork with Christian environmental activists affirms the suggestion that when attempts are made to mobilize religion in relation to environmental issues, reductive and essentialist understandings of religion can undermine efforts to engage with various religious publics.[16] The key point here is that religion has likely always been a heterogeneous force, and we are only just beginning to outgrow narrow late-modern characterizations and appreciate the richer work involved in religious forms of knowing and belonging.

With this definition of religion as full of play and novelty in mind, I'd like to promote a description of religion as *vernacular* or *folk*, and this description applies not just to new religious movements but also to various forms of more supposedly conventional religions, such as Christianity. A key scholar of vernacular religion, Marion Bowman, points out:

> There has been growing academic recognition of the need to challenge the supposed homogeneity of any so-called religious tradition. While we conventionally talk about Christianity as if it is self-evidently one thing, it would probably be more helpful

and more correct to talk about "Christianities." Similarly, to talk about Catholicism, Orthodoxy, Protestantism obscures the considerable variety to be found within such denominations according to time, place, sociopolitical and cultural contexts. Such terms are used as helpful labels, but we should not be fooled into thinking that they represent neat packages of uniform ideas, beliefs and practices that constitute "pure" or "real" religion. Religion is not monolithic. What is nominally the "same" religious tradition turns out differently in different times, cultures and contexts.[17]

For the sake of this chapter and this volume, a focus on folk religion implies a much wider field of conceptualization, including concerns such as hybridity, ritual and other religious practices, material culture, affect, play, and the production of lay knowledge outside professional or scholarly oversight. This approach also commends a different kind of attention to extinction. Rather than looking for what extinction means for some form of enclosed religion(s), we ought to seek to find out what things in this supposedly secular discourse are *already* religious. It then becomes important to ask what it does for us to recognize these things as such.

It is worth noting that the same argument I have been making for an understanding of religion as vernacular, ad hoc, and dynamic has also recently been made with regard to scientific practice and knowledge production. In recent years, scholars across a range of fields have argued for a recovery of lay *scientific* practice with a similar sort of outcome. In some cases, particularly in relation to climate change, this has meant an emphasis on Indigenous forms of natural science and ethnobotany, which, as Timothy B. Leduc argues in his chapter in this volume, are often intertwined with religious or spiritual epistemologies. This shift can also be seen in attempts to champion and represent more localized forms of experience and vernacular understandings of environmental change. My argument for the inclusion of folk religion within environmental policy and environmentalism may seem unusual, but this push for diversity actually mirrors the shift across the environmental and social sciences toward an acceptance of the kinds of novel productions that result from folk science and lay knowledge.[18] This can be seen in the mainstreaming of "citizen science" initiatives that many environmental NGOs are promoting, not just because of an interest in stakeholder engagement, but because, in practice, laypeople are genuinely good at knowledge production. Given the resituated accounts of religion and environmental science that I have suggested, we might even want to accept that these two fields are, at least in these aspirational cases, seeking to participate in a similar epistemological field. It is worth considering whether these changed perceptions are, at least in part, because these two fields are confronting unanticipated forms and levels of novelty. In both cases, there were premonitions of absence that have given way to unexpected presences.

Having set the scene with regard to the study of extinction and religion and some deliberate entangling of these two themes, for what remains of this chapter, I will unpack some of the connections across these domains. In particular, I will explore some of the layers of (both current and potential) social response to extinction through, as Nongbri suggests, a new and provisional, if sometimes implicit, "religions" lens.

ABSENCES

As I noted earlier, our experience of extinction is often framed in terms of *dis*appearances, and further universalized toward a characterization of living in an *age* of disappearances. The news of the glacier Okjökull's memorialization was taken to be a novel event, on one hand because religion was appearing in an unexpected context and on the other because a creature like Okjökull can seem to be so permanent, huge, and slow but in the face of anthropogenic impacts had been rendered fragile and fast in its decline. I think that it is important to pause and reckon with the shock that is felt when our experience and self-perception shifts rapidly and unexpectedly from that of strength to fragility. In fact, I would argue that this sense of shock can serve as a lens for interpreting many of the Enlightenment reactions to technology and nature. Seen in this way, Okjökull is yet another recontextualized object in a long line of shifting perceptions, where one began with intense optimism about human enterprise and was overcome by a growing sense of fragility. We experience this with regard to individual creatures, landscapes, cultures, and, most recently, earth systems. Seen in this way, we might say that the late modern period has been characterized by an ongoing oscillation between high self-delusions of civilizational strength and low depths of revealed fragilities. Moreover, I would argue that this awareness of shock has been a catalyst for many (often temporal) human forms of reckoning, like nostalgia, anomie, and, to circle back around to our earlier example, mourning and memorialization.

Though memorialization has taken on what seem like novel forms in this episode with Okjökull and other departed or departing forms of life, it is important to take a broader view and acknowledge that this kind of reckoning with loss is actually not so original. The same juxtaposition of human strength with fragility and impending loss surfaced in a long-running documentary series produced by the BBC from 1970 to 1993, *Disappearing World*, which focused on *human* communities and cultural traditions that were under threat. This series formalized a key goal of the discipline of anthropology, which has from its earliest moments aimed to chronicle threatened cultures for the sake of either rescue or preservation in the context of archives. And even earlier, centuries before this, Bartolome de las Casas wrote one of the first narratives to warn of possible disappearances as a consequence of colonial expansion, *A Brief Account of the Destruction of the Indies* (1542). Across all these narratives, we find that the sense of a durable world initially open to violent exploitation has been overlaid with a sense of vulnerability and threat. Forms of presence that were taken for granted were suddenly—and, in many cases, shockingly so—called into question. In observing this juxtaposition of fear and optimism, it is important to note one crucial nuance: this sense of threat has largely been offered as a warning about what *might be* lost in contrast to memorializing what *has truly* passed. It is my conviction that this oscillation between anthropological optimism and grief or between a perception of strength and fragility produces a certain kind of proleptic (that is, anticipatory) grieving. And this specific kind of proleptic reckoning with loss, which often occurs in what can be either covertly or overtly secularized rituals of mourning, carries with it some fundamental problems.

Given the way that extinction has increased and sharpened our awareness of loss, it seems natural that the contemporary conversation about extinction should turn to grief. This has recently been formalized in an emerging literature on *solastalgia*, a term coined to refer to the forms of distress caused by environmental change.[19] In this way, as noted by Nita in this volume, lament and grief have entered the academic environmentalist mainstream. It is also worth noting that this turn is highly relevant to a volume like this one, given how the forms we give to mourning are often shaped in the context of religious rituals. I take this development to be a fundamentally good and important one, but I do want to pause and press some political theological questions in relation to the increased attention to and promotion of affective responses to ecological loss.

In particular, as I find more and more fellow scholars, artists, and activists beginning to grapple with these feelings of loss on a personal level and seeking to integrate these new sensibilities into their scholarly reflection, I want to ask what it is that we are lamenting. Is it the loss of specific species, as with Martha, the last passenger pigeon? Few of us will have had the privilege to live in biodiversity hotspots to tangibly and relationally witness species decline, so it is unlikely that we will have had any actual experience of these extinctions. If this is the case, then participation in this kind of lament might be a proxy for other kinds of personal losses: the loss of "home," the loss of access to rural landscapes, the loss of "familiar" things, or simply the loss of any forms of stasis in liquid modernity. As we suggest in our introduction, there is an often unwarranted sense of commonality concealing the numerous ways extinction is actually conceptualized by individuals, and it is perhaps the case that while we may have different sources of shock, we find solidarity in the broader shared experience of loss writ large.

There are also questions that need to be raised about exactly how pervasively the shock is felt. There are hazards lurking here that wrap around the anticipated absence of cultures, human peoples, and other animal and plant species. These hazards result from the entanglement of ecological sensibilities with colonialist notions of white supremacy. In one study, Patrick Brantlinger coins the term *proleptic elegy* to refer to the frequent response by colonizing societies to potential future loss. In *Dark Vanishings*, Brantlinger notes how the "future perfect mode of proleptic elegy" that "mourns the lost object before it is lost," such as the imagined extinction of Tasmanian peoples in 1876, "spurred home governments ... to support colonising projects" and "missionary efforts to save souls of last members of perishing races."[20] To bring Brantlinger's argument into the domain of political theology, proleptic elegies—when exerted on the level of social movements—can manufacture a political "state of exception" where the perception of imminent harm justifies the suspension of ordinary ethical and political apparatus. In a political moment in which far-right fascism has been increasingly visible, it is well worth noting how the political left has its own parallel legacies. In Brantlinger's analysis, proleptic elegies are often mobilized by settler colonists as *part of* and serve as an enabler for colonial projects.

It is important to appreciate this possible hazard, because mourning is often treated as a valorous undertaking, and by extension, the mourner can be placed in a protected, even sacred, category. My argument in this essay is not to dismiss mourning, even proleptic forms of it, but I do want to highlight the lack of questioning that happens with respect to ecological grief. There is room here for increased critical self-interrogation of mourning and mourners. In a corresponding way, the affirmation of the postsecular presence of religion in these environmentalist spaces allows us to mobilize forms of ritual critique and liturgical analysis (as modeled in the chapter by Nita). For the sake of this discussion, I need to first examine the wider critical context that preceded the resurgence of interest in mourning in order to observe some indications of how problems may have been embedded in this project for many decades now.

At the start of the twentieth century, scholarly attention returned to mourning in the work of Sigmund Freud. Freud is significant, not least because the psychoanalytic school he inaugurated began by formalizing what was an early modern disdain for mourning. Freud set up a now-classic contrast between mourning and melancholia. The latter of these represents a pathological condition in which we refuse to let go of the dead. Mourning, for Freud, is characterized by the detachment of one's affection from the person who has departed followed by reattachment to a replacement.[21] As Elissa Marder puts it, "Freud argues that normal mourning is a form of psychic work in which the self detaches from the world and retreats into itself so that it can, slowly and painfully, disengage the energy it has invested in a love object that no longer exists in order to be able to reclaim that lost energy for itself."[22] To be fair to Freud, his own account of these two modes of grappling with loss is much more complex (and ultimately inconclusive) than this neat scheme might suggest, but the schema stuck, and many contemporary interactions with mourning take this binary as given.

More than half a century later, in 1986, psychoanalysts Nicolas Abraham and Maria Torok took on this Freudian legacy and attempted to better account for the persistence of the dead and how departed persons can carry a spectral, haunting presence for mourners. In many ways, the experience of spectrality troubles easy distinctions between forms of life we take to be either "disappearing" or "appearing." Their account is complex, and I will only note two aspects of it that are germane to this discussion, particularly in light of their subsequent and sustained treatment by Derrida. As Marder notes, their account represents a modification of Freud inasmuch as they suggest that "mourning always entails taking the lost object into the self in one way or another."[23] For Abraham and Torok, grief can consist of two basic processes. The first (and, in their view, nonpathological response), which they call "introjection," is where "the mourner assimilates aspects of the other and makes them part of the mourner."[24] Here, "the departed object is successfully consumed: it is fully 'ingested,' 'digested' and 'metabolised' until it ultimately becomes assimilated into the self. The lost object is successfully mourned when it becomes an integral part of the 'me' who mourns."[25] Fundamentally, this mode of grief involves an *increased perception* of the object of mourning to such an extent that that other becomes a part of the self. In this account, the pathological response to grief is called *incorporation*, and in this mode of grappling, as Marder puts it, "the mourner refuses . . . to swallow the reality of the loss and so swallows the person instead. The departed other, neither living nor dead, disappears, as if by magic, into the hidden crypt which the self secretly builds for it within itself. The disappearance occurs in a flash, as if by magic, and seemingly leaves no trace."[26]

This notion of a crypt occupied Derrida, who suggested that "the inhabitant of a crypt is always a living dead, a dead entity we are perfectly willing to keep alive, but as dead, one we are willing to keep, as long as we keep it, within us, intact in any way save as living."²⁷ The crypt represents a place where, by force of will, we avoid the departed other and refuse to affirm our relation to them. As Derrida argues, "By resisting introjection, it prevents the loving, appropriating assimilation of the other, and thus seems to preserve the other as other (foreign), but it also does the opposite. It is not the other that the process of incorporation preserves, but a certain topography it keeps safe, intact, untouched by the very relationship with the other to which, paradoxically enough, introjection is more open."²⁸

For my purpose in this chapter, this concept of the crypt is especially important in helping us to understand the inner dynamics of these modes of proleptic mourning. What I would like to suggest is that grief can serve as a crypt where we bury the objects of our concern in such a way that, shielded by the dynamics of sacred mourning, they cannot be interrogated. In a sense, we silence the departed so that they cannot haunt us with their complex presence.

This problem comes into sharp relief when new elegies or rituals of mourning are constructed by privileged activists in response to "extinction" that do not arise from grief about actual material or specific losses experienced locally. These rituals can serve as modes of concealment or obfuscation, because while the real object of (perceived) loss is locked inside a crypt, mourning may actually serve as a proxy in which we covertly mourn the onset of negative feelings about the disruption of an everyday experience that is free from threat and disturbance. To put this another way, these projects of mourning can serve as ways to elegize threats to a privileged existence. So on one hand, the act of mourning actually marks a departure from our connection with the entities being lost and an obfuscation rather than the intensification of our relationship and collective memory of the entities and their presence. At the same time, ecological grief can often represent the deployment of half losses tangled up with personal experiences and entitlements. In this way, proleptic elegies risk magnifying only indirectly experienced losses—in contrast to, for example, persons whose homes have actually been destroyed by sea-level rise or subsistence societies who find that specific forms of life in which they are related have begun to vanish. Furthermore, these proleptic elegies may also impair our ability to connect with those forms of life that may, in the very midst of threat (like my mushy glaciers), sharpen in their more novel aspects.

In light of this critique, it is important to note that I am not calling for an end to the valorization or normalization of lament in ecological contexts but rather for a more critical but continued performance of it. In the best possible instance, these acts mirror the decline of the Earth and in turn provide ritualized expressions of solidarity with extinct and nearly extinct species. My hope is that we may find novel forms of solidarity that can emerge in these creative spaces of ritual performance, particularly in the midst of a potentially vanishing world. If we are to engage in these forms of solidarity, it is something that must be carefully conceived, lest it turn into an amplification of personal concern, a doubling down on (rather than a challenge to) existing privilege, or, as I will note further, an appropriation of the grief of others.

Part of the reason why this critical engagement with mourning and lament is important is because in many ways, grief and mourning are, as Timothy Morton puts it, "quintessential" parts of ecological concern.[29] Yet, as Morton goes on to suggest, in spite of the ubiquity of this mode of reflection—ever on the rise as anthropogenic impacts become increasingly evident—it is often paradoxical: "We cannot mourn for the environment because we are so deeply attached to it—we are it," and so "ecological discourse holds out the possibility of a mourning without end."[30] Morton wants to argue for a new kind of "dark ecology" that problematizes the sadism inherent in deep green eco-elegy, which "presupposes the very loss it wants to prevent" in a kind of "narcissistic panic" that "fails fully to account for the actual loss of actually existing species and environments."[31] Actual loss consists of things that are repugnant, possessing "sheer otherness," and so grappling with those things should lack the aesthetic comfort of mourning that (according to Morton) might be digested, whereas melancholia sticks in the throat.

In engagement with Lisa Sideris's book *Consecrating Science*, Courtney O'Dell-Chaib also recommends caution at the ethical possibilities of deep ecoreligious thought that work with "normative relationships . . . shaped solely around ideal visions of love, kinship, and wonder" as a way of teaching biological kinship.[32] In particular, agreeing with a critique voiced in the chapter in this volume by Sideris, O'Dell-Chaib notes how new cosmology promotes a kind of "deracinated wonder" that is "ripped from cultural and historical contexts, thus erasing embodied inequalities and the narratives" and by extension bracketing out the kinds of experienced negotiations with loss and grief that one finds in Black environmental imaginaries.[33] In her analysis, white privilege blurs and obscures the unequal distribution of environmental loss and the impact of ecological degradation. O'Dell-Chaib suggests that Black environmental imaginaries offer significant sharpening of this reflection on ecological loss. This is not to suggest that white scholars should appropriate Black experience but rather to note how existing Black commentaries offer a uniquely salient perception. This is a kind of mourning that has reckoned far longer with spectral presence; it is a "tricky kind of mourning . . . for what might have been but never was—a relationship with nature free from oppression, toxicity, and fear."[34] Following Morton's description, this is a melancholic subject that resists the goal of closure and relief. In a similar way, Jennifer James pushes back against Freud's insistence that "mourning is a necessary but temporary process of grieving" and instead calls for a privileging of lament for "black collective trauma," which she describes as an "inability or unwillingness to 'stop mourning' ecological loss and losses associated with 'the land' in a present where loss continues."[35]

Donna Haraway's insistence, laid out in the title of her recent book, *Staying with the Trouble: Making Kin in the Chthulucene*, hangs over all these arguments for ecomelancholia in the face of extinction. Rituals of mourning and lament can be seen to be problematic. In some cases, these rituals can be easily parodied. They may be found to be morally imperfect in their mobilization of privilege. Some observers may argue that they are ambiguously religious. The response to these challenges to what I would suggest is novel religious practice for a truly novel crisis, however, is not to shrink away from them but to continue with forms of practice that are complex and imperfect. In my view, it is precisely in the repetition and regeneration of novel rituals of ecolament, in spite of their raw edges and possible shortcomings, that we begin together to develop new and more mature modes of social response to the extinction crisis. There is a deliberate repudiation of the kind of satiation that might be granted by these new rituals of solastalgic lament. One also finds a kind of authenticity and immediacy to such an approach, particularly because extinction hovers over our present in a way that does not fully settle or arrive. This is captured in the growing awareness of "living dead species," those flight ways that persist in contemporary landscapes but are doomed to inevitable extinction given the irrevocable loss of necessary habitat range and creaturely population.[36]

Yet there is also a tension among the accounts of elegy and melancholia I have summarized. We may want to go with Haraway's suggestion that we find ways to *resist* the horrors of the Anthropocene and the concomitant temptation to adopt a "game over" attitude, yet it would be equally problematic to pursue a cheery enthusiasm for a more open future full of novel appearances. So how can creative grappling with loss engage the contemporary theopolitical imaginary? The answer lies, at least in part, in the methods of care that we extend to those forms of life that do persist and emerge and modes of political life that integrate more dynamic types of reckoning with presence and absence.

An embrace of these modes of care will require a shift in our configurations of lament, especially inasmuch as they might be entangled with the epistemologies of white frailty and given the focus on an assimilation of the spectral other. Though it might be taken as an exclusive affective mode of response to extinction, solastalgia also represents a set of incomplete temporalities—that is, those that entrench our resistance to uncertain and undetermined futures. However, before I offer a tentative constructive proposal, I want to briefly spend some time dwelling with this juxtaposed instance of novelty.

UNEXPECTED PRESENCES

I have already highlighted how novel modes of religion, though always present, have increasingly occupied the scholarly *consciousness* over the past century, from global Pentecostalism to Neopaganism. However, it is of further interest to note that novel appearances have also mobilized the biological sciences. In particular, conservation biologists have been forced to grapple with unexpected novelty and weird presences in recent decades. This comes in particular as restoration ecologists—who are in the midst of formalizing codes of practice that might guide their work in degraded landscapes—keep finding unanticipated ecological innovations.[37] This presents a significant challenge inasmuch as environmental management as a form of landscape practice fundamentally tends to work toward some kind of predetermined baseline, so that as the work of conservation or restoration proceeds, successful outcomes are measured against a return to some kind of former state of equilibrium or aesthetic. Yet, practitioners often find outcomes that undermine the baseline expectation. In a broader sense, we might say that the perception of novelty relies on the production and maintenance of a sensibility about what is "normal" against Queer presences and temporalities that are "strange," "unexpected," or "unconventional."

One example of the appearance of ecological novelty in environmental conservation work can be found in the work under way on coastal ecosystems in the Southeastern United States with the declining freshwater alligator population. A range of interventions have been attempted and in some cases have resulted in a rebound of alligator populations. Beyond these successes, however, researchers were surprised to find a reappearance of alligators in saltwater habitats—an environment that is supposedly hostile to the species. It has been generally assumed that the ability to live for long periods in saltwater was a key point of difference between crocodiles and alligators.[38] Alligators are not the only species to settle into novel ecological contexts in this way, as Brian R. Silliman and coauthors observe; this behavior seems to be occurring across a range of species: "River otters are now commonly found in many marine wetlands, orangutans are found in disturbed forests, coyotes, bobcats, jackals, wolves and hyenas are foraging on beaches and rocky shores, pumas are moving into grasslands, and killer whales have been observed in freshwater rivers."[39]

There are a range of hypotheses that have been generated in response to these seemingly strange behaviors. Certainly, climate change is playing some role here, as even familiar ecosystems are being altered for these "re-inhabitations" as temperatures range more widely and weather shifts into unexpected new patterns. It may also be the case that some of these sightings are idiosyncratic—that is, that some of these animals have wandered into hostile habitats and may not settle there successfully. While these possibilities are plausible, Silliman and colleagues dismiss them and argue that these creatures might be "recolonizing formerly inhabited ecosystems in which their populations once thrived, but were more recently extirpated by human hunting."[40] As the authors observe, this represents a challenge to the very narratives biology deploys about the normativity of contemporary "large consumers" or about exactly how static behavior patterns are for a given species. In his chapter, Stefan Skrimshire notes similarly the recent (and ambiguous) appearance of grolar bears. Silliman and his coauthors provocatively titled their essay "Are the Ghosts of Nature's Past Haunting Ecology Today?" And this question also presses the question of temporal scale—is normativity about proximate history? Or do we risk more ancient ghosts showing up to haunt our landscapes unexpectedly?

It is important to note that these novel ecological effects are felt at multiple scales. It is a recently observed paradox in environmental science that it is not only individual species that can take unique directions; whole ecologies can do the same, and they do so in ways that are not simply an aggregation of the development of individuals within the system. These two scales of activity can be working out concurrently in an interdependent way. As Shahid Naeem puts it: "Biodiversity is a product of its environment, and the antithesis, that the environment is, in part, a product of the organisms within it, is also correct."[41] The appearance of novel ecosystems at the level of landscape has been so significant that a range of environmental scientists came together to produce an extensive edited volume theorizing novelty at this scale.[42] Here, researchers have identified the development of ecological novelties at the level of a particular landscape (e.g., on urban roofs or surprisingly lively brownfield sites) and the emergence of unexpected ecosystems with their own unanticipated (and perhaps less aesthetically pleasing) forms of equilibrium. These developments are less often linked at the level of local ecologies to more historically distant precedents, but in many ways, the sense of temporal disruption is shared.

The trouble here is that novel forms of equilibria and of life are emerging at the same time that familiar forms of both equilibria and life—"flight ways"—are experiencing mass death and decline. We find increasingly pronounced indicators of extinction and in response put more energy into the formation of culturally situated ways to process and respond to mass death, including religious forms of ritual and lament. At the same time, our barely managed discomfort at the sharp increase of species and habitat loss is compounded by the arrival of new life-forms. In marked contrast to the naive optimism of our nineteenth-century lay-scientific predecessors—who formed "introduction societies" to introduce flora and fauna poached while traveling abroad to British parks, now often enclosed as botanical gardens—we Anthropocene dwellers can find ecological novelty unsettling and unwelcome, something around which to design interventions. What we confront in our response to these manifold appearances and disappearances is not just a matter of concurrency but also of intensification. These incursions of death and novel life in an age of extinctions can be sudden, unexpected, and accelerating. This presents a kind of double disorientation, as we concurrently grapple with phenomena arriving and disappearing in such sharp ways.

My reason for noting this juxtaposition between concurrent ecological departures and arrivals is that conservation efforts can be framed in multiple ways: Is conservation about holding back decline? Or is it about preventing the emergence of novelty? These are two different kinds of work, but they are often deployed in an entangled way, and the conservative expression of this reaction—especially when regimes of suspicion, control, and eradication are directed at new arrivals, as my coauthor, Skrimshire, observes—is not always benign. Moreover, I would suggest that the work of finding an appropriate response to the appearance of novel forms of life is intertwined with our attempts to fashion a response to other forms of encroaching novelty (e.g., cultural, religious, etc.).

One can find an example of this symmetry in the response to postsecular religion. The results of a quick internet search for the terms *religion* and *extinction* will reveal that the secularization thesis still holds strong in certain digital quarters. Across chat boards and news media, the rise of religious nonaffiliation is often taken as an indication that religion is facing a similar existential threat of extinction.[43] There is no denial that particularly in Europe, affiliation with institutional religions and weekly attendance at places of worship are generally in decline. Yet here, too, we find the confluence of a perceived decline-toward-extinction with the emergence of novel forms. This can be seen particularly in the rise of new religions, which, though numerically small, are nonetheless a significant phenomenological challenge to the notion of a secular nonreligious future. Further, as the study of lived religion has emphasized, experimentation, bricolage, and novelty—unexpected encounters—are at the core of everyday religion for many practitioners of supposedly "traditional" religion in the twenty-first century, as well. This can be seen in the increased number of people who will claim adherence to a religion while not attending weekly worship, a phenomenon Grace Davie calls "believing without belonging."[44] So, we find the perception of religion in decline in tension with the proliferation of novel forms of belonging and belief; our perception of decline is complicated by the appearance of new forms of religious life. Here, too, novelty—what I have called *folk religion*—both in the context of playful approaches to well-established religions and in the appearance of new religions, is often (perhaps ironically) not seen as welcome but is instead subjected to contestation, eradication, or control.

THEORIZING AT THE CONFLUENCE OF NOVEL LIFE AND MASS DEATH

In my arguments so far, I have called for a reorientation toward novel presences, especially inasmuch as our attitudes toward new life are sharpened by the specter of extinction. Furthermore, I have suggested that attitudes toward religion and ecology, especially as they both experience similar disorientations, have some symmetries, particularly in the conservative ethos that seeks to avoid or contest unexpected and novel phenomena. The kind of reorientation that I want to argue for should, I hope, be the embrace of new modes of care and collaboration, what the editors of one volume call the *Arts of Living on a Damaged Planet*.[45] With many of the other authors in this volume, I want to suggest that religion has much to offer as we seek to find viable theoretical frameworks amid the paradoxes of extinction. What I want to prescribe is not simply the appropriation of religious practices, such as lament, in new formulations—though these are definitely welcome. What I would like to suggest is that a turn to religions in the midst of extinction offers us an opportunity to acknowledge the inextricably cultural aspect of our responses to the "scientific" phenomena of ecological decline and extinction and to think in more critical ways *about* the form and content of the practices we adopt.

I have already hinted that part of my emphasis on providing a place for novelty can be described as reaching for a kind of Queer ecology. This is one key starting point toward my suggestion that we need to adopt new forms of care and collaboration. A range of scholars including Morton have called for precisely this kind of thing—particularly because Queer ecology can help us attend to the radical otherness of the unexpected other, even as we seek to repair our damaged planet through fuller collaboration with nonhuman forms of life. What has not been emphasized as fully is the potential for a Queering, not just of relations and spaces, but also of temporality. This is important given the many ways that the various phenomena I have engaged with so far—rituals of lament, conservation strategies, attitudes toward novel ecosystems, and so on—confront us most sharply in terms of the ways in which we reckon with time. So, in my call for a new attention to the place of emergence and novelty, I want to emphasize how this appeal is for a temporal reorientation away from a focus on the past and its ability to determine our present and toward an indeterminate future and the forms of cosmopolitics that can grasp at the ways that our present situation is a matter of unexpected "becoming."[46] What I'd like to tentatively suggest is that we need to connect process philosophy with Queer temporalities.[47]

In one classic treatment, in *The Legitimacy of the Modern Age*, Hans Blumenberg suggests that a defining feature of late modernity is the attempt to flatten out our understanding of time into a linear sense. Blumenberg and Reinhart Kosselek suggest that this reorientation occurs in the nineteenth century. Fundamental to this kind of time reckoning, which sees time as extending outward in a linear way (potentially in engagement with some form of "progress"), is the identification of a "zero point." This is a point in which all subsequent things find their reference and flow forth.[48] Whereas Christian theology has historically identified the Christ event as a zero point (leading to the formation of *BC* and *AD*), modernity supplants this notion, taking revolution as its founding moment, whatever that revolution happens to be, as the new zero point. As Karl Marx observes, "Just when they seem engaged in revolutionizing themselves and things, in creating something that has never yet existed, precisely in such periods of revolutionary crisis they anxiously conjure up the spirits of the past to their service and borrow from them names, battle cries and costumes in order to present the new scene of world history in this time-honored disguise and in this borrowed language."[49]

The point here to be appreciated is that many quite different political philosophies share this linear orientation. One moves forward into the future with some deference toward the traditions of the past, all while assuming that there is only one temporal horizon, which, while complex and textured, is nonetheless shared and experienced by all life. We can see the imprint of this way of thinking in the well-embedded emphasis in conservation biology on the normativity of past ecosystem states. What Blumenberg and many other philosophers of history observe is that subsequent ideologies, such as Marxism or, in my way of thinking, conservation biology, simply take the linear orientation and shift the normative zero point to some other position. At the heart of these reactions is the observation that the revolutionary aspect of modern discovery tends to generate and reify its own sense of subsequent historicity. This is what Eric Hobsbawm and Terence Ranger have called the "invention of tradition." To get back to my wider argument, in the context of this kind of temporality, we find that a constructed notion of tradition is used to defend the programs of a current regime from the threats posed by new approaches and phenomena. I would assert that this is the source of the broader cultural reflex that can be found in the struggles of conservationists to integrate novel species in the midst of decline and also with the ways that new religious expressions, including those being formulated in response to mass extinction, struggle to be even categorized as religious.

Seen in this way, reactions to extinction mobilize an intertwined set of commitments. History and the instruments of (albeit selective) archaeological excavation of these pasts can serve as a key ideological tool for hegemonic regimes of control and management.[50] We can find a shared ethos—*Things should continue this way because they have always been this way*—across a number of different domains; as examples, consider the matter of preserving statues of slave traders in public places as "history," the assumption that the use of fossil fuels for transportation is inevitable, the resistance to new forms of liturgy and ritual, or the attempt to preserve familiar species regardless of their impact on a given ecology. My emphasis on folk religion and folk science represents a deliberate attempt to challenge the institutional enclosure of both religion and science.

Novelty and the unexpectedly present *other* is often framed as encroaching on this repristinated past and subsequently managed present. There have been a variety of attempts to undermine the normativity of history when it is used in this sense. One exemplary account is the work of French Caribbean writer, poet, philosopher, and literary critic Édouard Glissant, who coins the term *nonhistory* in reaction. Glissant argues for a more encompassing philosophy of history that can still do the possibly restorative and creative work of collective memory. He also observes that our different histories, just like our different social experiences, can vary quite widely, not just in content but also in structure. Afro-Caribbean history, he notes, is not simply linear in the way that white history tends to present itself; it is a "history characterised by ruptures."[51] The challenge that Glissant issues is for white historians and historiographers to set aside what they think of as history and pluralize it.[52]

It was a similar sort of anxiety about history—or (anti)history that is not "regulated by archetypes," as Mircea Eliade said—that led to a program to recover the temporalities of so-called traditional societies.[53] Eliade argued that these societies worked with a cyclical temporal myth of "eternal return" and that this could offer a kind of countertemporality to overly linear and progress-oriented accounts of time that can underwrite technocratic destruction of the biosphere.[54] There are problems with Eliade's account, particularly the homogenization and simplification of "traditional" societies (which is subject to helpful critique in the chapter by Leduc), but this program has proven influential.[55] For my own constructive account, I want to affirm the kind of critique being offered, which calls for a reconsideration of temporality, but follow Glissant instead of Eliade and explore whether and how we might look toward the future in a more anarchistic and nondetermined—perhaps even utopian—way.

It is important to emphasize that I do not mean to suggest that we should watch the passage of anthropogenic extinction and mass death with benign acceptance. There is room for contestation of extinction rather than acceptance in this way of thinking, precisely because this is a (playful) counternarrative. As I see it, the upside of this kind of cosmopolitical approach is that it offers a dual engagement with these themes of extinction both in play or experimentation *and* lament. In this way of thinking, as

Anna Tsing puts it, "freedom emerges from open-ended cultural interplay, full of potential conflict and misunderstanding. I think it exists only in relation to ghosts. Freedom is the negotiation of ghosts on a haunted landscape; it does not exorcise the haunting but works to survive and negotiate it with flair."[56] There is an aspect here of, as Haraway puts it, "making-with" or "staying with the trouble" of environmental degradation in order to resist the "the horrors of the Anthropocene and the Capitalocene."[57] By embracing novelty, we open up a more provisional and proximate historical anchoring, a kind of *being with* whatever sort of "oddkin" we find ourselves sitting next to.[58] But taking up this different kind of frame does necessitate a similarly different kind of engagement with loss.

I think that this work of reckoning with loss can be opened up in significant ways if we accept that it will have a religious valence (taking the term *religious* in its widest possible definition): an awareness of and desire to grapple with fleeting presence and haunting, ritual engagement with the dead and an openness to connection with an unexpected and lively biosphere across transcendent avenues of relation. There are battle lines within religious studies to be aware of here—in particular, a tendency to claim dynamism and flexibility as a characteristic exclusive to certain forms of religion. In one example, Bron Taylor has advanced an argument for "deep green" religion, suggesting that implicit and new religious movements have greater flexibility and thus enable more radical forms of environmental work. Fieldwork with Christian activists seems to contest this suggestion, however. As highlighted in the chapter by Nita, her ethnographic research has found a range of more hybrid configurations at work. What I am getting at here is that it is not merely enough to make the environmental humanities more religious or to promote more frequent engagement by environmental charities with religions. There is a need to engage with contemporary sociology of religion in order to grasp at exactly what contemporary religions *are* and then on this basis seek to reintegrate religion with these fields, including extinction studies.

In seeking to draw this chapter to a close, let me briefly summarize where I have gotten to so far. I think that the crucial task facing extinction studies is not merely confronting extinction as a simple phenomenon. There is a need to look at other intersecting (or intertwined) phenomena when one faces extinction. More specifically, I have suggested that one needs to understand the intertwining of response to mass death with the emergence of novel forms of life. This also makes it necessary to grapple with religion in a more complex way, not merely as something with instrumental value. In many ways, religious epistemologies help us to confront the extinction crisis, particularly if we broaden the scope of what we mean by *religions* and ensure that the contents of this category are actively informed by everyday experience. I would also urge readers to consider how generous expectations can reveal forms of everyday religious performance, belief, and experience that are far more improvisatory, playful, and ad hoc than one might expect.

In light of this renewed and broadened attention to religion in an age of extinctions and my earlier comments regarding the intertwining of these fields of religion and extinction, it is interesting to observe a possible pattern wherein (as is the case with our glacier ceremony) religious performance follows environmental decline. There is something intuitive about the grasping toward ritual and religious alterities that has begun to surface in various contexts, from activist front lines to weekly worship. In this way, I want to celebrate the work being done by Icelandic mourners at the edge of Okjökull.

This reassessment of religion, especially in terms of its everyday character, and my related emphasis on lay experience and forms of expertise resonate with a much broader interdisciplinary reconfiguration underway, which has also prompted reconsiderations of the notion of *expertise* and, by extension, configurations of hierarchy and power relations in conservation science. There is a claim to be made for much more robust integration and exchange between these two fields of knowledge (e.g., ecology and the study of religion), particularly in "tricky" spaces like extinction studies. One benefit that religious studies may bring to the mass extinction crisis, as several of my coauthors observe, is explicit permission to give our attention to affective responses and spaces in the midst of what we are bearing witness to.

There is a corresponding need to offer constructive critique of the ritual responses to environmental crises that ensue, including the new proliferation of rituals of loss and lament. I have highlighted two specific issues that bear further scrutiny as they arise in this particular expression of lament: My first concern lies in the proliferation of forms of proleptic elegy and other related forms of mourning of losses that are not losses. While on one hand, I want to affirm this new emphasis on the ritual arts relating to mass death, on the other hand, I want to also draw attention to the dynamics of privilege that are at play here and, by extension, the incidence of fetishization and appropriation of rituals of lament that have been fashioned by those who are not privileged and live at the more acute end of ecological impact. I think that we should definitely take note of the salience of the collective trauma endured by Black people, Indigenous people, and Persons of Color and its sharpening in the context of mass extinction, but white scholars (like me) should be careful not to seek to step into that experience without also interrogating the tacit modes of fragility and guilt that will arise alongside their affective response to extinction.

My second concern relates to the problems that lurk in our construction of the subject of lament, particularly in the latent assumption that the object of lament must be assimilated or destroyed. I think that mass extinction has generated a very real need to contend with ghosts, and the function of lament, as Nita suggests, is not merely therapeutic. While many scholars have drawn attention to the spectral quality of extinction, I want to place particular emphasis on how this is not merely metaphorical. I want to argue for abjection and melancholia not in a way that centers the impacted human person but in one that centers the other-than-human victims of extinction. This is a situation where relationship, attention, and care can and should persist beyond the horizon of death, and I would argue that religion provides resources here that may require reintroduction. We experience and should seek continued communion with those things that are "gone" beyond the human.

Contrary to Freud's theory of grief, I want to argue that if we are able to provide space for those beings who have died, this will also open up our relations for those who continue to live, including those who arise unexpectedly and whose lively presence may initially seem unwelcome. Developing a holistic orientation toward novel life is equally crucial in this Anthropocene age of mass extinctions. And achieving this requires some careful critical thinking about our temporalities. Against certain forms of nostalgia that center the self and fixate on invented traditions and imagined histories, we may draw some benefit from the nonhistory of Glissant. So, in my suggestion that we pursue process-oriented philosophies, I do not propose that we abandon history, but rather that we take up practices of history that take seriously the limits of our horizons and leave open possibilities for the future.

In several decades, when I am able to return to my mountains and their lurking glaciers, when I can venture back into the North Cascades and sit at the mountain's edge where my glaciers once sat, I hope that I can sit with my two sons and that we can tune our attention to those massive beings that have departed and attend to how their spectral presence continues to press upon those mountains with their silence. I hope that we can inhabit all the feelings that arise from that continued communion, including rage at the indifference of generations that altered a global climate system and destroyed them preternaturally. But I also hope that we can inhabit that new world together. Fundamentally, I hope that this inhabitation of a world scarred by mass extinction is one characterized by new forms of solidarity—a world where justice is sought while knowledge of the differential experiences of oppression and privilege is maintained, a world that stretches across the boundaries of life and death and where we are able to *feel* the full spectrum of loss together.

JEREMY KIDWELL is Associate Professor of Theological Ethics at the University of Birmingham. His research is action-oriented and interdisciplinary, engaging environmental ethics with geospatial data science, activist and multispecies ethnography, critical work in religious studies, and constructive moral theology. His first book, *The Theology of Craft and the Craft of Work*, explored an ecological theology of craft and was developed in conversation with ancient accounts of craft work and contemporary writing on work and design.

NOTES

1. See "Un-glacier Tour 2019," accessed June 13, 2022, https://www.notokmovie.com. Dozens of examples of contemporary requiems for extinction can be found at the independent artist database bandcamp.com, ranging from work by hard-core metal group Infernal Outcry to electronic music and classical pieces such as Christopher Tin's "The Lost Birds" (2022).
2. Peter Berger, "A Bleak Outlook Is Seen for Religion," *New York Times*, February 25, 1968.
3. Peter Berger, *The Desecularization of the World: An Overview* (Grand Rapids: Eerdmans, 1999), 2.
4. Jürgen Habermas, "Religion in the Public Sphere" (paper presented at 4th annual Kyoto Laureate Symposium, University of San Diego, CA, March 4, 2005).
5. Michael Walzer, "Islamism and the Left," *Dissent* 2, no. 1 (Winter 2015), https://muse-jhu-edu.ezproxyd.bham.ac.uk/article/565371.

6. Jonathan Z. Smith, in "Religion, Religions, Religious," in *Critical Terms for Religious Studies*, ed. Mark C. Taylor, 269–284 (Chicago: University of Chicago Press, 1998).

7. Brent Nongbri, *Before Religion: A History of a Modern Concept* (New Haven, CT: Yale University Press, 2013), 16.

8. Nongbri, *Before Religion*, 18.

9. Nongbri, *Before Religion*, 20.

10. I provide further commentary on some of these configurations in "Mapping the Field of Religious Environmental Politics," *International Affairs* 9, no. 2 (March 2000), https://doi.org/10.1093/ia/iiz255.

11. Christiana Figueres, "Faith Leaders Need to Find Their Voice on Climate Change," *The Guardian*, May 7, 2014.

12. Figueres, "Faith Leaders."

13. Nongbri, *Before Religion*, 155.

14. Cited in Nancy T. Ammerman, *Everyday Religion: Observing Modern Religious Lives* (Oxford: Oxford University Press, 2007), vii.

15. Wolfgang Vondey, "Religion as Play: Pentecostalism as a Theological Type," *Religions* 9, no. 3 (2018): 1, https://doi:10.3390/rel9030080.

16. Kidwell, "Mapping the Field." See also Chris Ives and Jeremy H. Kidwell, "Religion and Social Values for Sustainability," *Sustainability Science* 14 (February 19, 2019), https://doi.org/10.1007/s11625-019-00657-0.

17. George D. Chryssides and Benjamin E. Zeller, eds., *Bloomsbury Companion to New Religious Movements* (London: Bloomsbury, 2014), 253–254.

18. Catherine Brace and Hilary Geoghegan, "Human Geographies of Climate Change: Landscape, Temporality, and Lay Knowledges," *Progress in Human Geography* 35, no. 3 (2010); Douglas L. Medin and Scott Atran, eds., *Folkbiology* (Cambridge, MA: MIT Press, 2000).

19. Glenn Albrecht et al., "Solastalgia: The Distress Caused by Environmental Change," supplement, *Australasian Psychiatry* 15, no. 1 (February 2007): S95–98, https://doi.org/10.1080/10398560701701288.

20. Patrick Brantlinger, *Dark Vanishings: Discourse on the Extinction of Primitive Races 1800–1930* (Ithaca, NY: Cornell University Press, 2003), xxx.

21. Sigmund Freud, "Mourning and Melancholia," in *The Standard Edition of the Complete Psychological Works of Sigmund Freud*, trans. James Strachey, 237–258 (London: Hogarth, 1966).

22. Elissa Marder, "Mourning, Magic and Telepathy," *Oxford Literary Review* 30, no. 2 (December 2008): 185.

23. Marder, "Mourning," 185.

24. Michelle Ballif, "Regarding the Dead," *Philosophy & Rhetoric* 47, no. 4 (2014): 461.

25. Marder, "Mourning," 185.

26. Marder, "Mourning," 185.

27. Jacques Derrida, "Fors: Les Mots Anglés De Nicolas Abraham Et Maria Torok," in *The Wolf Man's Magic Word: A Cryptonymy* (Minneapolis: University of Minnesota Press, 1986), xvi.

28. Derrida, "Fors," xvi–xvii.

29. Timothy Morton, "Guest Column: Queer Ecology," *Proceedings of the Modern Language Association* 125, no. 2 (2010): 251. Thanks are due to David Farrier for pointing me toward Morton's work on elegy.

30. Morton, "Guest Column," 253.

31. Morton, "Guest Column," 255.

32. Courtney O'Dell-Chaib, "The Shape of This Wonder? Consecrated Science and New Cosmology Affects," *Zygon* 54, no. 2 (2019): 4.

33. O'Dell-Chaib, "The Shape of This Wonder?," 388.

34. O'Dell-Chaib, presentation at European Academy of Religion (2019), unpublished, 9.

35. O'Dell-Chaib, presentation at European Academy of Religion (2019), unpublished, 10.

36. I take the term *flight ways* from Thom van Dooren, who uses it to refer to a more expansive sense of "species" in light of relationships, novelty, and extinction, in his book *Flight Ways: Life and Loss at the Edge of Extinction* (New York, Columbia University Press, 2014).

37. On this, see R. J. Hobbs, Eric Higgs, and Carol M. Hall, eds., *Novel Ecosystems: Intervening in the New Ecological World Order* (Oxford: Wiley-Blackwell, 2013).

38. P. V. Wheatley et al., "Estimating Marine Resource Use by the American Crocodile *Crocodylus Acutus* in Southern Florida," *Marine Ecology Progress Series* 447 (2012): 211–229, https://doi.org/10.3354/meps09503.

39. Brian R. Silliman et al., "Are the Ghosts of Nature's Past Haunting Ecology Today?," *Current Biology* 28, no. 9 (2018): R533–534.

40. Silliman et al., "Are the Ghosts," R534.

41. Shahid Naeem, "Ecosystem Consequences of Biodiversity Loss: The Evolution Of A Paradigm," *Ecology* 83, no. 6 (2002).

42. Hobbs et al., *Novel Ecosystems*.

43. cf. Daniel M. Abrams and Haley A. Yaple, "Dynamics of Social Group Competition: Modeling the Decline of Religious Affiliation," *Physical Review Letters* 107 (2011).

44. Grace Davie, *Religion in Britain: A Persistent Paradox* (Malden, MA: Wiley-Blackwell, 1994).

45. Anna Lowenhaupt Tsing et al., eds., *Arts of Living on a Damaged Planet: Ghosts and Monsters of the Anthropocene* (Minneapolis: University of Minnesota Press, 2017).

46. Kidwell, "Re-Enchanting Political Theology," *Religions* 10, no. 10 (September 2019).

47. I am indebted to the work of Catherine Keller, Isabelle Stengers, and William E. Connolly, which has brought insights from the process philosophy of Alfred North Whitehead, particularly around his later work *Process and Reality* (1929), back into the frame of scholarly discussion around ecotheology and environmental philosophy. Space in this chapter does not permit a proper summary of how process philosophy has reemerged in this particular scholarly context, but I hope to provide some preliminary suggestions here as to how we might understand religion not just as a form of social organization but as a more dynamic social *process* in this chapter.

48. Peter Osborn, *Politics of Time: Modernity and Avant-Garde* (London: Verso, 2011), 67.

49. Cited in Hans Blumenberg, *The Legitimacy of the Modern Age*, trans. Robert M. Wallace (Cambridge, MA: MIT Press, 1985), 93.

50. See Skrimshire, chapter 5, this volume, for more on this point.

51. Édouard Glissant, *Caribbean Discourse*, trans. J. Michael Dash (Charlottesville: University of Virginia Press, 1989), xxxii.

52. I provide further engagement with Glissant's work and Afro-Carribean philosophy of history in "Reconfiguring Deep Time," *Worldviews* 26, no. 3 (2022): 216–227.

53. Mircea Eliade, *The Myth of the Eternal Return: Cosmos and History* (Princeton, NJ: Princeton University Press, 2005), xi.

54. Eliade, *The Myth of the Eternal Return*, xi.

55. For more on Eliade's account of temporality, see Simone Kotva, "Cosmopolitical Spiritualities of Deep Time: Reading J. G. Ballard's Mystical Impulse," *Worldviews* 26, no. 3 (2022): 228–241.

56. Tsing et al., *Arts of Living*, 76.

57. Donna Haraway, *Staying with the Trouble: Making Kin in the Chthulucene* (Durham, NC: Duke University Press, 2016), 3.

58. Haraway, *Staying with the Trouble*, 2.

THREE

SACRED WATERS, SACRED EARTH

*Contemporary Paganism inside Extinction Rebellion:
A Relational Analysis of Protest Death Rituals*

MARIA NITA

INTRODUCTION

In this chapter, I address the interface between religion and extinction by looking at protest rituals in extinction activism and their connections with Contemporary Paganism as a post-Christian new religious movement. My focus here on protest death rituals arises from the way Extinction Rebellion (XR) rituals use images that symbolize death to "talk" about extinction. In this guise, protest death rituals become a modality for exploring extinction at the boundaries of death, particularly because extinction, like climate change, is simply too vast to represent. By examining XR's eco-protest rituals and representations in connection to one of its key countercultural roots, Contemporary Paganism, I address questions about religion and the valuation of nature and the planet while offering a theoretical model of relational analysis for investigating ritual. I show that the use of death rituals and funeral rhetoric in XR engages protesters and their audience with a complex symbolism intersecting a wide array of themes at the boundary of death, such as illness, healing, vulnerability, murder or the culpability for murder, suicide, sacrifice, and the absence of memorialization. This investigation will shed light not only on the Contemporary Pagan and Christian heritages in XR but also on the possibility of ritual to challenge, provoke, and empower us to contemplate and hopefully avoid extinction.

The dramatic arrival on the British and global eco-protest scene of the highly ritualistic and performative XR movement in 2018 was amplified by the preceding period of dormancy inside the climate movement that followed the 2015 Paris Climate Accords. Although XR looked in many ways like a repackaging of the older climate movement—the one that emerged in Britain in 2005[1]— much had changed. The colors on its mast had been changed from pale blues and greens to deep reds and black. The annual Day of Climate Action became the daily climate action. Its old poster animal, the polar bear, had been retired and exchanged for a new poster animal, the human: human skulls, human bodies floating in water, unborn humans drowned in oil.

Eco-Paganism, a key subculture in Contemporary Paganism, is dispersed inside the XR movement; a core Eco-Pagan methodology developed during the 1990s road protests[2]—nonviolent direct action (NVDA)—is now at the heart of XR. Moreover, as (I would argue) a post-Christian movement, Contemporary Paganism is in a dynamic relationship with Christian theology and praxis.[3] This is shown in several ways—in the intricate syncretic links within the contemporary Green Christian movement,[4] as well as in the common roots of the nineteenth-century Romantic movement and twentieth-century Celtic revival.[5] It is thus no wonder that we find at the more mystical end of the Green Christian spectrum, such as the Forest Church movement, a tangible Contemporary Pagan material culture made up of worshiping in nature, summoning or meditating on the elements during rituals, hosting rituals near waters and involving bodies of water, or connecting to the Earth by walking barefoot.[6]

XR's roots can be traced back to the British and transatlantic 1960s counterculture, the antinuclear protests of the 1970s and

1980s, and the road protests of the 1990s. When I first started investigating the climate movement in 2008, I had found an "open plan" Green spirituality and Celtic and Indigenous material culture that had visible influences from Contemporary Paganism; protest actions were organized according to the elements (earth, air, fire, water), Celtic-inspired dragons were being crafted and processed inside protest camps, and activists danced for the Bolivian fertility goddess, Pachamama.[7] Building on scholarly work on British Contemporary Paganism,[8] I offer here a discussion of Contemporary Paganism inside the XR movement in the United Kingdom, both as an inherited ethos through the historical roots of eco-protest culture and as a contemporary influence on eco-protest rituals in relation to two core ritualized cosmological categories: sacred waters and sacred Earth. This chapter draws on empirical studies, scholarly findings, and my own theoretical model for examining ritual to investigate public protest rituals gathered during my recent ethnographic work inside XR (2019–2022).

Contemporary Pagans' beliefs and practices about death are often portrayed in comparative scholarship as being in contrast with Christian, post-Christian, and Western attitudes, whereby Pagans accept death and decay as ordinary and natural while not necessarily ruling out the hope of life continuing in some form after death.[9] Yet such beliefs would clearly clash with the symbolism of what I call here protest death rituals. This tension leads to a cascade of questions: How are protest death rituals used in XR, and what can they tell us about extinction? Moreover, what can they tell us about religion in a post-Christian society? What exactly is the relationship between funeral rites and Contemporary Pagan and Christian/post-Christian attitudes toward death and extinction? Can funeral rites help the protesters and their audience and media contemplate extinction?

I begin by proposing a relational analysis approach to ritual and a discussion of death rituals. I follow this with a scholarly examination of XR's dual Contemporary Pagan and Christian inheritance, which will provide a basis for discussing wider cultural attitudes in Britain and beyond toward the sacredness of bodies of water and of the Earth.

WHAT CAN RITUAL TELL US? A RELATIONAL ANALYSIS OF RITUAL

An examination of ritual can offer us a unique perspective of the influences and directions inside the XR movement. Ritual can be investigated as a "type of communication" that enables experiments with alternative outcomes and power dynamics.[10"] My approach for analyzing rituals, as well as other performative and representational actions in my field of research, combines a biosemiotics approach to stories—which includes the ritual story—with relational identity theory.[11] First, biosemiotic and ecosemiotic approaches to culture understand stories and rituals to be intricately connected with the landscape,[12] given that place itself is produced by stories and in turn generates stories. Second, relational identity theorists postulate that our identity consists of the sum of our relationships,[13] with those key central relationships with caregivers shaping later relationships through different identity repertoires. However, I have argued that our surroundings, nature, and the landscape—waters, fields, cities, skyscapes—are also part of our relational identity. We form relationships with our home, our garden, our immediate landscape, or the sky in a very material fashion; these are places of refuge, rest, comfort. Moreover, we also form relationships with imagined places and remembered places through story and rituals. Therefore, an ecological approach to relational identity should consider how stories and in particular rituals enable the extension of our identities by forging new relationships with both real and imagined places and landscapes.[14]

My model proposes that discourses about invoked and evoked landscapes or skyscapes—be these stories, prayers, or rituals—construct relational identities and can be understood as narratives of empowerment. These narratives can be viewed, from the perspective of biosemiotics and relationality, as modalities to establish a place-identity connection, whether these landscapes are imagined or real, invoked or evoked. The cosmological elements in stories and rituals about the Earth and sky shape our relational identities and power relations, acting as narratives of empowerment that define and redefine our place and relationships with what surrounds us. We thus examine the relationships inside the ritual space—the relationships with other humans, nonhumans, real and imagined places and landscapes—while asking the following questions: What do these relationships reveal for the key actants in the story—the officiant, celebrant, or those represented inside the ritual space? What do the relationships represented inside the ritual space imply for the nonactants in the ritual—the onlookers, the audience, the congregation? When we investigate the relationships described by the semiotics of ritual space, we can find that rituals can be surprisingly similar and thus easily understandable or translatable in a post-Christian society. For example, I found that climate activists used coal or a symbol for fossil fuels, such as black molasses, in many of their ritual and performative spaces. In one XR protest I observed, held in North Somerset in 2019, activists poured black oil on a globe situated in front of a poster that said "12 years to Mass Extinction." I interpreted this placing of a negative charge inside the center of the performative or ritual space as a challenge to authority; by polluting the central space or at times altar, activists engaged in reclaiming this center and redressing their own (traditionally) marginal, countercultural status. Their marginal status is linked to the early beginnings of the Green movement. Although on one hand, the climate movement is a self-identified middle-class movement, thus enjoying a privileged status, the hippies in Britain have been marginalized, ridiculed, and vilified since the 1960s and even earlier and surprisingly continue to be ridiculed in "mainstream" circles.[15]

Ritual offers a delineated space where such an analysis can be (more easily) done, yet we can investigate any discourse for the relationships it displays and their implications for actants and nonactants. Given that one of the XR rituals I will discuss is a protest ritual at the Bath Spa "sacred" spring, I would like to first discuss the meaning of *sacred spring* if we apply the model of analysis I propose here. First, sacred springs in our secular society can be investigated in connection with a multitude of concepts, including religion, ethnicity, natural heritage, pilgrimage, belonging, ecological values, globalization, local economies, tourism, health industries, and so on. For example, in my native Romania, Techirghiol Lake, whose Turkish name—meaning "striped lake"—was connected with Marian veneration during the Ottoman Empire,[16] is considered to have healing properties even today and supports a quasimystical health and cosmetic industry. In contrast, the Bath Spa spring, the United Kingdom's only thermal spring, makes an important case study for examining secularization in Britain given that in the United Kingdom, important bodies of water progressively lost their official status as holy or healing waters after the nineteenth century, owing to increasing secularization. As I will show here, Contemporary Pagans in the United Kingdom have reclaimed certain bodies of water as sacred—such as the Chalice Well in Glastonbury—but the Bath Spa springs are not as easily accessible, as they are contained by a museum. Thermae Bath Spa, the health spa in Bath that also makes use of the thermal springs, represents the equivalent relic for the healing discourses of the Bath springs. In the United Kingdom, these waters are *not* presented as miraculous or healing but are connected to discourses of physical, mental, and emotional well-being.

To understand how the word *sacred* is used in relation to the Bath springs, we can engage in a relational analysis by considering how their status is constructed in conjunction with actant and nonactant relationships. For example, the Bath Spa springs are presented as sacred in promotional online material produced by Thermae Bath Spa: "Where the Cross Bath now stands, the Celts revered their goddess Sul, in whose honor the Romans named their spa town Aquae Sulis. The Cross Spring is now recognized as an official sacred site."[17] In a contrasting example, a website for the equivalent of a health spa at Techirghiol Lake notes that the "spa treatments [were] considered to be miraculous and unique in Europe, [their] key factor is the mud from Techirghiol Lake, a result of the fauna and flora of the lake."[18] What is immediately apparent about these contrasting examples of promotional materials about sacred waters from the United Kingdom and Romania is that the relationships that justify the sacredness of the waters are different: in the United Kingdom, the Romans and the Celts are an invocation of the powerful and represent the authority of heritage. Interestingly, in Romania—which has been in this millennium (mostly) an enthusiastic supporter and beneficiary of the European Union—"Europe" represents this connection with power and credibility. In both cases, the sacred is constructed by connecting the waters with particular people who used the waters—people who can be trusted because of their past and present power. This reflects the more general trends toward secularization and the passing of important "sacred" places into a sense of shared heritage.[19]

Before going any further and attempting to investigate protest death rituals in the XR movement, I would like to examine death rituals. Death rituals are different from other types of rituals, and this becomes clear when we employ the relational analysis I discussed earlier. Before we look at *how* these protest rituals are used, we need to first understand *why* death rituals are used inside the XR movement.

WHAT CAN DEATH RITUALS TELL US ABOUT EXTINCTION?

Death rituals can be a key to understanding societal or community attitudes toward the Earth. For example, scholars claim that Contemporary Pagans see death as part of a seasonal life cycle, which has implications for climate change and its disruption of

Figure 3.1. February 2020 Green Christian Protest, London. Photo by the author.

the seasonal order of the Pagan ritualized year. For Contemporary Pagans, death correlates with the winter season, and it is honored or celebrated as part of that life cycle and anticipation of the coming spring.[20] In contrast, in the context of the Christian tradition, death is part of a complex eschatological belief system, with the apocalypse being the closest contemplation of extinction in Western cosmology and a potentially dangerous self-fulfilling prophecy.[21] For example, Val Plumwood traces the Christian apocalyptic "master story" back to Plato and his dualistic "philosophy of death"[22] as she warns, "If we are to survive into a liveable future, we must take into our own hands the power to create, restore and explore different stories, with new main characters, better plots, and at least the possibility of some happy endings."[23] Thus, the use of what I call here protest death rituals in XR in the context of vigils, coffin processions, or die-ins needs to be investigated on the backdrop of Western, and thus

Christian and post-Christian, rhetoric relating to death and attitudes toward death.

Figure 3.1 comes from a protest funeral ritual held in February 2020 by the Christian Climate Action network outside the Church of England General Synod. The protesters, Rebel Christians or XR Christians, gathered in the morning wearing funeral clothes and processing four small children's coffins, three white and one black, to the ritual space outside the Synod. Asking the Church to disinvest from fossil fuels, the protesters sang heartfelt hymns, brought flower offerings, and knelt down in front of the coffins, which represented the children who died because of climate change and future children whose lives will be cut short due to the crisis. A small wicker cross inside the central ritual space was the only Christian symbol, while XR Christian symbols—the hourglass and the cross—were visible on the main protest banner.

Death rituals are often discussed by scholars as rites of passage in the context of rituals concerned with birth, initiation, marriage, and death, rituals that mark the transition and journey to new identities.[24] The context of extinction presses us to scrutinize death rituals as a discourse in their own right.[25] My contention is that death rituals are not just rites of passage and that it is limiting to see them as just another type of ritual on that journey from birth to the grave. As both Eastern and Western European folklore show us,[26] death is not just an event in one's life; it is always there and thus cannot be completely unexpected, even when someone "unexpectedly" dies. Hence, in his ethnographic study of the Romanian funeral, Simion Florea Marian shows that the rituals that herald death are on a continuum with other death rites and display a complex repertoire that can include signs of death in dreams, like losing one's teeth or having a nosebleed, personal and household objects breaking down unexpectedly, animals, like cats or birds, behaving in strange ways, and so on.[27] Therefore, death rituals can be understood to belong to a temporal axis that begins with the anticipation of death or premonitions of death (like the banshee in Irish folklore, whose presence is always anticipated) and is followed by death itself, funerary rites, and finally long-term memorialization rituals after the dead person is buried. Of course, death rituals, including mourning and remembering the dead, are not only a part of "human" culture.[28] Animals—elephants, dolphins, chimpanzees—mourn and remember their dead. Thus, death rituals are different from other kinds of rites, including so-called rites of passage. For humans, they maintain a constant boundary between life and death and between this realm and the other. This timeline on which death rituals can be placed can depict the relationship between the departed and the living, both for the individual and the community, for life on Earth and life beyond it.

Romanian funeral rites are worth examining, given how they provide a classic example of how death rites are structured in many European cultures and preserve important elements of Roman rites,[29] which would have influenced Western attitudes to death and the treatment of the dead body.[30] First, once the person dies, they are ritualistically washed, which begins the process of getting them ready for their journey.[31] In parts of Romania, the pot that was used to wash the body is buried alongside the body so that the soul, which first "runs around the body," can wash as well.[32] The women who wash the body cannot touch food until they wash themselves nine times. The dead body is not just a body but, as I show elsewhere,[33] since this entity now becomes *mortu'* (the dead one), it is an ambivalent, transitory being, sometimes cautiously mentioned as *it* or *one*, that is capable of harm (i.e., it can contagiously attract others to join it in death if they are not careful and do not guard themselves by observing ritual interactions with *it*) while still representing the beloved. Mortu' is dressed in new, beautiful clothes that are sometimes changed if the face of the dead person looks sad and unhappy. As it even was in Neolithic burials, the body is adorned with important objects for their journey to the *other world*; in the case of Romanian rites, these include money (to pay for the crossing), a comb, and a hat. Mortu' is then watched by the family for the duration of the wake, sometimes lasting three days. During this time, mortu' is ritually "washed" with the light of candles by being surrounded both morning and night with a candle. Eventually, once all the Christian prayers for the dead have been said by the priest, mortu' is taken outside with a flag or a tree and processed to the place where they will be buried. Here, they are then ritualistically "cried," and like in many other cultures, the wailing is sometimes staged with the help of professional wailers. Although mortu' is a potentially harmful being against whom the living must be guarded ("Never turn your back to *it*!"), it is also called by the name of the deceased, as the wailers will sometimes ask the dead person to wake up, "speak to us," or "say a few words."[34]

Remembering what the deceased person did and how they were when they were alive and recalling others who have died are the main activities during the wake. Women who are sat around mortu' will ask, "If where you go you will find my children, tell them I miss them."[35] In the center of the ritual space, the body is surrounded by candles and light, while the mourners sitting around the coffin wear dark or black clothes. During the last hours before the funeral, Mortu's centrality is accentuated when *it* is adorned with jewelry or more makeup, such as red powder on their face and lips, indicating a transition of the body into a puppetlike state, which precedes the final separation. After the funeral, the deceased will be remembered ritualistically forty days after the burial and then one, three, five, and seven years after death, as well as on all the holy days around the year designated for remembering the dead. During the first forty days, there are numerous water rituals to look after the soul of the departed.[36] Young women take water to the house of the deceased, counting up to eighty buckets and finally blessing the water with frankincense. It was customary for wells to be dedicated to the dead so that travelers drinking from these would bless their souls.[37] A cup of water is left hanging on the door with a towel for forty days so that the soul, which visits all the places that were important to the deceased in his or her life, can come back at the end of each day and drink. Death rituals can be elaborate narratives; they are performances in which water/blessed water/sacred water—from the first washing of the body to the final water offerings to the soul—plays a key part. The purification through water implied by these rituals sets the deceased apart, intensifying their separation from the community of the living.

As opposed to other types of rituals—marriage rites, for example—death rituals are *not* what I call narratives or rituals of empowerment.[38] While most rituals can be said to have as a central concern empowering the celebrant—be this the priest, groom, bride, and so on—this is not the case with death rituals. In contrast, death rituals might be seen as the most "selfless" of rituals, as they are focused on expressing grief rather than dealing with the anxiety of living—although, as we can see with the ambivalent status of mortu', that anxiety of living and elements from various empowerment narratives do seep through. For example, anxiety is apparent in the concern with avoiding the potentially contaminating or contagious power of mortu' by maintaining boundaries between *it* and the living. Yet the identity of the person performing the ritual, who is covered in black, is obscured or cut off, so that the deceased becomes the most vibrant, lifelike, or beautiful thing in the ritual space; young women, for example, would be dressed as brides and adorned with flowers and jewels. The funeral's staged ritual space allows the mourner to appreciate the soon-to-be departed for one last time. For the most part, death rituals are not about self-empowerment but are decentering, as they celebrate somebody other than the person enacting the ritual (whom we can think of as the officiant) or even another living person occupying the center stage in the ritual (whom we can understand as the celebrant). As such, death rituals are the least celebrant- or officiant-centric rites; they are self-denying rituals. Certainly, we can think of the dead person occupying the place of the celebrant, and this is quite clear with death rituals for young people, who, in many European death rites, are treated as brides or grooms and are sometimes either married (to God or to trees) or prepared for their marriage in the other world as a means of protecting the community from their potential desire to choose another living person to join them in death.[39] However, we can also recognize that this important role of the celebrant appears to be either absent or reversed in the case of a funeral, which is a ritual not of celebration but of lamentation. This decentered aspect makes death rituals particularly useful for XR activists seeking ecological rituals, given the symmetrical possibility of challenging anthropocentric relationships. So, just as the dead body is decorated and adorned, we see coffins in the climate protests that are adorned with images of the other-than-human species threatened by extinction, such as insects and birds. The main purpose is to shine a light on what will soon be forever lost and enable the audience to see it, grieve it, and remember it.

This account of death rituals leads to a key point vis-à-vis extinction: although death rituals mark a separation, this separation is not an end but an integration through memorialization of the deceased inside the family of ancestors or a community of the living and the dead. In contrast, the extinction that XR activists struggle to portray is not a "natural" end of a cycle, like death, but it is caused by violence, greed, and indifference and is self-inflicted; as such, it can be seen to share more territory with rituals and narratives concerned with suicide and sacrifice. Thus, protest death rituals need to employ both the poignant rhetoric of loss found in funerary rites and the themes at the boundary of death, such as murder, suicide, and sacrifice, to help us contemplate extinction. For example, in die-in rituals, when XR protesters voluntarily fall or collapse to the ground and lie there motionless in complete silence, the audience is reminded that with extinction, nobody is left behind to mourn and remember. To represent murder in a post-Christian society, the crucifixion is of course a powerful and pivotal symbol of destruction of the sacred. Conversely, sacrifice itself is understood by some as a form of suicide—this time not of an individual but as a self-destructive attitude of the entire community.[40] Suicide has added Christian resonance, since, in some traditions, it is seen as a mortal sin that prevents a transition to the other world.

XR'S OVERLAPPING ECO-PAGAN AND CHRISTIAN INHERITANCE

To better understand the dynamics at play in cultural or artistic responses to death and extinction, it is important to examine what I call XR's overlapping Contemporary Paganism and Christian inheritance. This is important because Christianity and Paganism have different attitudes toward death and, by extension, the neighboring connotative field—suicide, extinction, murder, sacrifice, and so on. It would be reductive to look at these traditions' respective theologies or rites of passage; instead, I aim to offer an analysis of Contemporary Paganism on the backdrop of ethnographic, literary, and historical accounts. In 2009, while doing ethnographic research at the Kingsnorth climate camp in Kent in the United Kingdom, I interviewed Contemporary Pagans at the protest camp. My interviews were in-depth and unstructured, as I asked the participants to tell me about coming to and being at the protest camp in relation to their religious or spiritual beliefs and practices. As an example of the complex narratives of identity Contemporary Pagans constructed in these interviews, consider this excerpt from an interview with a middle-aged man I call Kevin:

> I discovered deity through meditation. I think that each person creates their own deity, projects their own image upon deity.... I spent all my life being connected to nature. It's been here forever

so [how] can we own it? So, it seems we are all connected, we are part of it, yet we separate, we divide, our ego is the reason why we have all these problems. We have a task to do which is to look after all of creation. I don't own or control anything, everything belongs to God. In order to be a Christian, you need to let Jesus live through you, or to be a Buddhist you let Buddha live through you. You are only a Druid if you have respect for all of life, all of the creation, for all of the beauty and abundance of nature. Having respect means going beyond our comfort zones in order to look after it, protect it. I am surprised at how few Druids there are in a place like this. I was born a Druid if that makes sense, and I hang around with Christians and Buddhists and others. (Climate Camp, Kingsnorth, Kent, 2009)

The interviews reveal both the complex, emergent nature of identity and the hybrid nature of individual religious identities that scholars of religion have long pointed to.[41] As I discussed in my book on Environmental Christians,[42] Contemporary Paganism as a reified scholarly category is as monolithic a category as Christianity or any other religious tradition. As we can see from Kevin's account, Contemporary Pagans in Britain make use of plural religious and cultural references, have been exposed to a nonconfessional religious studies education, and can easily share in a deeply inculcated Christian discourse of stewardship, with Kevin even saying that we have to look after "creation."

Similarly, XR can be understood first and foremost as a British-born movement, and as such, it needs to be seen against the backdrop of Britain's countercultural repertoire and landscape. In Britain, from the point of view of broad trends,[43] Contemporary Paganism is growing while Christianity is declining, and both are currently influential in their pulverized forms and material dimensions (i.e., place organization, dress, makeup, media, food, vernacular) through a myriad of cultural and countercultural influences. Pagan and New Age ideas in Britain are on showcase during major festivals like Glastonbury and, particularly post-COVID-19, online via a growing number of channels. The

XR movement has clear roots in the transatlantic 1960s counter-cultural movements; communes and free festivals had a similar mix of civil disobedience, "artivism"—or artistic activism—cooperative ethos, and communalism and anticipated a future world in deep crisis that the communes could withstand.[44] Moreover the "protestival," a favored type of protest action in XR, is also rooted in the 1960s counterculture and has been central to movements of artistic social reform and the alter-globalization movements that have begun to develop since the 1980s. The 1960s transatlantic counterculture represents an important root for Eco-Paganism,[45] among other radical environmental networks inside the alternative milieu. Hence, although key Paganism scholars tend to use it as an umbrella designation and include Eco-Paganism with other forms of contemporary Paganism (e.g., Wicca, Druidism, Shamanism, Heathenism, Goddess spirituality) or as a part of a broader lexicon,[46] Andy Letcher locates Eco-Pagans within their own subculture of radical environmentalism and Goddess spirituality.[47] As such, Eco-Paganism itself becomes more clearly visible as a distinctive subculture or religious movement that emerged in the context of the religious change that dominated the 1960s.[48]

Letcher's ethnographic work on Eco-Paganism in the 1990s road-protest movement offers some important coordinates in the context of British eco-protest culture.[49] Importantly, Letcher shows that the Pagan road protests of the 1990s were influential in propelling radical environmentalism and its methodology of NVDA into the (greater) public consciousness. This new heroic type of environmental activism is millenarian and Tolkienesque,[50] as there is a strong narrative of the protest as "the last pitched battle of some ancient tribe against the relentless advance of modernity."[51] Millenarianism is of course an important Christian root that has implication for extinction, since it promises a resurrection. The movement had a long-lasting influence on Pagan theology, with the "thealogies" of such prominent Pagans as Starhawk and Carol Christ forged into Goddess Spirituality in the context of the antinuclear and antiroad protests.⁵² Starhawk, an influential Pagan witch and activist, explained at the beginning of the millennium: "A deepening earth-based spirituality led me into environmental and antinuclear activism, out of the sense that if the earth is sacred, we should prevent idiots from destroying her and us. Throughout the eighties and nineties, I engaged in many nonviolent direct actions on the issues of nuclear power and weapons, and later on militarism, intervention in Central America, the clearcutting of redwood forests, AIDs, and other issues. I was part of a collective of nonviolence trainers and also helped to organize many of the actions."⁵³

Green Christians share significant similarities and cultural territory with Eco-Pagans. As I show in my own ethnographic work on Green Christianity in Britain, the opposition toward modernity (with common roots in the Romantic movement) and the adherence to a back-to-nature discourse are also present in Christian models of a pastoral reimagination of the Early Church. This is evident both at a level of discourse and of material culture—for example, at Greenbelt, the annual British arts and performance Christian festival (1974–present). Here, the landscaped gardens of the festival fields have names such as the Mount or the Grove, and in 2014, there was even a sermon on the Mount, though this was discontinued in later editions of the festivals due to health and safety concerns over climbing the landscaped hill.⁵⁴ In Britain, this identification with the Early Church has long roots and many political implications. Hence, the town of Glastonbury has been a center of pilgrimage in Britain since the thirteenth century precisely because it was claimed to represent the Early Church established by Joseph of Arimathea, the man who took Jesus down from the cross and arrived in Glastonbury two years after the crucifixion.⁵⁵ The claim that Glastonbury represented a direct link with the Holy Land and the Early Church became a local and national symbol of resistance against other Christian dioceses and Rome itself, particularly around the sixteenth-century Reformation. The town of Glastonbury, with its plural symbolism as "Ancient Avalon, New Jerusalem, Heart Chakra of Planet Earth,"[56] represents a clear example of the shared territory and diachronic continuity between Christian and Pagan discourses (as well as New Age influences), their opposing Earth-versus-Sky orientations notwithstanding.[57] This allows us to see Contemporary Paganism in relation to national and place identity and in continuity with what can be understood as the identity-reclaiming processes that were made evident during the English Reformation.

Although the nineteenth-century Romantic movement had already rejected modernity through its nature writings,[58] it is particularly post-1960s that back-to-nature discourses become visible in Britain in more than just poetry. Hence, Sharif Gemie and I have argued that early festivals in Britain drew on a Christian vernacular and the antimaterialism of a simple Eden imagery to reframe festivals as a return to a sacred nature.[59] Recent work on Green Orthodoxy in Romania suggests that despite the lack of political opportunity, the cultural isolation, and the restrictions on freedom of expression during the country's communist regime, Christian discourses offered an intuitive path to Green concerns, even in the absence of a vocabulary to express this as a countercultural reformulation.[60] Conversely, Contemporary Paganism in Britain is the result of the political and religious freedom that enabled a radical reformulation. Thus, it can be claimed that Contemporary Paganism in Britain has links or roots in the Christian Reformation, whereby Contemporary Paganism is also a part of the reclaiming of local identities and the rejection of "outside" or "distant" power structures.

This slightly different origin story for British Eco-Pagans shows that they share more territory with Christianity than with early Wicca and even other contemporaneous North European Paganisms that emerged post-1960s (i.e., Icelandic), which were understood as a Norse, rather than Celtic, revival.[61] Thus, the alternative counterculture that emerged in the 1960s, after the hippie trail or journey to India and the East of the 1950s, had a deeply rooted, dynamic, and reciprocal relationship with Christianity in Britain.[62] Gemie and I assert that we can discern in this British alternative hippie culture of the late 1960s and 1970s much stronger Christian undertones and a religiously inflected language of Christian antimaterialism that led to the establishment of the early festivals as alternative spiritual pilgrimages at a time of growing secularization. Importantly, the festivals during this time allowed for an encounter between hippies and Christian clergy, who also recognize and affirm their shared Christian values.[63] As such, it can be argued that Eco-Pagans themselves share more cultural territory with Christians than with fellow Contemporary Pagans—such as Wiccans—particularly when we consider other common roots in the nineteenth-century Romantic tradition and the Celtic revival. The same can be said of Green Christians, like the Forest Church movement and other "post-material religionists."[64] The links between Eco-Paganism and the Christian tradition are further deepened by a major literary influence for Paganism and Eco-Paganism in particular—this being J. R. R. Tolkien's fiction[65]—given that Tolkien was raised and remained a devout Roman Catholic. Letcher shows how this powerful Tolkienesque aesthetic and millenarian "final battle for Middle Earth" narrative simply became a live stage at Eco-Pagan protest camps, where protesters were blocking the advance of tree-felling machinery:

> A long ribbon of trees had been cleared to make way for the oncoming road, the area now fenced off as a security compound. Noisy generators powered bright arc-lights that lit up an activity of security guards in fluorescent jackets, standing vigilantly in the mud and debris. In stark contrast, on the other side of the fence and stretching up the opposite side of the valley, obstructing the oncoming road, an array of candles and lanterns had been hung

crookedly among the treetops. Treehouses and aerial walkways could just be discerned in the gloom, with people murmuring and moving among them, their faces painted with symbols and "Celtic" spirals. The sound of a tune played on a tin whistle floated down from the canopy. It was, for an observer on the ground, and however cliched, a scene like that from a fairy tale. I felt at the time that I was witnessing something more Tolkienesque than real, the last pitched battle of some ancient tribe against the relentless advance of modernity.[66]

We can recognize in XR a dual, overlapping Eco-Pagan and Christian inheritance that helps situate XR protest rituals inside a broader cosmology, material culture, and emotional matrix.[67] We can clearly recognize the elements of a Christian affective repertoire—the heroic sacrifice and vulnerability that come with getting attested. We can also identify elements from the Eco-Pagan, eco-protest material culture that are affectively steeped in Christian pilgrimage praxis through practices of deprivation, for example. Although Contemporary Paganism is a post-Christian movement and hence Christian influences and countercultural reformulations are to be expected, my argument is that post-1960s Eco-Paganism in Britain is distinct in affective ways and should be viewed as a hybrid New Christian movement. We can see this by looking at its discourses, material culture, and emotional landscape and in particular its sacrificial and heroic character, which is qualitatively different from earlier British movements (e.g., Wicca) or even concomitant movements (e.g., Nordic Paganism).

ECO-PAGANISM AND CHRISTIANITY IN RELATION TO SACRED WATERS AND SACRED EARTH

The link between Eco-Paganism and Christianity in Britain can be illuminated further by examining their relations with sacred waters and sacred Earth on the backdrop of wider trends of religion and secularization in Europe. Attitudes toward nature are intricately connected—meaning both influencing but also facing opposition—with religious attitudes, past and present.[68] The process of secularization in Europe in the modern and postmodern eras is often understood to be concomitant with what German philosopher Max Weber (1864–1920) called *entzauberung* (disenchantment or a loss of nature's enchantment). We can see this quite clearly in the status of sacred waters in Britain. In the United Kingdom, the nineteenth-century status of such previously venerated waters (both in Roman times and subsequently via the belief in the healing properties of the waters) as the Bath waters in England declined progressively, these springs being currently only of historical interest.[69] Thus, this city had an important tradition of balneotherapy (water therapy) that advertised the waters as having unique healing properties, a tradition that (albeit controversially) still survives in Eastern Europe.[70] In the United Kingdom, balneotherapy was eventually replaced with hydrotherapy, which does not consider the waters to have any unique healing or curative properties but aims to help rehabilitation through mechanical processes alone. For example, the former Royal Bath Mineral Hospital, first opened in 1742, presently includes a museum where one can see how various ailments were treated there in the past, when patients came to "take the waters." The only institution that provides access to Bath Spa's thermal waters presently is Thermae Bath, a deluxe spa offering health and beauty treatments. Thermae's advertising material talks about the history of the springs, including the fact that the Cross Spring in Bath was considered sacred by the Celts, who worshiped the goddess Sul, in whose honor the Romans called this antique city Aquae Sulis. This reflects the more general trend toward the "heritagization" of religion, which includes the passing of important sacred places into a sense of shared patrimonium.[71]

Contemporary Paganism is perceived as a movement of resistance against secularization and disenchantment,[72] and we can extend that to this trend of heritagization, whereby the recognition of important sites is purely historical or connected to a national identity rather than inherently sacred. With new religious movements and alternative spiritualities arriving on the British and global scene in the twentieth century, some springs regained their "healing" status; such is the case with the Chalice Well spring in Glastonbury, considered sacred by Contemporary Pagans. Although Contemporary Pagans reach out to pre-Christian traditions, such as Druidism, it is important to note that beliefs in the protective spirits of places and waters, those *genii loci* from pre-Christian times, have survived for many centuries in folk vernacular, even when these beliefs were not in agreement with official or institutional Christian beliefs. The convergence I have talked about between Eco-Paganism and Christianity is thus not that surprising if we consider that vernacular or folk Christianity in Europe preserved some Pagan customs and attitudes toward nature. Thus, the pre-Christian customs of tree worship,[73] or revering sacred and healing waters, continued under different guises through associations with Christian figures, particularly in the context of Marian veneration, in the case of European healing waters.[74] Many of the healing waters of Europe continue to be associated with Mary, as is the case with the Lady of Sanctuary in Lourdes, France, which remains a thriving pilgrimage center to this day. Moreover, pilgrimages often involved practices of body deprivation that are very similar to those deprivations endured as actions of resistance (i.e., not eating, not washing, being cold, sleeping outside, etc.) by those involved in the radical eco-protest culture. It is these affective and material realities of deprivation and sacrifice in the eco-protest culture that can be investigated for their links to Christianity. XR activists often orient their protest actions toward waters, even if these are just fountains in an urban environment, which gains new meaning when we juxtapose these two types of experiences—Christian pilgrimage to sacred sites and waters on one hand and eco-protest actions oriented toward waters on the other.

The valuation of sacred waters and the sacred Earth is further linked to the local and global dimensions in the Green movement and the increasing emphasis on the importance of "thinking globally and acting locally" in many Green initiatives.[75] The alternative globalization movements of the last four to five decades have often addressed the local-global dynamic through festivals and protestivals that have *glocal* relevance; they share global trends but are oriented toward localities.[76] The emphasis on locality and bioregions is also obvious in XR, which resembles the organization of the 2005 local-global Transition Towns movement in terms of its emphasis on local regeneration groups. We can credit Eco-Pagans for their leading role in striking a local-global harmony though their construction of Gaia.[77] Through their leading role inside the antiroad movement, their concern with resisting modernity, and the valuation of "local" environments, Eco-Pagans made it clear that they opposed globalization, yet at the same time, they were able to "connect" with both local (sacred waters like the Chalice well in Glastonbury) and global (the Earth) environments. My contention is that in this construction of Gaia as one encompassing divine entity, Eco-Pagans were able to draw on a Christian monistic model of divinity and relationality, just as Green Christians themselves were.[78]

One important question here concerns the relevance of the word *sacred* in this field. What relationships does it tend to describe? As I indicated at the beginning of the chapter in regard to the recognition of Bath waters as sacred in various local publications, we need to pay attention to the relationships described by this term or engage in a relational analysis of the text in order to discern its dynamic (not static) meaning. The fact that the waters were considered sacred by the Celts points to a recognition of their historical significance, and this has monetary value, since it attracts visitors to the town of Bath. However, a recognition of their sacred status simply lacks the "numinous," mysterious, or mystical quality that early scholars of religion attempted to identify when they discussed this category of the sacred.[79] Kate Rigby, in her own chapter in this book, talks about the official recognition of the Bath waters as a sacred site in connection with a revival of interest among Contemporary Pagans in these waters. Rigby shows that the waters are once again being revered by Contemporary Pagans, since for them, their ecospiritual experience is interlinked with ecopolitical praxis, and thus the quest for personal healing is interwoven with a collective responsibility for healing the waters. Rigby provides the example of Margaret Marion Stewart, a devotee of Celtic goddess spirituality whose work led to the recognition of one of the main geothermal springs, the Cross Bath, as a sacred site.[80]

Although Rigby's example appears to indicate a postsecular change of attitude toward the Bath waters and even a change of flow (or a double flow) in the healing attributes that circulate from the waters and toward the waters, I would like to suggest that such a revival or re-enchantment is *not* happening. A revival might mean that the waters are capable once again of producing new miraculous stories by inspiring activists and demonstrating a special kind of agency. Contemporary Pagans, with their "capital" in Glastonbury, do not connect with middle-class, gentrified Bath in the same manner, and the rivalry between Bath and Glastonbury has a long history that goes back to the thirteenth century, with the Glastonbury Abbey "frantically trying to assert its autonomy from the bishop of Bath and Wells."[81] I will discuss the protest ritual that took place inside the Roman Baths, or what was considered the sacred spring in Roman Britain, later in this chapter, but I would like to emphasize here that while it may be possible for Contemporary Pagans to visit and connect with the sacred sites in Glastonbury (like the Chalice Well), Bath's waters are completely encased in the museum site and commercialized; there is simply no possibility of approaching these without paying for it or being surrounded by kids on a school trip or tourists listening to a tour guide.

The biosemiotic categories of *sacred waters* and *sacred Earth* represent rather magical processes—processes of stories that make places and places that make stories. While waters are visible and can easily "make stories" and "be storied," the Earth as a totality arrives in human consciousness particularly after the iconography of the planet developed after the 1969 moon landing. The image of the planet is "storied" by the 1960s transatlantic counterculture and the 1970s Earth movement. It is chiefly art and iconography of the goddess as a Gaia, the Earth, often appearing as a pregnant woman or in reference with the Greek Goddess, that develops a consciousness of the sacred Earth—with such influential public sites as the Whole Earth festival, which began in 1969 in the United States. It is important to note that while this Earth consciousness was taking root in Western Europe, countries in Eastern Europe were also experiencing a back-to-nature movement,[82] though they lacked an explicit environmental art and a proper vocabulary to express these concerns for nature.[83] Contemporary Paganism's role in the construction of the Sacred Earth and Gaia consciousness in the West simply through representing the Earth as sacred in their artworks cannot be overstated; it is through the graphic representations of the Earth that the Earth can be seen and storied. In figure 3.2, a Pagan poster from 2008 entitled "Gaia and the Spirit of Activism," we can observe a representation of the planet as if transposed on a classic Christian icon, with the halo and the mystical, saintly hand gestures symbolizing divine blessing and authority.

When considering how Eco-Pagans connect or relate with sacred waters and sacred Earth, we can more clearly see the continuum between vernacular forms of Christianity and Contemporary Paganism. The notion of sacred waters, which was widespread in Europe and declined vertiginously after the nineteenth century, may have been rekindled by (some) Eco-Pagans

Figure 3.2. A Pagan poster (Pantheacon, 2008). Courtesy of the Bath Archive for Contemporary Religious Affairs (BACRA).

(i.e., the Chalice well is considered to be a sacred spring), but only a contextual analysis can reveal the dynamic meanings of this term. While Eco-Pagans can be credited for the construction of the sacred Earth, this model of relating to the planet as one divine entity contributes to my general argument for understanding Eco-Paganism as a Neo-Christian movement. Furthermore, my contention has been that one ought to be cautious when examining the meaning of sacred waters in 2019 Bath and even Glastonbury in light of contemporary processes of heritagization and secularization. To what degree are these waters truly considered healing, miraculous, and powerful? Are they merely recognized for their historical significance, and for what purpose?

If the former is the case, then we can talk about a revival of their sacred qualities—which I argue we might equate with a sort of present fecundity, endowing them with a special agency in being able to generate or inspire *new healing stories* and thus create new relationships. If the latter is true, we are only talking about old stories; albeit important, these are stories from the past.

PROTEST DEATH RITUALS AND EXTINCTION

Given the abundance of opportunities to study XR public rituals, my data is diverse and extensive; it covers more than fifty protest actions lasting anywhere from a few hours to a few days, ten extended interviews with XR activists between twenty-one and sixty-five years old, XR online material and databases (Basecamp), weekly meetings with XR Rebels in Bath (2019–2020), literary and cultural activities, social media communications (Facebook), choir singing groups, yoga in the park, cooking for communal meals, workshops, and lectures. For my discussion in the present chapter, I draw mainly on participant observation during public rituals, among which I will consider examples from an XR protest ritual at Bath Spa sacred spring in 2019, an Earth pilgrimage from Cardiff to London in 2019, and a series of cultural events, entitled Letters to the Earth (2019), organized by XR's Regenerative Culture networks. Additionally, I draw on an online series of workshops organized during the COVID-19 lockdowns by a Green Christian UK charity called Radical Presence. My proposed model of analysis[84] draws on biosemiotics and relational identity approaches[85] to consider the instrumental function of ritual and other discourses in the construction of empowered identities.

As I showed at the beginning of this chapter, death rituals encompass a huge repertoire of affective performances that are concerned not only with death itself but with a whole human existence, both invisibly and visibly connected with death—the anticipation of death (in illness), premonitions of death, funerary rites, memorialization after the death of a beloved. These rituals may reflect many themes that are found in the vicinity of death (suicide, murder, sacrifice, illness) and a Christian point of view of resurrection and healing (e.g., the story of Lazarus). Illness and healing are, as I have shown, a major attribute of sacred waters and a key concern in ritual, be it in their ability to actually cure or purify and create a boundary between life and death, as my examples of funeral rites showed. As the COVID-19 crisis has made a lot more obvious for us modern people who grew up without such major health emergencies, death, illness, and healing can eclipse all other activities, particularly when there are no available cures. Certainly, pre-COVID-19, these concerns might have appeared rather distant in our modern world,[86] yet religious traditions and contemporary spirituality are fundamentally preoccupied with death, illness, and healing, and vice versa. Illness and healing are contexts in which religion and spirituality gain major importance.[87]

Death rituals are for the most part reverent treatments of death, with some exceptions, such as the pre-Christian relics in some localized funerary rites that make fun of the dead body, treating it like a puppet and frightening unassuming visitors.[88] Thus, funerary symbolism can easily evoke elements of grief and loss, but the rite itself implies a process of memorialization, which becomes impossible with extinction. Thus, XR death rituals explore extinction by working with the rich symbolism in death rituals in an artistic way, not just as the art that one would find in a gallery or museum but as a new type of engaged "radical art" that provokes the onlooker and aims to stimulate a civic response.[89] This can be done through art and performance by surprising the audience with the removal or addition of elements that are found in this vast semiotic field representing death rituals. For example, a key embodied XR ritual, the die-in, represents the more morbid version of the sit-in, which involves sitting down and thus

Figure 3.3. Fountain Ritual Red Brigade 2019, Bath Spa, UK. Photo by the author.

refusing to be moved by police. Yet during a die-in, everyone is on the ground and there are no mourners; the only people standing are the audience, the onlookers who see this spectacle through the lens of the future and thus are not able to intervene.

The color red, which symbolizes the blood of the species that have been and will be lost, is complementary to the funeral black in XR.[90] The XR Red Brigade (XR activists dressed in red gowns whose street-theater activism has become iconic for the movement; see fig. 3.3) attempts to perform this collective and irreversible kind of death alongside a funerary material culture in XR that is made up of coffins, flowers, wreaths, and black clothes. Striking images—a lonely human handprint on a black canvas, for example—remind the onlooker of humanity as a species whose future hangs in the balance. Although activists are naturally concerned about the extinction of all these other disappearing species, with XR, an emphasis on human extinction becomes central to rituals and art. For example, an image of the human skull may be printed in a pattern of bees and insects as a symbol of our interdependent relationships, yet there is also an emphasis on human extinction, possibly as a means of addressing the unengaged public. Human extinction juxtaposed with the extinction of other species can also be understood as a radical art tactic through which human extinction, as the natural consequence of other species' extinction, is the sort of bang at the end of the performance.

The protest ritual at the Bath spring involved activists infiltrating the museum and floating in the pool of water that once was the sacred heart of the baths. The ritual is of particular interest because, as I showed in the previous section, these waters have lost their traditional healing status. Instead, their sacred status is now part of their heritagization—a trusted brand, a way of adding to the status and reputation of the waters, and a promise of physical, mental, and emotional well-being added to the mix. My data suggests that the XR activists conducting this protest ritual inside the Roman Baths in Bath Spa (2019) did not think that these waters were indeed sacred in this magical and healing sense of the word.[91] I interviewed the person who organized the protest action, and she was not a Contemporary Pagan, nor was she religious, yet she told me that she had a degree in religious studies and "loved ritual." As I pointed out in my introduction, the celebration of the elements—earth, air, fire, water—is a taxonomic category in the Green and climate movement, with numerous actions following these patterns. For example, in an early climate protest action aimed at closing the Kingsnorth power station in Kent (2009), protesters descended on the power station in four groups representing the elements; a fire dragon led the procession. The dragon, called Kingsnorth, "had eaten too much coal and had gotten sick," and he was made better by the procession, laughter, and conversation with the children at the protest camp.[92] A humorous tone often permeates protest rituals as part of a countercultural strategy of distinguishing eco-protest culture from the buttoned-up mainstream culture the former is attempting to provoke and challenge, since eco-protest ritual, like art and performative actions in this field, will seek to challenge the nonactant/audience/onlooker. The floating bodies of XR activists in the sacred pool and the other activists forming a protective circle around them illustrate how symbols of death—in this case a floating body holding a flower—are used to portray extinction. Yet this is not a reverent representation of death but a portrayal of climate change, rising seas, and flooding.

One final step in this chapter is to ask how XR activists can be understood to relate to the Earth, considering this repertoire of illness, healing, death, and extinction. An important symbol in the semiotics of ritual space at climate protests is coal. Coal and fossil fuels are associated with illness, pollution, and degradation. Coal and oil were present very early in my research data,[93] with coal often being placed at the center of a ritual space (i.e., on the altar), which is of course an unexpected and provoking object to see in the middle of a traditionally pristine space.[94] I argued that coal was used as a negative charge in a traditional model of sacred space in order to articulate a different power dynamic, whereby the center of sacred space was no longer pristine and powerful but equally contaminated or polluted. In contrast, the marginal become powerful.

Often, symbols of regeneration and healing, such as apples and living plants, are part of climate protest rituals. When cut flowers are used, they are often a symbol of death and funerals. In one ritual, Green Christian protesters prayed around a charcoal-colored effigy of a power station (2009), yet they also placed a red apple on top of the effigy as a symbol of creation and regeneration. The Christian activists were going to read the power station its last rites, which is reminiscent of the Christian Sacrament of the Sick that is offered to the ill and dying, but there was opposition to doing that, as some members felt it would be disrespectful or sacrilegious.[95] Yet, when looking at prayers as narratives of empowerment in a Green Christian context,[96] we see that they reflect a transformed cosmology, with community and creativity leading to salvation (as opposed to pursuing empowerment by relating to the sky/God/the heavens or by accessing the vertical axis of power that permeates the Western cultural tradition). And we see this represented spatially in a "de-evolution" of the Green Christian altar, which is increasingly set directly on the ground, rather than on a table; the altar has become the ground, or the ground the altar. Like Contemporary Pagans, Green Christians set altars that are decorated with cones, stones, sticks, and other such natural objects, literally changing the content of the altar with nature itself. During Radical Presence 2020, an online workshop on climate activism that took place amid the COVID-19 lockdown, one Green Christian explained her new interest in the Forest Church movement thus:

> If we worship in a way that reminds us that we are creatures of the Earth, you know, the way out of Adam, then we will be sort of better connected with the Earth. We will see our health and our well-being as part of the Earth. The pandemic is teaching us to worship in a different way, how to express longing for God by reaching out to God as people of the Earth as through ritual. And there were a couple of groups that talked about Forest Church... being a model for the future. So that's something. That's something to think about as a way of emerging from this.

My data suggests that during public events, XR activists do not tend to talk about the Earth as sacred or with any particular reverence associated with sacredness, though Pagan songs invite those present to "remember that you're walking on sacred ground." During a Letters to the Earth event put together by the XR Regenerative Culture networks, activists addressed the Earth and expressed their feelings toward it, but these interventions were quite removed from the reverence of the Deep Ecology rituals of Joanna Macy and other earlier ritualists.[97] Hence, activists who addressed the Earth were often addressing humans in statements that were self-referential and sounded more like confessions to those present: "I'm sorry as humans that we had the nerve to call this destruction part of nature," or "I'm sorry, I'm sorry that as humans, we've been using you as a credit card with no spending limits." If sacredness is/was associated with power and healing properties, it follows that illness would be somewhat difficult to reconcile with the sacred nature of these waters and that of the Earth. Yet, the illness of the Earth—oftentimes represented through artistic means (i.e., the planet is feverish)—was described by climate activists through personal statements: "It's possible to understand you're ill, but it's impossible to live with you being ill, all the time, every second of every day." The illness and healing/regeneration dimension that is present in some Green Christian climate rituals is not evident in XR public protest death rituals.

CONCLUSION

Rituals of death, illness, and healing are often repurposed and explored by activists to represent extinction, pollution, and regeneration. Through their use of radical artistic methods, death rituals provide the opportunity to contemplate extinction without the possibility of salvation and memorialization. The content of XR rituals is varied, but some rituals may display a story arc that is characteristic of a certain mode of empowerment, which I have found in my research with Green Christian activists and defined as empowerment through vulnerability.[98] Although I have shown that XR protest rituals do not really focus on healing, we still find here a Christian-inspired countercultural model of repositioning the performer and the audience through the actant's vulnerability and representations of fragility and illness—the Earth globe has been encaged (in a greenhouse), or wrapped in lace, or tarnished with molasses. Similarly, the act of being arrested and carried away by police can also be investigated as a form of empowerment through vulnerability. The dichotomous nature of the construction of such narratives of empowerment by representations of fragility and vulnerability (i.e., die-ins) illuminates an important connection between Contemporary Paganism and Christianity. I suggested that it is particularly this common emotional and relational landscape that indicates a continuity (rather than a countercultural reformulation) between Christianity and Eco-Paganism. Thus, we can regard Eco-Paganism as distinct from other types of Contemporary Paganism and understand it as a New Christian movement. This Christian heritage helps XR communicate with a (post)Christian audience. During a die-in, it is the audience who is made to reflect on their responsibility as upright (standing-up) humans. Similarly, although XR activists are being arrested, it is the onlookers who are given the opportunity to feel uncomfortable as they reflect on their role as oppressors.

So, what can XR's rituals tell us about religion or about how we should understand religion in an age of extinctions? Although I argued in my discussion of the Bath Spa XR protest action that we should not search for traditional models of sacredness (i.e., associated with healing through miraculous powers or properties) in XR protest rituals, I am not suggesting that sacredness is altogether lost to us Anthropocene humans. I argue that we need to reconceptualize our models of sacredness if we are to understand contemporary ritualized behavior in the context of mass extinction(s). My own notion of the sacred here, which I arrived at by engaging in a relational analysis of ritual space, is that it should be understood as a fecund generatrix of new stories, new relationships, and new identities. This can help us distinguish between sites and landscapes that have this property in the present tense and those that have now become relics. Our endangered Earth and its polluted waters appear to have lost their voice and inherent power to generate beautiful, sacred stories.

Yet it is activists who are using their bodies and their voices to stand in and tell the story of the Earth with letters, prayers, art, street theater, silent cries, and floating bodies. XR activists draw on a Christian affective repertoire to communicate extinction. Relating to the Earth and its waters may enable the creation of a planetary identity among activists and—it is hoped, before it is too late—their audiences.[99]

MARIA NITA is a Lecturer in Religious Studies in the Faculty of Arts and Social Sciences at the Open University. Her research interests encompass cultural theoretical approaches to religion and climate activism, with a particular focus on rituals and protest actions. She is author of *Praying and Campaigning with Environmental Christians: Green Religion and the Climate Movement*.

NOTES

1. Maria Nita, *Praying and Campaigning with Environmental Christians: Green Religion and the Climate Movement* (New York: Palgrave Macmillan, 2016).

2. Andy Letcher, "'If You Go Down to the Woods Today...': Spirituality and the Eco-Protest Lifestyle," *Ecotheology: Journal of Religion, Nature and the Environment* 7, no. 1 (2002): 81–87; Letcher, "'Gaia Told Me to Do It': Resistance and the Idea of Nature within Contemporary British Eco-Paganism," *Ecotheology: Journal of Religion, Nature and the Environment* 8, no. 1 (2003): 61–84.

3. Please see John. P. Newport, *The New Age Movement and the Biblical Worldview: Conflict and Dialogue* (Grand Rapids, MI: William B. Eerdmans), 274–278.

4. I have claimed that despite the heterogenous Green Christian praxis from a great variety of networks, such as the transatlantic Creation Spirituality or Green Christian in the United Kingdom, we can identify common hubs (e.g., the Greenbelt festival in the United Kingdom) and a shared vignettes of material culture, which suggests that we are talking about a movement. See Nita, *Praying and Campaigning*.

5. Nita and Gemie Sharif, "Counterculture, Local Authorities and British Christianity at the Windsor and Watchfield Free Festivals

(1972–5)," *Twentieth Century British History* 31, no. 1 (2020): 51–78; Nita, "Christian Discourses and Cultural Change: The Greenbelt Art and Performance Festival as an Alternative Community for Green and Liberal Christians," *Implicit Religion* 21, no. 1 (2018): 44–69.

6. Nita, "Christian Discourses."

7. Nita, *Praying and Campaigning.*

8. Letcher, "If You Go Down"; Graham Harvey, *Listening People, Speaking Earth: Contemporary Paganism* (London: Hurst, 1997).

9. Harvey, *Listening People.*

10. Roy A. Rappaport, *Ritual and Religion in the Making of Humanity* (Cambridge, UK: Cambridge University Press, 1999); Victor Turner, *Ritual Process: Structure and Anti-Structure* (London: Aldin Transaction, 1969); Catherine Bell, *Ritual Theory, Ritual Practice* (Oxford: Oxford University Press, 1992).

11. Nita, "Sky vs. Earthly Empowerment: From Angels and Superheroes to Humans and Community in the Marvel Universe and Green Christian Cosmology," *Journal of Religion and Popular Culture* 31, no. 3 (2019): 236–249.

12. Yi-fu Tuan, *Space and Place: The Perspective of Experience* (Minneapolis: University of Minnesota Press, 2005); Almo Farina and Andrea Belgrano, "The Eco-field Hypothesis: Toward a Cognitive Landscape," *Landscape Ecology* 21, no. 1 (2006): 5–17; Kati Lindström, Kalevi Kull, and Hannes Palang, "Landscape Semiotics: Contribution to Culture Theory," in *Estonian Approaches to Culture Theory*, ed. Valter Lang and Kull, 110–132 (Tartu: University of Tartu Press, 2014); Serpil Oppermann, "From Ecological Postmodernism to Material Ecocriticism: Creative Materiality and Narrative Agency," in *Material Ecocriticism*, ed. Serenella Iovino and Oppermann, 21–37 (Bloomington: Indiana University Press, 2014).

13. Susan M. Andersen and Serena Chen, "The Relational Self: An Interpersonal Social-Cognitive Theory," *Psychological Review* 109, no. 4 (2002): 619–645; Daniel L. Shapiro, "Relational Identity Theory: A Systematic Approach for Transforming the Emotional Dimension of Conflict," *American Psychologist* 65, no. 7 (2010): 634–645; Helena Lopes and Teresa Calapez, "The Relational Dimension of Identity—Theoretical and Empirical Exploration," *Review of Social Economy* 70, no. 1 (2012): 81.

14. Nita, "Sky vs. Earthly Empowerment."

15. Nita and Gemie, "Counterculture"; Nita, "Where Are Extinction Rebellion's Cultural Roots?," *Contemporary Religion in Historical Perspective* (blog), Open University, 2019, accessed May 24, 2022, http://www.open.ac.uk/blogs/religious-studies/?p=980.

16. Nita, "'Inside Story': Participatory Storytelling and Imagination in Eco-pedagogical Contexts," in *Storytelling for Sustainability in Higher Education: An Educator's Handbook*, ed. Petra Molthan-Hill et al., 154–167 (London: Routledge, 2020).

17. "Britain's original natural thermal spa," Thermae Bath Spa, accessed June 1, 2019, https://web.archive.org/web/20211027123629/https://www.thermaebathspa.com/news-info/about-the-spa/spa-history/.

18. "About Us," Sanatoriul Balnear și de Recuperare Techirghiol, accessed June 1, 2019, https://sbtghiol.ro/en/acasa/about-us/.

19. Marion Bowman and Tiina Sepp, "Caminoisation and Cathedrals: Replication and the Heritagisation of Religion," *Religion* 49, no. 1 (2019).

20. Harvey, *Listening People*.

21. Val Plumwood, *Feminism and the Mastery of Nature* (London: Routledge, 1997); Anne Primavesi, *Gaia's Gift* (London: Routledge, 2003); Donna Haraway, *Staying with the Trouble: Making Kin in the Chthulucene* (Durham, NC: Duke University Press, 2016).

22. Plumwood, *Feminism*, 69–103.

23. Plumwood, *Feminism*, 196.

24. Arnold van Gennep, *The Rites of Passage* (Chicago: University of Chicago Press, 1960); John Bowker and Jean Holm, eds., *Rites of Passage* (London: Pinder, 1994).

25. Nita, "Humour, Concealment and Death Mindfulness in Romanian Funerals," *Contemporary Religion in Historical Perspective* (blog), Open University, 2018, accessed May 24, 2022, http://www.open.ac.uk/blogs/religious-studies/?p=676.

26. Patricia Lysaght, *The Banshee: The Irish Supernatural Messenger* (Dublin: O'Brian, 1986); Simion Florea Marian, *Înmormântarea la Romani* (Bucharest: Grai și Suflet, 1995).

27. Marian, *Înmormântarea*, 8.

28. Margo DeMello, ed., *Mourning Animals: Rituals and Practices Surrounding Animal Death* (East Lansing: Michigan State University Press, 2016); Pauline Delahaye, "Ritual Mimicry: A Path to Concept Comprehension," *Biosemiotics* 12, no. 1 (2019): 175–188.

29. Marina Cap-Bun, "Attitudes towards Death in Romanian Culture and Civilization," *Philologica Jassyensia* 8, no. 2 (2012): 151–157.

30. Philippe Ariès, "Western Attitudes toward Death: From the Middle Ages to the Present," trans. Patricia Ranum (Baltimore: Johns Hopkins University Press, 1974).

31. Marian, *Înmormântarea*, 36.

32. Marian, *Înmormântarea*, 36.
33. Nita, "Humour, Concealment and Death Mindfulness."
34. Marian, *Înmormântarea*.
35. Marian, *Înmormântarea*, 77.
36. Marian, *Înmormântarea*, 254.
37. Marian, *Înmormântarea*, 256.
38. Nita, "Sky vs. Earthly Empowerment."
39. Marian, *Înmormântarea*, 46–47, 68.
40. René Girard, *Violence and the Sacred* (1988; repr., London: Continuum, 2005); James George Frazer, *The Golden Bough: A Study in Magic and Religion* (London: Macmillan, 1960), 366.
41. Bowman, "Vernacular Religion, Contemporary Spirituality and Emergent Identities: Lessons from Lauri Honko," *Approaching Religion* 4, no. 1 (2014): 101–113.
42. Nita, *Praying and Campaigning*, 166–167.
43. "How Religion Has Changed in England and Wales," Office for National Statistics, June 4, 2015, https://www.ons.gov.uk/peoplepopulationandcommunity/culturalidentity/religion/articles/howreligionhaschangedinenglandandwales/2015-06-04.
44. Timothy Miller, *The 60s Communes: Hippies and Beyond* (Syracuse, NY: Syracuse University Press, 1999).
45. George McKay, *Senseless Acts of Beauty: Cultures of Resistance since the Sixties* (London: Verso, 1996).
46. Harvey, *Listening People*; Ronald Hutton, *Pagan Britain* (Oxford: Oxford University Press, 2013).
47. Letcher, "If You Go Down."
48. Grace Davie, *Religion in Britain since 1945* (1994, repr., Oxford: Blackwell, 2004).
49. Letcher, "If You Go Down."
50. In the 1960s, people began to profess historical belief and spiritual attachment to Tolkien's fiction, while a second wave of Tolkien spirituality, with a strong focus on Elven spirituality, started after the release of Peter Jackson's films. The Tië eldaliéva, the Elven Path, use *The Silmarillion* as their sacred text and believe it to hold spiritual truths.
51. Letcher, "If You Go Down," 64.
52. Greenham Commons was a key British protest site for the development of Goddess spirituality.
53. Starhawk, *Webs of Power: Notes from the Global Uprising* (Gabriola Island, BC: New Society, 2003), 4.

54. Nita, "Christian Discourses."

55. Adam Stout, *Glastonbury Holy Thorn: Story of a Legend* (Glastonbury: Green & Pleasant, 2020).

56. Bowman, "Ancient Avalon, New Jerusalem, Heart Chakra of Planet Earth: The Local and the Global in Glastonbury," *Numen International Review for the History of Religions* 52, no. 2 (2005): 157–190.

57. Nita, "Sky vs. Earthly Empowerment."

58. J. Andrew Hubbell, "A Question of Nature: Byron and Wordsworth," *The Wordsworth Circle* 41, no. 1 (2010): 14–18.

59. Nita and Gemie, "Counterculture."

60. Maria A. Asavei, *Art, Religion and Resistance in (Post-)Communist Romania: Nostalgia for Paradise Lost* (New York: Palgrave MacMillan, 2020).

61. See Hutton, *Pagan Britain*; Stefanie von Schnurbein, *Norse Revival: Transformations of Germanic Neopaganism* (Leiden: Brill, 2016).

62. Gemie and Brian Ireland, *The Hippie Trail: A History* (Manchester: Manchester University Press, 2017); Nita and Gemie, "Counterculture."

63. Nita and Gemie, "Counterculture."

64. Mika Lassander, "From Security to Self-Expression, the Emergent Value Pattern and the Changing Role of Religion" (unpublished PhD thesis, Milton Keynes, Open University, 2010).

65. Markus A. Davidsen, "The Spiritual Milieu Based on J. R. R. Tolkien's Literary Mythology," in *Handbook of Hyper-real Religions*, ed. Adam Possamai (Leiden: Brill, 2012).

66. Letcher, "If You Go Down," 62.

67. Douglas Davies discusses understanding religion in relation to a specific emotional matrix. See Davies, *Emotion, Identity, and Religion: Hope, Reciprocity, and Otherness* (Oxford: Oxford University Press, 2011). An examination of this emotional matrix can provide further information about religious and cultural syncretism.

68. Lynn White Jr., "The Historical Roots of our Ecological Crisis," *Science* 155 (1967): 1203–1207; Plumwood, *Feminism*; Primavesi, *Gaia's Gift*.

69. Bowman, "'The Need for Healing': A Case Study in Bath," in *Health and Religion*, ed. Bowman, 96–97 (Enfield Lock: Hisarlik, 2009).

70. Nita, "Balneoterapia în Europa," *Techirghiol* IV, no. 12 (October 2018), https://sbtghiol.ro/wp-content/uploads/2018/10/techirghiol12-site.pdf, 2018.

71. Bowman and Sepp, "Caminoisation and Cathedrals"; Simon Coleman and Marion Bowman, eds., "Religion in Cathedrals: Pilgrimage,

Place, Heritage, and the Politics of Replication," special issue, *Religion* 49 (1): 74–98.

72. Harvey, *Listening People*.

73. Stout, *Glastonbury Holy Thorn*, 18–19.

74. Nita, "Balneoterapia in Europa."

75. Eric Helleiner, "Think Globally, Transact Locally: Green Political Economy and the Local Currency Movement," *Global Society: Journal of Interdisciplinary International Relations* 14, no. 1 (2000): 35–51.

76. Graham St. John, "Protestival: Global Days of Action and Carnivalized Politics in the Present," *Social Movement Studies Journal* 7, no. 2 (2008): 167–190.

77. Letcher, *Gaia*.

78. Nita, *Praying and Campaigning*, 205–225.

79. Rudolf Otto, *Mysticism East and West: A Comparative Analysis of the Nature of Mysticism* (New York: Macmillan, 1932); Mircea Eliade, *The Sacred and the Profane: The Nature of Religion*, trans. W. R. Trask (New York: Harcourt, Brace & World, 1959).

80. Rigby's chapter in this volume, "Oceanic Extinctions and the Dread of the Deep."

81. Stout, *Glastonbury Holy Thorn*, 14.

82. Asavei, *Art, Religion and Resistance*.

83. The niches of alternative cultures that opposed the mainstream in Eastern Europe and the alternative texts and artwork that developed in Eastern Bloc countries before 1989 had limited circulation in the public domain.

84. Nita, "Sky vs. Earthly Empowerment."

85. Andersen and Chen, "The Relational Self"; Shapiro, "Relational Identity Theory"; Lopes and Calapez, "The Relational Dimension of Identity."

86. Ariès, *Western*.

87. Nita, "Spirituality in Health Studies: Competing Spiritualities and the Elevated Status of Mindfulness," *Religion and Health* 58, no. 1 (2019): 1605–1618, https://link.springer.com/article/10.1007/s10943-019-00773-2.

88. Nita, "Humour, Concealment and Death Mindfulness."

89. Agnes Czajka and Aine O'Brien, eds., *Art, Migration and the Production of Radical Democratic Citizenship* (London: Rowman and Littlefield International, 2021).

90. Red and black are of course anarchist colors, but that association seems accidental.

91. In contrast, in Romania beliefs, the healing properties of the waters continue to thrive in the context of a contested therapy: balneotherapy, a water therapy based on the chemical properties of certain springs and lakes.

92. Nita, *Praying and Campaigning*.

93. A function of rituals involving coal is to educate and offer a public pedagogy on climate change and carbon literacy (and to further an understanding of—and acceptance of responsibility for—the effect of carbon emissions on the global climate system). For example, the public may be confronted by a sack of twenty kilograms of coal and told that this would be the equivalent of carbon dumped into the atmosphere by one passenger flight.

94. Nita, "'An Altar inside a Circle': A Relational Model for Investigating Green Christians' Experiments with Sacred Space," in *Material Religion: The Stuff of the Sacred*, ed. Timothy Hutchings and Jo McKenzie, 133–151 (London: Routledge, 2018).

95. Green Christians often distinguished between their own Christian rituals and Pagan-inspired ones that had to do with invoking the elements—for example, as *serious/in spirit/in truth* versus play. See Nita, *Praying and Campaigning*.

96. Nita, "Sky vs. Earthly Empowerment."

97. See, for example, Joanna R. Macy, "The Council of All Beings," in *Encyclopedia of Religion and Nature*, ed. Bron Taylor, 425–429 (London: Thoemmes Continuum, 2005).

98. Nita, "Christian Discourses."

99. Nita, *Praying and Campaigning*, 240.

FOUR

REPLANTING A TREE OF PEACE
Naturalizing Relations in an Age of Extinction

TIMOTHY B. LEDUC

> Today the Sun dissipated all these clouds to reveal that beautiful Tree of Peace which was already planted on the highest mountain of the earth.
>
> —Wendat Chief Kondiaronk, 1701.[1]

OVER THE PAST TWO DECADES, I have stood many times with my back against a tall strong *onerahtase'ko:wa* (white pine), letting my urban mind sink into the land. Groves of these tall, straight evergreens stretch across Turtle Island (North America), from the Kaniatarowanenneh (St. Lawrence River) east of Montreal, where I was born, across Lake Ontario, whose shores I currently live on, into the other Great Lakes and southeastern Manitoba. Their green boughs can reach skyward a couple hundred feet, while the branchless space between their straight trunks opens my eyes to lower vistas. Each breath inspires a distinct peace-filled calm, especially in the summer months, when the sandy soil and decomposing pine needles fill the air with a pungent aroma that I wait all year to smell again. When I slow into relation with this presence, stories arise that would not cross my mind without being here.

On this day, I am haunted by the words of Wendat Chief Kondiaronk when he asked those who had gathered on the isle of Montreal in August 1701 to help him lift a tall onerahtase'ko:wa, "that beautiful Tree of Peace which was already planted on the highest mountain of the earth."[2] Under these shady boughs, thirty-nine Indigenous nations helped lift up this tree and then listened as French Governor Louis Hector de Callière supported the vision: "I today ratify the peace we have made. I attach my words to the wampum belts I give to each of your nations so that the elders may have them carried out by their young people."[3] After walking through "the darkness of war" for the first century of colonial contact, Kondiaronk wanted to work with others in soothing the pain of loss with a vision that would renew an old story.

The eldest onerahtase'ko:wa can reach five hundred years, an age that gives it a long view on the Tree of Peace that preceded colonial relations and Kondiaronk. Picking up a cluster of pine needles, I am drawn by their number of five to Haudenosaunee stories that tell of five nations who gathered under just such a Tree of Peace. Long before the arrival of colonists, these nations who became the Haudenosaunee Confederacy had been at war and killing each other until the Peacemaker arrived from the north shores of Lake Ontario. This legendary Peacemaker was a Wendat who came to the Haudenosaunee with a vision to bury the weapons of division under a great white pine and to do so in a way that would affirm the unique gifts of each nation. In the words of the late Cayuga Chief Jacob Thomas: "Five bound arrows symbolized the complete union . . . they had bound themselves together in one mind, one body, one head, and one heart to settle all matters."[4] A diversity of nations coming into peaceful union would be the source of strength for this Tree of Peace, this onerahtase'ko:wa.

Following the protocols of the land, the negotiations in Montreal were suffused in the teachings of wampum (whelk shell) belts

Figure 4.1. Uprooted white pine. Photo by the author.

like the Haudenosaunee Gayensra'go:wa (Great Law or Tree of Peace) and the Sewatokwa'tshera't (Dish with One Spoon), with its white background and purple center. This "big dish" represented all the lands that would be shared through, in Callière's words, "a misouaine [large spoon] to eat the meat and drink the broth all together."[5] In contrast to sharp knives, the *misouaine* signified the intention to be careful in how the gifts of lands that were held in common and could never be owned were shared.[6] For Kondiaronk's Wendat descendent Georges Sioui, this event in Montreal "still serves today as a most significant illustration of one of the most positive expressions of the meeting of the Europeans and Amerindian."[7]

Unfortunately, the reality is that from the beginning, the misouaine was not held with care by the French and subsequent generations of Canadians. Over time, I have become haunted by the ancestors of a Montreal peace who are connected to the relations I am trying to reconcile within myself. My mother is French Canadien with connections to Catholic missionaries while my French Canadien father carries ancestral relations to Haudenosaunee and Wendat mission communities along the Kaniatarowanenneh.⁸ My situation highlights one dimension of the truths I am trying to reconcile by reflecting on this colonial story in relation to our present moment of turbulent changes.

A cold north wind swirls me out of this remembrance from an earlier time, when I could still stand under this onerahtase'ko:wa and imagine what might have been with a lifted Montreal Tree of Peace. Now there is only a chill as I stand near a crusty layer of snow and ice that covers the tree's fallen trunk and a root mound reaching twenty feet in the air. I was guided to continue my relation with this uprooted tree by Haudenosaunee (Cayuga) elder and teacher Gae Ho Hwako Norma Jacobs, who was aware of my history with it; thus, when the tree fell in May 2018 due to an extreme windstorm, she advised me to go there, offer thanks, and listen for what it can still teach. In her culture, the Ganǫhǫnyǫhk (Thanksgiving Address) is a way of expressing gratitude for all the relations that make our lives possible, from the people, to Mother Earth, to the plant medicines, animals, and forests, and all the way up to the celestial bodies and Creator. Giving thanks is the first order in any activity, whether it be treaty negotiations in Montreal or knowledge creation in the midst of a pine.⁹

Standing in the icy hole that remains, I am awed by the extent to which, in four centuries, we have moved from what the Jesuits, who were the translators in Montreal, saw as an uncultivated wilderness into our era of the Anthropocene, a time when nothing is untouched by modern progress and its impacts. The windstorm that toppled this tree also caused four hundred million dollars of damage to surrounding urban areas. Though extreme storms have long been part of these forests, their frequency is increasing. Along the Kaniatarowanenneh, the river's flow has been altered while many beings are challenged by "habitat fragmentation, pollution and . . . habitat loss."[10] The average annual temperature has increased by 1.1 degrees Celsius, resulting in ice-cover decreases, precipitation increases, and more extreme storms, with projections of another rise of between 1 and 3 degrees Celsius by 2050.[11] All of this will deeply impact many habitats and species. These local changes are a reflection of global climate processes that have led the Intergovernmental Panel on Climate Change to state that we must phase out fossil fuels by 2030 to limit catastrophic changes.[12]

We have moved into a time when the effects of modern ways, from intensifying extreme climate events to the expanding losses of habitat and species extinction, can be seen everywhere on the planet. From a Western conservation science perspective, *extinction* is a term descriptive of an irreversible situation whereby every member of a particular species has died. According to geological studies of the Earth, there have been various periods of time when a mass extinction of biological beings (plants, insects, and animals) has occurred due to various natural phenomena, and today we are undergoing what scientists describe as our planet's "sixth mass extinction event," due this time to industrial, modern, and colonial expansions.[13] This uprooting of so many relations who are honored in the Thanksgiving Address is the central concern of this book, and for me, the stories of the Montreal Tree of Peace offer one way of seeing the colonial depths of these losses.

The ghosts that gather around me at this fallen tree offer a different view on the roots of extinction and on the spirit needed to sustain a response to so much loss. The words of Gae Ho Hwako reverberate: "When we see everything as a resource, we lose that sense of what is sacred in our everyday lives. We forget the importance of Thanksgiving, and thus uncertainty and confusion grows for future generations."[14] Extinction and climate change arise, in her perspective, from broken cultural protocols that were meant to guide human ways of relating with the world that sustains us.

She is not alone in this view, as a recent special volume on Indigenous peoples and extinction highlights: "From many Indigenous perspectives, addressing existential threats to lifeforms means remaking protocols and repairing relations through direct engagements with more-than-human communities in the specific places where these bonds are made and broken."[15]

In the wake of giving thanks to this uprooted tree, I cannot help but notice the array of trees that lie across the ravines around me. These are not simply the result of the increase in extreme windstorms in the area but also of an urban forest canopy that is more open to the sky due to growing human pressures. With each new opening, the forest and its community of relations becomes more vulnerable to the intensifying storms. Sitting with these changes, I cannot help but think about what Deborah Bird Rose learned with her Indigenous teachers from Australia about extinction today. With more species departing than coming into creation and more habitats becoming vulnerable, she says we are becoming intimate with a new kind of "double death" that is "unravelling the work of generation upon generation of living beings."[16] Those modern and colonial processes that have been bringing about the death and extinction of species are now far outstripping the capacity of habitats, like this urban forest, and the Earth itself to renew in the face of unrelenting, ever-growing modern pressures.

The "Anthropocene," Rose writes, "is bringing us into a new era of solitude, one marked less by our fragmented vision of ourselves than by the actual loss of co-evolved life."[17] But there is another dimension to this issue that I sense in these roots. The gratitude that I have learned to offer at this onerahtase'ko:wa is also being unraveled, and with such lost relations, our capacity to envision a way out may be constricted. As I note in these pages, the relational nature of our double death moment means that the current dwindling of capacities to renew in the face of accruing losses can also be seen to have internal dimensions for us—individually, culturally, and spiritually. There is a tension I am concerned with here

Figure 4.2. Red-tailed hawk feather. Photo by the author.

between the legacy of *religion* as a colonizing force that is related to extinction dynamics and the potential of "religious" ceremonies like the Thanksgiving Address in fostering viable ways of living relationally. The story of what was offered in the Montreal Tree of Peace and its subsequent rejection have slowly unraveled for me teachings about the intertwining of extinction and religion and how we are ancestrally entangled in our double death times.

A coarse call followed by squeals of fledglings draws my eyes up to the flash of a red-tailed hawk's feathers gliding into the nest atop a neighboring onerahtase'ko:wa about twenty meters to the south. Looking up at this soaring presence, I recall Jacob Thomas's teaching about how an eagle sits atop the Tree of Peace, serving as a guardian who can see "far into the distance."[18] Eagles are at home in a variety of forest habitats, where they nest in tall trees, often near the hunting grounds of a large lake or river like the Kaniatarowanenneh flowing around Montreal. With the gift of high flight and keen vision, the eagle—*shöndahkwa'* in Kondiaronk's Wendat language—is responsible for warning people when danger approaches that may threaten the peace.

Kondiaronk could see the importance of renewing such a broad vision, especially after having witnessed many of his Wendat communities "die out through war and epidemics."[19] Born in 1625, he was a child when the Jesuits came to live among the Wendat in the 1620s and created their first mission, Sainte-Marie-Aux-Pays-Des-Hurons (Wendat), in 1632. In the words of Jesuit Father Pierre-François-Xavier de Charlevoix, "The missionaries were convinced that by fixing the Centre of their Missions in a Country (Wendake) which was at once the Centre of Canada, it would be easy for them to carry the Light of the Gospel to every part of this vast Continent."[20] Across the river from Montreal, the Jesuit mission to the Haudenosaunee (Mohawk) of Caughnawaga (Kahnawá:ke) experienced similar dynamics as converts were separated from their communities so as to uproot cultural ways that were seen as sinful. But without the suffering and confusion brought by the epidemics, the Jesuits would have had limited success. As Indigenous peoples had no previous contact with smallpox, measles, and tuberculosis, millions died, with some nations experiencing a 75 percent loss.[21] While some colonials used smallpox-infected blankets as weapons to further political interests, the Jesuits simply saw the unfortunate upheaval as divine confirmation of their mission.

The winds still carry the hope-filled words offered by Kondiaronk as he asked those gathered to help "dissipate all these clouds" while moving through the loss of his own life. As Kondiaronk was "mortally sick from an epidemic disease which ... was raging in the Montreal region," his words "moved many people to tears, even his lifetime enemies, the Iroquois, the very ones who, the next day, carried his coffin and performed the traditional Hodenosaunee Condolence ceremony for their departed brother, Kondiaronk."[22] Callière ordered a state funeral that began with a silent procession along the streets with thirteen hundred Indigenous delegates and most of the village's two thousand habitants watching as they entered Notre Dame de Montreal. The multifaith ceremony had been initiated by Kondiaronk, who had requested that Haudenosaunee Condolence and French Catholic funeral rites be observed out of an intention "to create unity between all traditions present."[23]

In using his own death as a means to heal disrupted relations by weaving together elements of both Indigenous and French ceremonies, Kondiaronk was drawing from a central teaching of the original Tree of Peace. The Haudenosaunee story told by Gae Ho Hwako tells of a Peacemaker who traveled south from his Wendat homelands to bring a message of peace to five nations who were killing each other.[24] While on this journey, he came across a man, Ayenwatha, at the forest edge of a village and could hear him grieving the loss of his daughters. The Peacemaker approached and repeated with care the words he heard Ayenwatha speak, then wiped his tears, gave water to clear his throat, and used an eagle feather to clean his ears. As Ayenwatha began to feel better, the Peacemaker asked him to help bring peace to others who were also lost in this violence. Approaching the forest edge of other communities, they offered this Condolence ceremony to those who needed to be heard and renewed, and thus the Haudenosaunee Confederacy "buried their weapons beneath a Great Tree of Peace."[25]

What seems to my modern mind to simply be a political negotiation in Montreal was wrapped up in a ceremony that had a more spirited intention. I can almost see Miskouensa of the Fox nation approach the French donning a white powdered wig and a red-painted face along with others who wore hats and embraced other European styles. Miskouensa had, in the words of the Jesuits, "made himself an ornament of it to follow the French manner ... and, wanting to show that he knew how to act, he saluted the Chevalier de Callière with it."[26] The Indigenous intention, Gilles Havard explains, was "to appropriate otherness in order to eradicate it"; to enact ways of "adopting them [colonials] as their own."[27] On the surface, the French reciprocated, as Callière attached his words to wampum belts he gifted to the nations to convey respect for the protocols of these lands.

Despite the intention to share that was indicated by the Sewatokwa'tshera't, it would not take long for some to sense the semiconcealed sharp words of disrespect carried by French officials like the Jesuit missionaries who translated in Montreal. As Charlevoix reported in the *Jesuit Relations* following the Tree of Peace agreement: "This ceremony, as serious as it was for the Savages, was for the French a kind of comedy, which they enjoyed very much."[28] Speaking directly to the adoptive actions of Miskouensa, Charlevoix wrote, "We could not help but burst out laughing ... [at] his horrible and ridiculous appearance."[29] An air of European superiority is what many Jesuits carried with them as they learned the Indigenous languages and established missions. In contrast to the Indigenous intention to share the land, this dismissive attitude was connected to a view of those same lands as a "menacing wilderness" that was home to *sauvages* who were "like the uncultivated landscape."[30]

Noticing a few white-rust plumes that had fallen from the nest above, I recall that in Kondiaronk's Wendat culture, the high-soaring guardian clan is represented by the hawk, *yändehsonhk*. But as Sioui clarifies, this being is broader than modern taxonomies. The clan's origin story "does not describe the bird ruler as a hawk, but as 'the Ruler or Mighty Chief of all the Eagles, Hawks, Owls, and other birds of prey'"; it is this "Big Bird" who came into relation with the human spirit to cocreate the beings we relate with as hawks, eagles, and others.[31] While onerahtase'ko:wa and yändehsonhk are viewed in modern times as primarily natural phenomena or mental symbols that hold some abstract meaning and potential use value,[32] they carry something else in many Indigenous traditions. As Sioux scholar Vine Deloria Jr. explains, "there are no symbols in the Western sense" being held up in an Indigenous ceremony like the multifaith Condolence that suffused Montreal.[33] Rather, in this context, a Tree of Peace with soaring yändehsonhk "represents" the ceremonial opening of space for "spirit(s)" to attend "in the same way that people represent an interest group."[34]

In trying to approach the spirit of Montreal, it is helpful to consider how critical anthropologist Nurit Bird-David shifts earlier dismissive perspectives on animism toward a "relational epistemology." The classic anthropological definition of *animism* as a mistaken personification of nature was limited by Western assumptions like those of an objective observer rationally distanced from phenomena—assumptions knotted with the European sense of cultural and racial superiority that distances them from Indigenous relations. In contrast, Bird-David shows that people "do not first personify other entities and then socialize with them but personify them as, when, and because [they] socialize with them."[35] A clan animal or sacred tree is much more than a symbolic association but rather reflects how Indigenous peoples "engage in and maintain relationships with other beings" and, through these acts, "make them 'relatives' by sharing with them."[36] A relational epistemology, a ceremony like the Thanksgiving Address guides us to talk with trees and animals rather than objectively dissecting them, and this quality of behavior is how we come to know and live with each other peacefully

On a now faded yellow parchment, the Jesuit translators documented the French understanding of the Montreal Tree of Peace. It begins with a preamble by Callière that concludes with the words: "I invite you all to smoke this calumet [pipe] . . . and to eat the meat and broth that I have had prepared for you."[37] The oral speeches of the Indigenous representatives were affirmed in pictograph signatures that represent their name, nation, or clan association. The clan animals many signed with attach them to "a way of life in terms of character and respect" and thus can help people "learn how to comfort and support one another during times of need."[38] A crane was drawn by the Ojibwa delegate to reflect the fact that it was "the most prestigious clan and thus the one overseeing relations with the Europeans."[39] Others drew thunderbirds, sturgeon, a wading bird, a turtle, and a host of other animals, all of which have connections to images on older rock carvings and birch-bark scrolls.

In the wake of death, Kondiaronk signed the agreement with an image that represented the meaning of his name and was also evoked in the epitaph for his burial at Notre Dame: "Cy git Le Rat, chef des Hurons" (Here lies the Muskrat, chief of the Hurons).[40] His name calls to mind the shared Wendat and Haudenosaunee origin stories about Sky Woman's fall from the spirit world and the pivotal role Muskrat played in helping life flourish.[41] It is said that as she fell from above, a host of marsh birds carried her softly from the heights onto the back of Turtle. Meanwhile, a council of marsh animals realized the survival of spirit here depended on retrieving mud from the depths. In many versions, the great lodge builder Beaver and swift Otter made the first attempts with no success, and then Muskrat, the weakest and most modest of the deep divers, asked to try. After a long absence, his dead body floated to the surface, his paws holding the sacred mud that life needed to be planted. Now on the edge of death, Le Rat also carried forth teachings about death, humility, and how the "weakest are sometimes the most capable."[42]

Back in the present, the signature call of a red-tailed hawk—*kee-eeeee-arr*—reminds me to let myself be drawn into the spiritual ecology of this onerahtase'ko:wa treaty, an agreement more mysterious than the political, economic, and symbolic assumptions of land treaties in the colonial and modern mind. The Montreal Tree of Peace does not signify some kind of transfer of land ownership or war alliance as is often assumed but rather clarifies the responsibilities I need to uphold if I am to help foster peace across human,

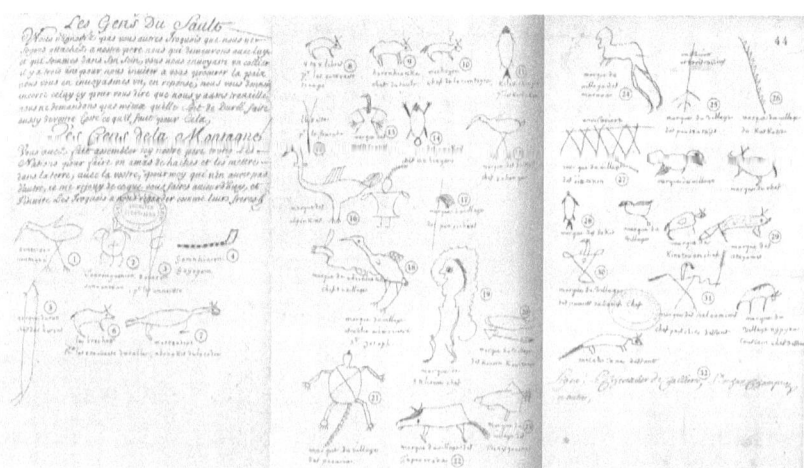

Figure 4.3. Montreal Tree of Peace treaty, signed August 4, 1701. Archives nationales de France, Fonds de colonies, CIIA, vol. 19, folios 41–44. Courtesy of National Archives of Canada.

ecological, and cosmological communities. To violate this agreement is to undermine the relational spirit of a Sewatokwa'tshera't; this is exactly what the colonial missions began doing, thereby contributing to our era of mass extinction. To follow the keen sight of yändehsonhk on the roots of our present moment, I need to look more closely at what my French Canadien ancestors and Catholic religion brought across the ocean to Montreal and Turtle Island.

We are in a world where, as Sioui writes, "life triumphs without eliminating death," a place that "is supremely beautiful and good, but also harsh, mysterious, and dangerous."[43] His words reverberate as I look back on the mound and recall first noticing an oak sapling of about twenty feet intertwined in the roots of the fallen onerahtase'ko:wa. It lies parallel about five feet away from the trunk I stand upon. For the first couple years, the oak's leaves remained green over the summer and into the autumn, its roots still intact. But as the mound's soil dried and stressful times took their toll, this life also departed. Something in these entangled roots haunts me with older stories from before Kondiaronk's vision and birth—religious stories about origins and the role of death in how we have come to live amid so much loss.

"Every living being on this continent might have shuddered with foreboding when that first tiny sail appeared over the Atlantic horizon."[44] This is how Catholic ecotheologian Thomas Berry describes the fateful meeting that brought a storm of change to Turtle Island. Contemplating the origin of this situation, he concludes that those on the European ships brought with them a desire to transcend natural relations and thus turn away from creation. It is a tendency that Berry observes both in his Catholic tradition and in the materialistic consumerism that is prevalent today. While there are sustainable alternatives viable in Christianity for Berry and others in this book, there is also a clear pattern of uprooting tendencies that I want to reflect on more fully before returning to what this all means for living in an era of extinction.

Kondiaronk was a child in 1636 when the now-canonized saint Jean de Brébeuf was guiding the mission of Sainte-Marie while translating and transcribing the Wendat creation story of Sky Woman's fall. Sioui describes this rendition as an accurate telling of life's sacred origin, including the fall from the Sky World to Turtle's back, but notes that it is told with that tone of superiority Charlevoix displayed in Montreal.[45] This can be seen as Brébeuf tells of Sky Woman having a daughter and eventually two grandsons who help to cocreate all life, including our human ancestors. His difficulty was that there was no male present for conception to occur. "If you ask them how this could happen, you will make them very uncomfortable," Brébeuf wrote, adding that if pressed, they will say "she was pregnant" before the fall.[46] Blocking the path to a meeting of minds around this mysterious (virgin) origin were various beliefs, including the male-centered and universalizing Christian view of such an event as exclusive to the Christian savior.

Contrasting the progressive evolutionary view of our modern era, the Jesuits inherited a Wild Man myth common to Europe that suggested Indigenous peoples in the Old Testament past had separated from their origins in the Judeo-Christian tradition.[47] This extended separation fostered their wild descent away from Biblical teachings. For the Jesuits, the belief in this common origin was discernable in various cross-cultural similarities. For example, the fall and virgin birth in the Christian tradition had a certain resonance with Sky Woman's fall and virgin birthing of creation. Brébeuf also noted a similarity in the appreciation both traditions have for the heavens and the sun as representations of divinity, but he critically clarified his view: "There are some indications . . . that in the past they had some knowledge of the true God that was more than merely natural."[48] In other words, a descent away from "the true" faith had occurred, and in this context, these similarities were then utilized with the arrival of colonial epidemics like those that killed Chief Kondiaronk as a means to reverse this descent through conversion. Bringing this colonial tendency forward in time, Bird-David highlights how subsequent generations of anthropologists also disregarded the relational cosmologies of Indigenous peoples, but this time it was because they were seen as representing earlier developmental forms of cultures that were on the way to becoming modern.[49]

Despite the change from regressive to progressive views, what remains unquestioned is the fundamental belief in the European conception of civilization as being culturally superior—a view that lacks the humility of Le Rat (Kondiaronk). Wanting to understand the origin of these tendencies, Berry goes back to the Black Death that plagued fourteenth-century Europe with a one-third loss of the population.[50] Over a couple of centuries, the spread of disease interacted with the climate changes of a Little Ice Age that brought cool wet weather that impacted harvests. These interactive changes increased the death toll to the point that whole communities disappeared.[51] The response of European power structures to the uncertainty was, in Berry's words, to increase "control of the physical world to escape its pain and to increase its utility to human society."[52] Supporting this view is David Herlihy's study of the Black Death that identified a cluster of trends, including "more intensive use of capital, a more powerful technology, and a higher standard of living" for survivors.[53] These dynamics informed innovations like the construction of ocean-crossing ships that would foster ways of transcending natural relations—ways that would fuel colonial violence.

To engineer the oceangoing vessels, larger oaks were grown in open spaces so as to expand hulls that could carry back to Europe more resources and wealth that would temporarily buffer a fear of death and loss of control.[54] It is from these colonial ships that the English term *bottom* came into common use to describe broad deep hulls; in time, it was also connected to shallow individuals "having no bottom."[55] The straight trunks of the onerahtase'ko:wa from Turtle Island were also harvested as tall masts for the oak-hulled ships. Their strength, straight height of up to two hundred feet, and sparse lower branches made them ideal for the European navies of the seventeenth and eighteenth centuries,[56] and as such, the oldest were harvested. A carrier of peace was converted into a resource for colonial nation-building that would relentlessly violate the values of the Montreal Tree of Peace.

Cupping my hand around the oak's slender trunk, I can see the young roots were not given time to reach any depth. This shallowness speaks not only to the desire to appropriate wealth but also to a fear of strangers that intensified with the uncertainty and loss of the Black Death. Scapegoating those who were different grew to be more common as Europe became embroiled in the Inquisition, which saw many women tortured and killed, particularly if they still practiced land-based traditions of Indigenous Europe in a Christian context.[57] This was soon followed by "the violent wrenching of African people away from their homes to become slaves in the New World" and the colonial conversion of Turtle Island.[58] It is in this context that the Jesuit missions first emerged among the Wendat, when Kondiaronk was a child.

The conversion of Indigenous peoples intensified into the modern era as Jesuit missions mutated into a Canadian residential school system run by various Christian orders and denominations. Their intent is hauntingly epitomized in the 1920 words of then Deputy Minister of Indian Affairs and national poet Duncan Campbell Scott: "Our object is to continue until there is not a single Indian in Canada that has not been absorbed into the body politic."[59] As with the preceding missions, the focus was on swooping up the land's wealth by uprooting children from mothers, family, culture, and land. Speaking of the residential school system, Canada's Truth and Reconciliation Commission states: "The Canadian government pursued this policy of cultural genocide because it wished to divest itself of its legal and financial obligations to Aboriginal people and gain control over their *land and resources.*"[60]

From fish and fur to forests, minerals, and energy (hydro and oil), resource extraction has been connected to Canadian identity since colonial times. The nation's political and economic expansion followed an east-west line that began with the canoe passages of the Kaniatarowanenneh, Great Lakes, and waterways westward; these were in time industrialized and modernized. Subsequent initiatives were often financed by colonial governments, as epitomized in the building of canal systems and then railways that instituted the "transfer of large areas tributary to the fur trade to the new industrialism."[61] According to Harold Innis's classic analysis, Canada's historic focus on staples reflected "an economically weak country" whose wealth and character depended on providing resources to a more industrialized Europe and later the United States.[62] These origins have continued to paralyze Canada, which oscillates between taking a leadership role in the 2016 Paris Climate Treaty and fighting Indigenous/environmental protests of oil pipelines.

There is so much more to Kondiaronk's Montreal vision of a Sewatokwa'tshera't than the unending cornucopia of resources desired by colonial and then modern nations. Without Turtle offering a back, Muskrat (Le Rat) deep diving for mud, and the gifts of many others, Sky Woman would not have found a place to plant the life she carried from above. As Potawatomi environmental scholar Robin Wall Kimmerer notes, Sky Woman did "not come empty-handed," as "grasses, flowers, trees, and medicines spread everywhere."[63] These cocreative acts are consistent with a relational epistemology that Bird-David tells us assumes "as human agents appropriate their shares they secure further sharing."[64] This is the vital source of the Sewatokwa'tshera't, and this is what was being renewed with the planting of a Montreal Tree of Peace by Wendat, Haudenosaunee, Fox, French, and many others, including Kimmerer's ancestor, Potawatomi Chief Onanguicé, who offered support from "all the nations of Lake Huron."[65]

Looking at the bottomless ship's ever-expansive desire to consume and uproot relations, Kimmerer offers an Indigenous diagnosis of the same estrangement observed by Berry: we have become *windigo*. This shadowy presence is described in Anishinaabe tradition as having an insatiable hunger for human flesh and is linguistically rooted in "'fat excess' or 'thinking only of oneself.'"[66] Drawing on ecological science, Kimmerer tells us that windigo embodies a positive feedback loop wherein its hunger fosters more eating; it is never satisfied, and the greed grows into "an eventual frenzy of uncontrolled consumption."[67] While the stabilizing nature of negative feedback loops tends toward decreasing hunger by promoting a dynamic balance, the fear-based windigo disease grows relentlessly almost in lockstep response to the way it destabilizes relations. The relational epistemology described by Bird-David and practiced in Indigenous ceremonies like the Thanksgiving Address is in this sense meant to align our ways of living with creation and thus inoculates people from the fear and isolation of becoming windigo.

In the midst of these knotted roots, it is clear various events fostered the spreading estrangement that has progressed into the extinction crisis of our time. While Berry highlights the Black Death, others delineate different key moments. Paul Shepard connects it with the dawn of agriculture,[68] and Haudenosaunee scholar John Mohawk roots it in a succession of Western philosophies that emphasize abstracted human ideals over natural relations.[69] Complementing these views are ecofeminists like Val Plumwood and Vandana Shiva, who outline a system of intersecting dualities in Western culture (e.g., male/female, civilized/Indigenous, society/nature, spirit/creation) that have fostered hierarchical violence against the most marginalized.[70] This is today epitomized in the experience of Indigenous women who are the traditional center of their matrilineal cultures and have thus suffered the brunt of colonial impacts,[71] as documented by Canada's 2019 National Inquiry into Murdered and Missing Indigenous Women and Girls.[72] Intersecting with this gendered and racial violence is the Indigenous connection to land and the related losses that are still escalating in today's environmental changes.

Circling the mound once more, I notice the oak's presence is almost impossible to detect amid the numerous tendrils of the elder onerahtase'ko:wa. Colonial missions and extinction are knotted in these tangled roots. One cluster tells of the first Jesuit missions and their transformation into Canadian residential schools and a contemporary child welfare system that continues to sever Indigenous children from culture and land. Then, in the blink of an eye, I am drawn to an interconnected tangle that tells of animal and plant species that are being displaced by our ever-growing desire to consume. What makes this all so troubling for Kimmerer is the way this windigo disease seeps into our lives through these disruptions, thus making us "all complicit."[73] We are being suffocated by assumptions and systems that choke out the capacity to imagine different ways of relating in this world.

Drawing my eyes up from these intertwined roots once more is the flashing red tail of a yändehsonhk. A century of urbanization around the Kaniatarowanenneh and Great Lakes impacted the bald eagle that for a long time watched over these lands and the Tree of Peace. By the 1980s, a combination of habitat loss due to shoreline development, deforestation, bioaccumulation of pollutants like DDT, and hunting had led to their local extinction in Ontario and reduction to six nesting pairs in Quebec.[74] To be clear, bioscientists usually employ the term *extinction* in reference to the total loss of a species from the planet, but from a relational epistemology perspective, the complete localized loss of a relation and its gifts is an extinction of relational potentiality for ecology and culture. It is in this sense that the colonial violence against Indigenous peoples has coincided with the extinction of many local relations that are vital to cultural and ecological integrity.

While environmental cleanup and reintroduction programs eventually changed the local Endangered status of the bald eagle to that of a species of Special Concern in Canada as they began returning to these lands, their sensitivity to ecological changes have led conservationists to describe them "as a bio-sentinel species" whose health reliably indicates "the health of aquatic ecosystems."[75] Even the absence of the bald eagle flying overhead is like the haunting whisper of a guardian yändehsonhk warning that peace for all is endangered—that if the double death diagnosed by Rose comes to outstrip the vitality of life's renewal, we are all in trouble. From this perspective, we can think about global "extinction" as a continuum of relational losses that range from localized dimensions that can be temporary (as has been the case with the bald eagle), to the complete and permanent global extinction of a species, to mass extinction, to the more extreme double death.

—⁂—

As I rub the dried ground from one curved root of the onerahtase'ko:wa, I am called back to Kondiaronk's multifaith

Figure 4.4. Sewatokwa'tshera't (Dish with One Spoon) wampum belt. Photo by the author.

Condolence ceremony as a reflection on what is needed to carry up the much-needed grief-soaked mud from the depths. At the core of this ceremony is a recognition that "a person in grief is not in their right mind . . . [they cannot] treat others with the kindness and respect necessary for peace."[76] Those who sailed across the ocean were searching for the safety of resources and wealth, and thus, such a relational peace would be difficult to plant without cultural healing. In the words of Berry, his and my Catholic ancestors "might have learned from the peoples here how to establish a viable relationship with the forests" but instead could only see a land that needed "to be conquered and brought under human and Christian discipline."[77] Being out of "their right mind," those at the helm of the colonial ship chose missionizing behaviors that have fueled a still-intensifying windigo storm of loss relations, extinctions, and double death rather than being adopted to the Sewatokwa'tshera't that holds this now fallen tree.

Each winter's erratic oscillation through heavy snow, -30 degrees Celsius weather, and quick melts takes its toll on the onerahtase'ko:wa; its remaining green needles first brown and then simply fall before decomposing. As for the oak, spring continued renewing its first buds for a couple years, but the fact that it was rooted in an eroding mound of soil meant this was borrowed time. In the presence of these dying roots, it is difficult to sense what could have been if the gift of being adopted to these lands, as modeled by Kondiaronk and Miskouensa, had been received with Muskrat humility. While French officials followed these land protocols by imitating the gestures of Indigenous representatives, Havard concludes that "they were imitating the Other only for the purpose of manipulation."[78] Affirming this recognition does not lead to the assessment that Kondiaronk and Miskouensa were naive of colonial intentions. Rather, the living religious cosmologies that they and others etched on the Montreal parchment inclined them toward "adopting" rather than subjugating allies and thus needed to be affirmed even in the face of colonial disregard and violence.

What was offered to my French Canadien ancestors in Montreal was an opportunity to bring their roots into relation with all the beings of the Sewatokwa'tshera't, and the death of Kondiaronk modeled the existential spirit of this giving act. I can hear this intention reverberating through time as Sioui advises Indigenous people "to get busy with the task of . . . Indigenizing the non-Indian society, and thereby avoid what is coming our way if we keep on with this linear thinking, this path of destruction."[79] To sign this agreement was to spiritually commit to an adoptive process that is akin to what Kimmerer describes as becoming "naturalized to place." As she explains, this means relearning "to live as if this is the land that feeds you. . . . Here you will give your gifts and meet your responsibilities."[80] There is an inclusive spirit being expressed in the adoptive intention of Montreal that is vitally different from the universalizing approach to colonial conversions.

As I contemplate this sense of adoption, my attention is drawn from the uprooted tree to a new growth of plants, including the broad-leaved common plantain that comes from European shores. While this plant carries antimicrobial medicinal properties useful as a poultice for wounds, this is not the only reason it is today included in Indigenous medicine bundles, according to Kimmerer. The common plantain has found a niche among the land's original inhabitants. It carries a cultural medicine that models for settlers how to be adopted or "naturalized" into local relations, to "give your gifts and meet your responsibilities."[81] So while Indigenous people are responding to the colonial storm by decolonizing and creating space for their Indigenous cultural renewal, those of colonial descent are called to take in this plantain medicine to renew their gifts and responsibilities to what was rejected in Montreal.

A sign of what taking the plantain's medicine looks like can be seen in the apology of the United Church of Canada to Indigenous nations for its role in the residential schools and colonialism: "We tried to make you like us and in so doing we helped to destroy the vision that made you what you were.... We ask you to forgive us."[82] Considering what such an apology means for a faith that promoted universalizing conversions, Marilyn Legge asks whether Christianity can "attempt to disentangle churches from a concept of mission as 'civilizing'" and wonders if we can "reframe [the] mission in terms of negotiating our place in 'the family of things,' to discover how to live in right relation."[83] This was the hope of Kondiaronk and Miskouensa as they modeled what it means to appropriate otherness by asking the French to bring their gifts into these relations—a transformative process that recognizes death's role in reconciliation and renewal. In this sense, the missions of capital R Religion that prioritize particular institutions and dogmas as holding "the truth" need to be pruned back into "right relation," and this may partly entail reviving small r religious practices that can foster Le Rat's humble sense of our place in relation to the gifts of others under the Tree of Peace envisioned in Montreal.[84]

Beyond the mound with its patches of plantain, I can see spreading into the ravine the nonindigenous garlic mustard that at the height of summer will sprawl over the forest floor. Just as the expansion of modern systems creates less space for biodiversity and leads to the loss of many species, garlic mustard expands its range by poisoning the soil and spreading roots that crowd out native plants. For Kimmerer, this invasive presence carries teachings about the difficulty of pruning windigo ways, for the act of trying to pull out its roots actually fosters garlic mustard's proliferation. I can sense these choking knots in the expanding colonial missions; in the growth of my Canadian social work profession through residential schools and a child welfare system that is composed of more than 50 percent Indigenous children,[85] in the economization of conservation responses to our climate of extinction,[86] in the way increasing natural disasters foster what some refer to as "disaster capitalism,"[87] and, as Lisa Sideris's chapter in this book explains, in the wonder of a de-extinction technology that upholds modern assumptions of unending technological prowess over relational responsibilities.

I recall that it is through lifelong relations with the bald eagle or yändehsonhk that Indigenous stories teach of their roles as a peace-guardian whose broad vision is needed to hold in check appropriative behaviors. In a similar spirit, some Western mystics describe the eagle as being kin to those messengers known as angels, who, in the earliest texts, had elemental associations with wind, heat, and all-seeing eyes.[88] For the fifth-century elder of Christian mysticism Dionysius the Areopagite, the eagle is a "representative" of the "swift in flight, and quickness, and wariness, and agility, and cleverness in search of the nourishment which makes strong; and the unimpeded, straight, and unflinching gaze towards the bounteous and brilliant splendor of the divine rays of the sun."[89] A line of Christian mystics, such as St. Teresa of Avila, subsequently experienced the broad vision of this guardian: "This powerful Eagle rising and bearing you up on its wings ... carries [us] away you know not where."[90]

Opening to such heights humbles our limited knowledge so we can walk in the world with an unknowing spirit, a *via negativa* that, with some decolonizing, can perhaps foster a naturalizing capacity. For Dionysius, the spiritual heights inspired by the eagle would bring one to an unknowing of our knowledge and of the relations from which that knowledge arises. In his words, since the Creator is "the Cause of all beings, we should posit and ascribe to it all the affirmations we make in regard to beings, and, more appropriately, we should negate all these affirmations, since it surpasses all being."[91] Meanwhile, the Indigenous approach of yändehsonhk similarly offers a broader vision for unknowing many beliefs that can impact our relations, but the engagement of spirit occurs in the context of our created relations and not outside them. We need a guardian vision for unknowing that which can limit us and the broader peace, but this is to be done as a means for deepening our relations with the medicines of the animals represented in clans or plants like the plantain.

Rather than as a *via negativa*, perhaps we can conceive this unknowing approach through our relations as a kind of *via naturaliza*. I can sense this potential in the "briny watery depths" that Kate Rigby descends into in her chapter. The oceans are suffering from pollution, a loss of life, and the extinction of species, and Rigby draws out some ancestral roots of these impacts in Christianity's "dread and loathing of the watery deep," which came into prominence in the second century CE with "the doctrine of creatio ex nihilo" and its belief in divine omnipotence and the "hierarchical (and highly gendered) spirit-matter dualism." But simply critiquing these limitations is not her primary concern. Looking for an alternative to creatio ex nihilo, Rigby follows Catherine Keller and related feminist, liberation, and via negativa theologies in describing a vision of *creatio continuo ex profundis*—"a theology of continuous cocreation ... [that calls] those made in the divine image to act creatively, compassionately, and justly to help sustain the potential for continued cobecoming."[92] Swimming into those dark briny depths like Kondiaronk and bringing up some mud ultimately requires leaving behind much, though not all, of what we hold dear.

In the presence of the fallen tree, the via naturaliza teachings I sense around me do not ask us to leave the body of this world for some transcendent spiritual ideal. Rather, we are called to unknow many assumptions, beliefs and practices of our modern lives so as to foster a continuous cobecoming or cocreation. A ceremonial spirit is needed to energize this work, and it is in this way that I attend the yändehsonhk guardian above me. Powerful ceremonies are meant to broaden our vision so we can see all that we need to die to if we are to live a more peaceful life on these lands. Much in modern society needs to be made smaller, composted to the language of where we live. So much of what the modern mind thought was certain increasingly seems incompatible with the sharing of the Sewatokwa'tshera't. This is apparent in the localized losses of many relations that were once directly or indirectly represented on the yellowing parchment of the Montreal Tree of Peace, but added to these losses is the global extinction of species and habitats. Beyond this is what Rose describes as double death, an emotion-filled time of escalating losses that is marked by the way death is seemingly eclipsing the capacity of life to renew. We need a vision not only for seeing all this but also for staying with the grief-soaked pain that will arise when we do so—a via naturaliza.

The adoption enacted in Montreal attempted to "appropriate the otherness" of colonists in an effort to encourage them to bring their cultural ways into relation with the Tree of Peace, which needs everyone to lift it up. It is a violation to convert others and to appropriate the culture and religious practices of another. Rather than taking up specific Indigenous ceremonies, as a French Canadien, I can learn from "Indigenous worldviews" about the values they model.[93] While I have long appreciated hearing stories of the Haudenosaunee Tree of Peace and Condolence ceremony, I am more rooted when learning about a Montreal Tree of Peace that I was never formally educated about and yet grounds all my ancestors. By renewing these roots, I can listen carefully to the earlier stories of a Tree of Peace and focus on the values they contain and what they teach about approaching a via naturaliza of my cultural responsibilities in this cocreation.

By coming to this onerahtase'ko:wa in a spirit of thanksgiving, I learn that our vision of what we rationally know becomes broadened by a heart warmed with gratitude for our relations. I am reminded of Gae Ho Hwako's Haudenosaunee approach to imagination as "a homing device for finding a way into the sacred unity of time, mind, spirit, and place."[94] In contrast to the dominant modern view of nature as a resource, many Indigenous people approach "this mysterious energy differently, by recognizing it first in personalities, then in the motions of the natural world."[95] A personal relation with this sacred energy is fostered as we embody Muskrat's humility, the broad vision of the yändehsonhk, the medicine of the plantain, or the sharing of the Sewatokwa'tshera't. The acts enshrined in the Montreal Tree of Peace are relational, not symbolic. To emphasize this point, Deloria notes the tendency for Western symbols to lose their "potency primarily when we become over-familiar" and wear them out, whereas Indigenous traditions foster ways of relating wherein "spirit can intervene to remove the power from the ceremony or withhold the representatives of that power."[96] Many modern symbols have stopped being renewed through a lively ritual relation with their source in a mysterious cocreation. From this perspective, I cannot help but agree with James Hatley that the term *extinction* "proves itself to be antiseptic and distant," a word symbolic of "policies and lists, when one determines dates and definitions."[97]

If I recall the many representatives on that faded Montreal parchment, I begin to sense the relational depth and profound mystery that goes so far beyond what an antiseptic term like *extinction* can evoke. Each time I watch a muskrat swim by in the pond not far from this tree, I remember the need to humbly bring up the mud of life with our own death. The glimpse of red tails above reminds me of the bald eagle I have yet to see return to these lands and the importance of coming to a broader vision of my place and responsibility in all this. There is a generative spirit that comes with living with familiar yet autonomous relations and that is not expected of modern nation-states and corporations focused on controlling creation so as to accrue wealth and political power. Rather than encouraging a world built on the shaky foundation of unending economic growth and fixed national borders, the Sewatokwa'tshera't affirms that multiple nations and species can learn to share lands in ways that are culturally and ecologically unique yet mutually beneficial. The only control I have in this quality of creation is the discipline of returning to this fallen tree to offer thanks, opening internal space by evoking a via naturaliza, and then following the relational imaginings.

Our unfolding knowledge depends on a cosmos that is responsive to how we embody values like sharing, respect, humility, and peace in our acts. The physical benefits of affirming such a relational cosmology can be seen today in research on the positive health effects of being intimate with a diversity of natural realities, from green spaces, to water, to mud.[98] What becomes clear as I spend time with this fallen tree is that these natural capacities are extended through the practices of Indigenous ceremonies like Condolence or Thanksgiving. Such acts are meant to nurture our flowing connection to the vital energy of life as we become "active participants in this wholeness."[99] They renew our knowledge, inform treaties, and heal individual suffering or great traumas like that of Canada's colonial legacy.

Just as I feel choked up with pessimism, I imagine Kondiaronk once again carrying from the depths mud that affirms that even in our death, we live in a give-and-take world. In receiving Condolence from his enemies the Haudenosaunee and French Catholic rites from those who missionized his confederacy, Kondiaronk models the difficult task before us. letting go of so much in the hopes of renewal for future generations. There are other dark dimensions to the task of carrying this gift from the depths that Rose helps to clarify: "As living beings come into life collaboratively and mutually, their fates are intermeshed; we live and die together, and no one, ultimately, is isolated from calamity."[100] We are interconnected in our origins, and now our entangled deaths are revealing that codependence in the more haunting methods of mass extinction and double death.

Long recognizing our modern trajectory, Sioui summarizes the counsel of his Wendat elders: "This way that the Strangers are living and . . . treating life cannot last for a very long time. One day, soon, the Strangers will be frightened by the consequences of their actions."[101] And yet the relentless pull we feel toward so much estranging loss may still remind us of something forgotten but held in all our cultures, families, and lives: the renewal ancestral ceremonies in the spirit of Condolence, Thanksgiving, or a via negativa may still have vital power for naturalizing our place in this cocreation. We need to recover such ways of reconciling ourselves to a life that is sustained by our deaths but yet mysteriously not limited by them.

―᚜―

After three days of speeches and sharing, on August 4, 1701, the Montreal Tree of Peace was signed by the gathered representatives. This agreement is a spiritual contract between human nations, the beings of creation, and the land's spirit and thus goes beyond so many modern assumptions. In affirming these relations, we agree to embody life-affirming ways that stretch back to Sky Woman's reciprocal acts with beings like Muskrat and Turtle. It was through such give-and-take relations that, Kimmerer writes, "the original immigrant became indigenous," learning

Figure 4.5. Standing white pine. Photo by the author.

in relation with so many others "to take care of the land as if our lives, both material and spiritual, depended on it."[102] The same care-filled intention must be fostered as we "naturalize" modern ways, especially after so much death.

What was agreed to in Montreal was meant to blow like a soothing summer wind across the generations for those who live on the Sewatokwa'tshera't lands. The agreement did provide a half-century of peace until the resumption of French and British hostilities saw the end of Nouvelle France, thus setting the stage for the American Revolution and subsequent founding of two colonial nations, the United States (1776) and Canada (1867). While the Sewatokwa'tshera't was later reaffirmed in the 1764 Treaty of Niagara that came to inform Canada's constitution, the reality is that the intervening centuries have been marked by intensifying treaty violations, missions to convert, cultural misunderstandings, successive waves of land appropriation, systemic extinction of so much life, and a relentless march into our era of double death. As Sioui writes, the unfortunate reality is that "an authentic meeting between the heirs of the two worlds whose destinies were united long ago on American soil still has not occurred."[103]

Sitting with these severed roots, I wonder whether a Tree of Peace can be replanted in today's climate of uncertainty and whether any of the atrophied tendrils have enough life to take root. This is what Kondiaronk's Condolence evokes in chorus with other Indigenous ceremonies, like those half a world away in Australia, where Rose learned from her elder, "Old Tim," that ceremonies of death and grief are ultimately "about coming into being."[104] Through patient attention, we foster a "turning toward life that connects species and generations and brings death into dialogue."[105] We ritually engage our ancestral guides to learn ways of participating in this death with the life-giving spirit of reciprocity, and such acts are especially needed when we are faced with injustices that intensify the experience of life's existential challenges.

Back at the mound, I see one of four Mother roots is severed in the hole's southern edge. Putting my hand to this pliable strong root that for a time flexibly anchored this tree in storms, it becomes clear that I want to be responsible to the guidance of ancestors like Kondiaronk. Though I cannot fully know his intentions, everything about his accord with the humility of Muskrat, vision of yändehsonhk, and peace of the onerahtase'ko:wa asks me to help him by naturalizing cultural ways of relating that I have inherited. As an ancestor who I have adopted by trying to live the Montreal Tree of Peace, Kondiaronk reminds me that if we are to sink into the muddy depths, we need the life-giving energy of ceremonies like Condolence, Thanksgiving, or a via naturaliza.

With the choking windigo knots intensifying in our time of double death, we each need to summon a vital living energy for facing a deep internal denial that keeps us distant from these dying relations and what they teach about renewal. The twofold nature of this denial is first related to how I often look away from my participation in the loss of so many relations, an act that increases the externalization of the suffering of and injustices faced by others. From this emerges my denial of a growing double death that is surpassing the generative power of life and the sustainability of modern societies. There is a physical rawness to the task of responding to this denial that I find highlighted in Hatley's chapter as he guides us with the salmon migrations into spawning grounds that are filled with their own death. He writes: "even as the next generation is called into existence, the present one is being actively consumed. Eagles descend on the river, as do bears and ravens.... In the end, the entire river stinks for days of rotting meat" (see chap. 7, this volume).

Religious ceremonies have long helped peoples from around the world to look at such death rather than deny, and we will need to renew that energy if we are to find our way back into a relational cocreation. When we forget the life-giving gifts of Le Rat, the vision of yändehsonhk, and the other ancestral roots held in the Montreal Tree of Peace, the spirit of these relations also depart and forget us in a kind of creation-based via negativa of us, modern society, our cultures, and even humanity. This is the deep source of the double death that I hear whispers of around this fallen tree.

We are being called to embody relational values that can guide us toward sharing what we hold in common, even amid a numinous double death. In the silence of this great onerahtase'ko:wa, I listen to the land and give thanks for the relational medicines it offers in the wake of our windigo storm. I will follow Kondiaronk and wade into the mud of double death with the hopes of replanting "that beautiful Tree of Peace which was already planted on the highest mountain of the earth." With that, I follow the ways of

Gae Ho Hwako Jacobs in concluding by saying *merci*—thanks—to all who gather around these roots and their diverse teachings for affirming life in the face of death.

ACKNOWLEDGMENTS

I give thanks to a few Elders and traditional teachers whose teachings guided this chapter, including Norma Jacobs, William Woodworth, and through them, Jacob Thomas, as well as Banakonda Kennedy-Kish (Bell) and her teacher Jim Dumont Onaubinisay. I also acknowledge that I published a short piece of prose in the book *Rising Tides* that began my writing relation with Kondiaronk.[106]

TIMOTHY LEDUC is Associate Professor in land-based social work at Wilfrid Laurier University, not far from his home in Toronto, Canada, which he shares with his partner and two children. He is author of three books, including *Climate, Culture, Change: Inuit and Western Dialogues with a Warming North* (short-listed for 2012 Canada Prize in the Social Sciences) and *A Canadian Climate of Mind: Passages from Fur to Energy and Beyond*. Most of his writing arises from the time he spends walking in the forests and along the lakes, rivers, and ponds that are the root of his life in southeastern Ontario.

NOTES

1. Cited in Gilles Havard, *The Great Peace of Montreal of 1701: French-Native Diplomacy in the Seventeenth Century* (Montreal: McGill–Queen's University Press, 2001), 201.
2. Havard, *The Great Peace*, 201.
3. Cited in Havard, *The Great Peace*, 136.
4. Jacob Thomas, *Teachings from the Longhouse* (Toronto: Stoddart, 1994), 17.

5. Cited in Havard, *The Great Peace*, 147.

6. See Havard, *The Great Peace*; Susan M. Hill, *The Clay We Are Made of: Haudenosaunee Land Tenure on the Grand River* (Winnipeg: University of Manitoba Press, 2017), 43.

7. Georges Sioui, *Histories of Kanatha: Seen and Told* (Ottawa: University of Ottawa Press, 2008), 284.

8. See Timothy B. Leduc, "Falling with Heron: Kaswen:ta Teachings on Our Roughening Waters," *Social and Cultural Geography* 21, no. 7 (2020): 925–939; Leduc, *A Canadian Climate of Mind: Passages from Fur to Energy and Beyond* (Montreal: McGill–Queen's University Press, 2016).

9. Gae Ho Hwako Norma Jacobs, *Q da gaho dẹ:s: Reflecting on Our Journeys*, ed. Timothy B. Leduc (Montreal: McGill–Queen's University Press, 2022). Also see Noah Theriault et al., "Living Protocols: Remaking Worlds in the Face of Extinction," *Social & Cultural Geography* 21, no. 7 (2020): 893–908.

10. "Watershed Report: The St. Lawrence River," WWF-Canada (2015), accessed May 24, 2022, http://watershedreports.wwf.ca/#sws-020/by/threat-overall/threat.

11. "State of Climate Change Science in the Great Lakes Basin," Ontario Climate Consortium (2014), accessed May 24, 2022, https://climateconnections.ca/app/uploads/2014/07/OCC_GreatLakes_Report_Full_Final.pdf.

12. "Summary for Policymakers," Intergovernmental Panel on Climate Change, October 8, 2018, accessed May 24, 2022, https://www.ipcc.ch/2018/10/08/summary-for-policymakers-of-ipcc-special-report-on-global-warming-of-1-5c-approved-by-governments/.

13. Theriault et al., "Living Protocols." Also see Anthony D. Barnosky et al., "Approaching a State Shift in Earth's Biosphere," *Nature* 486 (2012): 52–58; Rodolfo Dirzo et al., "Defaunation in the Anthropocene," *Science* 345, no. 6195 (July 2014): 401–406.

14. Jacobs with Leduc, *Q da gaho dẹ:s*, 38–39.

15. Theriault et al., "Living Protocols," 899.

16. Deborah Bird Rose, "Double Death," accessed March 1, 2019, https://web.archive.org/web/20190402000224/https://deborahbirdrose.com/144-2/.

17. Rose, *Wild Dog Dreaming: Love and Extinction* (Charlottesville: University of Virginia Press, 2011), 10.

18. Thomas, *Teachings from the Longhouse*, 17.

19. Sioui, *Histories of Kanatha*, 284.

20. Cited in Sioui, *Histories of Kanatha*, 119.

21. See Hill, *The Clay We Are Made of*, 86–90; Sioui, *Huron-Wendat: The Heritage of the Circle* (Vancouver: University of British Columbia Press, 1999).

22. Sioui, *Histories of Kanatha*, 284.

23. Havard, *The Great Peace*, 4.

24. Jacobs with Leduc, *Q da gaho dẹ:s*. Also see Thomas, *Teachings from the Longhouse*; Brian Rice, *The Rotinonshonni: A Traditional Iroquoian History through the Eyes of Teharonhia:wako and Sawiskera* (New York: Syracuse University Press, 2013).

25. Jacobs with Leduc, *Q da gaho dẹ:s*, 9.

26. Cited in Havard, *The Great Peace*, 138–139.

27. Havard, *The Great Peace*, 139.

28. Cited in Havard, *The Great Peace*, 137.

29. Havard, *The Great Peace*, 139.

30. Allan Greer, *Mohawk Saint: Catherine Tekakwitha and the Jesuits* (Oxford: Oxford University Press, 2006), 199; Carole Blackburn, *Harvest of Souls: The Jesuit Missions and Colonialism in North America, 1632–1650* (Montreal: McGill–Queen's University Press, 2000), 42.

31. Sioui, *Huron-Wendat*, 42–43.

32. Some possible points of connection can be made with the work of Ian McGilchrist, *The Master and His Emissary: The Divided Brain and the Making of the Western World*, new ed. (New Haven, CT: Yale University Press, 2019).

33. Vine Deloria Jr., *C. G. Jung and the Sioux Traditions: Dreams, Visions, Nature, and the Primitive* (New Orleans: Spring Journal, 2016), 192.

34. Deloria, *C. G. Jung and the Sioux Traditions*, 192.

35. Nurit Bird-David, "Animism Revisited: Personhood, Environment, and Relational Epistemology," *Current Anthropology* 40 (1999): 78.

36. Bird-David, "Animism Revisited," 73. Also see Tim Ingold, "On the Social Relations of the Hunter-Gatherer Band," in *The Cambridge Encyclopedia of Hunters and Gatherers*, eds. R. B. Lee and R. Daly, 399–410 (New York: Cambridge University Press, 1999); Roy A. Rappaport, *Ritual and Religion in the Making of Humanity* (Cambridge, UK: Cambridge University Press, 1999).

37. Cited in Havard, *The Great Peace*, 211.

38. Thomas, *Teachings from the Longhouse*, 146. Also see Sioui, *Huron-Wendat*; Edward Benton-Benai, *The Mishomis Book: The Voice of the Ojibway* (Minneapolis: University of Minnesota Press, 2010).

39. Havard, *The Great Peace*, 188.
40. Havard, *The Great Peace*, 3.
41. For examples, see Robin Wall Kimmerer, *Braiding Sweetgrass: Indigenous Wisdom, Scientific Knowledge and the Teachings of Plants* (Minneapolis, MN: Milkweed, 2013); Leduc, *A Canadian Climate of Mind*.
42. Rice, *The Rotinonshonni*, 42.
43. Sioui, *Huron-Wendat*, 19.
44. Thomas Berry, *The Great Work: Our Way into the Future* (New York: Bell Tower, 1999), 40.
45. Sioui, *Huron-Wendat*.
46. Cited in Greer, ed., *The Jesuit Relations: Natives and Missionaries in Seventeenth-Century North America* (Boston: Bedford/St Martin's, 2000), 43.
47. Blackburn, *Harvest of Souls*; Olive P. Dickason, *The Myth of the Savage: And the Beginnings of French Colonialism in the Americas* (Edmonton: University of Alberta Press, 1984).
48. Brébeuf (1636), cited in Greer, ed., *The Jesuit Relations*, 41.
49. Bird-David, "Animism Revisited."
50. Berry, *The Dream of the Earth* (San Francisco: Sierra Club, 1988), 125.
51. Brian Fagan, *The Little Ice Age: How Climate Change Made History, 1300–1850* (New York: Basic Books, 2001); David Herlihy, *The Black Death, and the Transformation of the West* (Cambridge, MA: Harvard University Press, 1997); Emmanuel Le Roy Ladurie, *Times of Feast, Times of Famine: A History of Climate Since the Year 1000* (Garden City, NY: Farrar Straus & Giroux, 1988).
52. Berry, *The Dream of the Earth*, 125.
53. Herlihy, *The Black Death*, 51.
54. William Bryant Logan, *Oak: The Frame of Civilization* (New York: Norton, 2005).
55. Logan, *Oak*, 197.
56. S. A. Rogers, "The Tree that Sparked the Revolutionary War: Eastern White Pine's Colonial History," 2013, accessed May 24, 2022, https://web.archive.org/web/20220123004815/https://easternwhitepine.org/the-tree-that-sparked-the-revolutionary-war-eastern-white-pines-colonial-history/.
57. For more on this, see Celeste Ray, *The Origins of Ireland's Holy Wells* (Oxford, UK: Archaeopress, 2014); Wolfgang Behringer, *Witches and Witch-Hunts: A Global History* (Cambridge, UK: Polity, 2004); Keith Thomas, *Religion and the Decline of Magic: Studies in Popular Beliefs in*

Sixteenth and Seventeenth Century England (Harmondsworth, UK: Penguin, 1973).

58. Banakonda Kennedy-Kish (Bell) et al., *Case Critical: Social Services and Social Justice in Canada*, 7th ed., 52–53 (Toronto: Between the Lines, 2017).

59. Cited in "Executive Summary Report," Truth and Reconciliation Commission of Canada (2015), 2, accessed May 24, 2022, http://www.trc.ca/websites/trcinstitution/File/2015/Exec_Summary_2015_06_25_web_o.pdf.

60. "Executive Summary Report," 1–2.

61. Harold A. Innis, *The Fur Trade in Canada: An Introduction to Canadian Economic History* (1930; repr., Toronto: University of Toronto Press, 1999), 400–401.

62. Innis, *The Fur Trade*, 401.

63. Kimmerer, *Braiding Sweetgrass*, 4–5.

64. Bird-David, "Beyond the Original Affluent Society: A Culturalist Reformulation," *Current Anthropology* 33, no. 1 (1992): 32.

65. Cited in Havard, *The Great Peace*, 205.

66. Kimmerer, *Braiding Sweetgrass*, 306.

67. Kimmerer, *Braiding Sweetgrass*, 305.

68. Paul Shepard, *The Only World We've Got: A Paul Shepard Reader* (San Francisco: Sierra Club, 1996).

69. John Mohawk, *Utopian Legacies: A History of Conquest and Oppression in the Western World* (Santa Fe, NM: Clear Light, 1999).

70. Val Plumwood, *Feminism and the Mastery of Nature* (New York: Routledge, 1993); Vandana Shiva, *Monocultures of the Mind* (London: Zed, 1993).

71. Bonita Lawrence, "Gender, Race, and the Regulation of Native Identity in Canada and the United States: An Overview," *Hypatia* 18, no. 2 (2003): 3–31.

72. "Reclaiming Power and Place: The Final Report," National Inquiry into Missing and Murdered Indigenous Women and Girls (2019), accessed May 24, 2022, https://www.mmiwg-ffada.ca/wp-content/uploads/2019/06/Final_Report_Vol_1a-1.pdf.

73. Kimmerer, *Braiding Sweetgrass*, 307.

74. "Watershed Report"; R. J. Galbraith, "Quebec's Bald Eagles Return from Verge of Extinction," *Montreal Gazette*, August 8, 2014, accessed May 24, 2022, https://montrealgazette.com/news/blue-skies-ahead-for-quebecs-bald-eagles.

75. "Bald Eagle Populations in the Great Lakes Region: Back from the Brink," Environment Canada (2001), accessed May 24, 2022, http://publications.gc.ca/collections/Collection/En40-222-13-2001E.pdf.

76. Hill, *The Clay We Are Made of*, 39; Rice, *The Rotinonshonni*; Thomas, *Teachings from the Longhouse*.

77. Berry, *The Great Work*, 41.

78. Havard, *The Great Peace*, 139.

79. Sioui, *Histories of Kanatha*, 97.

80. Kimmerer, *Braiding Sweetgrass*, 214–215.

81. Kimmerer, *Braiding Sweetgrass*, 214–215.

82. Cited in Marilyn Legge, "Negotiating Mission: A Canadian Stance," *International Review of Mission* 93, no. 368 (2004): 124.

83. Legge, "Negotiating Mission," 130.

84. The approach to religion that I discuss here is largely informed through learning with Indigenous teachers, like those I mention in this chapter, who talk about spirit and ways of life as opposed to directly mentioning religion as a separate category. During his keynote at the 2018 World Parliament of Religions in Toronto, Anishinaabe Elder Jim Dumont Onaubinisay talked about the importance of letting go of the concept of religion in the wake of colonialism; this supports the approach I am taking. See Jim Dumont, "Onaubinisay at the 2018 World Parliament of Religions," YouTube video, posted November 26, 2018, accessed April 1, 2023, https://www.youtube.com/watch?v=AB-Fi31klTs. In relation to scholarly publications on these issues, from an Indigenous Studies perspective, I find the thought of Deloria Jr. on Western religions suggestive of these issues. See Deloria Jr., *God Is Red: A Native View of Religion* (Golden, CO: Fulcrum, 1994); and Deloria Jr., *C. G. Jung and the Sioux Traditions*. From a Religious Studies perspective, these ideas are consistent with Brent Nongbri's research on the evolution of religion in Western traditions as an isolated institution or object of study that supplanted earlier senses of *religio* as simply "worship practice" or "rite" that did not "delineate "religious" from "non-religious." See Nongbri, *Before Religion: A History of a Modern Concept* (New Haven, CT: Yale University Press, 2013), 30, 45.

85. See Kennedy-Kish (Bell) et al., *Case Critical*; Cindy Blackstock, "The Occasional Evil of Angels: Learning from the Experiences of Aboriginal Peoples and Social Work," *International Indigenous Journal of Entrepreneurship, Advancement, Strategy, and Education* 1, no. 1 (2009): 1–24.

86. See Theriault et al., "Living Protocols."

87. Naomi Klein, *The Shock Doctrine: The Rise of Disaster Capitalism* (Toronto: Random House of Canada, 2007).

88. See Michel Serres and Philippa Hurd, *Angels, a Modern Myth*, (Paris: Flammarion, 1995).

89. C. Luibhéid and P. Rorem, eds., *Pseudo-Dionysius: The Complete Works*, Classics of Western Spirituality, vol. 54 (New York: Paulist, 1987), 188–189.

90. Teresa of Avila, *The Life of Teresa of Jesus*, trans. and ed. E. A. Peers (1565; repr., New York: Image Books, 1960), 189–200.

91. "Pseudo-Dionysius," in Luibhéid and Rorem, eds., *Pseudo-Dionysius*, 136.

92. Rigby, chapter 6, this volume.

93. Cindy Baskin, *Strong Helpers' Teachings: The Value of Indigenous Knowledges in the Helping Professions* (Toronto: Canadian Scholars' Press, 2011), 10–11.

94. Joseph Sheridan and Daniel Longboat, "The Haudenosaunee Imagination and the Ecology of the Sacred," *Space and Culture* 9, no. 4 (2003): 375.

95. Deloria Jr., *C. G. Jung and the Sioux Traditions*, 187.

96. Deloria Jr., *C. G. Jung and the Sioux Traditions*, 193.

97. James Hatley, "Walking with Ōkami, the Large-Mouthed Pure God," in *Extinction Studies: Stories of Time, Death, and Generations*, eds. Rose, Thom van Dooren, and Matthew Chrulew (New York: Columbia University Press, 2017), 26.

98. See Kimmerer, *Braiding Sweetgrass*, 236; Florence Williams, "This Is Your Brain on Nature," *National Geographic Magazine,* January 2016, http://www.nationalgeographic.com/magazine/article/call-to-wild; C. A. Capaldi et al., "Flourishing in Nature: A Review of the Benefits of Connecting with Nature and its Application as a Wellbeing Intervention," *International Journal of Wellbeing* 5, no. 4 (2015): 1–16.

99. Deloria Jr., *C. G. Jung and the Sioux Traditions*, 155.

100. Rose, *Wild Dog Dreaming*, 11.

101. Sioui, *Histories of Kanatha*, 105.

102. Kimmerer, *Braiding Sweetgrass*, 9.

103. Sioui, *Histories of Kanatha*, 29.

104. Rose, *Wild Dog Dreaming*, 133.

105. Rose, *Wild Dog Dreaming*, 133.

106. Catriona Sandilands, ed., *Rising Tide: Reflections for Climate Changing Times* (Halfway Moon Bay, BC: Caitlin, 2019).

FIVE

A WORLD IN EXILE?

Extinction, Migration, and Eschatology

STEFAN SKRIMSHIRE

LOSING HOME

There are few environmental metaphors more compelling and, in conjunction with our current assault on the biosphere, *condemning*, than that of the Earth as our house, dwelling, or abode. This Earth is, in the words of Pope Francis, "our common home," and we have "turned [it] into a pile of filth."[1] "We Are Destroying Our Only Home" was the headline that accompanied several media releases of the United Nation's 2018 global assessment report on biodiversity.[2] The statement that "it is time to stand up and save our home" has been a prominent slogan at Extinction Rebellion protests.[3] At a profound level, it is also surely *more* than a metaphor to call Earth our home. Psychoanalyst Shierry Nicholsen says that we initially experience home via our first enclosure, the womb. This then becomes the family, and finally the Earth itself becomes known to us as that which encloses and encompasses and is thus, in a profoundly primordial sense, our home.[4] If the concept is radically straightforward, it is also conceptually radical. Etymologically, the concept of household is evoked, via their root in the Greek *oikos*, by the terms *ecology* and *economy*, both forms of knowledge about the management of our household. It is, moreover, an association resonant in religious traditions for which creation is narrated as a fitting abode, or home, for the human. The Abrahamic faiths are not unique in this regard, but they are certainly representative. The scriptural expressions of creation as the fitting abode for creaturely existence is a fundamental feature of Islamic, Jewish, and Christian scripture. And the legacy of such thinking to secular environmental narratives is very clear and now calls for reexamination. Christian ecological theology, which will be the predominant focus of my chapter, comes under particular strain and is called to respond to the sense of *loss* of Earth as home being generated by ecological crisis.

The concern at the heart of this chapter is that the current global extinction crisis troubles this seemingly stable conceptualization of Earth as our home. Anxiety over losing place has been discussed for some time in relation to climate change, of course. A dominant feature of environmental reporting in the last decade has been the shock of extreme weather hitting homes that might have once imagined themselves impenetrable. For instance, wildfires in California and flooding in Miami have made some of the most affluent parts of the world unlivable. Amitav Ghosh noticed how such a concept struggles to register: "For most governments and politicians, as for most of us as individuals, to leave the places that are linked to our memories and attachments, to abandon the homes that have given our lives roots, stability, and meaning, is nothing short of unthinkable."[5] It is the sentiment behind some of the starker reporting on climate crisis, such as David Wallace-Well's *The Uninhabitable Earth*. Extinction discourses, on the other hand, have been predominantly fixated on the permanent loss of individual species and biodiversity and tend not to be associated with this broader sense of the loss of home and habitat.[6] As a report on vertebrate extinctions argued, media attention on lost or highly endangered species has come at the cost of the public appreciating the extent of local population extinctions, decreasing geographic ranges for certain species, and the linked destruction of ecosystems and displacement from natural habitats, including the disruption to human dwelling and livelihoods, as a result.[7] These latter disasters seem less easily identifiable as extinctions. Nevertheless, as Willis Jenkins notes in chapter 1, biologists are calling for a shift of emphasis precisely in this direction: from extinction of species to that of "ecological interactions ... relations and processes," which generally occurs at higher rates.

The authors of the report just cited are right on scientific grounds to want to widen the public's perception of an extinction crisis. But a further reason for doing so is to make more explicit the relationship between extinction and another definitive phenomenon of our time, forced migration. There are clear empirical reasons for establishing this relation in our minds. Climate-related migration is increasingly seen as a survival strategy for local populations or species.[8] Those ill-equipped to increase their range or relocate are most vulnerable to extinction. Conservation strategies to combat species extinction have increasingly turned to the possibility of assisted migration, or relocation (I discuss the example of the proposal to relocate polar bears to the Antarctic later). Alongside such observations, I shall argue that understanding these phenomena together prompts us to revisit environmentalism's relationship with the concept of Earth as home. Conversely, critically refining what we mean when we talk about Earth as home—with the help of theological distinctions—should aid our understanding and responses to the global extinction crisis.

I acknowledge the fact that the words *home* and *migration* can serve radically different purposes in different contexts. Home can indicate a point of *common* ground with other beings, an interdependence with the natural world. Pope Francis's use of the metaphor is an appeal to a new sense of openness to the others that share our place in the world. On the other hand, home can in other contexts signify isolation, a position of security, and a *fortress* to be defended (against others). I wish to critique the tendency for the idea of the fortress to predominate in responses to the global extinction crisis and to find resources by which the understandings of *common* is stronger. It is this former model that I want to argue is more fit to reflect the conditions of life during this extinction crisis—that is, a notion of home that is in solidarity with those forced to seek refuge, those who become "strangers in a strange land." Nonetheless, we need to be careful about too quickly appropriating a sense of sojourning as an individual experience of movement and mobility, as this can result in us becoming caught up in privilege and capability. There is an important distinction to make here between the free mobility of privileged "cosmopolitan" humans around the globe and the movement of peoples seeking refuge who are seen by those on the political right as a *threat* to the security of the globe. It is in the light of the latter phenomenon that I believe religious traditions have a unique potential to inspire ethical responses to the extinction crisis. I will suggest giving prominence to a narrative that is certainly shared by the Abrahamic faiths and has resonance far beyond these—that of being "in exile" or "sojourning" on the Earth. This is a focus that is all but missing from ecotheological discussion, perhaps because of its perceived tension with the dominant narrative of creation as the fitting abode for humanity.

EXTINCTION AND MIGRATION

The relationship between species extinctions and migrations is complex. We might note first that the extinction crisis in its many forms is closely tied to the violent legacies of settler societies and continuing fossil fuel extraction; for example, consider how global warming, habitat destruction, resource extraction, and the killing of Indigenous people affect biodiversity. We might see in this association a very particular valorization of the global mobility of certain humans and an assertion of their right to travel, settle, and pollute at will at the expense of other species. But there is a further, different association. Arguably, we are already witnessing both the forced and unforced movement of peoples from their homelands to avoid extinction. For example, Pacific Islanders in Tuvalu and Kiribati are facing the near-extinction of their state as the low-lying islands on which they live begin to disappear.[9] Theirs is a very different sense of movement and mobility. The current extinction crisis is also bound up in hostile and defensive attitudes toward the movement of those who are now increasingly referred to as "climate refugees." Fears about waves of human migrants thus also play on a very specific conceptualization of extinction. Reporting on the impact on human and other-than-human migrants at sites of the US-Mexico border wall, Megan Perret has observed that white anti-immigrant protesters in the United States also invoke a sense of existential threat to their (white) identity.[10]

Extinction and migration are also implicitly linked through their respective representation in catastrophic, end-time political imaginaries. The relations here are intriguingly inverse. On the one hand, mass extinction is frequently narrated in terms of what Ursula Heise calls a "declensionist" framework, aesthetically represented through the fear of a great emptying of the planet of life-forms, or what Edward O. Wilson dubs the "Age of Loneliness."[11] The impact of ecological collapse on human migration, on the other hand, is mediated through an opposite end-time aesthetic of swarming (in a very different sense to that explored by Jenkins in this volume) that includes the images and rhetoric of nameless and numberless masses of people and the concept of an overcrowded, shrunken planet.

Even in these inverse terms, the stories of mass extinction and migration both tell us something important about the conceptualization of Earth as home, focusing on the threat to terrestrial security. *National Geographic* concluded from a survey of four thousand species that "half of all life is on the move" due to climate change and the knock-on effects of species extinctions.[12] This very connection highlights the problematic way in which both extinction and migration are narrated as crises. As is now frequently noted, reporting on "the climate refugee crisis" can reduce complex and multiple social and political drivers of migration—ethnic cleansing, economic and gender inequality, religious and racial prejudice—by referencing a physical, external knock-on effect of climate.[13] The "refugee crisis" is increasingly referred to as an objectified, threatening force of nature that will quickly accompany the ecological disaster of extinction and biodiversity loss. This passive description is aided by the maritime metaphors of flows, tides, and waves (of migrants) that threaten to engulf neighboring lands. A headline story about a US defense secretary's warnings in the *Guardian* serves as a familiar example: "Disaster Alley: Australia Set to Receive New Wave of Climate Refugees."[14]

There are important parallels between this framing of unsanctioned creatures "on the move" in supposedly hazardous ways and the narration of subjects in the "sixth mass extinction crisis" using passive terms. Both evoke the sense of home as fortress—that is, they depict species as in need of saving, enclosing, or relocating. An increasingly prevalent critique of the political discourse of extinction has been that it recommends interventionist forms of biodiversity conservation. These include the placing of endangered animals in captivity, the controversial "half Earth" thesis of Wilson (denying access to certain human populations of half the planet for the sake of the life of the planet), and the forced relocation of certain species to more favorable climates. Julian Reid has criticized the "neoliberal regimes of governance" that underpin such strategies, and they apply to both phenomena.[15] The politics of both migration and conservation are often underpinned by a benevolent fortress logic of intervening in, halting, or enclosing life for the sake of the "survival" of life itself.[16] Both extinction and migration can be conceived as problems of mass movement whose solution must come in the way of managing, redistributing, and repolicing geographical space. Consider as a specific example the proposals to relocate polar bears from the Arctic, where melting sea ice is preventing hunting, to Antarctica.[17] The focus on polar bears is significant, embodying some of the more general contradictions of the mediation of ecological crisis in general.[18] They are the iconic endangered species, the barometer of global warming. Aesthetically compelling photos of bears stranded from land through the breaking up of sea ice epitomizes the link between forced movement and extinction. Less commonly acknowledged, these bears are also part of the livelihood of some human groups (Indigenous communities in Nunavut, for instance), whose physical and cultural existence are also threatened by climate change. Reid suggests that polar bears have come to symbolize the different ways in which life forms can be categorized as vulnerable, resilient, and endangered. Nature documentaries often note how polar bears are especially at risk of extinction due to melting Arctic ice because they are ill-equipped to adapt by migrating to warmer southern climates. They are, in other words, not "resilient" enough. But in fact, other adaptation techniques *are* being enacted by the bears. In media reports, one senses that such techniques are viewed with dismay in comparison to the "purer" versions of nature conservation and rewilding. There is a palpable aversion to hybridity in reports on, for example, interspecies breeding in the the case of the "grolar" bear (offspring of grizzly and polar bears), which the *Guardian* noted was the "result of climate change" and was an evolutionary "throwback."[19]

What could be problematic about the attempt to rectify, through forced relocation, a predicament of human making? Managed migration, at least as it is presented here, as a form of social and ecological engineering appears to be attempting to solve two perceived types of problem: hazard and hybridity. The first case involves the *hazard* of the incursion of foreigners, whether human or other, into the place one is protecting. This sense of a bad and dangerous type of mobility overlaps with anti-immigration rhetoric and the reference to "waves" of refugees set to overrun our societies. In the second sense, the perception of *hybridity* comes tainted with fears about how unnatural, "monstrous" adaptations of life pose threats to human societies. This fear is confirmed for slightly different reasons in Jeremy H. Kidwell's chapter in this volume. His treatment of the concept sheds further light on the broader problem of how extinction is narrated as the great emptying of life. Kidwell notes a tension, in the ecological literature, between the practice of restoration ecology and rewilding and the now-frequent discovery of novel ecosystems in the place of wilderness. Questions arise from these discoveries: What ecological base rates, or "normal" states of nature, do efforts at conservation aim to achieve? And what positions of privilege do such evocations of *normal* and *natural* betray?

I return to the comparison with migration narratives and note dangerous parallels in an aversion to hazard and hybridity. In both cases, the predominant political response appears to be driven by a highly controlled management of *certain* life forms—both human and other—and under strict conditions. Reid notes how support for the scheme to facilitate migration, which is assumed to be the only viable solution to guarantee this life-form's survival, reveals biopolitical assumptions about what counts as life worthy of mobility and reproduction and what does not. A starkly illustrative case in point can be made by comparing the portrayal of the migration of an iconic, mediatized, "in-favor" species (the polar bear) with that of a feared species (developing world humans) perceived as hazardous. In mainstream climate discourse, a polar bear's inability to adapt is attributed to its "highly specialized" nature as a top predator of a geographically and climatically specific location. By contrast, the forced migration of (typically rural and poor) humans is most often narrated as being the result of their *unskilled* natures. In both cases, migration is something that must be managed top-down in order to maintain security, but for crucially different reasons. In the case of the polar bear, it is to minimize the risk to human life (polar bears will actively attack humans they come into contact with.) In the case of climate refugees, it is to minimize threats—economic, ethnic, religious, physical—to the existence of sovereign nation-states. What such a comparison reveals is that the mobility, hybridity, and flux of species and lifeways are never valorized for their own sake. The relative benefits or value to life will always be conditional on *which* human lives movement will help and under which conditions such movement can be approved. In the case of the polar bear, even those who advocate for assisted migration appear motivated by a selective desire to preserve an iconic species. Christian theologian Christopher Southgate, arguing on behalf of the assisted migration of polar bears to Antarctica (where sea ice is currently in great supply), defends this highly selective and risky strategy on the grounds of ensuring the survival at all costs of a highly valued, "magnificent, iconic species."[20]

To be clear, it is certainly not my intention to dismiss all cases of assisted migration as examples of managerial, biopolitical governance. There might be very good reasons for adopting such schemes. The important question for me is, what sort of reorientation to notions of home, place, and belonging do such actions prompt? Is it a sense of solidarity with those who have become unseated from their habitats? Or is it what I described earlier—a colonialist mentality of home as fortress, solidifying "the human" as head of the household?

One way to encourage a deeper connection with the former perspective—solidarity—might be to think about displacement as an increasingly generalized condition of life. We are used to thinking about migration and displacement through the tragic lens of poor foreign people crowding onto tiny, perilous boats, threatening national border sovereignty, and demanding charitable hospitality. A different perspective is that displacement is now revealed to be not an exception but a more generalized condition of living from which many of us in the affluent Global North have been protected and that ecological and climate crises threaten to unravel this security. Clearly, affluent white communities continue to protect themselves (financially or in terms of mobility) from climate change in ways that poorer communities cannot. Still, this notion of the unraveling of a secure and privileged place was palpable in the apocalyptic framing that accompanied the devastation of Hollywood homes during the 2018 Californian wildfires.

Claire Colebrook takes this reasoning a step further and suggests that underpinning the narrative of the Holocene period of climate stability has been a myth of the permanence of place and sanctuary.[21] The Holocene was the age in which certain species, and certain peoples within those species, bestowed upon themselves the right to inhabit and conquer certain lands. Thus, Colebrook argues, we ought not characterize the figure of the climate refugee as the tragic loser in the harsh new reality of climate breakdown. Rather, the figure of the migrant reveals something of an original condition of life that might only have been previously understood by thinking within the context of deep time but has been thrust to the fore in an age of extinctions. Even though the "sixth extinction" is a story of "unnatural history" (to cite Elizabeth Kolbert's well-known work), Colebrook thinks that what these forced extinctions reveal is a condition of life as maintained through continual flux, displacement, and movement. Essentially, life is made and remade through the successive finding and losing of refuge. Only as a result of the violent colonization of habitable space by an elite race did the myth of stable, habitable space become the norm: "Rather than see nations as blessed spaces that accept refugees, one should see the nation as the outcome of a violent expulsion of the migratory movements that are its original *and* ongoing condition. The condition of life *is* migration and refuge, the searching out of hospitable conditions after metabolic processes exhaust or transform milieus."[22] I find Colebrook's thesis highly problematic for a number of reasons. In particular, one might draw the conclusion that taking a deep time perspective—considering the human over stretches of geological timescales—ought to inure us against the narrow-minded concerns of Holocene existence. She seems to advocate for an abstracted God's-eye view, taking in the deep time "bigger picture" precisely at a time when arguably we need the opposite—to focus attention on our present fragile and creaturely existence. And since the Anthropocene, which derailed that period of geological stability, was a creation of certain humans at the expense of others, why not fight for its return in our attempts to secure a more stable and livable planet? Nevertheless, there is a valuable point of critique that we might want to retain here: simply put, affluent societies are being forced to acknowledge that their sense of place as guaranteed, privileged, exclusive, and permanent is being radically pulled from under their feet. Bruno Latour's parallel observations can be of some help here. Latour argues that contemporary migrations, though the continuation of old problems (e.g., colonialism, neoliberal capitalism), finally signify that the world cannot be inhabited in the unequally distributed, bordered, and policed ways that it currently is. The Earth is already radically *uninhabitable* in that sense of inhabiting privileged space. Hence, we are today witnessing a change in the nature of what it means to be *at home*: "The soil of globalization's dreams is beginning to slip away. This is the truly new aspect of what is discreetly called the 'migratory crisis.' If the anguish runs so deep, it is because each of us is beginning to feel the ground slip away beneath our feet. We are discovering, more or less obscurely, that we are all in migration toward territories yet to be rediscovered and reoccupied."[23] Far from portraying the subjects of extinction and migration as tragic victims of an external force of nature (Gaia taking her revenge) we can understand both as crises in the sense that they reveal "our" current ways of living as unsustainable and incompatible with the material limits of one Earth—or at least *my* way of living. The material conditions of an affluent white male are still bound up with the identity of being globally mobile and able to travel, work, live, and relocate with relative ease. It is in this sense that there is no longer a guaranteed homeland: "It is a question of attachment, of lifestyle, that's being pulled out from under us, a question of land, of property giving way beneath us, and this uneasiness gnaws at everyone equally."[24]

We might suspect Colebrook and Latour are playing fast and loose with temporalities here. Of course, much can be said about the preeminence of migration and flux in the life of every living system, when viewed at a certain scale. Even mountains are constantly on the move.[25] But what does this have to do with the threat of extinction for those in flood- and drought-stricken parts of the world? One ought to be wary, too, of adding unreflectively to the commentary (often made, in my opinion, for a kind of shock value) that in a world of extinctions and ecological breakdown, we are increasingly becoming a world of refugees. One should exercise extreme caution in adopting such a view to avoid generalizing a condition that is still experienced in highly specific political, ethnic, and geographical contexts. Also to be resisted is the equally romanticized image of a globe that is suddenly in motion. We need to acknowledge the paradox, as Anna Rowlands attests from her work with destitute asylum seekers in the United Kingdom, that the condition of *immobility* through detention is one of the hallmarks of being a migrant in the twenty-first century.

On a further critical note, we should say that Latour's slippage into universals is also careless. It cannot be correct that a sense of loss of lifestyle "gnaws at everyone equally." A sense of entitlement is not equally distributed, just as the ability to leave home and take refuge is not. Nevertheless, I do think that a case can be made that in the context of our global extinction crisis, while the physical inability to take refuge is not an experience universally shared, localized examples are a reflection on the health of the whole. Donna Haraway, citing Anna Tsing, says that this generalized condition *is* perhaps definitive of an age of extinctions. The epoch that we are in is marked by the planetary loss of "most of the refugia from which diverse species assemblages (with or without people) can be reconstituted after major events (like desertification, or clear cutting, or, or . . .)."[26] The fear this loss conveys is not only about the literal ecosystem and habitat destruction. It is also about the possibility of recovery, the conceivability of future sanctuary and resilience in a self-replenishing Earth. Though the revelation of an *end of nature* is shocking, so too is the awareness that many human societies that weren't previously are now experiencing the *end of refuge* such as we have known it. But our response, says Haraway, should be to *rethink* the idea of refuge as the transcending of boundaries of kinship and living alongside (different species). Talk of a world "full of refugees" is, for her, part of a manifesto for radical multi- and interspecies coexistence, not a leveling out of the very unequal experience of displacement. Neither ought this prognosis encourage an abandonment of the idea of emplacement, or a sense of belonging to place. On the contrary, for Latour, it entails rethinking the relationship between politics and territory that avoids all the pitfalls that one might expect in such a relationship. We can conceive of our sense of political identity as the search for somewhere to land—reattaching oneself to "national" place but without the traditional associations of sovereign borders, blood, and soil. The challenge of thinking about homeland in the context of extinction echoes the political critique of tying sovereign rights to place of birth, or, as Giorgio Agamben puts it, tying *natio* to *nativity*.[27] It is precisely the concept of being in exodus or refuge that should be the principle that binds each member of the community rather than being its principle of exception: "The guiding concept would no longer be the *ius* of the citizen, but rather the *refugium* of the individual."[28]

What the arguments offered thus far suggest is that the way in which an age of extinctions and migrations has been portrayed in terms of an impending end, or collapse, of habitable space can be contested. The figures of extinction (emptying of life) and migration (surplus of life) have been imagined as opposite figures of a secular eschatological narrative. They are portrayed as the absolute or ultimate—the limit of our mode of existence and perhaps their telos or destination, if they are narrated as tragic inevitabilities to the current crisis. I would also like to note that both extinction and migration are narrated in apocalyptic terms—that is, they reveal something of the ultimate end of human life. The framing of migration and extinction in this way exposes something that I believe to be an unacknowledged aspect of extinction studies in general: what we often take to be thoroughly secular discourses, derived as they are from scientific categories of species, climate, and so on, are on closer inspection closely bound up in "theological imaginaries." This can be in the form of the prefiguration of apocalypse, as we have seen. But it can also produce alternative conceptions of life and human existence and remind us of our dispossessed, stateless, and nomadic humanity.[29] It is to such imaginaries that I turn next.

THEOLOGIES OF HOME/LESSNESS

To repeat the claim I began with, the belief in Earth as our home is theologically central to many religious traditions, including the three Abrahamic faiths. Jewish, Christian, and Muslim scriptures describe creation as a fitting abode for humans and other creatures to dwell in.[30] But it is this same scriptural focus that has historically been a primary target in the environmental critique of religion. Critiques of the negative impact of (mainly monotheistic) religion on ecological awareness—one thinks of the legacy of Lynn White Jr.'s thesis most obviously here[31]—have focused on those faiths' interpretations of creation as a temporary backdrop to the human's true eschatological destiny. The notion of the believer as a pilgrim on the Earth is present in numerous cultural legacies of religious narratives. A familiar phrase found in Christian hymns and spirituals is *This world is not my home; I'm just passing through.* The sentiment is found in many parts of scripture; in the Hebrew Bible, for instance, it says, "We are guests before you, as were all our ancestors, our days on earth as fleeting as a shadow" (1 Chron. 29:15, NRSV). In the New Testament, this eschatological sentiment takes on explicitly political language. The apostle Paul reminds his followers that "we have no lasting city, but we seek the city that is to come" (Heb. 13:14, NRSV), and the apostle Peter suggests that they are "sojourners and exiles" (1 Pet. 2:11, NRSV). There are parallels to be found in the Koran, in which the responsibility of humans, as khalifa or vice regents who serve as protectors of creation, is mitigated by the reminder of the transience of this world: "And the life of this world is nothing but play and amusement. But far better is the house in the hereafter for those who are Al-Muttaqun (the pious). Will you not then understand?" (Qur'an 6:32).

Placed in the historical context of a profound suspicion toward the legacy of religious traditions for the value of nonhuman life, these are highly partial interpretations of scripture. And contesting the focus on *pilgrimage* and *sojourning* has been one of the major contributions of ecotheological and feminist critiques of those narratives. As Grace Jantzen pointed out, eschatological narratives flourished in the context of a Western philosophical tradition for which all that is impermanent and subject to decay (which conceptually ties *Earth* to *women*) is less perfect than that which is disembodied, otherworldly, and eternal—the world to come. We recognize also the ideological context in which sojourner narratives have flourished. In the words of Brazilian liberation theologian Ivone Gebara, the dominant story of eschatological salvation has been one that, in denying people a true home in the "arms of the earth," acts instead to dominate and alienate human existence, leading to "human damnation in concrete history" for the world's poor in particular.[32]

It is not hard to see how this line of critique might continue to inform a theology fit to respond to ecological crisis—and mass extinction specifically—as the loss of home. Ecotheologians have hitherto sought religious foundations for ethical imperatives to conserve species based on the special type of harm of extinction—a harm based on the eternal, irrecoverable loss from the world of a particular type of living thing.[33] The duty of the religious ethicist in response to this situation is ongoing, never complete. And advocates of ecotheology will want to insist that the urgency of this task is not hindered by eschatological faith. On the contrary, a Christian might argue that a vision of the beatific end point of Christian faith ought to spur the believer to greater acts of mercy in the present. Nevertheless, the context of a mass extinction crisis places the long-term viability of Earth as a fitting dwelling place into question. Thus, it is easier to see how the narrative of sojourner existence might be viewed as a temptation toward apocalyptic fatalism.

The critique of sojourner theology is very much relevant for our times. It finds powerful targets in both religious and secular responses to global extinctions. For instance, we might consider the secularization of eschatological hopes through the promise of technological salvation as an appeal to a *literal* sense of leaving the Earth as home. The colonization of Mars is a fantasy not only explored in science-fictional thought experiments. It is now a heavily funded field of research by the likes of Elon Musk's SpaceX ("It's about believing in the future and thinking that the future will be better than the past"[34]) and Jeff Bezos's Blue Origins ("Building a road to space so our children can rebuild the future"[35]). Such ventures are increasingly presented as a response to the planetary emergency. Sarah McFarland-Taylor has identified a thinly veiled secularized salvation narrative operative for both venture capitalists, for whom the possibility of addressing the extinction crisis has now disappeared.[36] To these figures we should also add the target of Lisa H. Sideris's critique in this book—advocates of genetic de-extinction technology who similarly evoke a secularized salvation narrative as justification for their work. But specifically in relation to planet colonization, such fantasies manifest very clearly the sojourning desire—those who can afford it will effectively become exiles—in terms of literal escape and have nothing to do with the message of political liberation or hope for return with which much exilic political theology is concerned (I return to this later). Here, salvation is conceived as an escape from the possibility of human extinction. Planet colonization represents the desire for a literal exodus from Earth in order to save the species.

More generally, we should be wary of those traditions for which crises such as mass extinction represent further evidence of the hastening conclusion of the world's history. One still encounters forms of millennialist eschatology for which the longed-for destination is framed in terms of absolute rupture from the historical and ecological order rather than the fulfillment or redemption of the current one. In Christian history, such a position is represented by forms of premillennialist apocalypticism that are most prevalent in the United States. To those embracing such beliefs, ecological catastrophes (including extinctions) may represent the nearness of the second coming of Christ and the beginning of the millennium. It is important to note the environmental and social context of nineteenth-century America in which premillennialism first flourished. As Michael Northcott describes, premillennial preachers in puritan settler America capitalized on the experience of the Civil War, the Great Depression, and a series of cataclysms that included "agricultural catastrophes" and "increasing immigration" as the backdrop of a general mood of apocalyptic catastrophism.[37] If such a theology can be characterized as exilic, then it is with a view to "return" that has nothing to do with this world. An escapist eschatology hopes for a return to an Eden that is not the world renewed but is on the contrary a more literal understanding of a "new heaven and a new earth." (Revelation 21:1) The following words of nineteenth-century dispensationalist preacher Dwight L. Moody are interesting to read alongside consideration of contemporary ecological end-time rhetoric, including the secular prognoses of Elon Musk on the extinction crisis considered earlier: "I looked on this world as a wrecked vessel. God has given me a life-boat, and said to me, 'Moody, save all you can... the world is getting darker and darker; its ruin is coming nearer and nearer. If you have any friends on this wreck unsaved, you had better lose no time in getting them off.'"[38] Neither are contemporary versions of this sentiment hard to locate. Though they are not universally anti-ecological, there are still prominent dispensationalist Christian organizations (e.g., RaptureReady.com) that are increasingly looking to signs of mass extinction as the fulfillment of end-time prophecy and the nearness of the rapture for believers.

Feminist theologians have long been critical of the patriarchal and ecologically destructive implications of sojourner language for precisely these reasons. Sallie McFague's *Body of God* is a classic example of a Christian theology of being "at home on the Earth." She insists that "space is the central category, for if justice is to be done to the many different kinds of bodies that comprise the planet, they must each have the space, the habitat they need."[39] This prioritizing of spatiality over temporality is an attempt to counteract the eschatological connotations discussed earlier.[40] Sojourner narratives have, she argues, been at the expense of realizing that the earth is our home and that we belong here: "Christians have often not been allowed to feel at home on the earth, convinced after centuries of emphasis on otherworldliness that they belong somewhere else—in heaven or in another world."[41] Sin, within this re-*embodied* theology, is to be understood as a refusal of our place within the web of life. Turning away from sin would mean recognizing our codependence with humans and nonhuman others. Philosopher Mary Midgley is invoked by McFague precisely in these terms; she speaks of the fittingness of the ecosphere for human flourishing: "We are not tourists here. . . . We are at home in this world because we were made for it. We have developed here, on this planet, and we are adapted to life here. . . . We are not fit to live anywhere else."[42] We should also note that religious traditions have contributed profoundly to broader cultural associations of particular places, landscapes, and even ecosystems with a belief in the "dwelling place" of divinity or a sense of "the sacred."[43] The strength of this line of argument, it would seem, is that in a time of ecological crisis, we need to deepen, not problematize, religious modes of identifying with the suffering of the Earth and resist the causes of that suffering.

EXILIC RELIGION

These theological arguments are much needed against the macho cultures of salvation *from* the world that we have mentioned. Even so, how equipped are they to acknowledge the shifting sense of home that I have claimed lies at the heart of our extinction crisis? And which theological emphases do they sideline that might be better equipped to meet that crisis? Some ecotheologians insist that redefining the notions of sojourn and exile can and ought to be undertaken for an ecological age. Indeed, as I shall explain in more detail, the spirit of sojourning is not always cast in a negative light. American nature writer Annie Dillard, in her short essay "Sojourner," uses the biological phenomenon of mangroves, the migrant of the plant world, as a metaphor for a more generalized human condition. She follows this up with a theological reflection on the meaning of exile: "I alternate between thinking of the planet as home—dear and familiar stone hearth and garden—and a hard land of exile in which we are all sojourners. Today I favor the latter view. The word 'sojourner' occurs often in the English Old Testament. It invokes a nomadic people's knowledge of estrangement, a thinking people's intuition of sharp loss: 'For we are strangers before thee, and sojourners, as were all our fathers: our days on the earth are as a shadow, and there is none abiding.' We don't know where we belong, but in times of sorrow it doesn't seem to be here."[44] In a similar way and going against the grain of the focus on a theology of "enworlding" by McFague and others, some Christian thinkers question the implications of a theology of being at home on the Earth. Ernst Conradie, for example, argues that a theological overemphasis on being earthbound discourages resistance to the suffering and injustice that marks our material condition. Distinguishing *home* from *household*, Conradie believes it is possible to retain the sense of longing for a redeemed creation that is not yet enacted without succumbing to an escapist eschatology: "It is only through the Christian longing for the new earth that we can discover our *belonging*, in body and soul, to this earth. *The earth may therefore be our one and only house, but it is not our home yet.*"[45]

What might be made of this subtle theological shift in emphasis from home to house? And if this is something that resonates with religious believers, what new approaches to extinction might it open up? The focus on being pilgrims is, of course, deeply associated with that element of Christian eschatological belief in a world to come that has been the target of suspicion by environmentalists since White Jr. To see oneself as on the way to another world is surely to leave behind the concerns of the present crisis. Two points can be raised by way of response to this suspicion. First, there is nothing exclusively or quintessentially Christian about the idea that human existence is caught between the desire for belonging and a restless longing for that which transcends the world altogether.[46] Geographer Yi Fu Tuan asserts that a core thread of all major religions (of the Axial age, we might say) that broke away from the local specificity of place to the universal is the sense that for them, "humans are most deluded when they believe that they can feel, even in the best of times, at ease and at home on Earth."[47] There is nothing obviously eschatological in an escapist sense, or exclusively Judaeo-Christian, about such a sentiment.

Second, the theological concept of exile invokes a tradition in political theology that is grounded in the social and political experiences of the Abrahamic faiths. Explicit to Judaism, Christianity, and Islam are two core features in their founding narratives: stories of fleeing persecution, displacement, and wilderness; and the ethical imperative to welcome and make a home for the stranger. For instance, the story of the Exodus of the Hebrews from enslavement in Egypt is a central founding narrative of Judaism. The forced exile following the siege of Jerusalem by the Babylonians is what produces the distinctive literature and religious worldview of the exilic prophets.[48] Their quintessential condition is one of being cut off from their homeland and receiving the mercy of welcome and repatriation from foreign strangers. The founding texts of Islam also place the experience of exile and the mercy of strangers at its heart. This can be seen in the Hadith story of Hagar and Ishmael being abandoned at God's command by Abraham at the Ka'ba; the action of Hagar running between the Marwa Mountains and Safa to seek refuge and water for her son is still reenacted by Muslims performing the hajj. Another example is the account of the migration (*hijra*) of Muhammad and his followers from Mecca to Abyssinia (to seek refuge with a Christian king). Christianity also begins its story with a forced migration (to Bethlehem) and the experience of (Jesus's) self-isolation in the wilderness. Some telling moments in Christian scripture affirm this tradition of seeing the status of prophets as *essentially* one of migration and dispossession. In Paul's letter to the Hebrews, "Abel, Enoch, Noah, Abraham, Isaac and Jacob ... were strangers and exiles on the earth" (Hebrews 11:13). The exilic traditions criticize the idea of a stable home based on fixed imperial conceptions of place. Biblical scholar Casey Strine argues that even St. Paul's strongly eschatological reference to our homeless condition—we are strangers because "we seek a home (commonwealth/citizenship—πολίτευμα [*politeuma*]⁴⁹) that is not here" (Hebrews 13:14)—can be read in its emphatically political, historical context. To Paul's audience, the new sense of universal citizenship is a counterpoint to the exclusivity of *Roman* citizenship. To oppose an imperial logic of identity and difference, one must adopt a radical cosmopolitanism.

There are interesting connections between exile and exodus as twin biblical motifs that essentially express anti-imperial theologies; they call for reliance upon Yahweh alone in foreign environments rather than capitulating or recreating their own narrative of national sovereignty.⁵⁰

How might these foundational religious narratives help us engage ethically with the global extinction crisis? I have been arguing that the threat of an extinction crisis brings into sharp focus the fragility of our sense of place as we become aware of the constant relocation forced on humans and other species. We also fear the knock-on effects the extinction crisis will have on "our" patch of earth. Religious narratives of migration have the potential to help here, imaginatively and performatively. They help by redescribing this fragile condition of being forced into the path of strangers as a place of encounter with the other and with the divine. The scriptural stories I have briefly mentioned are well known, of course. But I am suggesting they need to take a more central place in ecotheological thought than they have done. What might this renewed focus look like? Peter Scott's commentary on the "Earth as home" debate comes close to the re-emphasis I am seeking here. The problem with a traditional theological defense of Earth as home, argues Scott, is their equation of salvation with a recovered "totality" in creation that has become deficient and must be restored. Scott calls this the "Eden-Exile-Return" model; it is the view that the destiny of human beings is to be "at home everywhere" and that what is sought is "the expansion of home and the overcoming of the loss of access to home."[51]

The "return" element of this account of home raises suspicions about what we take humanity's role (and capacity) in restoring that totality to be—*totality* here signifying a total occupation of all places. The extinction crisis describes an assault on the planetary commons by specific human groups that no efforts at rewilding or conservation will be able to fully restore.[52] If one is to avoid the concept of totality, *especially* in the context of extinctions in which relations between humanity and other creatures seem irreparably broken, then a faithful conception of exile would be one that affirmed the tragic element of the human's relation to the rest of creation rather than a promise of its mastery. Scott affirms precisely this, suggesting that the human may be homeless in the sense that it comes up against its other in nature just as much as it desires to be united with it. Resisting the temptation either to master nature or to escape it, we could say that the human is in the business of *rehoming* rather than *being at home*. This replaces the temptation to totalize with that of a circumscribed rehoming—precisely the sense of fortress I have been critiquing throughout. The theological notion of salvation, far from signifying a removal from this world and securing of one's place in the next, might be understood through the experience of making one's home with others and being at home *somewhere* (i.e., in certain places). Especially in the context of climate change, such a sentiment of rehoming implies a certain solidarity with and deep acknowledgment of the primacy of displacement in the fate of human existence. And it retains a critical element of feminist and liberation contributions to eschatology by implying its spatial—rather than purely temporal—dimension. Salvation is not only "elsewhere" in time; it is where encounter is opened up in space, where boundaries have been traversed.[53]

This attempt to paint an exilic condition in a more positive religious light seems a far departure from the critiques of sojourner theology I have summarized. Consider, by contrast, the use of the word *exile* by renowned eco- and liberation theologian Leonardo Boff in a first draft of the plenary speech he gave to the Earth Charter Continental Meeting in 1998: "We, human beings, men and women, have exiled ourselves from the homeland we shared in common, the Earth.... We must come back from exile to take care of the home we all share, which is the Earth, so that all humans and other beings, our brothers and sisters in this great terrestrial adventure, can all live happily in this home.... Never more shall we exile ourselves from the Earth again but we shall share life with her, in synergy and in solidarity."[54]

Though Boff's return from exile develops a slightly different emphasis than Scott's rehoming, the two positions do not seem to me to be incompatible. Indeed, Boff's perspective provides a crucial reminder to any such formulation of an exilic theology. With regard to the extinction crisis, humans do not simply find themselves in a position of exile from their homeland. *We exile ourselves* insofar as our actions collude in the poisoning of land, destruction of habitats, or violence against other living beings. In Boff's native Brazil, as I write this, an act of wholescale sabotage is taking place through the burning of the Amazon rainforest. Such an act surely represents the destruction of home in the two senses we have been considering—first, the literal home and ancestral place of its Indigenous humans and other creatures, and second, the habitability of planet Earth itself, which depends on that ecosystem for its storage of carbon, production of oxygen, and maintenance of biodiversity and climate stability. It is not, then, any passive or universal sense of exile that we are considering; it is certain humans in their pursuit of short-term gain who are exiling others, and eventually themselves, from their own home. And in response to such an assault on the commons, the appropriate response might well be mourning and seeking reparations. To the extent that mass extinction is an irreversible process (despite what the advocates of de-extinction discussed by

Sideris might think), then *exile* here evokes a real sense of being estranged from the good home of God's creation.

We might well consider, at this stage, whether any of this discussion of interdepence, refuge, and exile is a uniquely religious concern. Its ethical significance can surely be expressed quite easily in secular terms. There are clear parallels—for instance, with the expression adopted by scientists in relation to the extinction crisis: "Humanity's ongoing annihilation of wildlife is cutting down the tree of life, including the branch we are sitting on."[55] Nevertheless, I do want to claim that religious perspectives are capable of lending a very particular kind of urgency insofar as anthropogenic extinction must be seen as an act of exiling human existence from the gift of its integral home. It is essential to consider, as Noah Theriault et al. do in the context of writing about Indigenous perspectives on extinction, that extinction represents not only loss of home in this passive sense but also a form of "world breaking"—that is, as a willful neglect of the relationships and protocols between living beings upon which meaningful and flourishing existence depends.[56] Insofar as religions profess citizenship that is *truly* without borders, truly otherworldly, thus might they resource responses to the extinction crisis as the permanent seeking and embodying of refuge. An ethics of world remaking seems akin to the expressly religious belief that humans are called to be, through their actions, the presence of the divine on the Earth. In the Christian traditions of liberation and ecotheology, this means that making home is not simply a form of settling; it is a form of world-building in the sense of creating hospitable climates even where refuge is provisional and fragile. Making home is thus inseparable from acts of love and justice toward fellow creatures.[57]

Giving due attention to the figure of *exile* in religious narratives might also temper some of the more troubling aspects of a theology of *stewardship*. While the idea of a *steward* has been the favored mode by which ecotheologians interpret the command given to Adam by God to claim (as some translations of Genesis have it) dominion over the whole Earth, stewardship has also brought its own problems to recent ecological contexts. Reflection on the extinction crisis is one such context. Consider the case of the assisted migration of species that I mentioned earlier. Southgate's theological and ethical defense of such a scheme references the extinction crisis as living in the "new days of Noah" and requiring "large scale stewardship."[58] There are enormous hazards involved in such schemes (introducing bears to Antarctica might threaten the existence of penguins, who are unprepared for a new top predator). Nevertheless, humans, in Southgate's argument, are called to intervene in creation's suffering and contribute to the good of the whole community—in this case, the biotic community and not just the human community.

What some will find questionable about this use of theology, as well as its secular parallel in strong, interventionist forms of conservation practice, is its presumption of the human as the guarantor of a primal, Edenic harmony. Stewardship models will always enact, as Scott says, "the modern tendency that affirms the ascent to mastery of the human.... The relations between human creatures and nonhuman creatures are [in such theologies] one of hierarchy and management."[59] Such a danger is inherent and exemplified in the approaches to extinction I considered in the previous section. Moreover, the danger is amplified in considering them alongside similar approaches to forced migration. By shifting their theological focus from narratives of stewardship and management to those of solidarity through exile, religious traditions can better inspire an ethic of radical hospitality for an age of extinctions. By thinking of human existence as sharing a space of fragility and impermance with other life-forms, rather being their managers, religious traditions can inspire a different sense of home and dwelling as a mode of "living in turmoil."[60]

An exilic ecotheology might still be considered eschatologically oriented toward some *end*. In Jewish and Christian scriptures, the hope of the prophets is not for a romanticized, indefinite exilic existence. The prophet in exile is a mouthpiece for the people who hope for future *deliverance* from that homeless existence and the promise of their own land. Considered in this way, the scriptural narratives of exile I have mentioned straightforwardly oppose the destruction of habitats. By prophetically pointing toward their deliverance, eschatologies can inspire action to halt such practices in the present. But the main contribution of my chapter has been to suggest that this message of hope and deliverance isn't the only one that religious traditions can offer us in such times. They can also provide a form of alternative imagination by which to inhabit an age of extinctions.

My suggestion has been that religious traditions can help us to understand being at home on the Earth not as permanent, imperial, or sovereign masters but as impermanent, sojourning, and displaced citizens. I am not advocating a theology of fleeing—an eschatology that is really *escapology*—from the conditions of the Earth and its crises. I am looking instead to those religious narratives that express the human condition as in some sense un-Earthed, forced into the paths of strangers and called to solidarity with others who are also displaced. Both Jewish and Muslim (and to a different extent, Christian) histories have been profoundly shaped by the political experience of forced displacement and migration over centuries. In their religious privileging of the experience of homelessness, an active memory of life that is on the move suggests a theological reading of the condition of "unworlding" I have been developing. And such a religious perspective also lends an important nuance to our understanding of the threat of extinctions; it situates the decimation of species within a more generalized condition of threats to home and the ability to dwell.

The advantage of drawing on the religious traditions that I have engaged here—principally Christianity, but hopefully there have been enough references to Judaism and Islam to show how the theological moves being made are not the monopoly of this tradition—is that they are particularly suited to navigating the morally difficult tension between romanticizing exile and migration and portraying them as a sign of evil. In discussing the links between responding to biodiversity loss and responding to increased forced human migration, Rowlands, responding to Southgate's argument for assisted migration has pointed out that arguments for or against assisted migration tend to polarize the meaning of migration itself as either "unalloyed good or a pathological evil."[61] It can be good because migration can be understood as the expression of self-determination and resilience. It can be evil because it can equally be narrated as the destabilization of life—a strategy of last resort to preserve life—and a threat to place-based sovereignty. It is in religious traditions that one finds an account of human, earthly existence that encompasses both senses. Exile is both a blessed condition into which humanity is called, revealing God's purpose, and a tragedy or curse, the sign of fallen humanity.[62]

Though we should be careful not to romanticize it, we can see exile as revealing a crucial perspective of counterhegemonic existence. This perspective is affirmed by two of the most preeminent postcolonial thinkers on exile, Edward Said and Homi Bhaba. The former in particular wrote of the need to think about exile and return in literal terms (the urgency of struggling for the return of Palestinians to their homeland, for instance) but also about metaphorical exile, whose moral example will always be narrated and is thus a permanent resource. This essentially means that in a world in which injustice rules, one can never be at home.

One can see the fruits of navigating this tension in the experience of those who live at the intersection of political, ecological, and religious conflict. A distinctive faith-based practice and identity can draw on the experience of being strangers in a strange land as the basis for hospitality. Faith-based organizations responding directly to the increasing number of forced migrations across the world (but mostly in Islamic countries) draw increasingly in their literature on religious ethics of hospitality and duty toward the stranger. As David Hollenbach explains, Islam, Judaism, Christianity, and also (though less explicitly) Hinduism and Buddhism all contain sources from tradition and in some cases scripture that speak directly to the experience of forced migration/displacement and hospitality to the stranger. On a practical level, then, religious communities need to hold to account their national governments' records of the treatment of aliens and the effects of border policies, particularly in light of the pressures on movement caused by climate change and the extinction crisis. Indeed, as we have seen, the efforts of refugee support might in many cases be viewed as a response to the real threat of extinction to particular peoples as well as a response to the broader crisis of climate change in which extinctions occur. The politics of nationalism affects religious communities in every part of the world and is increasingly linked to the environmental pressures that lie at the root of displacement. The moral directives that are discernible from these traditions have been applied to the needs of nonhuman "strangers." For example, punitive border policing and technologies, and ecological destruction caused by border walls, produce injustices to both migrating humans and nonhumans alike.

CONCLUSION

The extinction crisis strikes at the heart of the concept that is most dear to many of us—the notion of Earth as our only home. We should not relinquish that notion. But we need a supplementary narrative that does justice to "the experience of being 'unworlded' by environmental change,"[63] that resists a securitized, biopolitical defense of homeland and a theology that underwrites the human as sovereign guarantor of that homeland. There are, I have argued, at least two ways that theology and religious studies ought to contribute to such resistance. The first is to critique the way eschatological imagination—imagination that is derived from belief in the end, or end-times—is in the service of a secular imagination or extinction-oriented catastrophe. A religiously inspired catastrophic imaginary is one that is routinely used to justify increased border security and the protection of certain (white) human populations from extinction and from the mythical incoming "swarm" of migrants. Second, religious traditions may play a role in resourcing the imaginations of their faithful, as well as of those who find themselves outside of religious tradition altogether but who look to them for moral inspiration. This very different form of eschatology could emphasize a narrative of being "human alongside," on the move, "in between worlds,"[64] in constant hope of a dwelling that cannot be guaranteed but whose very search produces ethical life in the form of new ways of welcoming the other.

All of this means overcoming the dominant security paradigm that is the main framework for thinking about both extinction and migration today. To live an exilic existence is today more than a reflection of hyperglobalization; it is also a necessary reflection on the shifting relationship between place and home in one's environment. We need to reevaluate the meaning of home to mean not fortress or settlement but "restless journey."[65] We need to describe a radical openness to encounters with loss and an inhabiting of the spaces of death and rebirth (through new life forms). Such a realization removes the temptations that have plagued climate migration discourses of describing "resilient" identities in simplistic terms as the stoic acceptance of whatever fate comes our way. The latter approach tends to favor those creatures who are either adaptive enough to weather the coming storms or iconic enough to merit human assistance in doing so. On the contrary, a migrant, exilic eschatology would be more sensitive than ever before to the vulnerability and fragility of all life and the need to bear that vulnerability within its ways of being a community.

In an age of extinctions, these crossing points of encounter are, very sadly, often sites of mourning as much as they are sites of encounter with other forms of life. As the opening of Kidwell's chapter powerfully attests, the absences of extinction are increasingly present in our worldly encounters with mountains as much as with fellow creatures. The task for which I have here sought the potential of religious belief and practice is to seek new modes of encounter in such contexts of loss and change. In the light of extinctions, let us do more to create refuge.

STEFAN SKRIMSHIRE is Associate Professor of Theology and Religious Studies at the University of Leeds. He researches the intersection of religious and political responses to the ecological and climate emergency. He is author of *Politics of Fear, Practices of Hope* and editor of *Future Ethics: Climate Change and Apocalyptic Imagination*. He lives in LILAC, the United Kingdom's first affordable, ecological cohousing community, in Leeds.

NOTES

1. Francis I, *Laudato Si'* (Vatican City: Vatican Publications, 2015), para 61.
2. Sandra Díaz et al., "Summary for Policymakers of the Global Assessment Report on Biodiversity and Ecosystem Services of the Intergovernmental Science-Policy Platform on Biodiversity and Ecosystem Services," Intergovernmental Science-Policy Platform on Biodiversity and Ecosystem Services (2019), accessed September 17, 2019, https://www.ipbes.net/news/Media-Release-Global-Assessment.
3. Jamie Bullen, "Extinction Rebellion: Shell HQ Windows Smashed as Climate Protest Blocks London Roads," *The Telegraph*, April 16, 2019, https://www.telegraph.co.uk/news/2019/04/15/extinction-rebellion-activists-threaten-bring-london-standstill/.
4. Shelley Nicholsen, *Love of Nature and the End of the World* (Cambridge, MA: MIT Press, 2001), 37.
5. Amitav Ghosh, *The Great Derangement* (Chicago: Chicago University Press, 2017), 54.

6. Audra Mitchell, "Beyond Biodiversity and Species: Problematizing Extinction," *Theory, Culture & Society* 33, no. 5 (September 2016): 23–42.

7. Gerardo Ceballos, Paul Ehrlich, and Rodolfo Dirzo, "Biological Annihilation via the Ongoing Sixth Mass Extinction Signaled by Vertebrate Population Losses and Declines," *Proceedings of the National Academy of Sciences* 114, no. 30 (July 10, 2017): E6089–E6096.

8. Martina Grecequet, Jack DeWaard, Jessica J. Hellmann, and Guy J. Abel, "Climate Vulnerability and Human Migration in Global Perspective," *Sustainability* 9, no. 5 (2017): 720.

9. James Ker-Lindsay, "Climate Change and State Death," *Survival: Global Politics and Strategy* 58, no. 4 (2016).

10. Perret, Megan, "Extinction in Public," presentation at online symposium hosted by Univeresity of Leeds, July 2020.

11. Edward O. Wilson, "Beware the Age of Loneliness," *The Economist*, November 18, 2013.

12. Craig Welch, "Half of All Species Is on the Move," *National Geographic*, April 27, 2017, https://www.nationalgeographic.com/science/article/climate-change-species-migration-disease.

13. Andrew Baldwin and Giovanni Bettini (eds), *Life Adrift: Climate Change, Migration, Critique* (London: Rowman and Littlefield, 2017), 3–5.

14. Ben Doherty, "'Disaster Alley': Australia Could Be Set to Receive New Wave of Climate Refugees," *Guardian*, April 4, 2017.

15. See Audra Mitchell, "Beyond Biodiversity and Species: Problematizing Extinction," *Theory, Culture and Society* 33, no. 5 (September 2016): 23–42; Brad Evans and Julian Reid, *Resilient Life* (London: Polity, 2014); Jamie Lorimer, *Wildlife in the Anthropocene* (Minneapolis: University of Minnesota Press, 2015).

16. For a critique of the logic of survival in state responses to extinction threats at the level of international politics, see Mitchell, "Is IR Going Extinct?," *European Journal of International Relations* 23, no. 1 (2017): 3–25.

17. Emma Marris, "Moving On Assisted Migration," *Nature Climate Change* 1 (2008): 112–113.

18. See Katherine Yusoff, "Biopolitical Economies and the Political Aesthetics of Climate Change," *Theory, Culture & Society* 27, no. 2–3 (2010): 73–99; Reid, "Climate, Migration, and Sex: The Biopolitics of Climate-Induced Migration," *Critical Studies on Security* 2, no. 2 (2004): 196–209.

19. Oliver Milman, "Pizzly or Grolar Bear: Grizzly-Polar Hybrid Is a New Result of Climate Change," *The Guardian*, May 18, 2016.

20. Christopher Southgate, Cheryl Hunt, and David Horrell, "Ascesis and Assisted Migration: Responses to the Effects of Climate

Change on Animal Species," *European Journal of Science and Theology* 4 (2008): 99–111.

21. Claire Colebrook, "Transcendental Migration: Taking Refuge from Climate Change," in *Life Adrift: Climate Change, Migration, Critique*, ed. Andrew Baldwin and Giovanni Bettini (London: Rowman and Littlefield, 2017), 115–130.

22. Colebrook, "Transcendental Migration," 119.

23. Bruno Latour, *Down to Earth: Politics in the New Climatic Regime* (Hoboken: John Wiley & Sons, 2018), 4–5.

24. Latour, *Down to Earth*, 8.

25. I owe this insight to Richard Irvine, who provided it during the symposium on which this volume is based.

26. Donna Haraway, *Staying with the Trouble: Making Kin in the Chthuluene* (Durham, NC: Duke University Press, 2016), 100.

27. Georgio Agamben, "We Refugees," *Symposium: A Quarterly Journal in Modern Literatures* 49, no. 2 (1995): 114–119.

28. Agamben, "We Refugees," 118.

29. Andrew Baldwin, "The Political Theologies of Climate Change-Induced Migration," *Critical Studies on Security* 2, no. 2 (2014): 210–222.

30. The reader should take note that while I refer to key parallels drawn from Islamic traditions with regard to the broad narrative of home and exile, I am not attempting to construct a comparative account of Abrahamic faiths here, and the theology from which I draw is predominantly Christian theology.

31. See Todd LeVasseur and Anna Pearson, eds., *Religion and Ecological Crisis: The "Lynn White Thesis" at 50* (London: Routledge, 2016).

32. Ivone Gebara, *Out of the Depths: Women's Experience of Evil and Salvation*, trans. Ann Patrick Ware (Mineapolis: Fortress, 2002).

33. See, for instance, Southgate, "The New Days of Noah?," *Creaturely Theology: On Gods, Humans, and Other Animals*, ed. Celia Deane-Drummond and David Clough (London: SCM, 2009).

34. "Mars & Beyond," SpaceX.com, accessed January 10, 2019, https://www.spacex.com/mars.

35. Hanna Miao and Michael Sheetz, "Jeff Bezos Says First Spaceflight Was "Tiny Little Step" in Blue Origin's Plan to Build a Road to Space," *CNBC*, July 20, 2021, https://www.cnbc.com/2021/07/20/jeff-bezos-says-this-is-a-tiny-little-step-toward-blue-origins-plan-to-build-a-road-to-space.html.

36. Sarah McFarland-Taylor, "No Planet B v. Disposable Planet: Self-Fulfilling Technocratic Apocalyptic Prophecies in the Marketing of Mars

Colonization," International Society for the Study of Religion, Nature, and Culture conference, Cork, Ireland, June 2019.

37. Michael Northcott, *An Angel Directs the Storm* (London: Bloomsbury, 2004), 59.

38. Quoted in Northcott, *An Angel*.

39. Sallie McFague, *The Body of God: An Ecological Theology* (London: SCM Press, 1993), 102.

40. For two further explorations of spatial eschatology, see Vitor Westhelle, *Eschatology and Space* (London: Palgrave, 2016); and Kathryn Tanner, "Eschatology and Ethics," in *The Oxford Handbook of Theological Ethics*, ed. G. Meilaender and W. Werpehowski, 41–56 (Oxford: Oxford University Press, 2010).

41. McFague, *The Body of God*, 102.

42. McFague, *The Body of God*, 111.

43. See Northcott, *Place, Ecology and the Sacred* (London: Bloomsbury, 2015); Sigurd Bergmann et al., eds., *Nature, Space and the Sacred: Transdisciplinary Perspectives* (Aldershot: Ashgate, 2009).

44. Annie Dillard, *Teaching a Stone to Talk: Expeditions and Encounters* (New York: Harper Collins, 2009), 148–149.

45. Ernst Conradie, *An Ecological Christian Apology* (London: Routledge, 2016).

46. This is what Bergmann, drawing on the German romanticist concept of *heimat*, calls the movement of Beheimatung—making oneself at home through movement and by embracing "turmoil." See Bergmann, *Religion, Space, and the Environment* (London: Routledge, 2017).

47. Quoted in Bergmann, *Religion, Space, and the Environment*, 45.

48. Peter Scott, "The Re-homing of the Human? A Theological Enquiry into whether Human Beings Are at Home on Earth," in *Christian Faith and the Earth: Current Paths and Emerging Horizons in Ecotheology*, ed. Ernst M. Conradie (London: T&T Clark, 2014), 124.

49. For a discussion of the significance of this translation, see Bergmann, "Places of Encounter with the Eschata: Accelerating the Spatial Turn in Eschatology," in *Embracing the Ivory Tower and Stained Glass Windows*, ed. Jennifer Baldwin (New York: Springer, 2016).

50. Alain Epp Weaver, "On Exile: Yoder, Said, and a Theology of Land and Return," *Cross Currents* 52, no. 4 (2003): 3.

51. Peter Scott, "The Re-homing of the Human?," 124.

52. Ashley Dawson, *Extinction: A Radical History* (New York: OR Books, 2016).

53. For a radical account of this view, see Westhelle, *Eschatology and Space*.

54. Leonardo Boff, "Alternate Earth Charter," *Petropolis*, November 13, 1998, https://cartadelatierra.org/wp-content/assets/virtual-library2/Images/uploads/Alternate%20Earth%20Charter%20Proposal.pdf.

55. Damian Carrington, "Humanity Is 'Cutting Down the Tree of Life,' Warn Scientists," *The Guardian*, October 15, 2018.

56. Noah Theriault, Timothy Leduc, Audra Mitchell, June Mary Rubis, and Norma Jacobs Gaehowako, "Living Protocols: Remaking Worlds in the Face of Extinction," *Social and Cultural Geography* 21, no. 7 (2020): 893–908.

57. Bergmann, *Religion, Space, and the Environment*, 42.

58. Southgate acknowledged that the practical and moral complexities of such a project would be significant. Nevertheless, Southgate suggests the thought experiment might be of value as a rhetorical device. In other words, it highlights the great effort and expense that would be required to reverse the threat of extinction and hopefully deter such an eventuality.

59. Scott, "The Re-homing."

60. Bergmann, *Religion, Space, and the Environment*.

61. Anna Rowlands, respondent, "The Suffering of Creation: Human and Nonhuman Migration," panel at Radical Ecological Conversion after Laudato Si': Discovering the Intrinsic Value of All Creatures conference, Pontifical Gregorian University, Rome, March 8, 2018.

62. Rowlands, "The Suffering."

63. Nigel Clark, "Strangers on a Strange Planet: On Hospitality and Holocene Climate Change," in *Life Adrift*, ed. Baldwin and Bettini, 134.

64. Cueto, quoted in Peter C. Phan, "Embracing, Protecting, and Loving the Stranger: A Roman Catholic Theology of Migration," in *Theology of Migration in the Abrahamic Religions*, ed. Elaine Padilla and Peter C. Phan, 77–110. London: Palgrave Macmillan, 2014.

65. Scott, "The Re-homing," 117.

SIX

OCEANIC EXTINCTIONS AND THE DREAD OF THE DEEP

KATE RIGBY

CURRENT EVOLUTIONARY THEORY TRACES THE remarkable emergence of life on this planet around 4.4 billion years ago to the primeval waters that began to pool on Earth's surface some five hundred years previously. While many mythic traditions have revered Mother Earth deities, with Christian writers of the Middle Ages still deploying the metaphor of *Terra Mater*, it seems that we living beings actually owe our existence to the watery deep, our ancient *Aqua Mater*. Recalling this renders especially appalling the multiple threats to marine life that are now coming to light, including industrial overfishing, plastics pollution, agricultural effluent, overheating, and acidification: the depletion of the oceans and the escalation of marine extinctions are turning Earth's ancient womb into an expanding death zone. Yet many of these adverse impacts have been escalating for some time, largely unseen—or at least unheeded—in a realm far from the lifeworld of landlubbing humans. While the movement to protect charismatic marine mammals and the efforts to safeguard commercial fisheries chalked up some early successes for conservation, it is only recently that the scale of problems threatening marine life has been brought to wider attention, not least through the prophetic witness of David Attenborough's spectacularly successful

2017 television series, *Blue Planet II*. In the catastrophic horizon of an unfolding oceanic ecocide, then, this essay considers theological, scientific, and poetic resources for reimagining human relations with endangered marine others. For Christians specifically, I argue, responding to the cry of the oceans, in collaboration with those of other faiths and none, entails revisiting the theology of creation, affirming our creaturely kinship with beyond-human others, and considering what it might mean to practice neighborly love toward fellow creatures, whose mode, time, and space of existence are so radically different from our own.

THE VIEW FROM BATH: HEALING WATERS, WOUNDED SEAS

In approaching the question of religion and extinction with respect to oceanic ecologies, I am mindful that I currently live and work near a town that owes its fame, indeed its very existence, to a once-sacred spring. Over a million liters of steaming mineral-rich water still surge up daily from some four kilometers below the city of Bath. Prior to the Roman invasion of Britain, the Celtic deity who was honored at this site was called Sulis—a name that tropes the spring as Earth's eye, an aperture where the land's hidden depths rise up to meet its sunlit surface (*súli* in Old Irish means "eye" or "gap" and is possibly derived from the proto-Celtic *sūli*, "sky"), and a hint, perhaps, that Sulis, presiding over the interface between worlds at this place, possessed powers of wisdom (insight) and prophecy (foresight).[1]

As was their wont, the Roman colonists assimilated this local deity to their own more urbane goddess Minerva, whose name had itself been swiped from the Etruscans and whose identity was modeled on that of the Greek Athena: a goddess of weaving and other crafts, music and poetry, wisdom and medicine, as well as commerce and military strategy. Whereas Sulis's life-giving waters nurtured an exclusively agrarian world, Sulis Minerva drew the sacred spring she presided over into the cultural, commercial, and military flows of an urbanizing empire. Between 60 CE, when work began on her temple, and the collapse of Roman rule at the beginning of the fifth century, the spring waters were channeled into a bathing complex for the benefit of a Romano-Celtic elite, who took to tossing clay tablets bearing curses against those who had wronged them into one of the pools in hopes that Sulis Minerva would punish the offending parties. During the Christian Middle Ages, the curative qualities of the spring waters continued to be valued, notwithstanding the expulsion of the pagan deities with which they had formerly been associated. Subsequently, in the eighteenth century, the Roman baths rose to renewed fame as a locus of urbane sociality and hoped-for healing for the beneficiaries of a new imperial regime—one that, with the arrival of the First Fleet bearing convicts and their captors in Botany Bay in 1788, extended even to the remotest ends of the inhabited Earth.

Today, visitors to the spring, which has been reframed as a museum site, are swiftly warned off if they dare to put so much as a finger into the waters for fear of imbibing harmful bacteria: these formerly healing waters, it is said, can make you seriously sick. You can nonetheless take a sip from a throwaway paper cup bearing metallic-tasting water from a tap proffering a suitably sterilized specimen. Largely (but, as we will see, not wholly) stripped of all sacred significance, Sulis's waters are now entering a very different world from the one they left behind when, falling as rain on the Mendip Hills some ten thousand years ago, they began their long sojourn below ground. Today, the waters that started their cycle early on in the Holocene are burbling back up into a profoundly anthropogenic world, overrun by the calamitous impacts of accelerating and still largely fossil-fueled industrialization. Today, it is the ocean into which they will eventually flow that is itself in need of healing.

The River Avon (from the Celtic *afon*, simply meaning "river"), into which the Roman drain still channels the spring waters once they leave the bathing complex, has long since been transformed from a series of braided streams, ebbing and flowing with the tides, pooling in ponds and swamps, into a navigable waterway. Its passage down to the sea, via a diversion leading to the Bristol harbor, is no longer guided into cleansing and modulating wetlands by industrious beavers but is instead interrupted by a series of weirs and locks engineered to prevent the river from spilling over into its ancient floodplains (not least those onto which the city of Bath now sprawls).[2] With the relocation of much manufacturing overseas, to countries with lower labor costs and environmental safeguards, the Avon is probably less polluted by industrial effluent than it was previously. But the runoff from the surrounding farmland is laden with excess nutrients and laced with toxic chemicals, and significant quantities of nonbiodegradable rubbish also end up in its waters. Like other rivers in the United Kingdom, the lifeworld of the Avon is afforded some protection, notably as one of the European Union's Special Areas of Conservation, on account of several endangered species for which it provides habitat—the whorl snail, the sea lamprey and brook lamprey, the Atlantic salmon, and a fish known as the bullhead.[3] Yet such local safeguards appear woefully insufficient when you recall that the waters of this river, like those of all Earth's seabound waterways, are heading into an abysmal oceanic "world of wounds."[4]

These wounds, inflicted with ever-greater intensity during the period of the Great Acceleration of global industrialization from the war-torn midpoint of the last century, are increasingly manifest in the lives of all sea creatures, from the greatest to the smallest. With respect to the former, while the heyday of whaling might lie in the past, many cetaceans, including some whose numbers have been recovering, are facing new threats. Six out of the thirteen great whale species are currently classified as endangered.[5] The conservation status of many other marine mammal species is uncertain, and where there are clear signs of trouble, the causes are not fully understood. Between January and May of

2019, for example, thirty-one emaciated Pacific gray whales were found dead along the West Coast of North America between Baja California and Puget Sound. Dozens more seen making their way south to their summer breeding grounds were also clearly malnourished. While the cause of their plight remains uncertain, climate change appears to be a factor; the receding Arctic ice cap is forcing the whales further north to breed and feed, thereby lengthening their journey to the Baja.[6] Some populations of orcas, too, appear to be in steep decline, but in their case, chemical toxins have been identified as the prime suspect—specifically, polychlorinated biphenyls (PCBs), organic compounds formerly used in capacitators, oil paints, and coolants. Although PCBs have been banned in many countries and are being phased out worldwide, they persist in marine environments, interfering with orca reproduction, harming their immune systems and altering their behavior.[7]

At the other end of the scale, microscopic organisms known as phytoplankton also appear to be declining due to the warming temperature of the ocean,[8] while the zooplankton who feed on them are threatened by increasing acidity levels arising from marine absorption of human carbon dioxide emissions, which interfere with the formation of their calcareous shells.[9] Since their shells comprise something akin to a mobile home for these tiny creatures, their plight might be considered emblematic of the dedomiciling trajectory of the (so-called) Anthropocene—an era in which people in industrialized societies, embedded in socio-ecologically damaging systems of capitalist production and consumption, have come to make themselves at home in the world in ways that are unhousing others (both human and nonhuman), as discussed further in this volume by Stefan Skrimshire. With respect to other creatures, this epidemic of unhousing (otherwise known as habitat destruction) is a major driver of the precipitously declining abundance and diversity of free-living plants, animals, and fungi, propelling ever more species toward extinction as the interconnectivities that enable their existence unravel around them.

This unraveling is the bitter truth lurking beneath the term *extinction*, a word that strikes me as almost euphemistic in its bland technicality, referencing merely the disappearance of a taxonomic kind while effacing the untold suffering endured by living creatures as the conditions that enable their lifeways are fatally eroded. In addition to whatever misery we might (with difficulty) imagine these tiny organisms to be experiencing as their world grows ever more inhospitable, marine plankton are also crucial members of the wider *oikos* of Earth, forming the base of the oceanic food chain, as well as absorbing carbon dioxide, releasing oxygen—providing some 50 percent in the air we breathe—and helping to regulate the climate.[10] In the interconnected living world of Earth's oceans, moreover, a myriad of other wounds too are coming to light, manifesting in declining fish stocks, bleached coral reefs, islands of trash, dead zones, undersea blasting, oil drilling, commercial and military traffic, and the plastics that variously ensnare, are ingested, form toxin-laden microparticles, and have been found even in the deepest depths of the sea.[11]

THE DREAD OF THE DEEP: BIBLICAL LEGACIES AND FAUSTIAN AMBITIONS

How has it come to this? As with all of the environmental—or, more accurately, socioecological—crises currently besetting our collective planetary home, the causes are complex and include an array of technoscientific, economic, political, and social factors. Underlying values, assumptions, and beliefs are also threaded through these material-discursive entanglements, and some of these have religious roots. While there is significant cultural variation in how different societies have historically construed human relations with the sea, Kimberley Patton has uncovered a widespread tendency, traceable across diverse religious traditions, to view oceans as "infinite and supremely cathartic, diluting and carrying off what is ritually impure in human religious systems and thus dangerous to human wellbeing."¹² This transcultural tendency has an experiential foundation in the perception of the vastness and constancy of the oceanic world, its perpetual motion and propensity for carrying things away, together with the cleansing and preserving qualities of salt. Yet, in Patton's analysis, the resulting sense of the unassailability of the sea and its infinite capacity to absorb all the contaminants we might cast upon its purifying waters has contributed to its treatment as a dumping ground, hindering our recognition of the finitude and fragility of oceanic ecologies.

While the narratives that Patton focuses on come from ancient Greek, Inuit, and Hindi religious traditions, she observes that the paradigm of the cathartic ocean also appears in the Hebrew Bible—for example, at the end of the book of Micah, where the prophet affirms his faith in a merciful God, who "will cast all our sins/into the depths of the sea" (Mic. 7:18–19). In fact, as Meric Srokosz and Rebecca Watson demonstrate in *Blue Planet, Blue God*, the sea appears in an array of different guises in the Bible: as a participant in the burgeoning of both aquatic and bird life on the fifth day of creation in Genesis 1 and as a vehicle for trade and imperial expansion; vast, yet potentially also vulnerable; sacred, yet sometimes also reviled.¹³ It is the latter view, arising from the association of the ocean with all that is chaotic, uncontained, and unconstrainable, that has been brought into focus by Catherine Keller in her diagnosis within Christianity of a certain dread and loathing of the watery deep that she dubs *tehomophobia* (from *tehom* in the Hebrew of Gen. 1). In her analysis, this dread of the deep lurks within the doctrine of God's creation of the world out of nothing (*creatio ex nihilo*), as it rose to theological orthodoxy from the second century CE, in association with ideas of divine omnipotence and the hierarchical (and highly gendered) spirit-matter dualism of Greco-Roman ontology. Keller argues that this doctrine occluded the possibility afforded by the biblical creation narrative of recognizing divine creative agency as always already cocreativity, actualizing the generative potential of that mysterious something characterized in Genesis 1:1 as a chaotic watery abyss. Over time, the theological model of solitary sovereign creation out of nothing became aligned with the privileging of permanence over transience, stasis over flux, *terra firma* over *aqua mater* and the imposition of order from without as opposed to working with the given, in ways that often also worked to subtly endorse social relations of domination, notably along gendered, classist, racist, and heterosexist lines.[14]

As Keller acknowledges, the narrative of creatio ex nihilo, which also informed both Jewish and Islamic thought, can nonetheless be told in different ways and to varied political ends, including emancipatory and ecological ones.[15] As Janet Soskice has shown, this doctrine, far from being an Hellenic import, can be traced back to far earlier Jewish texts, including some of the Psalms and the passages in Isaiah, the deuterocanonical books of Judith, and 1 and 2 Maccabees.[16] In her analysis, it enabled the early Church Fathers of late Antiquity, including Athanasius, the Cappadocians, John Damascene, and Augustine, to "slip the chain" of the "destructive dualism prevalent in late antiquity where matter was bad and spirit was good."[17] It does not "close the border" between Creator and creation, in her analysis, for the God who lovingly summons all things into being was also understood to be "always already there—nearer and more intimate to us than our own breath."[18]

It is not my purpose to enter the theological fray on this question. What concerns me here is the toxic cultural legacy of the unquestionably mixed messages regarding the briny deep that derive from biblical texts and traditions. At the same time, though, I think it is worth revisiting this ambivalent religious inheritance in search of potential sources of inspiration for Jewish, Christian, and interfaith practices of *tehomophilic* oceanic restoration in the perilous present as part of a wider movement to counter the growing extinction crisis.

My way into this discussion is not as a theologian or church historian but rather as an ecocritical scholar of literature and religion within the wider field of the environmental humanities, with particular expertise in European Romanticism. The cultural ferment of the decades around 1800, above all in Britain and the German region, erupted alongside, and in many ways in response to, the onset of that fossil-fueled process of industrialization, in conjunction with a new phase of colonial conquest, that has now delivered Earth into the era of the Anthropocene.[19] Germanists refer to this period as the "time of Goethe" (Goethezeit), and it is to the prophetic witness of Wilhelm von Goethe's remarkable two-part drama *Faust* that I now turn. In his Romantic rewriting of the Renaissance legend of Faust as a paradigmatic modern tragedy, the German author and polymath discloses the subterranean tehomophobia underlying the modern project of the technocratic mastery of nature in the historical course of what Theodor Adorno and Max Horkheimer would later diagnose as the "dialectic of enlightenment."[20] Unlike Adorno and Horkheimer, however, he also charts an expressly tehomophilic alternative that opens the prospect of renewed collective flourishing.

Unlike his legendary and literary predecessors, Goethe's Faust does not seek wealth, fame, and power but aspires rather to a perpetual process of self-realization powered by a sense of permanent dissatisfaction with the present. Accordingly, his bargain with Mephistopheles entails this pledge: "If ever to the moment I shall say: / Beautiful moment, do not pass away! / Then you may forge your chains to bind me, / Then I will put my life behind me" (I, sc. 7, 1699–1702).[21]

In *Part One*, it is the pretty village girl, Gretchen, who pays the price for Faust's classically modernist project of ceaseless self-development.[22] Having been left to deal with an illegitimate pregnancy alone, she is driven to the desperate solution of infanticide (not insignificantly, in view of Faust's later hostility toward the sea, by drowning) and dies in prison awaiting execution. Scandalously, the play ends with her redemption by an unconventional *deus ex machina*, a God of forgiveness rather than punishment who mercifully foils Mephistopheles's bid to claim Gretchen's soul. Having recovered from his feelings of grief and guilt about the death of Gretchen, the Faust of *Part Two*, the much later sequel to *Part One*, sets his sights on a higher quest, namely for the love of the legendary epitome of female beauty, Helen of Troy. In the play's third act, the union between Helen and Faust is eventually achieved, and they have a child, Euphorion. When their son, Ikarus-like, flies too close to the sun and falls to his death, however, Helen too returns to the Underworld. Distraught by their loss, Faust externalizes his urge for self-transformation into a quest to remake the world around him, eliminating in the process all traces of the premodern *oikos*, to which his first love, Gretchen, had belonged, and setting his sights on the mastery of the briny deep.

Act Four opens with a now aging and embittered Faust looking out upon the "high sea":

> It surged and swelled, mounted up more and more,
> Then checked, and spilt its waves tempestuously,
> Venting its rage upon the flat, wide shore
> And this displeased me
> [...]
> Landward it streams, and countless inlets fill;
> Barren itself, it spreads its barren will;
> It swells and swirls, its rolling waves expand
> Over the dreary waste of dismal sand;
> Breaker on breaker, all their power upheaved
> And then withdrawn, and not a thing achieved!
> I watch dismayed, almost despairingly,
> This useless elemental energy!
> And so my spirit dares new wings to span:
> This I would fight, and conquer if I can.
> (IV, sc. 14, 10198–10202; 10212–10221)[23]

Here, the ocean confronts Earth's self-proclaimed sovereign subject, in whom the religious inheritance of God-given dominion has been secularized into an anthropocentric aspiration to technocratic domination, as a primeval chaos monster that must be brought to heel.

Assuming an agro-industrial standard of productivity, moreover, Faust disregards the other-than-human life that flourishes in the liminal zone of the shoreline and reviles the coastal wetlands in terms that had long since become embedded in Western culture, namely as irksomely abject.[24] Determined to defy the waves by reclaiming the littoral zone for his own purposes, Faust also blinds himself to the cost entailed in the Mephistophelian realization of his new project to "ban the lordly sea" and "curb its force" (10229). In the dialogue between a shipwrecked Wanderer and his kind hosts, the shore-dwelling Philemon and Baucis, which opens act 5, it becomes apparent that this cost was borne not only by the more-than-human life of these coastal wetlands but also by those forced to perform the labor of turning them into a "garden" (V, sc. 17, 11085): "All night long we heard the cries / A canal was built by morning" (11129–11130). Behind the diabolical means that created what is, for Faust, a "paradisal scene" (11086) stand the historical realities of land reclamation and commodification at home, along with slavery and colonial conquest abroad—the "undivided trinity / Of war and trade and piracy" applauded by Mephistopheles as Faust's ships return to harbor laden with plunder from overseas (11187–11189).

Faust is dismayed when he learns that his appropriation of Philemon's and Baucis's dwelling place in order to create a viewing platform to admire his achievements cost them their lives. He nonetheless remains committed to his Promethean project, to which he now gives a utopian spin: Goethe's tragic hero dies dreaming of an expanded living space, created through his ambitious dyke, dam, and drainage scheme, for a manly breed of battlers against the elements. Scandalously, Mephistopheles fails to make off with his soul, having been lustfully distracted by the alluring boy angels, whose ministry helps to facilitate Faust's unorthodox redemption. This is not granted by the conventionally masculine deity of the Prologue in Heaven at the start of *Faust, Part One*, who agrees with Mephistopheles that the titular hero should be tempted, Job-like, to betray his soul to the devil. Rather, it is effected by the force of cosmic love, transcending the dualism of Eros and Agape, desire and compassion, which is personified in the closing words of the drama as "eternal Womanhood" (V, sc. 23, 12110). Meanwhile, in keeping with his self-designation in *Part One* as the "spirit of perpetual negation" (V, sc. 6, 1338), Mephistopheles has already foreshadowed the eventual ruination of Faust's earthly endeavors:

> And yet it's us you're working for
> With all your foolish dams and dikes;
> Neptune, the water-devil, likes
> To think of the great feast there'll be
> When they collapse.
> (V, sc. 21, 11544–11548).

According to one reading, Faust's hastily built canals are already collapsing, a phenomenon that was well known to Goethe and referred to at the time as "hydrological terrorism."[25] If so, the ending is profoundly ironic, as the "putrid puddle" (V, sc. 21, 11559–11560) that the dying Faust is set on draining is not a remnant of the original coastal wetlands but an unintended consequence of his attempted mastery of this aqueous terrain. Reread in the era of rising sea levels driven by anthropogenic planetary heating, the irony of Mephistopheles's chilling prediction only deepens.

The figure of Faust might have emancipated himself from the doctrines of the church; yet his tehomophobia bears the trace of a biblical inheritance, which, as Goethe shows, remains an undercurrent within modernity. In Psalm 74, for example, the hope for divine deliverance is tied to a recollection of YHWH's sovereignty over the ocean: "You divided the sea by your might;

You broke the heads of the dragons in the waters. You crushed the heads of Leviathan" (Ps. 74:13–14).[26] The anti-imperialist author of Revelation, otherwise known as the Apocalypse of St. John, goes one step further, imaging the longed-for coming of the Kingdom of God in terms of a "new earth" in which "the sea was no more" (Rev. 21:1).[27]

Not unlike the contrasting paradigm of the cathartic ocean, fear and loathing of the briny deep also have an experiential dimension. For all who breathe air, even a small quantity of water, relative to their size, carries the risk of drowning, and seas are not always placid neighbors. In conjunction with other elements, such as cyclonic storms or submarine earthquakes, oceans can wreak death and destruction on a massive scale. It was perhaps the story of one such extreme event, passed down through oral tradition from generation to generation, that informed the world flood narrative that found its way into the Bible. Framed as an act of redemptive violence in which "all the fountains of the great deep burst forth, and the windows of the heavens were opened" (Gen. 7:11), this great flood can also be seen to conform to the paradigm of the cathartic ocean in that it ends up enabling a new beginning under a new covenant—one that is made not only with humans but with "every living creature of all flesh that is on the earth" (Gen. 9:16).

As Keller observes, however, within the polylogical and polydoxical weave of biblical writing, it is possible to discern an ocean-loving, or tehomophilic, view of the briny deep, beginning, not least, with Genesis 1. In the version of the Hebrew creation narrative with which the Bible opens, in the beginning was not the Word, as Christians read at the start of John's Gospel—that only came later—but the waters; and the waters were *tehom* (deeps). Here it is in Keller's translation, with key Hebrew terms left in the original: 'When in the beginning *Elohim* created heaven and earth, the earth was *tohu va bohu*, darkness was on the face of *tehom*, and the *ruach elohim* vibrating on the face of the waters."[28]

Now, this first creation narrative was actually composed far later than the more conventionally mythic account of Adam and Eve that follows in Genesis 2, which imagines a solitary deity, *YHWH*, rather than the divine plurality, or heavenly collective, referenced in the plural term *Elohim*, pottering about in a primeval garden, fashioning the first human out of clay. This tale, almost certainly derived from oral traditions of unknown antiquity, has been dated by biblical scholars to the ninth or possibly even tenth century BCE, although this dating is by no means universally accepted. What is known with more confidence is that the poetically highly wrought text of Genesis 1 was composed considerably more recently, namely following the conquest of the Kingdom of Judah by the Babylonian empire in the sixth century BCE, and probably penned by a group of Jewish priests who were, or had been, held captive in Babylon.

Composed in the shadow of exile, this text can be seen to effect a subtly subversive form of decolonization in its transformative appropriation of the Babylonians' own creation myth—for the *tehom* of the Hebrew text (a feminine noun that, in the absence of a definite article, functions like a proper noun) is a cognate of the Akkadian *tamtu* and Ugaritic *t-h-m*, both related to the earlier Sumerian *Tiamat*, and this was the name given to the great mother of all the younger gods in Babylonian polytheism. A deity of the briny deep, ambivalently linked with both cosmogenesis and primordial chaos, Tiamat ghosts the Hebrew *tohu va bohu*.[29] In the Sumerian creation narrative, she is murdered by her own grandson, the warrior god Marduk, who fashions the separated spheres of sky and earth out of her dismembered body. Countering this distinctly misogynistic Bronze Age vision of creation through conquest, the Priestly authors of Genesis 1 instead imagine a magisterial—but nonetheless emphatically nonviolent—summoning forth from out of the formless (*tohu va bohu*) matter/

mater of the abyssal *tehom*, of distinct entities and diverse kinds, by means of the divine "breath" or "spirit." The Hebrew *ruach* was itself understood as something earthily material, for biblical Hebrew is innocent of the Greek matter-spirit dualism that infected Christian theology, as well as Hellenized Jewish thought, from at least the second century CE. Initially figured as "vibrating on the face of the waters," this divine breath then lends itself to that famous sequence of performative speech acts through which the created order is invited into being and becoming: "Then *Elohim* said, 'Let there be light'; and there was light. And *Elohim* saw that the light was good; and Elohim separated the light from the darkness. *Elohim* called the light Day, and the darkness He called Night. And there was evening and there was morning, the first day" (Gen. 1:3–5).

And following day and night, there was sky and sea, then sea and land; and on the land, and in the sea, and winging through the skies, multitudes of living beings were "let be," and all were invited to multiply and fill their respective realms; and finally, there were human beings also, made "in the image" of the transgender divine collective—that is to say, made to be in communion with the Creator/Creatrix, as was *Elohim* with the abyssal *aqua mater*, and thereby called to the service of ongoing creation in the role of regents:

> So *Elohim* created humankind in His image,
> in the image of *Elohim* He created them;
> male and female He created them.
> *Elohim* blessed them, and *Elohim* said to them,
> Be fruitful and multiply, and fill the earth and subdue it;
> and have dominion over the fish of the sea and over the birds of the air
> and over every living thing that moves upon the earth
> (Gen. 1:27–28)

The decolonizing impetus of this radical recasting of the tale of Tiamat and Marduk continues in the Priestly authors' construction of every single man and woman as "made in the image" of

God, for according to the politico-religious orthodoxy of their imperial overlords, only kings could be construed as gods. And yet, as has frequently been remarked, this passage, as it was inherited within Christianity, nonetheless laid the groundwork for another colonial venture: namely, the colonization of Earth and its diverse other-than-human denizens, along with peoples of many places with differing ontologies and spiritualities, by the dominant classes of those Western nations who mistook the Bible to authorize their hegemonic rule. First composed from a place of radical disempowerment, the vision of human dominion *within creation* began to be widely interpreted with the scientific revolution of the seventeenth century as licensing a project of human domination *over nature* in the Christian West. In the context of the growth of mercantile capitalism and colonial expansion, creation, traditionally understood as inherently good, albeit tarnished by the Fall, gets recast as Nature, conceived as so much mindless matter, a storehouse of resources for exclusively human benefit.[30]

Other biblical passages nonetheless not only reaffirm the originary and abiding goodness of the oceanic lifeworld summoned forth out of the primal waters, they also acknowledge the limits of human comprehension and control. One such passage surfaces, for example, in Psalm 104, in which praise for creation encompasses delight in the sporting of the archetypal chaos monster of the briny depths:

> O YHWH, how manifold are your works!
> In wisdom you have made them all:
> the earth is full of your creatures.
> Yonder is the sea, great and wide.
> Creeping things innumerable are there
> living things both small and great.
> There go the ships,
> and Leviathan that you formed to sport in it.
> (Ps. 104:24–26).

This reaffirmation of the manifest goodness of the multiplicitous creatures of the deep, as announced in Genesis 1:21, recurs in another book belonging to the ensemble of writings scattered through the Hebrew Bible known as the Wisdom tradition. In the book of Job, commonly dated to between the seventh and second century BCE, the divine voice that erupts from the whirlwind rebukes the beleaguered titular hero for his all-too-human assumption that the world was ordered for his benefit and that his virtue would inevitably be rewarded with good fortune. This voice exhorts Job to look up from his merely personal woes, grievous and undeserved as they were, in order to behold the vastly more-than-human world that bore everywhere the trace of its ever-attentive Creator. This is disclosed as a world in which myriad wild creatures—the lion and the raven, mountain goat and deer, wild ass and oxen, ostrich and eagle—were busy going about their own lives, facing their own challenges, independently from human interests and oversight (Job 38:39–39:18); a world where even domesticated animals, such as the undaunted horse, retain their own agency and seek their own satisfaction (39:19–25); a world in which the Lord causes it to rain in the "desert, which is empty of human life" (38:26), extending provision to all creatures equally and taking particular delight in those that elude human control—the Behemoth, hailed as "the first of the great acts of God" (Job 40:19), and the Leviathan, whose breaching and crashing cause even the gods to take fright (Job 41:25):

> Will it make a covenant with you to be taken as your servant forever?
> Will you play with it as with a bird,
> or will you put it on leash for your girls?
> Will traders bargain over it?
> Will they divide it up among the merchants?
> Can you fill its skin with harpoons...?
> (Job 41:4–7)

> It makes the deep boil like a pot;
> it makes the sea like a pot of ointment.
> It leaves a shining wake behind it;
> one would think the deep to be white-haired.
> On earth it has no equal,
> a creature without fear.
> It surveys everything that is lofty;
> it is king over all that are proud.
> (Job 42:31–34)

While acknowledging the potential, indeed propensity, for dominological readings of Job as ultimately affirming divine omnipotence, Keller counters by noting that the biblical "chaos monster does not seek vengeance but respect for its domain."[31] She concludes that, not unlike the author of *Moby Dick* in far more recent times, the "windy vortex mocks the powers of global commercialization; it puts into question the assumption of the exploitability of the wild life of the world—the 'subdue and have dominion' project." Yet, as Keller ruefully observes, the author of Job "could not have imagined the current human capacity to annihilate the whales altogether, or to turn the sea into a sewer."

GOING WITH THE FLOW: *CREATIO EX PROFUNDIS* AND OCEANIC COBECOMING

Against the doctrine of creatio ex nihilo, Keller advances a theology of *nova creatio ex profundis*. This is a theology of continuous cocreation "from the deep," in which Elohim figures as a "strange attractor," luring "self-organizing systems out of the fluctuating possibilities,"[32] delighting in their self-actualization, sorrowing in their stymieing, and calling those made in the divine image to act creatively, compassionately, and justly to help sustain the potential for continued cobecoming: "The *nova creatio ex profundis* requires our entire participation. In the beginning: a plurisingularity of universe, earth echoing chaos, dark deep vibrating with spirit, creates."[33]

Keller's theology of continuous cocreation is informed by contemporary science (especially the science of complex dissipative systems, popularized as chaos theory), poststructuralist thought, and a range of nonmainstream theologies (including older traditions of the *via negativa*, or "negative theology," which foregrounds the ungraspability of the divine, as well as current liberation, feminist, ecological, queer, and African American theologies). As a variant of process theology, it is premised on the "intuition that the universe itself is not most fundamentally a static being or the product of a static Being—but an immeasurable becoming. . . . The God of a universe in process may in powerful ways turn out to be a God in process: that is, in open-ended interactivity with each of the gazillions of us creatures."[34] While the death of individuals and the extinction of species are inherent to this process, human actions that precipitate the unraveling of those connectivities that make biodiverse life on this planet a going concern surely contradict our calling to be, and become, "in the image" of the Creator. This theology of continuous cocreation is indebted to the process philosophy of Alfred North Whitehead, crucial precursors of which can be found in those Romantic-era natural philosophies of interactive, evolutionary cobecoming that find poetic form in Goethe's *Faust*.[35]

From the perspective of modern evolutionary theory, the *tehom* of process theology, the metaphysical matrix of potentiality out of which the actual is forever being drawn into being—or rather, cobecoming—finds a material counterpart in Earth's ancient oceans. The premise of oceanic origins of life is also prefigured in *Faust, Part Two*. Here, Goethe signals the dubiousness of his tragic hero's tehomophobic project in a quirkily humorous yet philosophically profound subplot, which gets played out in the "Classical Walpurgis Night" scene of act 2. Across the Germanic cultures of Northern Europe, Walpurgis Night is celebrated on May 30, on the eve of the saint's day of the eighth-century Abbess Walpurga, famed for providing protection against witchcraft, but traditionally associated with the annual gathering of witches on the Brocken in the Harz Mountains: the *Hexennacht*. While a folkloric Hexennacht on the Brocken features in *Faust, Part One*, the Classical Walpurgis Night of *Part Two* draws back the veil on an Ancient Greek Underworld. Here, Goethe stages a debate between two of the earliest philosophers in the Western tradition regarding the formation of the Earth. While Anaxagoris (c. 500–428 BCE) celebrates the fiery volcanic forces that had raised the mountains, his pre-Socratic predecessor Thales (c. 624–545 BCE) professes a preference for the creative element of water: "In moisture all that lives originated" (II, sc. 10, 7856). This debate is interrupted when Mephistopheles appears with a half-formed test-tube baby, the fruit of a failed alchemical experiment by Faust's former student, Wagner, who holds the oldfangled sexual process of reproduction to be beneath human dignity. Thales proceeds to put his theory to the test by consulting the sea-god Nereus as to how Wagner's disembodied brainchild might acquire a corporeal existence. Nereus duly instructs him to take the hermaphroditic Homunculus, who appears only as a pulsing light, to Proteus. Manifesting intermittently as a dolphin—with some coaxing from Thales, who is not keen on talking to an entity that he cannot locate—Proteus declares that the Homunculus must be entrusted to the creative agency of the ocean if he wishes to become a man (while remarking misanthropically that things would be all downhill from there). Thales, giving a proto-evolutionary spin to Proteus's words, accordingly exhorts Homunculus to "seek the beginnings of creation" in the watery deep, in order to "move onward by eternal norms / Through many thousand thousand forms / And reach at last the human state" (II, sc. 10, 8322–8326).

For Goethe's Thales, then, if not for today's genetic engineers, including those critiqued by Lisa Sideris in this volume, for whom the answer to biodiversity loss is the techno-fix of de-extinction, there was no bypassing the generative processes of life and death that originated in, and were sustained by, Earth's life-giving oceans:

> In water all things began to thrive!
> By water all things are kept alive!
> Grant us your bounty for ever, great ocean:
> Send us clouds, for if you did not,
> Abundant streams, for if you did not,
> And rivers in meandering motion,
> And great waterways—for if you did not,
> Where would the mountains, the plains, and the world be then?
> By you fresh life lives and is sustained again.
> (II, sc. 10, 8435–43).

Ultimately, however, it is not Thales's wise words but the sex appeal of the sea-nymph Galatea who appears Venus-like in a seashell chariot that draws Homunculus into the waves. As s/he bursts orgasmically out of the confines of the test tube and flame and water are conjoined, the scene culminates with a chorus of Sirens singing the praises of Eros, to which "all" respond with adulation for the elements:

> Hail to the mild and gentle breeze!
> Hail, caverns rich with mysteries!
> Fire, water, air, and air as well:
> You elements all four, all hail!
> (II, sc. 10, 8484–8487).

In the wake of Charles Darwin's postulate of "natural selection" as the primary driver of adaptation and speciation (albeit now qualified by recent findings in the field of epigenetics), most modern evolutionary biologists would doubtless reject Goethe's talk of "eternal norms" as smacking of natural theology. There is nonetheless general agreement today that Earth's first living cells did indeed emerge in the ocean, as Thales had postulated and as the early evolutionary thinkers of the Romantic period, Goethe among them, concurred. Among them was Charles Darwin's grandfather, Erasmus Darwin, who set his version of this theory to verse in his *Temple of Nature; or, The Origin of Society* of 1803 (a work that is inclined to make one glad that scientists generally no longer try to share their findings in poetic form):

> Organic Life beneath the shoreless waves
> Was born and nurs'd in Ocean's pearly caves;
> First forms minute, unseen by spheric glass,
> Move on the mud, or pierce the watery mass;
> These, as successive generations bloom,
> New powers acquire, and larger limbs assume;
> Whence countless groups of vegetation spring,
> And breathing realms of fin, and feet, and wing.[36]

While the natural philosophers of the Romantic period thought they had found material evidence for Thales's postulate in the microscopic organisms that they mistakenly held to form spontaneously in standing water, the idea that life originated in the sea has considerably more ancient antecedents in the mythic creation stories of many cultures. These include the "earth diver" narratives of several Native American, Central Asian, and Finno-Urgic peoples, in which a divine being generally sends an animal of some kind into the primeval waters to find mud or sand with which to form dry land, thereby rendering Earth habitable for the emergence of terrestrial lifeforms.[37] In the biblical six days of creation, plant life and terrestrial animals are said to have burgeoned forth directly from the Earth in response to the divine summons. Yet here, too, the primeval seas come to cooperate with the Creator in birthing creatures of both air and water.

Although the mysteries of biogenesis have not yet been fully revealed (with seeding from the aerial depths of outer space remaining in contention), the scenario that is currently favored by evolutionary biologists gives a leading role to those thermal vents through which elements from the hot, steamy, and seething *tohu va bohu* beneath Earth's crust come into contact with salty waters, creating a warm, mineral-rich soup in which that as-yet-mysterious chemical reaction appears to have occurred, producing the building blocks of life. Yet contemporary science suggests that the sea not only birthed those first "forms minute unseen by spheric glass" (which is to say, long, long before the late appearance of humankind and the even more recent invention of microscopes); those briny deeps also created, and continue to sustain, conditions conducive to the burgeoning of terrestrial life. For it is the molecular structure of the waters covering some 71 percent of Earth's surface that makes our precious planet warmer and more hospitable to life as we know it than it would otherwise be, given its distance from the Sun. Meanwhile, the great ocean conveyor belt, in distributing heat north and south from the equator, plays a crucial role in transporting some of the immense warmth that the seas absorb toward the poles. Without our great Aqua Mater, then, Earth would be as inhospitable as Venus or Mars, and any organisms who came into being in the ocean would have been unlikely to have taken the momentous step that brought some of them, beginning with adventurous plants in partnership with their fungal friends, onto land. Life might have started, as it almost certainly has elsewhere; but it could not have got going in the gloriously biodiverse way that it has on our predominantly blue planet.

The processes of ancient oceanic cobecoming—as of today's rising tide of extinction—disclosed by science afford new perspectives on the earlier religious and literary texts and traditions discussed here. As I indicate in the concluding section of this essay, however, I do not believe that scientific accounts should supplant all others. For stories such as the biblical creation narrative and its refraction in Goethe's Faustian mythos of modernity are primarily concerned with questions that go beyond the brief of science per se—questions of meaning, value, and purpose that might inform how we conceive and conduct our relations with other creatures in the perilous present.[38]

SULIS RETURNS: HEALING THE SEAS, BEFRIENDING ALIENS

It is a peculiarly tragic irony that we should be enlarging our understanding of all that we owe to the seas, as well as witnessing some of the wonders of today's beleaguered ocean deeps on our TV screens, by virtue of the very technoscientific advances that have also enabled biodiversity-depleting industrial whaling, overfishing, and deep sea oil extraction, with its associated oil spills and plastics plague, along with greenhouse gas–driven oceanic overheating and acidification.[39] The perpetuation of these destructive practices, among many other planetary assaults, is being powered by a complex of actors and factors, including socioeconomic systems and political dynamics that demand to be tackled in the context of a wider agenda of ecopolitical change, as demanded by activists involved in movements such as Extinction Rebellion, as well as by Indigenous peoples seeking to resist the industrial ravaging of their traditional lands. This project nonetheless requires a corresponding cultural shift.[40] While "theism might be dispensable for ecological thought and practices," as Virginia Burrus posits, I share her view that "some form of piety or cultivated reverence is not."[41] In this needed transformation of cultural vision, values, and perceptions, religion and spirituality could play a key role, namely in the recovery, across and among diverse cultural traditions, of a sense of the inherent holiness of the living Earth in all of its domains, including its vast yet vulnerable oceans.

One instance of this ecoreligious insurgency is the US-based Interfaith Oceans campaign, which, as they state on their website, "encourages religious and spiritual communities to join with scientists to appreciate the gifts of the ocean systems, species, and coastal communities—and work together to protect and restore them . . . in responsibility to our Creator, the poor, our children, our brother and sister species, and future generations."[42] This organization originally grew out of the Jewish and Christian National Religious Coalition on Creation Care but now provides a venue for Jews and Christians to also make common ground, so to speak, with Muslims, Buddhists, Taoists, Confucians, Hindus, and Indigenous faith groups in seeking to advocate and undertake faith-inspired, scientifically informed, and ecosocially transformative works of ocean care.[43] Among the partners of Interfaith Oceans are secular environmental advocacy organizations and research institutions, such as the Ocean Conservancy and the National Oceanic and Atmospheric Administration, and their website provides a wealth of both scientific and religious resources. One of the cofounders of Interfaith Oceans is Jewish scholar and environmental activist David Krantz, whose "Psalm of the Sea" (*Tehillat HaYam* in Hebrew) echoes Psalm 104 but in a new key, indicating that we are now called not only to marvel at the oceans' "living things both small and great" but to actively "befriend" them:

> Our fate rests with the sea:
> With every breath
> We breathe air from the sea.
> Yet,
> Listen to the sea:
> It cries from overfishing—greed and gluttony.
> It cries from pollution—avarice and wastefulness.
> It cries from heat—carbon consumption and apathy.
> May we return to days of old:
> Let the sea and all within it thrive.
> Befriend the plankton and the minnow,
> The coral and the turtle,
> The seal and the shark,
> The dolphin and the whale;
> Like us, they are part of Creation.
> May the waves lap the shore
> As a mother cradles her child.
> Let the sea once again be filled with fish

As stars fill the sky.
Listen to the sea.⁴⁴

Back in Bath, meanwhile, Sulis is once again being revered, namely by contemporary pagans, for some of whom ecospiritual experience is necessarily interlinked with ecopolitical praxis, connecting the quest for personal healing from her waters with collective responsibility for healing the watery ecologies into which they flow. Thanks to the efforts of Margaret Marion Stewart, a devotee of Celtic goddess spirituality who founded the Springs Foundation in 1991, one of the three main geothermal springs in Bath, the Cross Bath, has been officially recognized as a Sacred Site as part of the Sacred Land Project. Although the water in the bathing pool is treated, the natural spring waters now rise into "a shallow circular steel bowl, bearing around its rim Ted Hughes's description of water as 'the ultimate life—the divine influx.'"⁴⁵

The medieval abbey that sits alongside the main Roman Baths, moreover, is also being allied with the waters of Sulis, albeit in a manner more pragmatic than spiritual, yet also ethical—namely, by means of an eco-friendly underfloor heating project encompassing both the abbey and the Baths, with the potential to be extended to other inner-city buildings. By contrast with the *macho* anthroparchal logic of domination driving the Faustian ambition to conquer the waves and drain the noisome swamp, this scheme embodies what socialist utopian philosopher Ernst Bloch (himself an inheritor of the Spinozan-inflected process thinking advanced by the likes of Goethe) termed a technology of "alliance" rather than "violation," entailing a creative collaboration with the *tehomic* energies manifest in the unstoppable upwelling of water from the earthen depths.⁴⁶ This project is part of a commitment on the part of the Church of England to shrink its carbon footprint to net zero by 2030. On the abbey's website, it is framed conservatively in terms of being "more responsible stewards of our planet's resources." In the Diocese of Bath and Wells Lenten Reflections for 2019, however, a more radical socio-ecological revisioning of Christian ethics made an appearance—namely, in the encouragement to consider the "neighbor" to whom we are beholden, following Luke 10:25–29, as including "our global neighbours, our future neighbours (grandchildren and beyond), *and our non-human neighbours*" (my italics).[47] From this perspective, to honor the gift of Sulis's largesse by enabling her warm waters to reduce the abbey's greenhouse gas emissions is to practice neighbor love toward all those whose lives are already, or potentially, placed at risk by climate change—and that includes those strange strangers, the oceanic microbiota, whom we are unlikely ever to encounter in the flesh and whose place and mode of becoming-with-others are unimaginably different from our own but whose future, along with that of all those, great and small, who are dependent on them, is now to a significant degree in human hands.

The voice that speaks from the *tohu va bohu* of the whirlwind in Job calls upon the decentered human subject to respect the independent agency and irreducible alterity of a plethora of free-living creatures, including those mighty denizens of the oceans who are presumed to be beyond human ken and control. On an anthropogenic planet, however, in an era of escalating extinctions, it seems that Christians are beginning (somewhat belatedly and still only patchily) to respond to what Pope Francis (echoing the Hebrew prophets) calls the "cry of the earth"—one that is issuing also from the deepest oceans.[48] Whether they, in consort with people of other faiths and none, will be able to respond in ways that are sufficiently transformative to disable the drivers of mass extinction remains to be seen.[49] In the process, however, they might just discover what it means to belong to a vastly more-than-human communion of creatures, rejoining the flow, however turbulent, fraught with risk, and tinged with anguish, of erotic-agapic cobecoming on this watery Earth.

KATE RIGBY is Alexander von Humboldt Professor of Environmental Humanities at the University of Cologne, where she leads the research hub for Multidisciplinary Environmental Studies in the Humanities. Her research lies at the intersection of environmental literary, historical, philosophical, and religious studies, and her books include *Topographies of the Sacred: The Poetics of Place in European Romanticism*, *Dancing with Disaster: Histories, Narratives, and Ethics for Perilous Times*, and *Meditations on Creation in an Era of Extinction*. She was the founding President of the Australia–New Zealand Association for the Study of Literature, Environment and Culture, and the inaugural convenor of the Australian Forum on Religion and Ecology.

NOTES

1. Marion Bowman notes that the word *sul* is "usually translated as 'gap, opening or orifice,' the interface between this world and the underworld, whence the extraordinary hot waters emerge." See Bowman, "Belief, Legends and Perceptions of the Sacred in Contemporary Bath," *Folklore* 109 (1998): 25.

2. Many thanks to Marybeth Lorbiecki for the reminder of the importance of beavers to aquatic ecologies. See Ben Goldfarb, *Eager: The Surprising, Secret Life of Beavers, and Why They Matter* (White River Junction, VT: Chelsea Green, 2018). I am also grateful to Marybeth for the extensive editorial suggestions on a draft of this chapter. Any remaining errors and infelicities of expression are entirely my own.

3. UK Government, Joint Nature Conservation Committee, Special Areas of Conservation, River Avon, accessed May 14, 2019, http://jncc.defra.gov.uk/protectedsites/sacselection/sac.asp?EUCode=UK0013016.

4. The reference is to Aldo Leopold's much-quoted observation that "one of the penalties of an ecological education is that one lives alone in a world of wounds." See Leopold, *Round River: From the Journals of Aldo Leopold*, ed. Luna B. Leopold (Oxford: Oxford University Press, 1972), 119. In the revised edition of her biography of Leopold, Lorbiecki extends his concept of the "land ethic" to our relations with the oceans. Lorbiecki, *A Fierce Green Fire: Aldo Leopold's Life and Legacy*, 2nd ed., (Oxford: Oxford University Press, 2016).

5. "Whale," World Wildlife Fund, accessed May 14, 2019, https://www.worldwildlife.org/species/whale.

6. A report in *Oceanography* from June 2019 indicates that endangered Atlantic right whales are also being adversely affected by warming oceans in the Gulf of Maine, where ecosystem change is driving the whales to alter their foraging behavior and bringing them into waters where they are at greater risk from ship strikes and gear entanglement. Nicholas R. Record et al., "Rapid Climate-Driven Circulation Changes Threaten Conservation of Threatened Atlantic Right Whales," *Oceanography* (June 2019): 163–169. In July 2020, the International Union for Conservation of Nature accordingly moved this species into the "critically endangered" category. "Almost a Third of Lemurs and North Atlantic Right Whale now Critically Endangered—IUCN Red List," IUCN, July 9, 2020, https://www.iucn.org/news/species/202007/almost-a-third-lemurs-and-north-atlantic-right-whale-now-critically-endangered-iucn-red-list.

7. Jean-Pierre Desforges et al., "Predicting Global Killer Whale Population Collapse from PCB Pollution," *Science* 361, no. 6409 (2018): 1373–1376, https://science.sciencemag.org/content/361/6409/1373. All parties to the United Nations Environment Programme's Stockholm Convention have been required to cease production of PCBs, but equipment contaminated by them can still be used up until 2025. "Overview," Stockholm Convention, accessed December 12, 2020, http://chm.pops.int/implementation/industrialpops/pcbs/overview/tabid/273/default.aspx.

8. John A. Gittings et al., "Impacts of Warming on Phytoplankton Abundance and Phenology in a Typical Marine Ecosystem," *Scientific Reports* 8, no. 2240 (2018), https://www.nature.com/articles/s41598-018-20560-5.

9. N. Bednarsek et al., "Extensive Dissolution of Live Pteropods in the Southern Ocean," *Nature Geoscience* 5 (2012): 881–885, https://www.nature.com/articles/ngeo1635. I was first alerted to the hidden plight of Earth's zooplankton through an article by ecophilosopher Freya Mathews highlighting the problem of what counts as newsworthy: "When the Media Won't Report the Environment, It's Time to Rethink the News," *The Conversation*, August 19, 2012, https://theconversation.com/when-the-media-wont-report-the-environment-its-time-to-rethink-news-8862.

10. John Roach, "Source of Half the World's Oxygen Gets Little Credit," *National Geographic* June 7, 2004, https://www.nationalgeographic.com/news/2004/6/source-of-half-earth-s-oxygen-gets-little-credit/.

11. The Intergovernmental Science-Policy Platform on Biodiversity and Ecosystem Services (IPBES) Global Assessment report released in May 2019 estimates that one-third of fish species are overexploited by industrial fishing, which now takes place in over half of the Earth's oceans; plastic waste affects 86 percent of marine turtles, 44 percent of seabirds, and 43 percent of marine mammals; and there are some four hundred "dead zones" caused by fertilizer runoff, affecting an area the size of the United Kingdom. Sandra Díaz et al., "Summary for Policymakers of the Global Assessment Report on Biodiversity and Ecosystem Services of the Intergovernmental Science-Policy Platform on Biodiversity and Ecosystem Services," IPBES (May 2019), accessed May 21, 2019, https://www.ipbes.net/news/ipbes-global-assessment-summary-policymakers-pdf. The discovery of microplastics in the Mariana Trench was reported in December 2018: Damian Carrington, "Plastic Pollution Discovered at Deepest Point of Ocean," *The Guardian*, December 20, 2018, https://www.theguardian.com/environment/2018/dec/20/plastic-pollution-mariana-trench-deepest-point-ocean?.

12. Kimberley Patton, *The Sea Can Wash Away All Evils: Modern Marine Pollution and the Ancient Cathartic Ocean* (New York: Columbia University Press, 2006), 9.

13. Meric Skrokosz and Rebecca S. Watson, *Blue Planet, Blue God: The Bible and the Sea* (London: SCM, 2017).

14. Catherine Keller, *Face of the Deep: A Theology of Becoming* (London: Routledge, 2003). On the historical emergence of the doctrine of *creation ex nihilo*, see 43–64.

15. Keller, *Face of the Deep*, 17–24.

16. For example, Janet Soskice cites Judith 16:14: "Let all your creatures serve you / for you spoke, and they were made." Soskice, "Why *Creatio ex nihilo* Today?," in *Creation ex nihilo: Origin, Development, Contemporary Challenges*, ed. Gary Anderson and Marcus Bockmuehl (South Bend: University of Notre Dame Press, 2018), 48.

17. Soskice, "Why *Creatio ex nihilo* Today?," 49. See also Soskice, "Creation and the Glory of Creatures," in *Being-in-Creation: Human Responsibility in an Endangered World*, eds. Brian Treanor, Bruce Ellis Benson, and Norman Wirzba, 143–158 (New York: Fordham University Press, 2015). In her more speculative exploration of "ancient Christian ecopoetics," Virginia Burrus revisits various formulations of creatio ex nihilo in Jewish and Christian thought of late antiquity in relation to the reception and reworking of Plato's concept of the *khora*, locating within this doctrine itself the lineaments of

what she calls an "ecochorology." Burrus, *Ancient Christian Ecopoetics: Cosmologies, Saints, Things* (Philadelphia: Pennsylvania University Press, 2019).

18. Soskice, "Why *Creatio ex nihilo* Today?," 50.

19. I explore these conjunctions and their legacies further in *Reclaiming Romanticism: Towards an Ecopoetics of Decolonization* (London: Bloomsbury, 2020).

20. T. Adorno and M. Horkheimer, *Dialectic of Enlightenment*, trans. J. Cunningham (1944; repr., London: Verso, 1979).

21. Goethe, *Faust, Part One*, trans. David Luke (Oxford: Oxford University Press, 1987), 52.

22. See Marshall Berman's interpretation of *Faust* as a "tragedy of development" in *All That Is Solid Melts into Air: The Experience of Modernity* (London: Verso, 1988). My comments on *Faust* in this essay draw on a prior reading of this text in relation to Romantic views of aquatic environments in Kate Rigby, *Topographies of the Sacred: The Poetics of Place in European Romanticism* (Charlottesville: University of Virginia Press, 2014), 202–214. See also Rigby, "Of Mice and Men and Surging Seas: Discerning Distributed Agency in Storm's *Der Schimmelreiter*," in ecocritical special issue of *New German Critique* 128 (2016): 153–176, eds. Heather Sullivan and Bernhard Malkmus.

23. Goethe, *Faust, Part Two*, trans. David Luke (Oxford: Oxford University Press, 1994).

24. Rod Giblett, *Postmodern Wetlands: Culture, History, Ecology* (Edinburgh: Edinburgh University Press, 1996).

25. Rigby, *Topographies of the Sacred*, 213.

26. Unless otherwise indicated, all biblical quotes are taken from *The New Oxford Annotated Bible* (NRSV), augmented 3rd ed., ed. Michael D. Coogan (Oxford: Oxford University Press, 2007).

27. It is hard not to read this image as consistent with the tehomophobia traced by Keller, but Celia Deane-Drummond has suggested that the disappearance of the sea in Revelation 21:1, in recalling the dawn of creation, reinforces the hope of the renewal of creation. Deane-Drummond, *Eco-Theology* (London: Darton, Longman and Todd, 2008). For a recent review of divergent readings of Revelation in the context of climate change, see Stefan Skrimshire, "Climate Change and Apocalyptic Faith," *WIREs Climate Change* (2013). See also Keller, *Apocalypse Now and Then: A Feminist Guide to the End of the World* (Minneapolis: Augsburg Fortress, 2004); and Keller, *Facing Apocalypse: Climate, Democracy and other Last Chances* (New York: Orbis, 2021).

28. Keller, *Face of the Deep*, xv. In the NRSV translation of the *New Oxford Annotated Bible*, these verses read: "In the beginning when God created the heavens and the earth, the earth was a formless void and darkness covered the face of the deep, while a wind from God swept over the face of the waters" (Gen. 1:1–2).

29. As Keller notes, the proposition that the Hebrew creation narrative is a demythologized version of the Babylonian epic was first put forward by biblical scholar Hermann Gunkel in *Schöpfung und Chaos in Urzeit und Endzeit* (1895). Keller, *Face of the Deep*, 106. See Gunkel, *Creation and Chaos in the Primeval Era and the Eschaton: A Religio-historical Study of Genesis 1 and Revelation*, trans. K. William Whitney Jr. (Grand Rapids: Eerdmans, 2007).

30. On the historical linkages between the interests of mercantile capitalism and the ways in which the project of scientific investigation and technological development were framed in the seventeenth century, not least in relation to earlier religious texts and traditions, see Carolyn Merchant's landmark ecofeminist history of science, *The Death of Nature: Women, Ecology, and the Scientific Revolution* (San Francisco: Harper and Row, 1980).

31. Keller, *Face of the Deep*, 138.

32. Merchant, *The Death of Nature*, 195.

33. Merchant, *The Death of Nature*, 238.

34. Keller, *On the Mystery: Discerning Divinity in Process* (Minneapolis: Fortress, 2008), xii. Keller's process theology is also in conversation with contemporary "new materialisms" that share an onto-epistemology of interactive cobecoming. See, for example, Keller and Mary-Jane Rubenstein, eds., *Entangled Worlds: Religion, Science, and New Materialisms* (New York: Fordham University Press, 2017).

35. See, for example, Robert J. Richards, *The Romantic Conception of Life: Science and Philosophy in the Age of Goethe* (Chicago: University of Chicago Press, 2002); and Dalia Nassar, *The Romantic Absolute: Being and Knowing in Early German Romanticism: 1795–1804* (Chicago: Chicago University Press, 2014).

36. Erasmus Darwin, *The Temple of Nature; or, The Origin of Society*, Canto 1, "The Production of Life," lines 295–302 (London: T. Bentley, 1803). Produced for Project Gutenberg by Stephen Gibbs and Christine P. Travers, October 9, 2008, http://www.gutenberg.org/files/26861/26861-h/26861-h.htm.

37. David Adams and Margaret Adams Leeming, *A Dictionary of Creation Myths* (Oxford: Oxford University Press, 1995), 79–80.

38. As exemplified by Rachel Carson's influential celebration of the life of the oceans in *The Sea Around Us*, first published by Oxford University Press in 1951, however, the genre of nature writing has emerged as a site where science is brought into conversation with affect, aesthetics, and ethics.

39. On the potential of visual media to enhance public appreciation of both the wonder and woundedness of Earth's undersea worlds, see Linda Williams, "Deep Time and Myriad Ecosystems: Urban Imaginaries and Unstable Planetary Aesthetics," in *The Aesthetics of the Undersea*, eds. Margaret Cohen and Killian Quigley, 167–179 (London: Routledge, 2019).

40. This appears to be acknowledged in the new IPBES report, which refers to the important role of the worldviews in either motivating or impeding biodiversity conservation. Díaz et al., "Summary for Policymakers."

41. Burrus, *Ancient Christian Ecopoetics*, 214. In their beautiful theologically informed meditation on our imperiled oceans, Jan Morgan and Graeme Garrett nonetheless incorporate an affirmative (albeit not unquestioning) discussion of Jean-Luc Nancy's emphatically atheistic *Adoration: The Deconstruction of Christianity II*, trans. John McDeane (New York: Fordham University Press, 2013). See Morgan and Garrett, *On the Edge: A-Way with the Ocean* (Reservoir: Morning Star, 2018), 187–195.

42. "About Us," Interfaith Oceans, accessed May 22, 2018, https://www.interfaithoceans.org/about-us.

43. As Lorbiecki explained in a private communication on August 30, 2019, "Interfaith Oceans began as an exploratory retreat [of the NRCCC] in Hawaii in 2012 to write a religious statement about the oceans . . . and was originally called the Interfaith Ocean Ethics Campaign." I am very grateful to Marybeth for alerting me to this initiative back in 2016 and for ongoing conversation about it.

44. David Krantz, "Tehillat HaYam: A Psalm of the Sea," AYTZIM: Ecological Judaism, Resources, accessed September 13, 2019, https://www.interfaithoceans.org/jewish. I am very grateful to David for directing me to these and other resources related to Jewish care for the oceans and for permission to cite his "Psalm of the Sea." On Jewish ocean care, see also Hillel Eckerd College's delightfully named Scubi Jew program, accessed October 2, 2019, https://www.eckerdhillel.org/scubi-jew.

45. Bowman, "A Tale of Two Celticities: Sacred Springs, Legendary Landscapes and Celtic Revival in Bath," *Journal for the Academic Study of Religion* 20, no. 1 (2007): 107.

46. Ernst Bloch, *The Principle of Hope*, vol. 2, trans. N. Plaice, S. Plaice, and P. Knight (Cambridge, MA: Harvard University Press, 1995), 686–690.

47. "How Do I Love My Neighbour?," Diocese of Bath and Wells Lenten Reflections—Living Well in God's Earth, April 3, 2019. I have written previously on the extension of the ethic of neighbor love to nonhuman (especially animal) others in Rigby, "Animal Calls," in *Divinanimality: Animal Theory, Creaturely Theology*, ed. Stephen D. Moore, 116–133 (New York: Fordham, 2014), especially 122–128.

48. Francis I, *Laudato Si': On Care for our Common Home* (Vatican City: Vatican Publications, 2015). Pope Francis's prayer intention for the month of September 2019 highlighted the threat to Earth's oceans and invited the faithful to pray that "politicians, scientists and economists work together to protect the world's seas and oceans." See "Pope's September Prayer Intention: For Protecting the Oceans," *Vatican News*, August 31, 2019, https://www.vaticannews.va/en/pope/news/2019-08/pope-francis-september-2019-prayer-intention-oceans.html.

49. For a critical overview of the claims for the "greening of religion," see Bron Taylor, Gretel Van Wieren, and Bernard Daly Zaleha, "The Greening of Religion Hypothesis (Part Two): Assessing the Data from Lynn White, Jr., to Pope Francis," *Journal for the Study of Religion, Nature and Culture* 10, no. 3 (2016): 306–378.

SEVEN

PRAISING SALMON
Creaturely Discernment in a Time of Species Metacide

JAMES HATLEY

> "In mercy do You give light to the earth
> and to all who dwell upon it,
> and in Your goodness do you renew every day,
> continuously, the work of Creation."
>
> Yetzer Or

> "I heard in the name of the Ba'al Shem Tov
> that making a window in [Noah's] ark [tevah]
> means making a window out of the word [tevah] of Torah and prayer,
> to gaze through it from the beginning of the world to its end."
>
> Or hame'ir, 57

בָּרוּךְ אַתָּה יְיָ אֱלֹהֵינוּ מֶלֶךְ הָעוֹלָם,
שֶׁהַכֹּל נִהְיָה בִּדְבָרוֹ.

THE SALMON SHOW UP

At first, there are green shadows hovering over green stones, ghostly blurs slipping among wavering fingers of light, there and gone. But within a few days, the salmon thicken the waters, churning the river with their massive bodies, second in size only to those of their Chinook cousins. The news spreads over networks both human and more-than-human: the chum have returned. Crowding the pathways along the river, visitors linger on a pedestrian bridge to gape, rubbing up against one another to get a better look at what is going on below. Yet other onlookers choose less accommodating perches for their viewing, braving thickets of devil's club and salmonberry to sit under the stands of hemlock skirting the river's edge. But wherever the vantage point, flashes of silver soon become visible as supple backbones, banded in olive and purplish-black, sinuously power through the current. Here and there, yellow dorsal fins, translucent and extended, cut into the surface of waves. From time to time, a thick ribbon of flesh smothered in glassy, cycloid scales flares upward from the depths as a salmon turns on its flank and arches sideways toward the heavens.

But more than a show is going on. The chum are settling in, finding their place under a clouded sun in the shallower waters of the lower reaches of what is known these days in Sitka as the Indian River. There, the innumerable members of a generation of a fellow living kind play out the dramatic last act of their lives. Amid the commotion, each female selects an appropriate spot in the channel and burrows into the riverbed, beating on the gravel with her tail and belly to hollow out a redd. Even as this is occurring, two or three males cluster around her, jostling one another; one sometimes swims upstream, then twists back and descends with the force of the current on the others, his teeth sinking into meat, tails thrashing the waters, the suitors jockeying for position. In the weeks directly preceding the run, those teeth have grown formidable in size, their structure not unlike the canines of a mammal. For this reason, the chum are also known as dog salmon.

The energy gathering in the river is intense but short-lived. The fish, both male and female, no longer eat, even as the oils stored in their muscles leach out to feed growing genitalia. Spawning females pump out roe, a thousand or more reddish translucent spheres the size of peas, to be bathed in clouds of milt by the males before burial in the gravel.

Yet even as the next generation is called into existence, the present one is being actively consumed. Eagles descend on the river, as do bears and ravens, all intent on feasting on their share of salmon. Each has its own manner of doing so. With expert precision, brown bears bite off a chunk of the skull, intent on the protein and fat in the brain, and another chunk of the belly in the case of the female, as her ovaries are charged with unfertilized eggs. Nearby, eagles dance around one another on the banks, taking turns stripping meat off the bones of a landed fish, even as the ravens are crowding in afterward for the scraps. All of this occurs over and over again for days, until all that remains are the emaciated bodies of salmon, their flesh growing leprous with ivory splotches, their muscles and organs shriveled, leaving only molting skin and protruding skeleton, their eyes caved in and glazed over in death—unless, that is, they have not already been pecked out by the beak of a raven. In the end, the entire river stinks for days of rotting meat.

By the next spring, the now-fertilized eggs, secreted over the winter in the gravel, hatch, the fry emerge, and a new generation— "a generation of orphans," as philosopher David O'Hara puts it— emerges in the light of day.[1]

IN PRAISE OF HUMANS PRAISING
SALMON PRAISING CREATION

What might it mean to be called into existence as salmon are, and what claims does this other kind of living kind make on us, as we, all-too-human in our own kind, come into its presence? That these questions and others might be raised when one frequents another creature's haunts is inevitable. In strolling along this river where salmon are spawning, one quickly finds gatherings of fellow humans eager to glimpse the salmon. Indeed, in these circumstances, we are becoming drunk on their very proximity, inspired by their ichthyic doings. And entailed in our desire to be in the company of another living kind—particularly one as charismatic, as gifted, and as gift-giving as salmon in their several varieties—are the modes of questioning that emerge in such circumstances.

As Emmanuel Levinas points out, for "the sages of the Talmud," attending to and assuring both the novelty and the particularity of the setting in which a question is raised in regard to a biblical text is crucial if the significance of that text is to remain alive for posterity. To this end, one's practice of reading scripture is called on to cultivate "the transfer to another climate of an idea," which in turn "wrests new possibilities from it."[2] In this legacy of transformative interpretation and commentary, termed *midrashic* by the Jewish tradition, "ideas do not become fixed by a process of conceptualization which would extinguish many of the sparks dancing beneath the gaze riveted upon the Real."[3] From the rabbinic perspective, one's ideas about the world are perpetually in danger of becoming modes of idolatry, modes of undoing what Levinas refers to as "the Real" by reifying and fixing it. The very import of the question—its vocation, then—is not to seek out a biblical authority that might in turn provide a closed response to it, one that fastens the meaning of the question to a text that already was assumed to be understood in its ultimate import. Instead, the question calls on the text to submit itself yet again to creation, to become vulnerable to being called beyond itself in order to signify the world in a manner that is sensitive concerning and remains true to meanings that were never one's own to master, even if one has been called irrevocably to attend to them.

In what follows, the very question of posing a question within the context of Jewish biblical tradition, as this might be understood broadly, finds its particular and novel setting in the circumstances of salmon. These in turn prove to be in themselves complex and fraught with newly emerging perils. For in a time of anthropogenic species extinction, although that way of putting the matter inevitably finds itself subject to yet further questions (for what might in truth be meant by a *species*, as well as by its *extinction*?), the manner by which proximity to another living kind refocuses one's thinking on the very reality of creation—a slippery but persistent concept permeating Jewish biblical texts—so that it might be unfolded and find itself emerging anew into the light of day is at issue. What becomes of the creaturely in the shadows cast by anthropogenic species extinction, and what becomes of anthropogenic species extinction in the light shed by creation? In the following remarks attending to these two questions, each an occluded mirroring of the other, salmon emerge as the protagonist and so the pivot by which received notions of creation and the creaturely within Jewish traditions are called on to be articulated de novo.

In her ecological reading of the biblical creation story, Ellen Bernstein notes how the fish of the sea, as they emerge into existence on creation's fifth day, are characterized as "swarming souls" (*sheretz nafesh*) whom the waters are called on to "let swarm" (*yishretzu*); the text doubles down in its formulation of this particular characteristic of a grand class of living kinds.[4] From this perspective, salmon emerge as creatures who are called into their peculiar mode of existence by the very fluidity of the earthly element in which they are to abide. The waters, in their capacity to flow and to stretch themselves across the face of the Earth, invite—indeed, incite—movement, particularly movement that directs itself sideways. Hence, the notions of creeping and swarming and of all manners of moving across the face of the Earth that are emphatically horizontal come into focus here.

In a more-than-human creation, Bernstein reminds her reader, the living kinds are rendered diverse through their distinctive manners of finding themselves at home in their particular place or places on Earth, meaning the salmon are called into a unique way of life by how they are called into attunement with their habitat. One's place on Earth matters so much so that evolutionary ecologists understand each living kind as an assemblage of characteristics called forth by the manner in which a particular place affords their intertwined existence with all else that finds itself at home there. This key insight is to a degree recognized and celebrated by no less a rabbinical authority than Akiva ben Yosef, who notes how "creatures that grow in the sea" immediately die when they "come up on the dry land," just as those that "grow on dry land" immediately die when they "go down into the sea"; "the place of death for one is the place of life for another."[5]

What is crucial for Akiva in making his observation is how this division of life, of the setting apart of those living kinds swarming in the sea from those creeping on the earth, calls in turn for our praise. To underline this, Akiva refers to these lines from Psalms 104: "O Lord, how manifold are thy works! In wisdom hast thou made them all; the earth is full of thy creatures." What renders this comment all the more remarkable is that in it, Akiva interrupts an ongoing exposition by other rabbinical authorities of a verse from Leviticus in which the discussion has been fixed on the uncleanness for human consumption of various creatures that are understood to be among those that crawl on land. In the midst of those considerations, Akiva changes the subject and in doing so reminds his interlocutors that what is unclean and inappropriate from one perspective becomes blessed and worthy of affirmation when viewed from another. Creation, it turns out, is manifold in its values!

David Abram, when he first encounters spawning salmon in their watery element, also cannot get enough of seeing them, so he finally wades in to be more in contact with them. He comments: "The stream was thick with Salmon, boiling with Salmon, all jostling and surging against the current in fits and starts—it was as if the stream was made of Salmon!"[6] Up to his knees in them, Abram notes how oblivious they are to his presence as they shove past him to get upstream so they can mate and spawn before "they fall apart and die."[7] The anomalousness of this vision—of too much movement in too small confines, of masses of living creatures bent on their shared moment of reproduction, which is immediately followed by their deaths—highlights the very manner in which the salmon as a living kind that swarms provoke distinctive modes of thinking in those humans who would spend time in their company. Indeed, the section in which Abram discusses his experience is titled "Lessons from the Salmon," and these lessons culminate for him in an extended meditation on how he is invited under the tutelage of salmon into a renewed understanding of his own human role in a world characterized by modes of reciprocity between diverse living kinds.

As Abram ruminates on his time spent in proximity to the salmon, he is moved to a series of insights in regard to the salmon as a way of life, a cascade of affirmations that are meant to be not only factual in content but also elevating in import. For instance, Abram entertains how the prodigious energy he is witnessing, bottled up and boiling as it is between the current's stony banks, leads one to appreciate and be thankful for the capacity of this living kind to move so fluently across great oceanic reaches. Roaming an arc of the planet running 2,300 miles, from the Aleutian Islands to the Kamchatka Peninsula to the coast of Japan, Abram notes, salmon gather the nutrients dispersed throughout these waters only to return them in concentrated form through their very bodies to the place of their own birth. In this way, their deaths become "an offering" that makes possible the flourishing of many other living kinds—indeed of the very ecosystem itself that is the Alaskan rainforest.[8] One is also called on by Abram to appreciate the anadromous intelligence exercised in this process by the salmon; they have the capacity to move between fresh and briny waters in their life cycle, to find their way home after thousands of miles of wandering over several years, and to do so in such a carefully calibrated time span that their widely dispersed kin show up within a few days of one another.[9]

What, then, draws the onlookers to a bridge arching over the waters of Baranov Island? While there are many ways in which this question might be answered, the one that is hoped for, if we are to take Bernstein's and Abram's remarks seriously, with the words of Akiva echoing in the background as our guide, is that people are there to praise the salmon. If one has shown up simply to gawk and be diverted and entertained, one has already lost track of the very thing that one has been invited to behold. A mode of discernment on the part of humans as they frequent the haunts of salmon is being called for. For salmon as a way of life constrain our approach of them precisely by how they differ from us as a living kind, even as they invite in that differentiation, indeed through that very differentiation, our reciprocity with them.

Hineni: Praising another involves mindfully beholding and so providing one's witness for how another is in some manner preeminent and commands through that preeminence one's own attention to them. Further, in becoming praise, this attention emerges as a liturgical response, as one's very words are elicited for the sake of that other. In praise, then, the very meaning of one's expressiveness emerges not as lying in one's own hands or resonating in one's own voice but rather as already having been offered for the sake of another. One does not speak in order to assure oneself that one is through this speech in command of its intent but rather paradoxically foregoes this very possibility. In praise, before one could have been responsible through one's own means for what one might mean by one's words, those words are revealed to have already been inspired and so claimed by another.

Hallelujah: In the concluding line of the concluding Psalm of the Book of Psalms, "all that breathes" (*chol han'shama*) is called on to "praise the Lord, Hallelujah" (*t'hallel Ja, hallelujah*) (Ps. 150:6). Here, *hallelujah*, the last word of creation—a word that is in fact doubled in its telling—is revealed to be the word *praise*, as all of creation is called on to give praise to the Creator. The rambunctious quality of this praise has been developed in more detail in the two preceding Psalms. Indeed, the very first line of Psalm 148 is "Hallelujah, Praise ye the Lord from the heavens; praise Him in the heights," and commentary in *Midrash Tehillim* notes that these words "are spoken to the creatures in heaven," the "ministering angels."[10] Even as there are "hosts of creatures" on Earth, their analogues are also to be found in the heavens. The hosts who praise the Creator then are doubled—they are hosts both of the heavens and the Earth—but it does not stop there; a few lines later, it turns out praise is to emanate not simply from one heaven but from "the heaven of heavens" (*sh'mei hashamayim*). From this, "you may learn," the rabbis argue, "that there are no fewer than three heavens."[11] Three heavens, then, and one Earth are consumed in praising the Creator—a noisy rambunctiousness, indeed.

But as creatures are also called on "from the earth" to offer their praise of the Creator, a list ensues in Psalm 148 that is surprising in its ordering, since humans remain unmentioned even as "the sea-monsters and all the deeps" are mustered. Then come "fire and hail, snow and vapor; stormy wind, fulfilling His word," followed by "mountains and all hills; fruitful trees and all cedars; beasts and all cattle; creeping things and flying fowl." Creature upon creature is praising the Creator before finally humans of all stations—"Kings of the earth and all peoples, princes and all judges of the earth, both young men and maidens"—are invited to join in. Perhaps in a playful mood, the commentary asks, in light of this odd, even scandalous way of proceeding: "After God's praises are sung from the heavens, who ought to be the first on earth to sing His praises?" The answer given is "He that is larger than his fellow creatures"—that is, "the sea monsters of whom it is said 'And God created the great sea-monsters'" (Gen. 1:21).[12]

This dizzying multiplication of praise is induced midrashically, not only by the words of authors of commentary on the Psalms but also through the very words of the Psalms themselves,[13] as they take up from other vantages the accounts of creation found in yet other biblical books. In line with this strategy, Psalm 148 offers commentary on other Hebraic accounts of creation through an exegesis that envisions a renewed (re)ordering of the creatures, one in which humans are imagined more as being at the end of the line than at the culmination of the proceedings. The effect of this inversion is to bring into focus what might be termed the reaches of creation. Creation's exuberance and its manifold dimensions of distinct creatures, elements, and processes are hinted at, even as the modes of praise respectively offered to the Creator by them are attended to.

Thus, while the Hebraic gesture of praise finds its exemplary end point in the Creator, in that terminus that is understood to transcend infinitely all that is creaturely, a strong argument can also be made for a mode of praise that is robustly attuned to the creaturely rather than one that is immediately theological.[14] In this attunement, the very speech emerging from one's mouth is revealed already to be an offering on behalf of another living kind for the sake of how that creature in its own way praises the Creator. It is not only humans who are involved in praising the Most High; salmon, too, must be attended to. Indeed, if the ordering of Psalm 148 is to be taken at its word, they are in line before us.

THE KINGDOM OF ENDS AND THE COVENANT OF CREATURES

One can certainly mark in Abram's words about salmon a fellow traveler in this tradition of praise and commentary. Yet in order to develop the full significance of the biblical invitation to creaturely praise, two additional points need to be acknowledged. First, one must consider how the praise involved here is not commanded by the ethical notion of respect for another's autonomy, through which one is called to live in what Immanuel

Kant famously terms a "kingdom of ends." Insofar as one's actions are praiseworthy in this arena, this is to be justified purely by whether one has chosen freely to act according to rational principles that prove consistent with themselves. What is commanded here is respect for lawfulness and, as a result, only for those beings for whom the matter of freely choosing to act lawfully arises in the very nature of their being who they are. Rather than praise for a living kind, Kant calls for respect for a reasoning kind, whether this be human, angelic, or the Most High, who in turn is only worthy of praise insofar as he, she, or it acts according to the rational nature they have already been given to be. One is understood to be autonomous precisely because one is given to oneself through the inherent capacity to set down the laws by which one's actions are in turn to be guided. The obliviousness of the salmon to their capacity to choose the principles by which their actions might proceed—whether these involve their driven rush to morbidity and death at the moment of spawning or their exuberant exploration of the oceanic reaches beforehand—rules out any respect due to them for the sake of their ethical autonomy. We humans do not join with salmon in a kingdom of ends and so are not called on to praise them in this context.

But this is not where the story finishes, for beyond any kingdom of ends postulated by human reason is the very covenant by which the living kinds as creaturely subjects have already been bound to one another before any human interjection in the name of reason might have occurred. This leads to the second point, which is that we must consider how the very notion of one's creatureliness entails the collapse of one's all-too-human autonomy and the rendering of it as abject in regard to its very emergence into existence within the frame of a living kind. Humankind, once it exists, constitutes a kingdom of ends, but its very emergence into existence as such a kingdom is dependent on its having been brought into being as a living kind as well. Yet, in emerging as a living kind, one does not choose one's own birth but rather finds oneself already having emerged, already entangled into the very fabric of a living world brimming over with other living kinds, all of whom are implicated through biogenetic evolution in the very possibility of each other's emergence.[15] In these circumstances, to speak of one's right to have emerged as a living kind is nonsensical, even if, in the wake of one's emergence as a reasoning creature, a whole range of inalienable rights might ensue.

One then does not possess a right to having been created, meaning to having emerged as a creature, a living kind among others. This insight offers the possibility for a critique of human doing in which the radical approach of Kant of insisting on questioning to their very root in human autonomy the values by which we are to proceed in filling out our way of life is interrupted and supplemented through one that is anarchical.[16] This means that critique begins not in seeking out a ground for how one can then proceed to evaluate what is to be affirmed through one's reason but rather in responding in faithfulness to an emergence into light that could never have been anticipated and could not have been evaluated as a choice of one's own beforehand. In creaturely praise, in reaching out beyond all of what is creaturely to acknowledge and be thankful for the very circumstances of one's creatureliness, humans become mindful of their helplessness and of a poverty without limit in regard to the very circumstances by which they have found themselves the recipient of their own capacity to have existed. Humankind, in the sense of its having been born into itself, finds itself without any root whatsoever in its own kind, anarchically unloosed from its moorings.

The enlightenment project, it turns out, involves a fatal and even catastrophic confusion of categories in which the creaturely is at best subsumed under the lawful or at worst simply dismissed. In this way, humans implicitly understand themselves as a necessary and inevitable element—indeed the necessary and inevitable element of the living world. One comports oneself as if (even if one does not acknowledge this) one's very presence as a reasoning creature were legislated metaphysically from eternity. In this frame of mind, one need not thank or praise anyone—not even the Most High—for one's very existence as a human being. Rather, one need only attend to how the very structure of one's autonomy, once one finds oneself to be human, calls on one to respect the autonomy of those others with whom one shares a capacity to reason. In this way, one becomes sealed up in one's reasoning through an obsession with the significance of one's own all-too-human humanity.

But in praising salmon precisely for their being salmon, the very thought of the priority of one's humanity and of one's own living kind to claim for itself solely through its own means its own spot under the sun is, at the very least, put on trial. This trial in turn need not be staged—indeed, it ought not to be staged—solely by a confrontation with the figure of the Most High, the theological Creator, but it can be supplemented, as suggested by Akiva, through a polyphony, or better, a heterophony, of living kinds whose very differentiation from one another is already enough to remind humans that they are not the masters of their own emergence as a living kind. Indeed, the respective indebtedness of every creature for having emerged as a living kind, whether this be human or otherwise, proves to be abject, a helplessness without limit.

Avivah Gottlieb Zornberg retells a midrashic Aggadah (story) in which the creation of Adam involves not only the Creator's breathing into the human form its very animation but also the Creator's immediately standing that human form upright on its legs.[17] In this way, the orientation of a humankind that is created and so creaturely is understood to be that of looking upward and downward (the vertical dimension), even as it is given a vantage, a stature (*komato*), to gaze across the face of the Earth and so witness all the creatures with whom creation is shared (the horizontal dimension). From the very position of the human as upright—keep in mind here how well this plays out in Abram's case as he wades into the waters with the salmon—praise for the Creator immediately emerges as a praise that calls on all other living kinds in the carrying out of its liturgical work. In a further twist to this insight, the midrashic Aggadah relates how the animals, fearful of the upright human posture and concluding that humankind is their Creator, approach the human in order to worship it. The human in turn responds by imploring all animals to join in putting on "the clothing of majesty and strength" so that the Creator and not the human is made "King over us, who created us all."[18]

CREATURELY DISCERNMENT ACROSS THE LIVING KINDS

In his mediations on the salmon, Abram is practicing what could be termed *creaturely discernment*. This entails becoming receptive to the agencies and intelligences of a more-than-human world so that one might be instructed by them and so interact with them more attentively, more thoughtfully, more justly, and, most importantly, more reverently. In creaturely discernment, the horizontal axis of creation and of how the diversity of living kinds calls for differentiated acknowledgment and response by humankind is taken carefully into account. For all of Abram's explicit and inspiring—although at the same time controversial and contested—dependence on Indigenous ways of thinking in pursuing this project, he is also implicitly practicing a mode of discernment in alliance with Hebraic tradition. In this latter understanding of his undertaking, the other, more-than-human living kinds, such as the salmon, function as modalities of Torah, meaning they offer modes of learning that open up how one is, in the Hebraic sense, called to acknowledge oneself as a creature, as an entity who is created.

Some further thought now needs to be given to what precisely is meant by acknowledging one is a creature, for in this a particular understanding of human exceptionality, especially as it is has been formulated since the Enlightenment, is put on trial. While the traditional Hebraic notion of how this trial should proceed is through an interrogation of the human by the Most High—an immediately vertical aligning of transcendence in which creature is confronted by Creator—room has also been made within that traditional approach, as the midrashic Aggadah already illustrates, for a horizontal axis. And no less than the Most High explicitly does so, for instance, when, in confronting Job, Elohim draws his attention to how creation is filled with creatures who put the very sense of a human claim on its ultimate intelligibility and justification into crisis. "Doth the hawk soar by thy wisdom, And stretch her wings toward the south?" asks Elohim.[19] Job is then directed to consider the ways of the vulture, who also flies where it will regardless of what humans might desire and whose very provision for its young turns out to be bloodied chunks of raw flesh, a meal that from a Hebraic perspective is fully unbefitting for human consumption and yet blessed nonetheless by the Creator.

What the Most High intends with this discourse, or, at the very least, what the all-too-human author of the Book of Job intends by placing this discourse in the mouth of the Most High, is to challenge Job in regard to that understanding of his own creatureliness that is so taken with its exceptionality, its height above creation, that he has failed to take seriously his kinship with and entanglement in all that is earthly. Throughout the book named after him, Job asks for an audience with his Creator, a request that fits solidly with the thought that Job and the Most High share membership in a kingdom of ends populated by reasoning and autonomous beings, only to be instructed, when the Creator finally appears, that this request requires Job to discern anew how the other creatures with whom he shares creation were already providing him counsel (although one of a different sort than Job had been soliciting). The living kinds serve at this moment as Torah, which is to say, as instruction into one's own creaturely dimensions, and a certain faithlessness in Job that was unremarked by him during his previous interrogation of the Most High is now put into relief.[20]

In a similar vein, Abram is concerned with putting into relief a contemporary version of our growing faithlessness in regard to the creatures with whom we share creation. Placing himself in proximity to another living kind, Abram finds he is being offered instruction on following a way of life that is not merely characterized as an existential ascent (as one is caught up in wonderment at one's own emergence into illumination and fluency) but also as a creaturely humbling in regard to others (as one is bowed down in thankfulness to powers that are not one's own to master). As Abram puts it, "Surely it is time to outgrow this most tenacious of modernist presumptions: for all our craftiness and creative ferment, we humans are by no means the sole, or even the primary, agents of the world's construction."[21]

Here, Abram is perhaps doing the rabbis one better, for it is not enough to invite the other living kinds to join humans in the praising of their Creator; one must also acknowledge how those other living kinds are providing yet other modes of praise of the Creator than those available to the human through its own means alone. We are called to praise how they in turn are called to praise. Here, our covenantal relationship with other creatures provides an anarchical supplement to the ethical notion of value enacted through a human kingdom of ends. The very terms by which creation elicits elevation and praise move us beyond the solely ethical and the securely human, involving us in a panoply of more-than-human qualities and activities by which we are instructed in regard to its very creatureliness. In this way, the reciprocity that Abram cultivates with salmon can be understood to be interrogative. The salmon call one to a reciprocity in which the very intelligibility of the terms by which that reciprocity is to be characterized is no longer simply in one's own hands (or emerging from one's own all-too-human mouth). As a result, we are called beyond even a radical humility in regard to what we might accomplish on Earth to one that is anarchical. In the latter prospect, one finds that what is to be affirmed through one's reason comes to be heard anew, as the very sense of that affirmation is altered and twisted through the manner in which other human beings and living kinds come to be involved in the matter. Here, one discerns that human affirmation alone is insufficient—even a human affirmation that takes upon itself the circumspection of reason. The ways of vultures, as much as of the salmon, are involved in how humans might be called on to make sense of their own comportment in regard to creation.

EATING THOSE WE PRAISE

One example of how one might be called to anarchical humility is provided by Abram as he meditates on how the thronging of the salmon as they move upstream, seemingly in oblivion to all that surrounds them, reminds him of similar tendencies in humans, although with some telling differences. Like the salmon, humans are capable of swarming behavior, of engaging in, as Abram puts it, "a steady, unending surge, a procreation and proliferation without bounds."[22] And yet this capacity, when left unfettered in the human, is of another order entirely than that of the salmon. For in the swarming of salmon, a "relentless sacrifice,"[23] as Abram puts it, is offered through which countless other species are nourished. Moved and humbled by this thought, Abram engages in a litany of creaturely praise as he recounts how salmon become "food for the bears, for the river otters, for raccoons, coyotes, skunks, bobcats and squirrels, food for eagles and red-tailed hawks and winter wrens, and for all the local corvids—ravens and crows and stellar jays and gray jays."[24] The run, it turns out, does not end in the waters where the salmon spawn but continues to eddy up the mountainside as the salmon's very flesh filters into the forested slopes, "gifting them with wild nutrients." Indeed, molecular remnants of the salmon's flesh have been found to be sequestered in the heartwood of the cedars and hemlocks standing on those slopes.[25]

As these remarks make clear, creaturely relationships are sustained via an ongoing offering of one's flesh, as one living kind becomes food for other living kinds, who in turn become food for yet others. In this manner, reciprocity between the human and the salmon is revealed to involve a heterociprocity,[26] an entanglement of multiple axes of reciprocity between a manifold of diverse living kinds. That Abram would offer his praise for these circumstances in which the salmon find themselves seems right and proper; yet, if the very same litany were to be offered on behalf of similar activities in the kingdom of ends, it would be nothing less than horrifying, a defiling of all that would be worthy of one's respect and praise. Indeed, as one Psalm succinctly puts it, most abhorrent to the Most High are "the workers of iniquity," namely, those who "devour my people like bread."[27] And yet everywhere one turns within creation, creatures are indeed being at least fed upon as if they were bread—and, to be sure, as if they were salmon. And this is precisely what one is being called on to praise.

This praise, unlike that on behalf of those of ethical agents acting responsibly in a kingdom of ends, involves subjects bound to one another through their very creatureliness rather than through their capacity to reason. In this regard, a point needs to be made clear that is not so obvious although perhaps still implicit in Abram's remarks about the reciprocity at work in the creaturely relations between the living kinds. In what is understood to be creation—which is to say, in the instantiation of our covenantal relationship with other living kinds—we find ourselves to be subjects beyond any means whatsoever of our having been the agents of our having become subjects. In creation, the very capacity to have a capacity is exposed as ultimately empty, as without a standing. Put in other words, as creatures, we are without a capacity to have had a capacity. Further, whatever reciprocity emerges between ourselves and the diverse living kinds who are also respectively without a standing in their very emergence as a living kind, the give-and-take between them and our all-too-human selves should be understood as occurring on the basis of an initial poverty, an inextricable helplessness in affirming one's standing among others through one's own agency.

In one's very creatureliness, one is called into a relationship with all the other living kinds that one could never have been in a position to have assented to. Yet precisely in these circumstances lies the notion of a covenant that is creaturely, meaning it is entered into in a manner such that the very incapacity of one's entering into it on one's own terms is the context by which the covenant is offered its meaning and paradoxically is found to be praiseworthy. Understood in this way, the very act of coming into covenant is the covenant offered by the covenant. The logic here, as recondite as that of Augustine's notion of *in-venire*,[28] of coming into oneself in order to be oneself, plays out in an allied strand of Latin roots, namely that of *con-venire*, "to come with or together." Creation, then, is a convening of the created in which the very incapacity to have been convened is reconciled by the gift of having been convened. In this way, one is called on to agree beyond one's capacity to have agreed! To affirm creation and to enter into the praising of it is to find oneself to have been vulnerable to what is to be affirmed or praised before one could have evaluated for oneself whether this should occur. Precisely in this slippage between a past that one could never have mastered and a present for which one could never have been prepared is offered a mode of affirmation that is not radical, that does not go to a root in order to sustain itself upon its origin, but that instead is anarchical and without precedent. One witnesses creation beyond one's capacity to ever have rendered it explicable merely in one's own terms.

That one is asked to live in a world in which one must eat other living kinds might seem, from the perspective of reason's partiality to its own autonomy, an odd and even monstrous thing to praise. And whether one might render such praise more acceptable simply by refusing to eat of the flesh of animals, preferring the tissues of plants, there exists an entire panoply of trophic relationships constituting life; as one gazes from the height of an all-too-human stature on the diverse living kinds feeding upon one another, the mother raven makes her way to her eager brood with bloodied pieces of rabbit or slivers of salmon in her beak.

But it is precisely in this context of how one is called on to praise the hunger of chicks for the flesh of other living kinds or indeed one's own hunger that a question of creaturely comportment emerges for humans for which their membership in a kingdom of ends could not have prepared them—namely, to what degree and in what manner is one required to digest the other living kinds in order to be who one is? The very condition of being a fleshly creature, one who must arise from the flesh of another in order to be born as oneself and who must then yet eat of others in order to sustain this birth, calls in turn for discernment and an openness in one's thinking and acting to modes of justice in which the very terms by which that justice is to be rendered must remain ambivalent and uncanny.

One needs, for instance, to become discerning concerning the distinction between one's eating of and one's devouring another living kind, or, more generally, between one's eating of and one's devouring creation itself. That another living kind can be devoured, can be eaten away so that its very being is consumed as a living kind and it is extinguished in its very kind, is a realization humankind, particularly in its European instantiation, has only come to in the last several hundred years.[29] When Psalm 53 fixes its regard on those among us who live absent of all humility as if they were gods unto themselves, it finds they are those "who eat up My people as they eat bread." We are only too familiar in our own time with political and economic regimes in which humans became fodder for the sake of the vaingloriousness of their oppressors. But Abram's meditation on spawning salmon asks whether an addendum to this insight is not urgently called for, namely that one lives in a perversion of creation and in abhorrent iniquity when one devours the entirety of another living kind as if it were merely one's own bread.

NOACH AND THE UNDOING OF CREATION

For most of the Abrahamic tradition, the willful extinction of a living kind was a sin one did not even know one might commit. While the Most High tinkers with the thought of the mass annihilation of all living kinds in the story of Noach, that power was laid squarely in Elohim's admittedly anthropomorphized hands and no one else's. Further, the rabbis are clear that Noach's act of tending to his shipload of living kinds during those forty days of shadows and storm functioned as a moment when he might finally be drawn near in an act of Imitatio Dei to the Most High, this occurring precisely in the ceaseless tending to the living kinds, no sleep or even a moment of inattentiveness possible,[30] while one was sharing with so many hungry mouths and defecating anuses, the ark.

The story of Noach, the rabbis inform us, is a meditation on what comes to pass when the lewdness of humans and their perversion of other living kinds through widespread fornication with them undo the very boundaries by which creatures are differentiated from one another.[31] The notion of this particular flood, given the Hebraic cosmology in which it finds its context, involved both a bubbling up from underneath the earth and a spilling down from overhead, so that the waters were undoing creation from both above and below, in the process overturning the very sense by which what is overhead and what is underneath are differentiated. The result is a world undone in its entirety, inundated in disorientation. Indeed, the Greek translation of *haMabal*, the Hebrew word reserved solely for the Noachic flood—a flood that is to be understood not as *a* but rather as *the* flood—was

Katachlysmos. This term is the root of the English word *cataclysm*, which indicates not only a watery deluge but also the intensifying of any calamitous act to the point of its irretrievability. In cataclysm, destructive forces are unleashed that cannot be called back, whose uncanny workings put into question the very sense of orientation by which creation is to be guided and sustained.³²

The elemental expression of the Most High's displeasure with humankind, the forty days of storm and shadow, can be understood both as an explicit punishment after the fact and a confirmation of what already was the state of affairs in which creation had found itself. The flood in the story of Noach in which creation is to be undone only occurs because it had already been preceded by a regime of undoing creation, a deluge of disorientation in which the very manner by which one kind is differentiated from another, so that each kind emerges in its own way of life as a living kind, was lost.

For the author of the story of Noach, or at least of a certain rabbinical reading of it, this particular mode of the perversion of creation in regard to the other living kinds is the worst that might be imagined and so is exemplary of precisely how creation is vulnerable to an undoing that threatens not only humankind but all the living kinds in their entirety.

Yet the current treatment of salmon at the hands of humankind—one moment in a vast array of moments of the undoing of a vast array of living kinds that have permeated human activity over the last two centuries, which is to say the regime of an era of widespread anthropogenic extinction of species—can also be characterized as cataclysmic, although in a manner that was not imaginable in the story of Noach. For here and now, the threat, rather than being that of a grandiose lewdness or of the desire to fornicate with the other living kinds below one's purported station as well as with the angels above it, now involves the wholesale de-animation of the creaturely world, the rendering of it as if it were a mere item to be seized and absorbed by one's all-too-human doing without any sense for the integrity of another's creatureliness or thankfulness for its unique contributions to a shared covenant, to a creation that inextricably involves more than humans, even if humans are, at least from a particular perspective—one needs to remember here G-d's fondness for Leviathan and insistence on praising vultures—to be viewed as creation's crown.

MORE THAN AN EXTINCTION MANIA

How one views and is claimed by the very emergence of life on Earth should not be discounted, even as one rushes to focus on the all-too-pressing issue of the ongoing human-caused undoing of a plethora of living kinds in every corner of creation. To entertain the latter thought, it turns out, is to find oneself already entangled in questions regarding the former, questions that would be imperative to consider even if the catastrophe that is currently unfolding had somehow been avoided. For if one is to learn from salmon regarding their plight in a time of mass anthropogenic species extinction, one must be first willing to learn from salmon simply because they are our fellow creatures, our kith and kin in creation. All too often, one comes to the question of how to respond to the threatened extinction of a living kind, as if what gave the question its heft and purchase was the very status in itself of being threatened with extinction. As a result, one proceeds as if the particular creature being focused on in this sort of discussion is extraneous to the very subject of it. What captures one's attention, instead, is demise pure and simple, even if it happens to be clothed in feathers or scales. One cultivates registries of annihilation and bemoans the numbers of threatened things, even as one calculates the relative importance of this or that instance of vulnerability, rallying support willy-nilly for this and that creature that one has determined is currently sitting at or near the top of a list.

In other words, one of the dangers of a species being threatened by anthropogenic extinction is that the very onset of this process all too often merely functions to fetishize a living kind, to register its significance not in its unique way of life and palpable entanglement with other creatures but in its terminating excision altogether from life, as if a living kind's ultimate significance is not in how it is a kind but rather in how, whatever kind it might be, it is vulnerable to ceasing to exist. This process of obsessive fixation redoubles and then redoubles in its redoubling; as a range of species are each entered singly into the many varieties of listings of extinction, the entirety of all living kinds, beyond any contingent itemizing of a set of particular species, is simultaneously being revealed to be vulnerable to excision. To enter the Anthropocene, in at least one of its senses, is to enter an era in which all living kinds are vulnerable to anthropogenic extinction, including humankind itself. The thought long cultivated by apocalyptic traditions of all earthly things being extinguished and of life itself dissipating altogether into the shadows suddenly finds a heft and purchase that is not so easily dismissed.

But if one is attentive to, for instance, salmon, two insights arise implicitly admonishing one to resist the tendency to render the current plight of the living kinds in a merely apocalyptic tone. The first involves our growing understanding of the evolutionary history of salmon, which, as with all other earthly species, is built on an edifice of extinct forebears. Salmon, particularly the *Oncorhynchus keta*, are born into existence precisely by their capacity to weather extinction and move beyond being one type of living kind into being yet others. Indeed, the genus *Oncorhynchus*, in its being genetically tetraploid, is particularly adept at moving along a path leading to species differentiation.[33] This capacity for a species to become other to itself proves to be part of a larger pattern, as we have come to discern that the lineage of any species currently inhabiting the Earth reaches back beyond itself to an origin in another living kind, even if it inevitably is more or less intimately related to one's own. Chickens are surely a kind of bird, but, as we are now discerning, they also prove to be a new iteration of dinosaur. Extinction, in this sense, does not so much excise a creature from creation as find its progeny, or, at the very least, its kin at one remove or another, emerging into something new under the sun.

The very notion, then, of what a species might be is anarchically unsettled by its entanglement in generative lineages pivoting on previous nonanthropogenic extinction events, whether the latter have been writ small (in the relatively low rate of ongoing, background extinction) or large (as in the case of a meteor striking the Earth and mass extinction ensuing). Extinction, insofar as it is part of a living complex that has led here and now to the evolution of human beings and our more-than-human fellow creatures, can even be argued to be positive and necessary. Further, the very fabric of intertwining lineages stretching across geological time leads to the emergence within creation of what Rolston Holmes III has described as an invitation to sympatry, to cultivating a feeling for and with all other creatures simply because they exist and also because we inevitably find ourselves to one degree or another in kinship with them.[34]

This idea is tied to a second insight, namely that as we become cognizant of how another living kind exists, the latter offers in its very way of life an invitation to humankind to learn anew of the engagement in our own manner of life and to become aware of the dizzying investment this involves in all other modes of life. This is not simply a matter of marveling at the difference between ourselves and other creatures, as if such wonder could simply feed upon itself, as if novelty were in itself its own reason for being claimed by another. The claim of other earthly living kinds on humankind is more personal, more intimate, and more unsettling than that; for these other, more-than-human modes of life, even as they are in kinship with the human, differ from that of humans in not only their empirical details but also in the very manner in which the world emerges as meaningful in them. The diversity of life, then, is both ontologically articulated and also semiotically communicated. Another way to put this is that there are not simply diverse kinds of life but also diverse worlds revealed through those kinds of life.[35] Life emerges both in the various kinds of beings and in the various ways in which these kinds render life as intelligible and meaningful, both to themselves and to others.

If one is to engage carefully in this mode of semiotic and ontological inquiry, then a notion of intelligibility is called for that is paranoetic,[36] that emerges neither straightforwardly nor even subtly, if by the latter one means through an extensive network of implications that ultimately can be discovered and eventually made explicit in fully human terms for oneself. Rather, one is called to know another living kind in a way that differs from how one was prepared to do so and could have ever been prepared to do so in the first place. In paranoiesis, one finds oneself engaged in a knowing of others that is hypersensitive to the blindness inherent in what can emerge as intelligible in one's always all-too-human knowing; this hypersensitivity is not the symptom of a pathological state, although it might at times resemble one, but is the very emergence of a responsibility that is creaturely. This means one is called on to know fully what one knows about another living kind and to simultaneously circle around one's knowing in order to outmaneuver it, so as to become, at the very least, aware of its blind spots. Yet even this is not enough. One must also be led to circle beyond the all-too-human circling of one's own knowing around one's own knowing of other living kinds so that the traces of these other creatures might begin to circulate from beyond one's own ken in one's knowing of them. The point here is that communication from another living kind concerning its significance is not simply to be facilely received and translated into one's all-too-human idioms; a radical and even anarchical sense to things is instead unleashed by the very approach of another living kind. In this way, one is brought to other manners in which the world offers its being made sense of lying beyond those rendering it intelligible that are held in the keeping of one's own kind.[37]

THE BLASPHEMOUS ARTS OF DEVOURING A LIVING KIND IN ORDER TO EAT IT

Wendell Berry surely has something like this in mind when he claims that eating other creatures, even those of flesh and blood, is to be praised insofar as one eats them "with understanding and with gratitude." [38] He adds that crucial to the goodness of this act is that it be framed by "one's accurate consciousness of the lives and the world from which food comes." In eating of the world from which food comes, Berry argues, we are called into an "extensive pleasure," one that entangles us in the manifold processes and living creatures by which our bodies and our lives are in turn to be nourished. In eating is enacted our perhaps most profound connection with the world, one in which "we are living in mystery, from creatures we did not make and powers we cannot comprehend."[39]

Yet this world is perhaps too narrowly conceived by Berry when he argues that one's eating of it is to be understood as an "agricultural act." In this formulation, the significance of eating, no matter how expansive and rich our interpretation of what is meant by agriculture might be, is not quite expansive and rich enough to account for the agencies and powers in play in the salmon run on Baranov Island. A bit of a sleight of hand is at work here, as Berry argues for the mystery involved in "creatures we did not make" even as he overlooks how the human pursuit of agriculture, in whatever form one contemplates it, inevitably involves profound alterations of living kinds as they come to be adapted to and dependent on human practices of husbandry and cultivation.

This is not to argue that the emergence of agriculture as a human enterprise, along with the immense burgeoning of hybrid and domesticated living kinds that accompany this, necessarily diminishes or perverts the mystery Berry would have us consider. But what does need to be acknowledged is that the notion of eating as an agricultural act is not enough to capture the full sense of what is suggested by eating as a creaturely act.

In the latter sense, our eating of the world involves participation in a covenant of diverse and heterogeneous living kinds rather than in a community of autonomous beings. In covenant, what brings creatures together with one another is not the similarity of their needs or even the possibilities of reciprocity between one set of needs and another. This covenant is not to be understood as the reciprocal exchange of mutually beneficial gifts between various living kinds but rather as the intertwining expression of a poverty that goes all the way down in the diverse ways of life with whom we share the Earth. In the context of creaturely covenant, nothing that is living proves itself capable of satisfying its own hungers through its own means or its own claim on itself or the world in which it is embedded. In this way, the very priority of autonomy as it is expressed in and structures a community of reason is anarchically disrupted and put on trial in a manner that a community of reciprocal ends could never have prepared itself for.[40] A community of reason is one based on respect for respectively autonomous actors, but a covenant of creatures is bound together precisely by the necessity that no living kind exists except through its feeding on and being nourished by yet other living kinds.

In the rabbinical discussion of the story of Noach, his caring for the other living kinds is based on the interaction of two virtues; the ceaseless discipline called for in the feeding of others is interwoven with an ongoing discernment as to precisely how these others are each in their own respective way in need of this care. That one shows up with persistence is not enough; one must also engage with another with sensitivity to the very manner in which the other might be nourished by one's approach. An interspecies or transhuman etiquette, as Anthony Weston has put it, is called for.[41] For this, one needs to cultivate both the commitment to be of help to other ways of life and the skillful means by which this help can be received. This cultivation in turn requires an ongoing and far-reaching curiosity regarding how other living kinds engage in their respective ways of life, as well as the capacity to judge when one's approach of these other living kinds is out of touch, or worse, at odds with their respective ways of life. This is what is meant in this essay by the notion of creaturely discernment.

Yet this discernment is called for not only in the matter of feeding others but also in the matter of how one how feeds upon others. This paradox leads to creaturely as opposed to ethical discernment. With this in mind, is it finally possible nearly at this essay's end to raise the question that all along has been simmering underneath its every word: How might one be called on to respond in one's all-too-human manner to the plight of being salmon in an age of anthropogenic mass species extinction? The question of how one might even raise this question regarding the circumstances in which another living kind now finds itself is itself one that calls for creaturely discernment. All too often, the very question of how other living kinds are threatened with extinction here and now is being raised without taking the proper time to cultivate one's sense of how one is compelled to attend to and affirm aptly the particular living kinds on the face of the Earth. We act like rescuers entering a burning building in which all the subtleties normally called for in the breaching of another's home can be dispensed with. The emergency alone is enough to provide a newfound relationship, an improvised utopic intervention in what is otherwise a cataclysmic circumstance.

Sadly, our obsession with the notion of an extinction emergency only exacerbates the extinction mania and serves as a sign of how lost we continue to be in regard to the plight of the living kinds in a time of mass species extinction. A state of emergency does indeed frame the story of Noach, as a flood demands human intervention in the lives of other living kinds. But this notion of emergency in our current circumstances promises a false sense of clarity in regard to what is going wrong, one that proves in itself to be the articulation of the very manner by which the cataclysm we are undergoing is being driven in the first place.

THE FATE OF CREATURELY DISCERNMENT IN A PLANET SCULPTED BY ANTHROPOGENIC EXTINCTION

So, given this lengthy preamble regarding the role of one's ethical and creaturely discernment in regard to the living kinds, some questions might now be provisionally posed: What, indeed, is the plight of salmon in an era of anthropogenic extinction? And how might we, in creaturely discernment, engage ourselves with it? How might we be called on to praise salmon-kind in the moment in which they, among so many other living kinds, are increasingly in danger of being lost to the Earth due to the negligence of our own all-too-human humankind?

These questions and the circumstances by which they come into being do not lend themselves to easy or clear answers. For instance, a recent study has noted that more salmon are populating the North Pacific fishery than at any time since records began being kept in 1925.[42] Further, the rise in these numbers has been especially pronounced for pink, chum, and sockeye salmon. If this is so, then the annual run of *Oncorhynchus keta* described at the beginning of this chapter might be understood to illuminate important aspects of our relationship with another living kind but hardly seems to demand our worried attention in a time of anthropogenic mass species extinction. If anything, the current conditions under the sun, which include warming arctic waters and the maintaining of hatcheries designed to intensify salmon numbers, have led to a wild salmon boom—"approximately 36% more Salmon than in the previous peak in the late 1930s."[43] The chum are doing well, and the pinks are doing better; the latter now account for 70 percent by number of the wild salmon fishery. Further, hatchery fish now make up 40 percent of the total biomass of all salmon free-ranging across the Pacific, "largely because of Chum Salmon that spend more years at sea."[44]

At the same time, the numbers and biomass of the other salmon species in this fishery—Chinook, coho, and steelhead—have been plummeting. So too have some populations of chum, including those emerging from Japanese watersheds.[45] To complicate this picture even more, the unprecedented number of free-roaming salmon now straining the carrying capacity of the Pacific has led to worry that these conditions are resulting in "reduced body size and survival of Salmon and lower survival of seabirds."[46] Yet another study found that the size of salmon who eventually make it back to Alaskan rivers has been diminishing over a sixty-year span. This includes Chinook, chum, coho, and sockeye. The factors driving these changes are complex but are generally tied yet again to global warming and increased competition from hatchery fish.[47]

Craig Medred, an independent journalist based in Alaska, points out that this situation has newfound negative implications for the spate of dam-removal projects that recently have been providing hope that once-extinct runs of various species of salmon across the Pacific drainages of the American West might be restored.[48] Indeed, even as these words are being written, Chinook salmon are being reintroduced into the Sanpoil River, a tributary of the upper Columbia under the auspices of the Colville people.[49] And while the tribe is hopeful that this run can be reestablished, the experience so far in the not-so-distant Lake Washington (bordering Seattle) suggests that as helpful as dam removal might be for restoring historic salmon runs, global climate change and the negative effects of the increasing prevalence of hatchery fish in these runs may be even more important factors undermining our efforts.

Indeed, to contemplate the plight of salmon in a time of anthropogenic mass species extinction is to confront a myriad of issues, including the extirpation of the genetic variability of individual species of salmon as the distinct heritages of genotypes that have coevolved over biogenetic time within the conditions offered by particular watersheds are lost. The loss of the coho or the Chinook or the steelhead proves to be not a single thing but a number of intertwined losses as the dance between salmon and their habitat so richly evoked in the words of Abram and others is brought into narrower and narrower confines until—and this threat continually hangs there—nothing at all like the dance that has been salmon is possible any longer.

To be clear, the loss that is being contemplated here is not simply that of anthropogenic species genocide, the human-induced wiping out of a unique living kind, or even that of serial genocide, as species after species succumbs to the current planetary regime framed by human doing. Rather, what calls for our all-too-human attention proves to be a regime of anthropogenic species metacide.[50] In this event, it is not merely a single or even a set of living kinds that are eradicated; instead, the very significance of being a creaturely living kind in itself is repeatedly undermined until the very significance of the creative entanglement of all living kinds with all others is thoroughly effaced. What is under attack in our time is not simply a specific lineage of salmon or of any other living kind, as they have each emerged in their own way and time through the creativity of evolutionary processes and the labors of succeeding generations. Rather, what is under attack is the very notion that it matters to be any kind of a way of life at all, meaning any kind of a way of emerging in biogenic time in order to weave the tangled fabric of a shared, creaturely, biogenic existence with all the other creatures thriving on Earth.

One irony of the regime of species metacide currently oppressing the living kinds of salmon is that their progressive transformation into an industrial commodity promises a world with a greater biomass of farmed salmon in it than heretofore could have ever been sustained by the waters of this planet.[51] Already, creatures who are understood to be salmon find themselves inhabiting the Southern Hemisphere in Chilean and New Zealand growing pens, locations that the warm equatorial waters of the Earth had served to deny entrance into by anadromous salmonid species, all of which had been previously confined to the frigid upper reaches of the Northern Hemisphere. And increasingly, the coastal waters ringing the Northern Pacific and Atlantic are home to vast stocks of genetically modified, farmed salmon, as they are confined to another sort of life than was possible heretofore in their free-roaming state. Indeed, as many as five hundred thousand Salmon have been recorded as being readied for market in one industrial rearing unit alone in Norway; this is, as Martin Lee Mueller points out, "roughly equivalent to all free-roaming Atlantic Salmon who returned to Norway's coast in [that same year]."[52]

On one hand, the introduction of salmon into new circumstances that require them to change their very manner of being a salmon is hardly a new thing under the sun. In fact, in our current moment in creation, the anadromous, free-ranging salmon whose various life cycles move them from fresh to salt water and then back again are arguably descended from distant generations that were previously confined in their way of being salmon solely to freshwater habitat.[53] Their evolutionary history undeniably involves successive radiations in which their respective kinds successfully adapted to the changing conditions of their habitat in order to thrive anew. Indeed, the fact that there are no less than six species of anadromous salmon populating the West Coast of North America (all belonging to the genus *Oncorhynchus*), whereas only a single species of yet another genus, *Salmo salar*, is to be found in the entire Atlantic, is in part attributable to a history within the Pacific region of more severe geological disturbances over the last twenty million years, particularly in the last two million. These included regimes of glaciation, volcanic eruptions, lahars (great mud flows), and megafloods (some of which involved in a single incidence more water than is found in all the rivers on Earth today).[54] Salmon indeed proves itself to be a shape-shifter, as Abram might put it, dancing down through the expanses of geological time, altering and renewing its forms of life in collaboration with the dynamic elements forming the diverse habitats of the planet.

Yet to understand salmon's sudden appearance in fish pens around the world as signaling another moment in which creation is emerging anew in its significance and a living kind is teaching humans something novel and unprecedented about what it means to be a creature is to have gotten something horribly wrong. In her admirable study of human-salmon interaction in the industrial feeding pens of Norwegian aquaculture of the last decade, Marianne Elisabeth Lien provides an arresting analysis of how the human attempt to control the lives of salmon in these circumstance is inevitably undermined, altered, and redirected by the very processes by which life sustains itself. And to a degree, her work demonstrates that penned salmon continue to exercise a creative agency as a living kind that inevitably amends the conditions under which its ongoing, so-called domestication is to occur and that invites new alliances and what she terms "assemblages" of living kinds to come into being. For instance, Lien discusses the transformation of two different species of wrasse as they are enlisted by humans to control the sea lice plaguing the fish pens and threatening wild runs of salmon swimming nearby. In thinking through the meaning of this relationship, Lien is taken by the renaming of the wrasse as *rensefisk* "cleaner fish" by their human collaborators. She argues, "Their new name seals their purpose and signals their new position: from an abundant and insignificant pastime prey for kids with a fishing pole, they have become a scarce commodity and an active agent in sea lice mitigation."[55]

Mueller is far less forgiving in his approach to these living assemblages, as Lien would have it, that are produced by the emerging regimes of salmon aquaculture. In his discussion of Lien's work and of the genetically modified salmon confined in their human-constructed pens, Mueller notes that Lien's account looks too quickly past the categorical imperative governing the activities of humans who have brought salmon into these circumstances in the first place—namely, unremittingly redefining a living kind as the availability of its biomass for human consumption. In industrialized food production, the remarkable agencies and promiscuous sociality of free-ranging salmon are reduced to a single activity: gaining weight as quickly and efficiently as possible. Mueller notes that while pockets of resistance enabling some degree of trans-species contact and creaturely agency might emerge in this process, particularly in the open-air pens characteristic of the final stages of farmed salmon rearing, the unhappy reality of the overall situation in which these salmon find themselves would have been more clear if Lien had been attentive to the salmon fry being reared in the inland water tanks, facilities in which they spend half their lives in the model of aquaculture Lien had been studying. As these make clear, the goal of the business of producing salmon ultimately is characterized by "a wish for absolute control with the fry's built environment."[56]

Indeed, the future of industrial salmon production, ever intent on its categorical imperative, envisions facilities, even now being planned and built, where salmon are to spend their entire life cycle before being slaughtered for human consumption in vast indoor tanks in which all aspects of their lives will be subject to an even more fine-tuned regime of control than was heretofore possible. As a result, the firm Atlantic Sapphire is confident of producing annually 222,000 tons of salmon, for which a mere 1.05 pounds of feed would be required for each pound of filet on a consumer's plate. This outcome would supply nearly half of the current US annual consumption. And all of this, it is proudly noted, would occur on a single "160-acre tract that once grew about 5,000 annual tons of tomatoes."[57]

Salmon are now being brought into existence whose life cycle will never have touched the oceanic reaches with whom heretofore they were as a living kind in such deep attunement. The one remaining connection will be in their feed, which will mostly be composed of processed wheat and rapeseed, though a third of it would consist of fish meal and fish oil from herring, among other species. Eventually, it is hoped even this contribution will be replaced by "some kind of microalgae."[58] In this development, salmon, a fierce carnivore in the wild, will have become in the tank fully vegetarian in its diet.

Who, then, are these salmon? As adults, their lives consist of being "crammed together even closer than feedlot cattle," Michael Grunwald notes, as they swim in tight, never-ending circles against an artificial current. Still, he is assured by a spokesperson that the salmon's ravenous appetites make clear "they're enjoying their South Florida lifestyle." Grunwald continues: "I saw hundreds of juveniles in one tank the size of an above ground swimming pool linked up directly below a horizontal bar that dispenses feed, as if they were queuing in a cafeteria. I then watched them swarm to the surface in unison as the feed hit the water."[59]

But the question of whether farmed salmon are thriving in their radically altered circumstances will increasingly become irrelevant, at least in the corporate eyes of Atlantic Sapphire, as future generations of these fish are shaped genetically by their human owners to conform increasingly to what humans have decided should be their allegedly "ideal conditions." As the chief technology officer of Atlantic Sapphire puts it in regard to the lives of these creatures: "They're only going to get better."[60]

This statement, offered so confidently and without any sense of irony, reflects an exasperating incapacity on the part of at least some of humankind to be discerning about the creaturely significance of salmon. As Mueller points out, the insistence of understanding salmon as a mechanism—in this case, as a set of genes to be tinkered with until the physiological processes and behavioral capacities of a living kind lead to the maximum output of biomass—empties out the very question of *Who is salmon?* In these circumstances, one answers it simply by responding *Whatever I need salmon to be!*

To this frame of mind, salmon becomes a kind whose very significance is to be found in its being rendered increasingly compliant to one's control over it. This kind emerges as meaningful solely through how radically it is open to taking on any qualities whatsoever, whatever one desires. The biotic processes by which this kind functions are determined to have nothing to teach one but everything to learn from how one decides to interpret and order them.

In a regime of species metacide, then, the very notion of a living kind becomes arbitrary beyond any limit. The danger that is to be confronted in regard to salmon, as well as all other living kinds in this moment, is not merely that one living kind after another is succumbing to anthropogenic extinction, as crucial and devastating as that knowledge might be. Beyond this, the very significance of being a creaturely kind whatsoever is becoming lost to our all-too-human human doing. The anarchic openness of the creaturely to renewal across the generations and to an emergence from out of its very kind of yet other creaturely kinds fails to command one's reverence and invite one's praise but rather merely proffers for oneself unlimited opportunity. In this way, salmon's standing as a unique living kind, not only differing from the human in its genotype and so in its empirical anatomy and physiology but also in the very manner in which the world—indeed, creation itself—emerges as meaningful through it, becomes lost to human discernment.

Mueller's diagnosis of this doubled extremity, deeply informed by Abram and an Indigenous understanding of creation, would address our current depredation through a reawakening of wonder at how "each landscape can simmer with its particular creativity, with its own swarm of voices that strive to make themselves heard."[61] And so we are invited by Mueller through our witnessing the "luminous embodiment" of salmon to enter fully into "the experience that the world is birthing itself,"[62] a world in which the diversity of living kinds announces a diversity of creaturely values. Modes of storytelling are called for, Mueller argues, that would offer a compelling alternative to "the narrative exceptionalism" of settlement culture. In the latter's telling of the story of creation, Mueller charges, a linear account of history is laid out in which "the world is to be remade through reason alone."[63] Finally, in lieu of a biblical notion of creation that has been characterized by its obsession with categories of transcendence, Mueller argues for one embracing creation's "radical immanence" and "palpable mystery."[64]

What is being argued in this chapter in regard to creaturely discernment, although deeply sympathetic to both Abram and Mueller on this question, also has insisted, in its retellings of the biblical story of creation, on the recuperation of a Hebraic notion of transcendence. That Indigenous peoples might be deeply suspicious of this project is all too understandable. Indeed, the insistence on transcendence lying at the very core of the Jewish tradition has all too often been misunderstood or misappropriated by Christian exceptionalism, which in turn has all too often led to Hebraic ways of characterizing creation becoming weaponized for the working out of the colonial projects of settlement cultures.

Yet, in this time of an unparalleled depravity in regard to the living kinds, humankind, mired in regimes of ecocide and species metacide, needs a renewed and renewing moment of *t'shuva*; we need desperately to be called back to a sense of our ethical obligations within a kingdom of ends and our creaturely vocation in regard to all the living kinds. But in order for this to happen, we must first be able to imagine what the creaturely as a category entails. In the Hebraic perspective on creation, as it has been developed in this chapter with the help of salmon, an alternative is being offered for this struggle that would supplement the radical immanence so persuasively argued for by Abram and then Mueller. Indeed, this supplement—namely, anarchic differentiation and the practices of heteroprocity that it invites[65]—proves already to be at work in Abram's own thinking, as Indigenous practices of storytelling find themselves at every turn intermixed with Hebraic modes of midrash and commentary.

Not only the Most High, it turns out, can be the subject of blasphemy. For this reason, the issue of our relations with the more-than-human living kinds in our time exceeds a merely ethical determination. Respect for the law and reverence for the unprecedented, for that which cannot be commanded by any human means yet ineluctably offers renewal, still inviting covenant in spite of our helplessness before it, are being proffered. Yet our forgetfulness of the creaturely and the discernment it requires from us is increasingly rendering the Earth a place of cataclysmic loss. In these dire straits, we are being called on to witness not merely the succumbing of living kind after living kind to regimes of human doing but also an infectious confusion in that doing regarding the very meaning of being a living kind. Ironically, given this confusion, the very attempt to account for what is being lost all too often only intensifies the disorientation that underlies all that is going amiss. What is called for in these uncanny circumstances is a humility that is anarchical and without limit in regard to the acknowledgment of its limits. Only then might modes of engagement with the other living kinds be sought through practices of paranoiesis, an ongoing and unceasing reorientation of the very manner by which the living kinds find their way into our all-too-human discourse. In this work, the reaches of creation might find expression within a human element that has become increasingly isolated from and hostile to its creaturely vocation.

The green shadows hovering over green stones, ghostly blurs slipping among wavering fingers of light, are there and gone. We are in this with salmon, and they with us. Perhaps, being already creatures of the waters, they did not need to find their way onto the passenger manifest in previous instantiations of the storied ark of Noach, and even now the very thought of salmon as passengers on any ark that humans might build for them is a disturbing one. But precisely in eliciting these reservations, the capacity of salmon to become a question that puts the human on trial is given yet another iteration. What must be thought through in all of this is how salmon share with humans both the vocation and the affliction of being creatures, of being born into poverty that goes all the way down. The praise due to salmon, then, is not only for their luminous, embodied powers, as formidable and shape-shifting as these might be. One must also attend to the manner in which salmon's vulnerability to emerging from out of other living kinds into its own unique rendering of the world confounds and alters our own all-too-human ways of affirming our shared creaturely existences. Without salmon and the other living kinds, humankind is fully lost to creation.

JAMES HATLEY is Emeritus Professor in both Philosophy and Environmental Studies at Salisbury University in Maryland. He is author of *Suffering Witness: The Quandary of Responsibility after the Irreparable*, a study of how one is called on to pursue philosophical questioning after the Shoah. He has also coedited one volume on the thought of Levinas and one on that of Maurice Merleau-Ponty. For the last decade, he has collaborated with the Extinction Studies Working Group, founded by Deborah Bird Rose, to publish essays addressing the plight, among the other living kinds, of buffalo, the Honshū wolf, ticks, and quoll in a time of widespread anthropogenic species extinction.

NOTES

1. David O'Hara, "Ash Wednesday, All Saints' Day, and the Bodies of Salmon, Given for You," Presented at the annual meeting of the Society for Nature, Philosophy, and Religion, November 1, 2019, Pittsburgh, PA.
2. Emmanuel Levinas, "To the Other," in *Nine Talmudic Readings*, ed. Annette Aronowicz (Bloomington: Indiana University Press, 1991), 21. The midrashic method of commentary employed in this chapter is inspired by and depends on the approach modeled by the writings of Levinas, particularly in the confessional essays stemming from his yearly presentations during the latter half of the twentieth century for *Le colloque des intellectuels juifs de langue française*. "To the Other" is among these. The midrashic writings of Catherine Chalier, who was Levinas's student, also frame the approach being employed here. See also note 31.
3. Levinas, "To the Other."
4. Ellen Bernstein, *The Splendor of Creation: A Biblical Ecology* (Cleveland: Pilgrim, 2005), 79.
5. Babylonian Talmud, Seder Kodashim, *Chullin*, 127a. William Davidson edition, trans. Rabbi Adin Even-Israel Steinsaltz, https://www.sefaria.org/Chullin.127a.10?lang=bi&with=all&lang2=en.
6. David Abram, "Reciprocity and the Salmon: Water-Borne Reflections from the Northwest Coast," *Tikkun* 16, no. 1 (May/June 2001), 21.
7. Abram, "Reciprocity and the Salmon," 21.
8. Abram, "Reciprocity and the Salmon," 22.
9. Abram, "Reciprocity and the Salmon."
10. William Braude, trans., *The Midrash on Psalms* (New Haven: Yale University Press, 1959), 375, 5.148.1. Discussions of the provenance of *Midrash Tehillim* agree that the commentary in the latter half of this document entailing Psalms 119 to 150, including the passages being discussed here, was written well after the rabbinic period, likely in the sixteenth century, perhaps by Rav Mattithiah Yizhari of Saragossa, who in turn was relying on material adapted from *Yalkut Shimoni*. See Wilhelm Bacher and Jacob Zallel Lauterbach, "Psalms, Midrash To (Midrash Tehillim)," in *Jewish Encyclopedia*, ed. Isidore Singer et al. (New York: Funk and Wagnalls, 1906), 248.
11. Braude, *Midrash*, 375, 5.148.2.
12. Braude, *Midrash*, 377, 5.148.5.
13. One should keep in mind that the Hebrew name for the Book of Psalms is simply *Tehlillim*, meaning "Praises." The Book of Praises, then, engages its subject precisely by enacting its call to praise in a series of

innovative reinterpretations of what praise itself might reveal. In this way, praise shows itself in Psalm after Psalm to be a mode of expression in which commentary erupts in the very manner that praise is elicited in and yet beyond one's own speaking by that which is to be praised.

14. This conclusion has been persuasively argued for in regard to Psalm 104 (yet another moment of the ongoing biblical reinterpretations of the meaning of creation) in Deborah Bird Rose's unpublished talk, "Two Laws: Steps toward Decolonisation in the Shadow of the Anthropocene." For *Global Ecologies—Local Impacts*, 6th Biennial Conference of the Association for Study of Literature, Environment and Culture, Australia and New Zealand, Sydney, AU, November 23, 2014. Rose argues there for a midrashic strategy (one involving an ongoing reinterpreting of all previous interpretations) so that one might move fluently and discerningly across the vast reaches of creaturely differentiation that characterize creation. In law that is attuned not only to humans but also to all other creatures, Rose argues, the full and robust sense of what creation demands of us emerges to challenge a purely secular thinking about how we are situated in regard to the earthly.

15. What is being argued for here finds a degree of correlation to Bruno Latour's suggestion that even if one were to remain fully secular in one's thinking about the human relationship with other living kinds, one still needs a paradigm such as James Lovelock's Gaia hypothesis in order to render that relationship as "messily providential," which is to say, as one's inhabiting an evolving yet encompassing providence sculpted by innumerable actants. In this view, the entanglement of all living kinds with one another suffuses the living world with intentionality. See Gerard Kuperus, "Listening to Salmon: Latour's Gaia, Aboriginal Thinking and the Earth Community," *Environmental Philosophy* 16, no. 2 (2019): 382. The claim being made here differs from those made by Latour and Kuperus in the insistence on the bottomless incapacity of any of the living kinds to have been born into itself through its own means. Rather than suffused with intentionality (or perhaps only in addition to this), creation is suffused with affliction, with poverty, with hunger. As a result, what Kuperus and Latour understand as the messily providential finds itself reframed as the anarchically differentiated.

16. The notion of the anarchical, understood as that which is without measure and whose significance lies beyond or is otherwise than the lawful and the rationally grounded, is an important concept in the thought of Levinas. The meaning that the anarchical gains in this discussion diverges from and innovates upon Levinas's emphasis on the anarchical as solely a

feature of the human-to-human relation as it is developed in his *Otherwise than Being*. In particular, see his discussion of this term in the section titled "Principle and Anarchy" in *Otherwise than Being, or Beyond Essence*, trans. Alphonso Lingis (Pittsburgh: Duquesne University Press, 1998), 99–102.

17. Avivah Gottlieb Zornberg, *The Beginnings of Desire: Reflections on Genesis* (New York: Doubleday, 1995), 21.

18. *Pirkei d'Rabbi Eliezer*, trans. Rabbi Gerald Friedlander (London: Keegan Paul, Trench, Turner & Co., 1916), https://archive.org/details/pirkderabbielioofrieuoft/page/n9/mode/2up.

19. Job 39:26.

20. See discussion of this point in Henry Bugbee, "A Way of Reading the Book of Job," in *Wilderness in America: Philosophical Writings*, ed. David Rodick (New York: Fordham University Press, 2017).

21. Abram, "Reciprocity and the Salmon," 25.

22. Abram, "Reciprocity and the Salmon," 22.

23. Abram, "Reciprocity and the Salmon."

24. Abram, "Reciprocity and the Salmon."

25. Dale Stokes, *The Fish in the Forest: Salmon and the Web of Life* (Berkeley: University of California Press, 2014), 4–7.

26. See discussion of this term in James Hatley, "Telling Stories in the Company of Buffalo," *Environmental Philosophy* 13, no. 1 (Spring 2016): 118.

27. Psalms 14:4. See also 27:2.

28. Augustine, *On the Trinity*, book X, chapter vii, paragraph 10, in *Nicene and Post-Nicene Fathers of the Christian Church*, vol. III, ed. Philip Schaff (Grand Rapids: William B. Eerdmans, 1980), 139.

29. See discussion of this point in the opening chapter of Mark V. Barrow, *Nature's Ghosts: Confronting Extinction from the Age of Jefferson to the Age of Ecology* (Chicago: University of Chicago Press, 2009), 19–23.

30. Zornberg, *The Beginnings of Desire*, 60–61.

31. See Rashi's commentary on Bereshit 6:11–12, in which the corruption of the Earth witnessed by the Most High is interpreted as involving sexual immorality on the part of humans, as well as idolatry. Rashi adds that "even domestic animals, beasts and birds had relations with those which were not of their own species." Rabbi Yisrael Isser Zvi Herczeg et al., ed., trans., *Rashi: Sepher Bereshit (The Torah with Rashi's Commentary Translated, Annotated, and Elucidated)*, ArtScroll Series (Brooklyn: Mesorah, 1995), 67. See also Zornberg's discussion of this issue in *The Beginnings of Desire*, 51–53.

32. The notion of cataclysm being developed here owes much to Catherine Chalier's discussion of the Hebraic category of *tohu v'bohu*, "the

formlessness and emptiness" over which the Most High hovers in the very first biblical account of creation in Genesis 1: "*Tohu v'bohu* is not in effect nothing, it is not simply a lack, or pure nonbeing, but rather a shadowy power of dislocation and confusion—that is to say, decreation—and it gives birth to nothing.... If speech is a light for us, this is precisely so because it grants being to differentiated creatures, and that it makes them emerge from out of shapeless magma" (translation mine). See Chalier, *La nuit, le jour: au diapason de la creation* (Paris: Editions de Sueil, 2009), 45.

33. Robin S. Waples, George R. Pess, and Tim Beechie, "Evolutionary History of Pacific Salmon in Dynamic Environments," *Evolutionary Applictions* 1, no. 2 (May 2008): 190. See also F. W. Allendorf and G. H. Thorgaard, "Tetraploidy and Evolution of Salmonid Fishes," in *Evolutionary Genetics of Fishes*, ed. B. J. Turner, 1–53 (New York: Plenum, 1984).

34. See Rolston Holmes III, "Values Gone Wild," *Inquiry* 26 (1983): 181–207. Also see my discussion of this point in Hatley, "Blood Intimacies and Biodicy: Keeping Faith with Ticks," in *Unloved Others: Death of the Disregarded in a Time of Extinction*, eds. Deborah Bird Rose and Thom van Dooren, *Australian Humanities Review* 50 (2011): 74.

35. Vinciante Despret, "It Is an Entire World That Has Disappeared," trans. Matt Chrulew, in *Extinctions Studies: Stories of Time, Death, and Generations*, eds. Deborah Bird Rose, Thom van Dooren, and Matt Chrulew, 220–221 (New York: Columbia University Press, 2017).

36. See discussion of this term in Hatley, "Telling Stories in the Company of Buffalo," 110.

37. The notion of intelligibility as it is being developed here owes much to Abram's turn to Spinoza in order to resist reductive, obsessively anthropocentric views of making sense of the world. Abram asks: "Once we acknowledge that our awareness is inseparable—even, in some sense, indistinguishable—from our material physiology, can we really continue to maintain that mind remains alien to the rest of material nature?" Abram, *Becoming Animal: An Earthly Cosmology* (New York: Pantheon, 2010), 109. In becoming open to the entanglement in the material and in the physiological of our very awareness of anything whatsoever, we might in turn become mindful of other living kinds in a manner that is increasingly apt in regard to how creaturely intelligibility emerges anew within the ambit of those other living kinds.

38. Wendell Berry, "The Pleasures of Eating," in *The World Ending Fire: The Essential Wendell Berry*, ed. Paul Kingsnorth (Berkeley: Counterpoint, 2018), 72.

39. Berry, "The Pleasures of Eating."

40. I am indebted here to Timothy Stock's reading of Levinas, in which "the alterity of hunger" is understood to be "proximal or 'at the core' of the subject." While Levinas characterizes hunger as initiating a dispossession of the human ego, leaving it bereft and fully attendant on the affliction of other humans, this insight is expanded on to argue for the trauma of this dispossession as permeating all creaturely relations. See Stock, "A Broken Fast in Advance: 'The Bread from My Mouth' as Ethical Transcendence and Ontological Drama," *Levinas Studies* 12 (2016): 165–184.

41. See his discussion of this idea in Anthony Weston, *Back to Earth: Tomorrow's Environmentalism* (Philadelphia: Temple University Press, 1994), 145–168.

42. Greg Ruggerone and James Irvine, "Numbers and Biomass of Natural- and Hatchery-Origin Pink Salmon, Chum Salmon, and Sockeye Salmon in the North Pacific Ocean, 1925–2015," *Marine and Costal Fisheries: Dynamics, Management, and Ecosystem Science* 10 (2018): 152–168.

43. Ruggerone and Irvine, "Numbers and Biomass."

44. Ruggerone and Irvine, "Numbers and Biomass."

45. These chum circulate in warmer Pacific waters and so have been negatively affected more quickly by global climate change. Unlike the chum of Indian River, Japanese chum are threatened, the annual catch there having plummeted by 70 percent in fifteen years. "Compelled to travel faster and farther to reach cooler northern waters, the young salmon use up stores of energy when they can least afford it." See Simon Denyer and Chris Mooney, "The Climate Chain Reaction that Threatens the Heart of the Pacific," *Washington Post*, November 12, 2019, https://www.washingtonpost.com/graphics/2019/world/climate-environment/climate-change-japan-pacific-sea-Salmon-ice-loss/.

46. Denyer and Mooney, "The Climate Chain Reaction."

47. "Alaska's Salmon Are Getting Smaller, Affecting People and Ecosystems," University of California–Santa Cruz, Phys.org, August 19, 2020, https://phys.org/news/2020-08-alaska-Salmon-smaller-affecting-people.html.

48. Craig Medred, "Losing Salmon," CraigMedred.news, January 7, 2021, https://craigmedred.news/2021/01/07/losing-Salmon/.

49. Eli Francovich, "Salmon Spawning in Upper Columbia River for First Time in More Than Eighty Years," *The Wenatchee World: The Spokesman Review*, December 17, 2020, https://www.wenatcheeworld.com/news/salmon-spawning-in-upper-columbia-river-for-first-time-in-more-than-80-years/article_fbba53a4-4155-11eb-808d-6bc4189e0971.html.

50. This term (*metacide*) is not one found in traditional midrashic sources but is rather an innovation required by the way in which the question of anthropogenic species extinction calls forth new senses of what is at issue in the context of these sources. This fits with the midrashic methodology of thinkers such as Levinas and Catherine Chalier.

51. See, for instance, Martin Berger, "Is Farmed Salmon Really Salmon?," *Nautilus* 30 (November 26, 2015), https://nautil.us/is-farmed-salmon-really-salmon-235688/

52. Martin Lee Mueller, *Being Salmon Being Human: Encountering the Wild in Us and Us in the Wild* (White River Junction, VT: Chelsea Green, 2017), 33.

53. This possibility has been openly discussed for several decades with no definitive answer in sight. What is not to be disputed is the capacity of some anadromous species of salmon to adapt to and thrive in solely freshwater habitats. See R. M. McDowall, "The Origin of Salmonid Fishes: Marine, Freshwater... or Neither?," *Reviews in Fish Biology and Fisheries* 11 (2002): 171–179.

54. Waples et al., "Evolutionary History."

55. Marianne Elisabeth Lien, "Unruly Appetites: Salmon Domestication 'All the Way Down,'" in *Arts of Living on a Damaged Planet: Monsters of the Anthropocene*, eds. Anna Tsing, Heather Swanson, Elaine Gan, and Nils Bubandt (Minneapolis: University of Minnesota Press, 2017), M114.

56. Mueller, *Being Salmon*, 41.

57. Michael Grunwald, "Will Your Next Salmon Come from a Massive Land Tank in Florida?," *Politico*, July 16, 2020, https://www.politico.com/news/agenda/2020/07/14/florida-bluehouse-fish-farm-352495.

58. Grunwald, "Will Your Next Salmon?"

59. Grunwald, "Will Your Next Salmon?"

60. Grunwald, "Will Your Next Salmon?"

61. Mueller, *Being Salmon*, 172.

62. Mueller, *Being Salmon*, 174.

63. Mueller, *Being Salmon*, 184.

64. Mueller, *Being Salmon*, 175.

65. *Anarchic differentiation* refers to how creaturely values and new and unique manners of making sense of creation emerge in particular living kinds as they evolve into their current lifeways from out of the lifeways of their previous generations.

EIGHT

RESISTING DE-EXTINCTION
The Uses and Misuses of Wonder

LISA H. SIDERIS

THE ANTHROPOCENE HAS EMERGED AS a staging ground for a variety of interdisciplinary debates and discussions about the past, present, and future of life on Earth. Among these are disagreements between environmentalists who adhere to traditional conservation practices and objectives—notably, protection and restoration of nature for its own sake—and proponents of what is called the *new conservationism*. New conservationists, who often identify or align with ecomodernists or ecopragmatists, prioritize economic development and human welfare above the preservation of nature, understood (problematically, perhaps) as pristine wilderness untouched by humans. When framed this way, new conservationism may sound like a benign or positive development, particularly in light of critiques that have shadowed the wilderness ideal for years.[1] This positive impression may be further strengthened by the new conservationists' penchant for the confident, buoyant language of humans' boundless innovation and creativity and of nature's resilience and almost infinite adaptability. As Eileen Crist observes, Anthropocene boosterism departs from environmentalism's traditionally "dark idiom" of nature's "destruction, depredation, rape, loss, devastation, deterioration," embracing instead the tame, palatable, and even upbeat vocabulary of humans "changing, shaping, transforming or altering the biosphere."[2] Humans, in this view, are now de facto planetary managers, and the sooner we embrace this reality, the more successful we will be at guiding the planet and its people toward a good Anthropocene.[3]

De-extinction, often referred to as *resurrection biology*, can be seen as one tool within a suite of strategies proffering an optimistic storyline, an upbeat narrative of humans' creative remaking of the planet. Here, environmentalism's traditionally dark idiom of destruction is replaced with language suffused with techno-triumphalism and excited awe. The popular media often contributes to the giddiness, of course, blurring the line between science and spectacle.[4] The prospect of de-extincting vanished species makes for arresting headlines, perpetuating what Stefan Skrimshire calls the "mythic narrativization of de-extinction."[5] These narratives—the combined rhetoric of scientists, journalists, entrepreneurs, and philanthropists—draw variously upon Faust and Frankenstein, the biblical story of Lazarus, and tired references to *Jurassic Park* and "playing God." Yet, as excitement about the possibilities of de-extinction grows, these narratives serve less as cautionary tales than as inducements to accelerate human manipulation of nature and the redirection of life processes. Metaphors of decoding and editing DNA readily lend themselves to envisioning nature as a book—an original, ancient text—whose sacred contents scientists not only access but boldly *rewrite* for future generations.

Visions of the Anthropocene are never merely descriptive. They actively engage their narrators and audiences in storytelling and even prophecy. More precisely, I argue, they engage us in an exercise akin to theological anthropology, however secular these narratives may appear on the surface. De-extinction is one chapter in a stubbornly forward-looking, upbeat narrative that positions the human as an innovative world-making species whose distinctiveness lies in our exceptional creativity.[6] For this reason, de-extinction is the stuff of excited TED Talks as scientists hold out the promise of atoning for past crimes by bringing back lost species. Favorite candidates for de-extinction include the once-ubiquitous passenger pigeon, charismatic Pleistocene megafauna such as woolly mammoths, and more recently vanished species like the Tasmanian tiger (aka the thylacine) or the humble but fascinating gastric brooding frog, whose ability to convert its stomach into a womb inspires visions of miraculous medical breakthroughs.

Allusions to potential medical benefits for humans point to the instrumental and anthropocentric values that often inflect the rhetoric surrounding de-extinction. Even rationales that initially appear compelling and ethically sound—recovery of ecological values, restoration of habitats and ecosystem function, concerns for species justice—begin to look suspect under closer scrutiny. Proponents also advance vaguely metaphysical arguments for de-extinction that invoke the "new" managerial role of humans vis-à-vis Earth and nonhuman life. Running through these various defenses of de-extinction are frequent claims on behalf of *wonder* as both a motivation and product of de-extinction technologies. Indeed, wonder often seems to be the overriding impulse. Wonder is not merely one justification among many but rather functions as a compelling *attraction* in its own right, diverting attention away from the very real risks—practical, moral, cultural, and political—of de-extinction technologies. In this sense, while it often appears as one item in a list of the "pros" of de-extinction, wonder functions in this discourse as an end to all arguments. Though it is often presented as a value that attaches to or inheres in the natural world and nonhuman creatures, the sort of wonder that recurs in arguments for de-extinction is not that of nature's terrifying sublimity or even delight in nature. It is a surprisingly superficial and unreflective variety of wonder that is evoked primarily by humans' presumed ability to perform feats of creation or "resurrection."

DENYING EXTINCTION

The upbeat storyline of de-extinction and its invocation of a problematic form of wonder reveal a great deal about the way in which the current crisis of mass extinction is framed in the first place. For good reason, extinction is generally seen as a declensionist narrative—a story of decline and failure. De-extinction therefore emerges as a strategy for enacting a kind of defiant hope, a rewriting of the tragic story. So averse are leading proponents of de-extinction to a narrative of failure that some, like maverick entrepreneur and ecopragmatist Stewart Brand, have denied the reality of widespread extinction. Brand believes the focus on extinction is wrongheaded, bringing with it an "emotional charge that makes the problem seem cosmic and overwhelming rather than local and solvable." He argues that nature on the whole remains "exactly as robust as it ever was—maybe more so with humans around to head off ice ages and killer asteroids." Conservation trends in the current century are "looking bright," he insists, and de-extinction technologies contribute to the sunny outlook.[7]

These denials of mass extinction can be seen as the secular (or quasi-secular) counterpart to a phenomenon Willis Jenkins addresses in his contribution to this volume—namely, the puzzling dearth of responses to mass extinction among religion scholars and religious ethicists, including those engaged in environmental ethics. As Jenkins's reflections on the saltmarsh sparrow suggest, a resistant strain of human exceptionalism in religious (and notably Christian) ethics may be one factor driving this oversight. Even in religious hymns featuring the sparrow as an object of God's loving care, references to this lowly and "disposable" creature merely serve to reassure humans of God's far greater concern for our own exceptional species. "His eye is on the sparrow, so I know he watches me," as the hymn goes. Extinction denial, whatever its root causes, appears to be on the rise at the very moment that exhaustive reports of mass extinction are circulating in the media. Scientists have recently warned of an emerging phenomenon of extinction denial akin to climate change denial in the wake of reports from the Intergovernmental Science-Policy Platform on Biodiversity and Ecosystem Services that millions of species are at risk of extinction worldwide. One study urges conservation scientists to use lessons learned from climate denial to "reclaim the narrative" from extinction denialists.[8]

But what if the narrative to be reclaimed is one that people do not want to hear? Resistance to reports of mass extinction is not simply a rejection of bad news, though it may partly be about that. It is also driven by a refusal to abandon bedrock beliefs regarding human exceptionalism and an overarching narrative of progress. If mass extinction positions humans ignominiously as purveyors of *de*creation, optimistic narratives of de-extinction reinstate humans as life-giving *creators*—a species whose capacity for innovation and ingenuity, exercised through cutting-edge technology, casts us once more in a divine light. As such, de-extinction participates in a secular theology of humans as creators, or *re*creators, of life, a comforting storyline that perpetuates belief in exceptionalism. Note, for example, how Brand's denial of mass extinction is coupled with a portrait of humans as nature's saviors, heroically defending the natural world against death-dealing asteroids or dramatic climate ruptures. With humans fully in charge, he suggests, both we and nature are safer than we have ever been.

There are other ways in which the framing of mass extinction makes de-extinction appear to be the obvious and inspiring "solution." Narration of extinction often reaches a poignant climax in tales of "endlings"—that is, organisms who are the last remaining survivors of a vanishing species. A species is usually considered extinct when its last member has perished (though it may be considered functionally extinct when its population has declined to the point that it plays a negligible role in an ecosystem). The sometimes inordinate focus on the death of sole survivors may distort our understanding of what it would mean to actually reverse species extinction once it has occurred—if such a thing were possible at all. The last individuals of extinct, or soon-to-be-extinct, species are often showered with scientific and media attention. As prominent "avatars of loss," endlings are invested with a kind of collective and concentrated pathos, as evidenced by the creation of commemorative shrines and monuments and the practice of christening endlings with personal names—Martha, the last passenger pigeon, or Lonesome George, the giant Pinta Island tortoise.[9] It's worth noting too that endlings, like favored candidates for de-extinction generally, skew toward charismatic fauna; there are few shrines to plants or insects, despite the vital ecological functions performed by these lowlier brethren.

Endlings may usefully draw attention to mass extinction, giving concreteness to a process of unraveling that generally occurs out of sight and on scales difficult to imagine. "The word recognizes the permanence of group extinction on an individual level."[10] The tangible sense of loss evoked by endlings may inspire efforts to put an *end* to endlings, to prevent them from occurring in the first place. But does it? It would appear that the very rarity of an endling—its *last of its kind* status—solidifies its supreme value, even (perhaps especially) when one encounters it as a museum artifact rather than a living being. More to the point, the attention paid to these pathetic icons of human failure may not challenge our imaginations enough, for endlings may make it too easy to ignore all that is truly lost when entire species vanish. This disconnection, in turn, fosters the illusion that "resurrecting" individuals of extinct species—engineered creatures that are at best proxies and at worst a bizarre genetic mishmash—somehow restores justice or redeems the loss.

The prospect of "resurrecting" these fetishized individuals also sets them up as creatures to be wondered at for the human technoprowess enshrined in recreated organisms, above and beyond their value as genuine repositories of evolutionary history. The preoccupation with the death and potential revivification of an individual creature also obscures the nature of extinction. As Thom van Dooren argues, extinction is not an all-or-nothing proposition; it has a dull and ragged edge, "a slow unraveling of intimately entangled ways of life that begins long before the death of the last individual."[11] The focus on the death of an individual "reduces species to specimens—reified representatives of a type in a museum of life, and in doing so ignores the entangled relations that are a particular form of life."[12] The framing of species as individual *specimens*, I would add, lends itself to the logic and rhetoric of de-extinction, which often treats a species as having been resurrected at the moment that a single individual has been "brought back." In other words, a focus on endlings may act as a goad, an incitement, to de-extinction. And that matters because, as we will see, de-extinction does not recover much of what is lost through extinction. Instead, it facilitates a redirection of wonder toward human creativity and ingenuity and their end products.

Yet another way in which the framing of de-extinction suggests its detachment from the crisis of extinction and its association instead with innovation is seen in arguments that align de-extinction technologies with tools applied in the realm of bioethics rather than environmental ethics. De-extinction is not a special case, this argument goes, but is continuous with interventions and novelties humans have introduced into crops or livestock or pests. On this view, revived species are "just another kind of genetically modified organism," no different in kind from hornless cattle, genetically modified soybeans, or mosquitoes genetically engineered not to carry malaria.[13] But to maintain this equivalency with GMO-style technologies is to obscure the causes of extinction as well as the affective and moral dimensions that ought to inform discussions of extinction and de-extinction. More specifically, a bioethics/biotech framing encourages excitement at the prospect of creating new forms rather than fostering the kind of reflection on anthropogenic extinctions and human complicity that might inspire species protection or activism to prevent further losses. This rejection of somber reflection on species loss in favor of excitement over the creation of new organisms is summed up in Brand's well-known injunction: "Don't mourn, organize."

The impulse to deny the full reality of extinction or simply scale it down so as to render it (ostensibly) manageable and solvable is intimately connected to the allure, the *temptation*, of de-extinction technologies and their shallow claims to wonder. The supposed irresistibility of de-extinction technologies is part and parcel of rhetorical appeals to wonder that reduce species to something like curios to be displayed and admired while exalting humans' life-giving powers. The temptation of wonder—at least, wonder as often invoked in de-extinction discourse—is itself a denial of humans' finite and fallible nature. Might wonder function more constructively, not as a goad to innovation but as a source of moral reflection on our fundamental relationality with the broader web of life? Can wonder be reclaimed within the narrative of extinction as a creaturely mode of being rather than an expression of excited awe at the creative technosolutions of one dominant species? This is what I intend to argue. What follows is a tour through arguments commonly presented for and against de-extinction, with particular emphasis on a suspect form of wonder that accompanies de-extinction advocacy. We begin with a primer on de-extinction technologies and the variety of concerns they generate, even among some advocates. This overview allows us to see more clearly that excitement about these technologies is excitement at the opportunity they present for humans to act as creators of life.

A PRIMER ON DE-EXTINCTION TECHNOLOGY

De-extinction science builds on developments in genetic engineering and synthetic biology as well as on long-standing breeding techniques. The various methods currently under development for reviving extinct species include selective breeding (or "back breeding"), cloning using somatic cell nuclear transfer (SCNT), and genetic engineering. Regardless of the method used, the creation of an identical copy of an extinct species may never be possible. Therefore, de-extincted species are regarded as proxies. Back breeding is a more traditional and lower-tech approach that entails selectively breeding close relatives of an extinct organism for signature traits of the extinct creature. As close relatives of mammoths, for example, elephants could be bred over time to recreate morphological or behavioral traits of their extinct relatives. Some limitations of this technology include the problem that not all extinct organisms have very close living relatives and the fact that back breeding can create inbreeding or concentration of particular traits that reduce the fitness of the de-extincted organisms.

Cloning via SCNT tends to get a lot of press, likely because of the popularity of *Jurassic Park* and the success of the cloned sheep named Dolly. But cloning is not a good option with many extinct species because DNA is unavailable or has significantly degraded. For species that have recently become extinct, clones can be created from cells collected from the last living organisms. In fact, as I will soon discuss, a recently extinct species of Pyrenean ibex, a type of wild goat, was briefly de-extincted in 2003 using skin cells collected from the last living ibex. In such cases, the cells are implanted into the egg cell of a living relative (a goat, in the case of the de-extincted ibex). The resulting zygote is then gestated and, if all goes well, birthed by a surrogate species. Again, this is only possible when researchers have access to entire cells of extinct species. When these are not available, as is the case with so many extinct species, other methods that combine SCNT and genome editing may be used. Researchers believe that they can reconstruct the full genome of extinct species using gene-sequencing technologies that splice the remaining DNA of the extinct organism with that of a related species. Using SCNT, a zygote is then formed that is gestated and birthed by an extant surrogate. This method is likely to be the most promising as a path to de-extinction, and a lot of attention is currently being paid to resurrecting mammoths whose DNA has been frozen in places like Siberia. Using the DNA of a closely related living relative—in this case, the Asian elephant—scientists can repair parts of degraded mammoth DNA by merging it with genetic material from the elephant.[14] Researchers using gene-editing technologies have already reconstructed full genomes for extinct species including mammoths and passenger pigeons.[15]

Other possible de-extinction techniques involving stem cells are still out of reach at the moment, but if we can preserve these cells now, it may be possible to save animals from extinction when the technology is perfected in the future (i.e., animals now on the brink of extinction whom future generations may choose to de-extinct). Stem cells can become any other sort of cell (they are "pluripotent"), so they could be used to create sperm and egg cells that could then be combined via in vitro fertilization to form an embryo that could be coaxed into existence. This is not achievable at the moment, but the Frozen Zoo in San Diego, which houses some ten thousand cell lines, is working on it. This initiative began in 1972—at the height of environmental legislation in the United States—and now holds the cells of 503 mammals, 170 birds, 70 reptiles, and 12 amphibians and fish. Similar "frozen ark" projects have sprung up around the world.[16] The selection of organisms generally skews, problematically, "toward charismatic megafauna and thus against the uncharismatic microfauna that keep the planet alive."[17]

Harvard scientist George Church is one of the most prominent researchers working on de-extinction and related technologies. Church is a media magnet who grabs headlines not only for his efforts at resurrecting the woolly mammoth but for such mad-scientist schemes as reversing the aging process—a technique he is currently testing on dogs. Widely circulated images of Church cast him as something like a hybrid of God and Charles Darwin with his trademark bushy white beard and a halolike radiance around his head. Through use of gene sequencing and editing, Church and his team believe that the creation (or revival) of a woolly mammoth is imminent.[18]

It is important to note that the creature produced by this technology would not *truly* be a mammoth but something "entirely new," namely, a *mammophant*, a hybrid creature with DNA patched together from Asian elephant and mammoth DNA.[19] Additionally, the newfangled mammoth would be raised by an elephant mother (in some scenarios), so there may be behavioral differences introduced by the parent. Given that Asian elephants are gravely endangered and thus not readily available as surrogates, Church and other de-extinctionists also envision artificial wombs, in which case, humans, presumably, do the actual raising once the organism successfully emerges from a high-tech gestational contraption. Imagine a mammoth-size artificial womb designed to facilitate a flawless elephantine gestation periods of two years producing an approximately two-hundred-pound baby. You begin to get an idea of the kind of time, effort, expense—and hubris—that often defines these endeavors.

Even supporters of de-extinction recognize a number of risks and downsides. In the first place, there is the likelihood of failed experiments and the suffering this might inflict on the animals involved. Working with very old DNA (in a method termed "deep de-extinction") can be an especially risky and error-prone process.[20] Even using recently harvested cell lines is no guarantee of success, at least at the moment. Consider the case, mentioned earlier, of the Pyrenean ibex that went extinct in 2000 and was briefly de-extincted in 2003. Scientists used a special hybrid goat as a surrogate mother. This surrogacy was the only promising outcome of fifty-seven attempts to implant embryos into surrogates. The "successful" baby ibex was delivered by C-section and lived less than ten minutes. Accounts of the animal's death often refer vaguely to lung issues or breathing problems. In fact, the baby ibex was born with a third lung. Complications associated with genetic technologies like cloning—shortened life spans, health problems, stillbirths—can be exacerbated by processes that create and gestate extinct animals in "close relatives rather than conspecifics."[21] De-extinction raises unique concerns about animal suffering, yet discussions of animal welfare are often absent in overviews of its pros and cons.

Even if animals whose cells are in deep freeze in places like the San Diego Zoo are successfully brought back in the future, introducing them into natural environments presents additional, potentially enormous technical challenges. The kind of data needed to give any reintroduction program a chance of succeeding—knowledge of habitat requirements and a species' former range, insight gained through trial and error with previous reintroduction methods, among others—might not be available for many extinct species. Researchers at the Frozen Zoo envision acclimating these newly created animals to their man-made zoo environment for years at a time, possibly without ever introducing them into the wild. It is difficult to see what is "natural" about these laboratory-produced, zoo-raised, or human-managed creatures. And should these organisms be successfully introduced, there are reasons to worry that de-extincted species might pose ecological or health risks. Organisms released into nature might spread out of control or prey on existing species. In short, conservation/ecological rationales are a stretch, and potential harms to animals likely.

In the face of these concerns about invasion or health risks, some scholars maintain that candidate species for de-extinction are not likely to pose these threats because "many revived species will be intended for research or exhibition, not release."[22] Moreover, the fact that these species have already gone extinct once and will have low genetic diversity suggests that they will *not be* highly adaptive, fecund, and successful at evading attempts to control their numbers "should they escape or be released." Note how the arguments offered to allay fears about ecological and health risks serve to underscore that de-extinction, especially deep de-extinction, bears little connection to conservation goals. For how can such goals be met with the production of organisms that exhibit nonadaptive characteristics and for whom integration into the wild is at best a secondary objective?

Other objections to de-extinction have to do with moral and existential risks for society at large. These generally fall under the category of the moral hazard argument. The concern is that de-extinction technologies and other nontraditional approaches to conservation create a false sense of security; if we can bring them back, or even think we can, we needn't worry about preventing extinction. Moreover, positive news stories about de-extincted animals may divert attention and resources away from conservation and species preservation. We may come to rely on these technologies as an insurance policy when subsequent species go extinct or their populations shrink. These arguments are worth taking seriously, especially in light of common references to how cheap and easy current gene-editing applications like CRISPR have become. Referring to a project to de-extinct the heath hen, a type of prairie chicken that went extinct in 1932, Church has remarked that this initiative is "basically a slam dunk. . . . As an engineering project, birds are easy."[23] Sentiments such as these that depict birds as simple technological feats gloss over the difficulties of achieving any meaningful conservation successes. They also hint at the impoverishment of the moral imagination of de-extinction, which reduces living creatures to engineering projects while positioning humans as life's engineers.

Having considered some of the major risks and downsides, we turn to some of the strongest arguments for de-extinction in order to discern how and where they meet up with invocations of wonder. When we review the full list of justifications commonly offered for de-extinction, it becomes clear that many of these fall apart under closer examination. Meanwhile claims on behalf of wonder and the seductive allure of the technology itself remain a significant, if questionable, motivation for this research.

THE CASE FOR DE-EXTINCTION

Some of the most powerful arguments for de-extinction have to do with restoring justice. Species are repositories of many different kinds of values. Perhaps humans are obligated to revive species that have gone extinct owing to anthropogenic causes, as a way of recovering those losses and compensating for wrongs humans have perpetrated. This argument has been advanced by some of the most outspoken advocates of de-extinction, including Michael Archer at the University of New South Wales, who spearheaded the Lazarus Project, as well as Brand with his Revive & Restore project.

Does the justice argument hold up? Typically, in cases of restorative justice, an individual or group is assumed to owe something to another individual or group who has been harmed or wronged. But de-extinction complicates this framework because extinction is a category that attaches to *species*. Individuals die, but only a species can "go extinct." As ethicist Ronald Sandler points out, a species (as opposed to an individual organism) cannot be said to suffer or to elicit welfare concerns. A species, as a category, "lacks psychological, biological, and teleological interests."[24] This is not to deny that *groups* of animals can have a welfare. It is rather to say that while "gray wolves" can be wronged, "*Canis lupus*" cannot properly be said to have been wronged. A species qua species "cannot be owed a debt of restorative justice."[25]

Whether or not one accepts this argument, it is certainly the case that if researchers successfully brought back individuals of an extinct species, these would not be the *same individuals* that went extinct. In many cases, particularly where the deep de-extinction of long-lost species is the goal, neither are the *human* perpetrators still alive—think of our ancestors who killed off the last of the Pleistocene megafauna. As Sandler puts it: "It is not possible for a debt of restorative justice, even if there were one, to be paid by those who owe it to those who are due it."[26]

There *is* a compelling and largely shared sense that it is wrong to drive species to extinction; otherwise, we wouldn't bother trying to halt it. So perhaps it makes more sense to think in terms of reparative justice rather than restorative. In a reparative framework, amends are made for past wrongs by reforming our current practices and minimizing ongoing effects of extinctions that *have* occurred. But it is questionable that de-extinction, and (especially) deep de-extinction technologies qua de-extinction technologies, can actually achieve these reparative goals, since the technology itself does not address the myriad underlying causes of extinction, such as habitat loss or climate change, or cultural values and may even divert attention away from extinction prevention, as noted earlier.

If, as many people likely believe, extinction entails a loss of something valuable, the key question is *valuable to whom or what?* Since arguments for de-extinction often invoke conservation or restoration rationales, this suggests that part of what makes a species valuable is its ecological or evolutionary context—both its historical trajectory and its embeddedness within a broader network of relationships. Species may appear valuable owing to a quality of wildness or their status as autonomous entities apart from human life and culture. These values are relational and tied to particular contexts, yet the relationships and contexts they depend on are not obviously restored or recreated by de-extinction, particularly in cases of deep de-extinction, where the habitats no longer exist. In other cases, as with more recent (or "shallow") extinctions, where environments still exist that resemble those of the lost species, de-extinction plus reintroduction *might* restore some of the lost ecological value because those relationships and contexts are still relatively intact. However, reintroductions are difficult under the best of circumstances, and reintroducing an organism created through genetic technologies and raised by humans in laboratory or zoo environments is an even more complex and precarious undertaking. In short, it is unclear how de-extincted organisms restore lost evolutionary and ecological values. As fellow travelers in the evolutionary journey, they arrive with "suspiciously blank passports."[27]

I would argue, then, that most current or emerging genetic technologies envisioned for de-extincting species are not easily justified on restoration or conservation grounds—that is, on virtually any grounds stemming from concerns about the state of the natural world and undoing harms humans have inflicted. Even if de-extinctions meet with technical success, these projects remain "ad hoc, opportunistic attacks on a systemic problem" that is unaddressed by the technology itself.[28] As Crist argues, clear conservation goals are necessary to frame efforts to apply biotechnology to endangered and extinct animals. Otherwise, these projects fall prey to "the ambitions of 'boys with their toys' and 'science for the sake of science.'"[29] Moreover, de-extinction is not a time-sensitive project; it is not as though organisms slated for de-extinction are in danger of becoming *more* extinct over time.[30] So why the urgency? Writing for popular audiences, one de-extinction enthusiast describes the motivations as follows: "Although [a mammophant] might not be exactly like the woolly mammoths of the past, it will be pretty close, and half a mammoth is better than no mammoth, right?"[31] This justification (if one can call it that) merely prompts additional questions that many advocates do not adequately address: Better for what? Better for whom? What is *good* about bringing back a woolly mammoth in the first place? We will see that these very basic questions often receive less attention than the technology itself. At the same time, the promotion of de-extinction often invokes a kind of helplessness in the face of great temptation; de-extinction is simply too irresistible to pass up.

Perhaps, then, what de-extinction actually does is *create* rather than restore value. If so, what kind of value does it create, and for whom or what? De-extinction technologies might generate additional scientific knowledge and applications. Indeed, this is one of the arguments presented by researchers at the San Diego Frozen Zoo who hope that these technologies will shed light on ways to prevent future extinctions.[32] Deep de-extinction in particular would be a "tremendous scientific and technological achievement" in and of itself.[33]

But what, exactly, does it achieve? Talk of *creating*, over and above conserving or restoring, brings us to the theme of wonder, for it is within discussion of values created by de-extinction that wonder of a particularly human-centered variety often makes a showing. References to wonder and awe entailed in de-extinction frequently align wonder, implicitly or explicitly, with largely anthropocentric values, including claims regarding economic or scientific benefits, or the sheer excitement of breaking through technological (and moral) limits. In the context of creating value, some scholars cite values associated with people finding it "wondrous" and "awesome" to see a living representative of an extinct species, "even if only in a zoo or wildlife park."[34] Moreover, this "wonderousness" [sic] might carry with it great economic value because people will pay "to see or own individuals of revived species."[35] Note especially the references to de-extincted creatures as possessions. Wonder's proximity here to enticements such as owning or selling revived members of a species is unsettling, for it treats these organisms as little more than a resource or means of entertainment. Here, arguments for the wonder of de-extinction shade into an endorsement of disaster capitalism— or biocapitalism—presenting the extinction crisis as an *opportunity* for "resource hoarding,"[36] profit, and increased biopower.[37] Sandler, for example, though he remains largely unmoved by key arguments for de-extinction, defends de-extinctionists against the charge that they view life in purely reductive terms, as mere matter that serves human interests and desires, by insisting that these researchers are "motivated at least in part by wonder."[38] The assumption here seems to be that wonder is somehow antithetical to a reductionist, hubristic, or arrogant stance, as if wonder automatically orients us in positive and responsible ways. The question that needs to be asked is, wonder at *what*, exactly? What kind of wonder is this?

WONDER AS DRIVING DE-EXTINCTION: SPREADING THE GOOD NEWS

If, as it seems, de-extinction is not a coherent conservation strategy, nor does it align with what we might call environmental values, nor is it obviously a means of restoring or repairing justice,[39] then why is it being pursued with such excitement? The answer often seems to lie in the excitement itself. Wonder often functions affectively in this discourse as something roughly synonymous with a state of optimistic excitement.

De-extinction enthusiasts often respond to concerns about these technologies (particularly the moral hazard concern) by insisting that stories of successful de-extinction will call *greater* attention to the extinction crisis. Moreover, they claim, tales of successful de-extinction will inspire the public who are desperate for good news stories to counter the grim headlines of the environmental crisis. I refer to this as the *good vibes* argument for de-extinction. This approach, which claims that de-extinction makes for a happy story, entails the advancement of an impoverished form of wonder.

Environmental scholar Ursula K. Heise has observed that narrators of the "new conservation," including some de-extinctionists, pride themselves on being *forward-looking* rather than backward-looking. To be backward-looking, it is implied, is to be glum and unimaginative, to wallow pointlessly in guilt or regret, rather than getting to work to fix the problem. For optimists who embrace an ecomodernist or new conservationist philosophy, the Anthropocene makes possible the reimagination of a *future* nature, not "as a return to the past or a realm apart from humans" but as one that is "reshaped by humans."[40] De-extinction projects in particular, as I have already suggested, tend to privilege the act of creation over acts of (backward-looking) restoration. In this sense, they are fundamentally keyed to an irresistible creative impulse. Creating is much more exciting than (merely) restoring something; where the former puts human powers on display, the latter might suggest that humans subordinate or accommodate themselves to a good whose locus of value is, in some sense, external to the human.

Seen in this light, de-extinction is largely about the making of worlds disguised as an "environmental" or "restoration" project.[41] As Frédéric Neyrat argues, the aims of synthetic biology stand radically opposed to "any kind of idea of conservation—of the environment or of a species. Why protect what we can improve, or reconstruct?" The exchange of conservation for creative synthesis is particularly apparent, Neyrat notes, "within current projects on 'de-extinction.'"[42] In aligning itself with synthesis, creation, and innovation, or what Neyrat aptly terms "the merchant desire of reformatting life,"[43] de-extinction challenges rather than accepts limits—both our own limits and those of the natural world. As such, it becomes a project that is fundamentally about us and our capacity to work wonders.

Indeed, for some in the good vibes camp, a planet remade by humans evokes feelings of "awed celebration."[44] Consider Diane Ackerman's rallying cry in her book *The Human Age*, where she triumphantly proclaims that humans are "not passive, we're not helpless. *We're earth-movers* . . . our mistakes are legion but our imagination is immeasurable." Humans, she argues, are "dreamsmiths and wonder-workers."[45] Warming to her theme of wonder and awe, she exclaims, "What a marvel we've become, a species with planetwide powers and breathtaking gifts."[46] *Dreamsmiths* do not look over their shoulder at the old world. They fabricate new worlds.

ADVANCING THE STORY

It may seem odd at first glance to think of de-extinction, of all things, and especially deep de-extinction, as primarily *future-* rather than past-oriented. But for many de-extinctionists, the prospect of reviving vanished species is valuable not for what it recovers or restores but for its intimations of humans actively shaping what comes next in a wide-open playing field. Ben Novak, the lead scientist at Brand's Revive & Restore project who often speaks passionately of his long-standing "secret and idle love of passenger pigeons," is surprisingly explicit about this future orientation.[47] "Contrary to the poetic nature of 'righting past wrongs' that some attribute to de-extinction," he says, "I view [it] as a project seeded in our present and future.... We are the drivers of change on this planet.... We ultimately write the story."[48] Similar sentiments are expressed in correspondence between Brand and Church in which Brand admonishes conservationists for having "mired themselves in a tragic view of life." He recommends the resurrection of the passenger pigeon as the cure for our malaise: "Wild scheme," he writes. "Could be fun. Could improve things. It could, as they say, advance the story."[49]

Advancing an exciting story—spreading good vibes—also appears to be a central preoccupation of Ben Mezrich, who has written an aggressively optimistic book called *Woolly* about the efforts of Church and others to revive the woolly mammoth. Mezrich is drawn to innovative thinkers—he gained fame for writing the book on which the film *The Social Network* (about Facebook and Mark Zuckerberg) was based. He worries that "there's this fear and dislike of scientists ... So I think [de-extinction] is one way of getting people to be more interested and optimistic." He continues: "If anybody's going to save the world it's going to be scientists coming up with big answers to these questions. . . . The future really lies in the hands of the scientists."[50] Mezrich's storyline here resonates with what some scholars have identified as the dominant narrative of the Anthropocene in which science and technology provide the arena for humans—or, specifically, scientists—to participate in the continuation of godlike creation and salvation. Scientists, as those who will shepherd the planet through the Anthropocene, "must take the lead and conjure up new green technologies."[51]

Often, as we see here, the good vibes rationale becomes indistinguishable from the promotion of science itself as a source of wonder, excitement, and good news. Beth Shapiro, a researcher of ancient DNA and author of *How to Clone a Mammoth*—a deceptively titled book, given that its contents are largely taken up with the obstacles to de-extinction—echoes these rationales in explaining why the mammoth is her favorite candidate for de-extinction (though the dodo, she concedes, would be more "fun"). In addition to what she believes could be positive environmental impacts, Shapiro praises the mammoth's potential "to inspire people to be interested in science and technology."[52] Note that the objective here is not necessarily to inspire people to act on extinction *prevention*. Nor is it even about spreading science literacy, which might be a worthy enough cause. It is rather about getting people excited and optimistic—*about* science. This is science evangelism, plain and simple. As one journalist aptly observes, "de-extinction can inspire a lot of hope—not necessarily about the species themselves, but for demonstrating how relatively fast an area of science can develop."[53]

Perhaps the best (or worst) illustration of the shallowness of so much de-extinction wonder rhetoric can be seen in the arguments advanced for de-extinction in a short, punchy essay titled "What if Extinction Is Not Forever?" The authors, Jacob Sherkow and Henry T. Greely, affiliated with Stanford University, make a case for what they call the *coolness* of de-extinction.⁵⁴ They rehearse the standard list of concerns regarding de-extinction: animal welfare and the ecological and health risks of the escape or release of de-extincted organisms. They gesture vaguely but predictably toward concerns about "playing God." Among what they consider the "pros" or "benefits" of de-extinction, they list increases in scientific knowledge, technological advancement, environmental benefits, claims for justice, and, finally, "wonder." Scientific and technological advantages include the possibility that "some revived species may be translated into *useful products*," such as new drugs.⁵⁵ In a culminating argument, they explain the "attraction" of wonder: "The last benefit might be called 'wonder,' or more colloquially, 'coolness.' This may be the biggest attraction, and possibly the biggest benefit, of de-extinction. It would surely be very cool to see a living wooly mammoth. And while this is rarely viewed as a substantial benefit, much of what we do as individuals—even many aspects of science—we do because it's 'cool.'"⁵⁶

This defense of coolness and wonder (or coolness *as* wonder) aligns with what Crist calls science for its own sake and boys with their toys. The authors conclude by noting that "de-extinction is a particularly intriguing application of our increasing control over life. We think it will happen."⁵⁷ But the critical issue is not *can* or *will* de-extinction happen, but *should* it happen? And if so, *why* should it happen? Is the claim here that we should pursue what is cool because we, and especially scientists, have always done cool things? These arguments about the coolness of de-extinction reach their nadir in commentary about de-extinction as sheer titillation. The irresistibility of de-extinction as a seductive taboo translates into its inevitability—de-extinction is "a topic so hot it sizzles."⁵⁸ It is simply "too sexy to ignore."⁵⁹

In *Resurrecting Extinct Species*, philosophers Douglas Ian Campbell and Patrick Michael Whittle give some sustained and apparently serious consideration to what they term "the argument from coolness." Coolness, they note, has two dimensions: the (supposed) restoration of the original coolness (awe, wonder) of an organism like a woolly mammoth and the coolness of the *act itself* of resurrecting such a creature. They argue that if a sufficiently large percentage of the public agree, on whatever grounds, that de-extinction is cool, these projects could have conservation value as a way of "getting the public excited about conservation."[60]

And yet, as we have seen (and as even many advocates of de-extinction attest), the conservation rationales remain weak, particularly for paradigmatically "cool" deep de-extinction projects like the mammoth. Moreover, as suggested by Novak, Mezrich, and Shapiro, the coolness and excitement factor attaches largely to the science and technology itself and the flattering portrait of humans as "drivers" of planetary change and "writers" of future life stories. Of course, the public may well experience coolness as a conservation value, an inspiration to care for nature and nonhuman life, regardless of whether scientists embrace de-extinction for the illicit thrill it affords. But the coolness of de-extinction as a pathway to conservation seems plausible only to the extent that researchers and journalists overstate the viability (as indeed many do) of de-extinction as a robust conservation tool and strategy. It is equally plausible that the wonder generated by this technology will undercut conservation efforts and concerns and engender overconfidence in our ability to bring back extinct species (as the moral hazard argument suggests).

At best, then, the forward-looking wonder narrative positions resurrected creatures as mascots of human achievement, reducing wonder to a species of the technological sublime, though without the gravitas that has traditionally defined conceptions of the sublime.[61] At its worst, the wonder of de-extinction functions as a diversion from serious moral deliberation about the causes of extinction, the dangers of these technologies, and their potential to reshape not just the world but the place of humans within it.

One of the most thoughtful inquiries into the wonder of de-extinction is voiced by environmental philosopher Ben Minteer. Minteer asks us to consider what de-extinction projects reveal about the values and moral character of those endorsing it. He notes that aspiring de-extinctionists view potentially resurrected creatures as objects of awe and wonder, but he worries that these advocates have misdirected their sense of wonder by substituting "aesthetic regard for the sublime qualities of wild nature for a celebration of our own technological ingenuity, power, and control."[62] The sublime, once associated with experiences of wonder that shade into reverence and even fear—"a reaction to power, mystery, and beauty of a world beyond human making, understanding, and control"—has now come to signal Promethean ambitions to bring that world within our control. "Wonder and respect once directed at nature has become instead a regard for our own technological prowess." Our foundational mistake was not that we caused extinction, Minteer argues. Extinction is a symptom of a more general disease—namely, a human-centered worldview in which "we see ourselves as masters of a world thought to be increasingly of our own making ... as all-powerful creators and presumptive governors of planetary life."[63] The Promethean expression of awe resides in, and is a response to, "our own mind," Minteer astutely observes. As a case in point, he cites Church's blithe assessment that "birds are easy." He also notes the way that would-be resurrectionists like Brand view traditional conservation and restoration as a depressing narrative, where de-extinction "promises a much cheerier story, a more uplifting narrative driven by sunny acts of biological creation and ecological recovery."[64] The backward-looking goal of recovery simply cannot compete with de-extinction's good cheer.

Minteer doesn't put it in quite these terms, but his analysis suggests an important distinction, about which I have written extensively elsewhere, between wonder turned inward, toward ourselves and our aspirations and creations, and wonder oriented to something beyond the self, something expressive of being in relation to other centers of value.⁶⁵ Internalized wonder reaches toward self-deification; "by *comprehending* the source of the wondrous, the thinking self in effect becomes the source of the wondrous."⁶⁶ Indeed, some advocates of de-extinction make it all too easy for critics to level charges of self-deification against them, given their express wish to deploy unlimited power, as reflected in Brand's oft-repeated claim, "We are as gods and we might as well get good at it."⁶⁷ With de-extinction, we might say that the human becomes the source of the wondrous not only in comprehending life's awesome power ("decoding" the book of nature) but in *rewriting* life's story. Nature no longer operates independently of humans as something that exceeds us; the biosphere is now subsumed under the human technosphere.⁶⁸ This denial of nature's exteriority and autonomy turns organisms into an extension of ourselves and our will—mere "bio-objects" created by humans for human interests and purposes, including our own redemption.⁶⁹ De-extinction as an instrument of internalized wonder is morally corrupting. It presents us with "no foil against which to evaluate our choices, no resistance that might set boundaries or limits, and no honest acknowledgement of an exteriority upon which we might gaze in awe," Christopher Preston states.⁷⁰ There is too much focus on us, as Preston argues, in the sense that de-extinction encourages a preoccupation both with our own ingenuity *and* with our own possibility of redemption through technology.

What is troubling about de-extinction goes beyond the various technical risks and costs or the confused and incoherent "ethics" of restoring versus creating nature, as worrisome as these are. De-extinction—and the excitement surrounding it—is troubling for what it reveals about its devotees. In a sense, then, it is both too much about humans and *not enough* about us, for it draws our energies away from genuine and sober reflection on the kinds of creatures we are and ought to be. Meditation upon loss and contrition confronts us with our own finitude and may encourage self-restraint. Attention to inwardness of this sort, we should note, is not the same as a preoccupation with our own redemption or atonement for human-caused extinction. A turn inward that prompts the desire to atone or be redeemed is or ought to be an expression of creatureliness. It is this recognition of our finitude and our sometimes powerlessness that atonement must acknowledge—and that the impulse to create and control too easily sidesteps. It is this finite and fallible human that the image of human as creator or world maker rejects. There is a sense, then, in which de-extinction really *is* far too easy. As a ritual of atonement, de-extinction wrongly assumes that loss is something that can simply be fixed, like a solution to a mathematical problem.[71]

RELIGION IN DISGUISE

The religion-resembling lexicon of de-extinction is often a mishmash of motifs of resurrection, salvation, redemption, sin, temptation, and atonement all tossed together in a prophetic, future-oriented narrative that ultimately advances a religion of limitless innovation. Aspirants of this religion stake out various roles in the narrative—often incoherently—as they present de-extinction researchers, or "humanity" generally, as both redeemer and redeemed, sinner and savior. Archer, the researcher who brazenly christens his work "the Lazarus Project," also draws freely on allusions to Eden and scriptural imperatives to defeat death. "If we destroyed part of Eden, we are responsible for fixing up that garden," Archer insists. "This idea of restoring things that have become extinct has actually a biblical sanction," he continues. To wit: "1 Corinthians, 15 verse 26 says that the last enemy that shall be destroyed is death."[72] Archer's case for de-extinction proceeds seamlessly from a "we killed these animals" lament to excited speculation about how we might "help ourselves" with medical breakthroughs, such as those to be wrested from a resurrected frog's uncanny gestational apparatus.[73]

It is also common for these narratives to track, albeit loosely, a Christian storyline of the seductive appeal of divine knowledge and power, suggestive of a fall into sin or punishment for dangerous and forbidden knowledge. As Sandra Swart argues, framing de-extinction technologies as some version of the Frankenstein myth—a story whose elements draw from much older myths like that of Prometheus, Icarus, and the biblical fall in paradise—is a widespread and perennial practice dating back to the 1980s, when a spoof news story reported the resurrection of the woolly mammoth by a Soviet scientist.[74] Invocations of the Frankenstein myth may be more accurate than some de-extinctionists would care to admit. Frankenstein, after all, is a story not of resurrection per se but of the creation of a wholly new entity from assembled lifeless parts. In any case, having gestured vaguely in the direction of forbidden knowledge, narratives of de-extinction then tend to veer off, vertiginously, into a framing of scientists as divine figures who have mastered the design of life. That is, rather than *chasten* would-be transgressors, the narrative urges them on with the promise of complete creative control and even apotheosis. Science writer Ed Regis and Church, in a book-length treatment of the promise of synthetic biology, describe the unprecedented "power and allure of redesigning life" on an ever-expanding canvas.[75] "We are already remaking ourselves and our world," they confidently write, "retracing the steps of the original synthesis—redesigning, recoding, and reinventing nature itself in the process."[76] Nature itself has ordained for us precisely this role, Church suggests. "We seem to be 'designed' by nature to be good designers."[77] Our innate propensity to engineer is what distinguishes us from most other animals.[78] Brand's diagnosis is even more bullish: "We are as gods and we might as well get good at it."[79]

As I have argued, the excited rhetoric surrounding remaking, designing, and especially *creating* testifies to motives that have little connection to recovering or restoring lost or threatened values or to concerns about the inherent worth of nonhuman life. As Britt Wray, author of *Rise of the Necrofauna* observes, many de-extinction projects are born of excitement about innovative possibilities and only later acquire environmental rationales to justify the technology. "Advocates of the project find a way to fit them into the ecological narrative."[80] For all their unclarity and imprecision, these narratives plainly position their protagonist—the de-extinction scientist who often stands in for humanity writ large—as a supreme world-making being. The wonder of the story ultimately redounds to the glory of this intrepid entity (and secondarily, to its manufactured curios)—an entity whose denial of finitude, frailty, or doubt and whose rejection of dependence on forces exterior to itself are proffered as grounds for a secular faith of excited optimism. The human-as-creator forms the center of value and wonder, and reclaiming wonder from these problematic interpretations has the power to reveal this religion for what it is: a religion by, about, and, ultimately, for the human.

In conclusion, then, I want to outline how wonder might more appropriately be understood in the context of humans' relationship to the natural world, with particular emphasis on conceptions of creatureliness. The condition of creatureliness is a fact of human existence, whether or not one subscribes to a religious interpretation or doctrine. Humans are mortal beings who share numerous behaviors, preferences, and evolutionary ties with other organisms. We exist within certain parameters over which we have limited control. To embrace creatureliness is to acknowledge our shared embodied nature, vulnerability, and biological fate. To present creatureliness as a natural fact is not to deny the belief that humans are the product of a Creator; but, as I see it, it is not necessary to affirm that doctrine in order to grasp the ethical import of our creaturely status. However, because de-extinction's rhetoric often mimics, albeit in a confused way, certain plot devices and discursive turns of the Genesis narrative and other biblical allusions to scientists as modern-day resurrectionists or Noah figures, it is useful to consider some perspectives on the human offered by Christian theologians, alongside insights from secular ethicists who "think with" recognizable elements of that tradition and its legacy.

Properly understood, wonder is a questing and questioning mode. Upbeat stories of the wonder of de-extinction seem designed, by contrast, to dodge all inquiries. Instead they *tell* us, dogmatically, authoritatively, who we are—we are wonder workers, earth movers, and creators. But de-extinction confronts us with questions: What does it mean to be human? What kinds of creatures do we *want* to be? These are questions about how humans and their knowledge fit into a larger context of a living world that humans did not bring into being. These questions often produce anxiety when they are asked and received in a genuine spirit of searching, rather than as a prelude to proclaiming all that we know, soon will know, or are capable of doing. They engage us in a difficult process of discernment that is never ending in a dynamic and changing world. We need to sit with these questions, uneasily.

Inquiries into the kind of creature we are and ought to be provoke anxiety, because when thinking about "the human" is framed as a question rather than an assertion, "one can begin to see the harm previous answers have caused."[81] These harms are apparent in the many ways in which the category of the human functions to exclude certain others from moral consideration, dignity, or worth, both within our own species and beyond it. Uneasiness in the face of this inquiry tempts us to banish the ambiguity in favor of closure. The desire for closure, I would argue, contributes to the framing of de-extinction as a solution to a tractable problem, a technology capable of engineering new marvels while also righting wrongs. In thinking about what it means to be human, theologians and scientists alike (though the latter might not realize or admit it) frequently gravitate toward an idiom of *imaging* God. In particular, as I have suggested throughout, the godlike dimension that humans are often assumed to mirror is the capacity to create and innovate.

But this move to define humans as creators often ignores what theologian W. Dow Edgerton heralds as the "wonderfully ambiguous language" of the Genesis story, which does not specify *what* about the human shows us to be in the divine image. This ambiguity is the ambiguity of wonder, and it can be highly generative, offering both a "source and limit" of what it means to be human and a "limit and a warning not to speculate upon the specifics but to receive and honor the mystery."[82] Wonder, as an interrogative impulse that resists closure, can help to hold the question open, to dwell in mystery, to engage in discernment. At the same time, however, what it means to be human is not a completely wide-open question. There are parameters. How might we recognize them? What we know with certainty is that we are creatures who exist among innumerable other living entities. A moral imagination grounded in creatureliness puts emphasis not on Ackerman's "immeasurable" scope of imagination and innovation but on conditions of what bioethicist Bruce Jennings calls "dynamic finitude and constrained becoming" developed within and through "relationships of accommodation with the limits and the gifts of evolved nature."[83] Contra Ackerman's dazzling portrait of us, the human imagination cannot function well on an unlimited canvas and immeasurable scale. This limitless imagination is not a moral imagination but at best an amoral one, for it does not recognize connection, interdependence, or relationality among humans and nonhumans or the profound debts we owe these myriad others.

Against the voices of technologists and Anthropocene boosters who urge us to embrace our unbounded creativity and its immeasurable scope, others point us back to our condition of creaturely finitude. For humans qua creatures, Wendell Berry argues, limitlessness is hell. He invokes a scene from Christopher Marlowe's telling of Faust in which Mephistopheles instructs Doctor Faustus on the basic characteristics of hell:

> Hell hath no limits, nor is circumscribed
> In one self place, but where we [the damned] are is hell,
> And where hell is must we ever be.

Limitlessness is the purview of gods alone. By normalizing a culture of limitlessness, we become convinced that all of our ills can be cured through more technology. "We are now, in short, coming under pressure to understand ourselves as limited creatures in a limited world," Berry writes.[84] In a similar vein Rowan Williams argues that to be human is to be engaged in a constant battle against "all those instincts in us that make us want to be God or make us want to be what we think God is."[85] The rejection of creatureliness is a refusal of limits and perhaps especially a refusal of death itself—and what is de-extinction but the refusal of an especially overwhelming and incomprehensible form of death?

Framed as a condition of being limited, creatureliness can sound too much like condemnation or confinement. But it is worth considering that a creaturely status *frees* humans from trying to be god, whether godlikeness is understood in explicitly religious terms or as a placeholder for aspirations toward omnipotence and control. Turning to the narrative of the Genesis "fall" in particular, Williams observes that Adam's resentment at not being God is what gives Satan power to tempt him to overstep his creaturely boundaries. The same resentment fuels our culture's widespread denial of death and aging, its aversion to risk, and its longing for security and technological control. "And when I read . . . in discussions of our environmental crisis, that we can be confident our technology will find a way, my blood runs cold," Williams confesses, "because I hear in that the refusal of real creatureliness."[86] I would argue that the rhetoric of wonder in de-extinction discourse functions in much the same way, as a temptation to deny limits and seize powers of technodivinity through the creation and resurrection of life rather than to confront the extinction crisis, and our role in it, with honesty. If this diagnosis is correct, then grappling with extinction does require an inward turn of sorts—not in the sense of cultivating new technologies as a path to redemption but in the recognition that something in *us* must change, in accordance with dramatic and destructive changes we have wrought. Otherwise, these tools are merely an extension of our self-regard.

Wonder, defined against the self-regarding, instrumentalizing impulse, may play an important role in recovering the lost art of being a creature.[87] Not only does wonder resist the closure of solutionist ideology; it also stands in opposition to exploitative and utilitarian valuing and the acquisitive impulse that characterizes much of the excitement surrounding de-extinction, notably in expressions of "coolness" at the thought of creating, owning, or displaying de-extincted creatures. Wonder involves a turning of the self toward the *other* in ways that refuse arrogant appropriation or mastery of another. The essence of wonder is its other-acknowledging quality. For this reason, as philosopher R. W. Hepburn argues, wonder is closely aligned with states of humility, empathy, and compassion and a general "concern not to blunder into damaging manipulation of another."[88] Wonder's refusal of mastery and its orientation toward the other bespeaks the wonderer's state of vulnerability and receptivity. Wonder shatters the illusion of, and desire for, total control.

CONCLUSION

Many features of wonder align it with the condition of creatureliness, which is similarly premised on an abiding and humble awareness of otherness and a shared sense of embodied vulnerability with other living beings. More broadly, to understand ourselves as creatures is to allow that the world confronts us as a mystery that cannot be resolved into its component parts and thereby solved like a mathematical problem. Perhaps, then, the primary challenge we face as human beings in an era of mass extinction is to understand how to honor our creaturely nature alongside a capacity for creativity and innovation. Humans' creative capacities must go hand in hand with, and be restrained by, responsibility and care. There is no formula for this balancing act. But wonder as an expression of creatureliness might counter the default to anthropocentricism that characterizes so many applications of biotechnology.[89]

Creaturely wonder as an antidote to de-extinction's defiant cheeriness might also complicate the storyline of mass extinction that reduces its incomprehensibility to a manageable engineering problem, as with Church's assessment of bird de-extinction as an "easy" fix. Put differently, if the denial of mass extinction is partly a function of human exceptionalism, then restoring humans to creaturely status might begin to chip away at this denial. We might start to look beyond competing narratives of salvation through innovation on the one hand and inevitable decline and failure on the other. Both narratives, in their own way, convey an excess of certainty—the certainty of optimism versus that of despair—that is not available to us as creatures. Hope (distinct from techno-optimism) and the ability to act locate themselves within the premise that the future is not already written. "We pretend that life like art has plots and we know how the story ends, whether it's an election or a cultural shift or the outcome of any major event," Rebecca Solnit writes, "and we often err not on the side of caution but on the side of conventionality: the future will look like the present."[90] Rejecting the closure of these narratives, we must then face the task of discerning how our agency aligns with other complex values with which we are embedded. Where the creator controls and perfects, the creature searches for an ethical mode of accommodation, of fitting into a world replete with wonders it did not make and cannot fully comprehend. This is not a science project. Berry refers to this mode as "propriety," a sense of *fittingness* that recognizes ourselves as part of a larger, irreducible whole.[91] Propriety presents us with a set of overarching questions in keeping with wonder's interrogative mode: Where are we? Who are we? What is our condition? To raise questions of propriety is to recognize an exteriority to which we are called to relate, rather than subsuming it within our ever-expanding technosphere. It might mean resisting the temptation to engineer the world around us and to remake it in our own image in favor of determining how we fit in and directing or restricting our creative powers accordingly. Propriety helps us to see de-extinction technology for what it is: a tantalizing impulse to make and remake worlds in search of an ecological rationale and ethical context. Creatures are beings who necessarily live, act, and create *in context*. The alternative, for us and the planet, is hell.

LISA H. SIDERIS is Professor of Environmental Ethics in the Environmental Studies Program at the University of California, Santa Barbara. From 2005 to 2021, she taught in the Religious Studies Department at Indiana University. Sideris is author of *Environmental Ethics, Ecological Theology, and Natural Selection* and *Consecrating Science: Wonder, Knowledge, and the Natural World* and editor, with Kathleen Dean Moore, of a collection of essays on the life and legacy of Rachel Carson, *Rachel Carson Legacy and Challenge*.

NOTES

1. See William Cronon, "The Trouble with Wilderness: Or, Getting Back to the Wrong Nature," *Environmental History* 1, no. 1 (January 1996): 7–28; Ramachandra Guha, "Radical American Environmentalism: A Third World Critique," *Environmental Ethics* 11 (1989): 71–89.

2. Eileen Crist, "On the Poverty of Our Nomenclature," *Environmental Humanities* 3 (2013): 133.

3. George Wuerthner, Eileen Crist, and Tom Butler, eds., *Keeping the Wild: Against the Domestication of Earth* (Washington, DC: Island Press, 2014).

4. Amy Fletcher, "Genuine Fakes: Cloning Extinct Species as Science and Spectacle," *Politics and the Life Sciences* 29, no. 1 (March 2010): 48–60.

5. Stefan Skrimshire, "Rewriting Mortality: A Theological Critique of Geoengineering and De-Extinction," in *Calming the Storm: Theological and Ethical Perspectives on Climate Engineering*, ed. Forrest Clingerman and Kevin J. O'Brien (London: Lexington, 2016), 103–126, 113.

6. Lisa H. Sideris, "The Human as World-Maker: An Anthropocene Dogma," in *Christian Theology and the Modern Sciences*, T&T Clark Companion Series, ed. John Slattery (London: T&T Clark, 2020).

7. Stewart Brand, "Rethinking Extinction," *Aeon Magazine*, accessed August 6, 2022, https://aeon.co/essays/we-are-not-edging-up-to-a-mass-extinction.

8. Alexander C. Lees et al., "Biodiversity Scientists Must Fight the Creeping Rise of Extinction Denial," *Nature: Ecology and Evolution*, August 18, 2020, https://www.nature.com/articles/s41559-020-01285-z.pdf.

9. Ed Yong, "The Last of Its Kind," *The Atlantic*, July 2019.

10. Dolly Jørgensen, "Endling: The Power of the Last in an Extinction-Prone World," *Environmental Philosophy* 14, no. 1 (2017): 119–138.

11. Thom van Dooren, *Flight Ways: Life and Loss at the Edge of Extinction* (New York: Columbia University Press, 2014), 12.

12. Van Dooren, *Flight Ways*, 58.

13. Henry T. Greely, "Is De-extinction Special?," *Hastings Center Report* (July/August 2017): 30.

14. Note that SCNT is not an option for egg-laying animals like birds and reptiles because their reproductive process makes it very difficult to access eggs in their earliest stages of development. However, other techniques involving the germ cells are available. See Beth Shapiro, "Pathways to De-extinction: How Close Can We Get to Resurrection of an Extinct Species?," *Functional Ecology* 31, no. 5 (2016): 996–1002.

15. Shapiro, "Pathways to De-extinction," 999.

16. Jenny Graves, "Saving DNA: The Frozen Ark Project," Australian Academy of Science, accessed August 6, 2022, https://www.science.org.au/curious/earth-environment/frozen-ark-project.

17. See David Bielo, "Will We Kill Off Today's Animals if We Revive Extinct Ones?," *Scientific American*, March 19, 2013, https://www.scientific

american.com/article/de-extinction-to-bring-back-extinct-species-but-challenges-conservation/.

18. George Church's lab claimed in 2017 the mammoth would be de-extincted within two years, but this has not occurred.

19. Mary Beth Griggs, "No, the Woolly Mammoth Won't Actually Be Resurrected by 2019," *Popular Science*, February 17, 2017, https://www.popsci.com/wooly-mammoth-will-not-be-resurrected-in-two-years/.

20. *Deep de-extinction* is a term used by Ronald Sandler to describe the effort to bring back species that have not existed for anywhere from several decades to millennia. Deep de-extinction cannot qualify as reintroduction, since environments may have changed dramatically in a species' absence.

21. Heather Browning, "Won't Somebody Please Think of the Mammoths? De-Extinction and Animal Welfare," *Journal of Agricultural and Environmental Ethics* 31 (2018): 785–803.

22. Sandler, "The Ethics of Reviving Long Extinct Species," *Conservation Biology* 28, no. 2 (2013): 358. Sandler does go on to say that it is possible that there could be "unintended negative consequences" of deep de-extinction, but these risks are also present, he notes, with other kinds of conservation programs that involve, for example, breeding programs and relocations; moreover, some de-extincted organisms might even bring ecological benefits to their environments. Yet the frequent hypothetical phrase "*if* they are released" and reminders that these organisms will have low genetic diversity cast doubt on de-extinction as a conservation practice. This impression is reinforced by the example of the Frozen Zoo, where there is little likelihood that a successfully produced organism would ever live beyond the confines of the zoo.

23. Nathaniel Horwitz, "Heath Hen's Boom Could Echo Again on Martha's Vineyard," *MV Times*, July 16, 2014, http://www.mvtimes.com/2014/07/16/heath-hens-boom-echo-marthas-vineyard/.

24. Sandler, "The Ethics," 355.

25. Sandler, "The Ethics," 355.

26. Sandler, "The Ethics," 355.

27. Ben Minteer, *The Fall of the Wild: Extinction, De-Extinction, and the Ethics of Conservation* (New York: Columbia University Press, 2018), 112.

28. Bruce Jennings, "The Moral Imagination of De-extinction," *Hastings Center Report* (July/August 2017): 58.

29. Crist, "Cloning in Restorative Perspective," in *Restoration and History: The Search for a Usable Environmental Past*, ed. Marcus Hall (New York: Routledge, 2009), 284–292, 288.

30. Browning, "Won't Somebody."

31. Stephen Fleischfresser, "What Is De-extinction and How Do You Do It?," *Cosmos Magazine*, March 7, 2017, https://cosmosmagazine.com/nature/woolly-mammoth-what-is-de-extinction-and-how-do-you-do-it/.

32. Creation of value might occur ethically alongside restoration of value. For example, the overriding goal might be to restore a species, with a side effect of creating knowledge to better enable us to prevent extinction.

33. Sandler, "The Ethics," 356.

34. Sandler, "The Ethics," 356.

35. Sandler, "The Ethics," 356.

36. Sandler, "The Ethics," 359.

37. Ashley Dawson, *Extinction: A Radical History* (New York: OR Books, 2016).

38. Sandler, "The Ethics," 359.

39. One exception might be the Zimov project of Pleistocene Park, where efforts to resurrect mammoths are motivated by the possibility of creating favorable impacts in terms of climate control—recreating a "mammoth steppe" ecosystem that might keep permafrost from melting further and releasing potent greenhouse gases. Here the goals are ecological—climate change mitigation—and de-extinction is a means to that (still somewhat anthropocentric) end. "I'm doing this for humans," Nikita Zimov says. "I've got three daughters. I'm doing it for them." Ross Andersen, "Welcome to Pleistocene Park," *The Atlantic*, April 2017.

40. Ursula K. Heise, *Imagining Extinction: The Cultural Meanings of Endangered Species* (Chicago: University of Chicago Press, 2016), 203.

41. Frédéric Neyrat refers to this project of world making or remaking as "geo-constructivism," dubbing its biological counterpart, as with de-extinction, "bio-constructivism." Neyrat, *The Unconstructable Earth: An Ecology of Separation* (New York: Fordham University Press, 2019).

42. Neyrat, *The Unconstructable Earth*, 53.

43. Neyrat, *The Unconstructable Earth*, 53.

44. Heise, *Imagining Extinction*, 206.

45. Diane Ackerman, *The Human Age: The World Shaped By Us* (London: W. W. Norton, 2014), 309.

46. Ackerman, *The Human Age*, 308.

47. Ben J. Novak, "Flights of Fancy," Project Passenger Pigeon, accessed August 6, 2022, http://passengerpigeon.org/Flights-Stories/Novak.html.

48. Quoted in Skrimshire, "Rewriting Mortality," 112.

49. Quoted in Nathaniel Rich, "The Mammoth Cometh," *New York Times Magazine*, February 27, 2014, https://www.nytimes.com/2014/03/02/magazine/the-mammoth-cometh.html.

50. Angela Chen, "Will Bringing Back the Woolly Mammoth Save Humanity from Itself? A Chat with Author Ben Mezrich about Bringing Back Long-Extinct Animals," *The Verge*, July 27, 2017.

51. Christophe Bonneuil, "The Geological Turn: The Anthropocene and Its Narratives," in *The Anthropocene and the Global Environmental Crisis: Rethinking Modernity in a New Epoch*, ed. Clive Hamilton, Christophe Bonneuil, and Francois Gemmene (New York: Routledge, 2015), 17–31, 23.

52. Elizabeth Quill, "These Are the Extinct Animals We Can, and Should, Resurrect," *Smithsonian Magazine*, May 2015, https://www.smithsonianmag.com/science-nature/these-are-extinct-animals-we-can-should-resurrect-180954955/.

53. Rachel Riederer, "The Woolly Mammoth Lumbers Back Into View," *The New Yorker*, December 27, 2018.

54. Greely has a ten-minute TED talk that reiterates all of these points, including the one he considers most important—"wonder." Greely, "De-Extinction: Hubris or Hope?," April 1, 2013, YouTube, accessed August 6, 2022, https://www.youtube.com/watch?v=HuRkoV2LoMY.

55. Jacob S. Sherkow and Henry Greely, "What If Extinction Is Not Forever?," *Science Magazine* 340 (April 5, 2013): 33.

56. Sherkow and Greely, "What If," 33.

57. Sherkow and Greely, "What If," 33.

58. Barbara Kiser, "Books in Brief," *Nature*, October 19, 2017, https://www.nature.com/articles/550331a.

59. Philip J. Seddon, "The Ecology of De-Extinction," *Functional Ecology* 31 (May 8, 2017): 994.

60. Douglas Ian Campbell and Patrick Michael Whittle, *Resurrecting Extinct Species: Ethics and Authenticity* (Cham, CH: Palgrave Macmillan, 2017), 98.

61. Shlomo Cohen asks whether technologically revived mammoths would retain the ability to evoke the sublime, given that they are human creations. He notes that the fact that we can create something does not mean we can control it and that in the face of the fearsome power of a de-extincted woolly mammoth (particularly one raging out of control), an experience of the sublime is arguably still possible. See Cohen, "The Ethics of De-extinction," *Nanoethics* 8 (2014): 165–178.

62. Minteer, "The Perils of De-Extinction," *Minding Nature* 8, no. 1 (January 2015): 13–14.
63. Minteer, *The Fall of Wild*, 110–112.
64. Minteer, *The Fall of the Wild*, 109.
65. Sideris, *Consecrating Science: Wonder, Knowledge, and the Natural World* (Oakland: University of California Press, 2017).
66. Mary-Jane Rubenstein, *Strange Wonder: The Closing of Metaphysics and the Opening of Awe* (New York: Columbia University Press, 2008), 16.
67. John Brockman, "We Are as Gods and Have to Get Good at It," Edge.org, August 18, 2009, https://www.edge.org/conversation/stewart _brand-we-are-as-gods-and-have-to-get-good-at-it.
68. Christopher Preston, "De-extinction: A Tale of Two Visions," *Humans and Nature*, September 9, 2015. Minteer, *The Fall of the Wild*, 117.
69. Lucia Martinelli, Markku Oksanen, and Helena Siipi, "De-extinction: A Novel and Remarkable Case of Bio-objectification," *Croatian Medical Journal* 55, no. 4 (August 2014): 423–427.
70. Preston, "De-extinction," 117.
71. Jennings, "The Moral Imagination."
72. Michael Archer, quoted in "The Scientist Trying to Reverse Extinctions (Think 'Jurassic Park')," *FiveThirtyEight*, November 25, 2015, https://fivethirtyeight.com/features/the-scientist-trying-to-reverse -extinctions-think-jurassic-park/.
73. Archer, "How We'll Resurrect the Gastric Brooding Frog, the Tasmanian Tiger," TEDxDeExtinction, March 2013, accessed August 6, 2022, https://www.ted.com/talks/michael_archer_how_we_ll _resurrect_the_gastric_brooding_frog_the_tasmanian_tiger.
74. Sandra Swart, "Frankenzebra: Dangerous Knowledge and the Narrative Construction of Monsters," *Journal of Literary Studies* 30, no. 4 (December 2014): 45–70.
75. Church and Ed Regis, *Regenesis: How Synthetic Biology Will Reinvent Nature and Ourselves* (New York: Basic Books, 2012), 201.
76. Church and Regis, *Regenesis*, 13.
77. John Brockman, "Constructive Biology: George Church," Edge, June 26, 2006, http://www.edge.org/3rd_culture/church06/church06 _index.html.
78. Peter Miller, "George Church: The Future Without Limits," *National Geographic*, June 2, 2014, https://www.nationalgeographic .com/science/article/140602-george-church-innovation-biology-science -genetics-de-extinction.

79. Brand originally proposed that humans are as gods with the first publication of *Whole Earth Catalogue* in 1968. He has since updated this diagnosis to say, "We are as gods and *have* to get good at it." Brand, *Whole Earth Discipline* (New York: Viking, 2009), 20.

80. Nicole Faires, "Can De-extinction Save Our Planet? An Interview with Brit Wray," Eartheasy, October 13, 2017, https://learn.eartheasy.com/articles/can-de-extinction-save-our-planet-an-interview-with-britt-wray/.

81. W. Dow Edgerton, "Asking About Who We Are," *Theology Today*, January 1, 1994.

82. Edgerton, "Asking About Who We Are."

83. Jennings, "Unnatural Selection," Center for Humans and Nature, June 21, 2017.

84. Wendell Berry, "Faustian Economics," *Harper's Magazine*, May 2008, https://harpers.org/archive/2008/05/faustian-economics/.

85. Rowan Williams, "Creation, Creatureliness, Creativity: The Wisdom of a Finite Existence," in *Being-in-Creation*, ed. Brian Treanor, Bruce Ellis Benson, and Norman Wirzba (New York: Fordham University Press, 2015).

86. Williams, "Creation, Creatureliness, Creativity," 35.

87. Williams, "On Being Creatures," Eric Symes Memorial Lecture, delivered at Westminster Abbey, May 15, 1989.

88. R. W. Hepburn, "Wonder," in *"Wonder" and Other Essays: Eight Studies in Aesthetics and Neighbouring Fields* (Edinburgh: University of Edinburgh Press, 1984), 131–154, 146.

89. Jennings, "Unnatural Selection."

90. Rebecca Solnit, "On Letting Go of Certainty in a Story that Never Ends," Literary Hub, April 23, 2020, https://lithub.com/rebecca-solnit-life-inside-this-strange-new-fairytale-doesnt-have-to-be-lonely/.

91. Berry, *Life Is a Miracle: An Essay Against Modern Superstition* (Washington, DC: Counterpoint, 2000), 13.

BIBLIOGRAPHY

Abram, David. *Becoming Animal: An Earthly Cosmology.* New York: Pantheon, 2010.

———. "Reciprocity and the Salmon: Water-Borne Reflections from the Northwest Coast." *Tikkun* 16, no. 1 (May/June 2001): 21–26, 54.

Abrams, Daniel M., and Haley A. Yaple. "Dynamics of Social Group Competition: Modeling the Decline of Religious Affiliation." *Physical Review Letters* 107, no. 8 (2011).

Ackerman, Diane. *The Human Age: The World Shaped By Us.* London: W. W. Norton, 2014.

Adams, David, and Margaret Adams Leeming. *A Dictionary of Creation Myths.* Oxford: Oxford University Press, 1995.

Adorno, Theodor W., and Max Horkheimer. *Dialectic of Enlightenment.* Translated by J. Cunningham. London: Verso, 1979. First published 1944.

Agamben, Georgio. "We Refugees." *Symposium: A Quarterly Journal in Modern Literatures* 49, no. 2 (1995): 114–119.

Albanese, Catherine L. *Nature Religion in America: From the Algonkian Indians to the New Age.* Chicago: University of Chicago Press, 1991.

Albrecht, Glenn, Gina-Maree Sartore, Linda Connor, Nick Higginbotham, Sonia Freeman, Brian Kelly, Helen Stain, Anne Tonna, and Georgia Pollard. "Solastalgia: The Distress Caused by Environmental Change." Supplement, *Australasian Psychiatry* 15, no. 1 (February 2007): S95–98. https://doi.org/10.1080/10398560701701288.

Allendorf, Fred W., and Gary H. Thorgaard. "Tetraploidy and Evolution of Salmonid Fishes." In *Evolutionary Genetics of Fishes*, edited by B. J. Turner, 1–53. New York: Plenum, 1984.

Ammerman, Nancy T. *Everyday Religion: Observing Modern Religious Lives*. Oxford: Oxford University Press, 2007.

Andersen, Ross. "Welcome to Pleistocene Park." *The Atlantic*, April 2017.

Andersen, Susan M., and Serena Chen, "The Relational Self: An Interpersonal Social-Cognitive Theory." *Psychological Review* 109, no. 4 (2002): 619–645.

Asavei, Maria Alena. *Art, Religion and Resistance in (Post-)Communist Romania: Nostalgia for Paradise Lost*. New York: Palgrave Macmillan, 2020.

Augustine. *On the Trinity*. In *Nicene and Post-Nicene Fathers of the Christian Church*, vol. III, edited by Philip Schaff. Grand Rapids: William B. Eerdmans, 1980.

Babylonian Talmud. Seder Kodashim, *Chullin*, 127a. William Davidson edition, translated by Rabbi Adin Even-Israel Steinsaltz.

Bacher, Wilhelm, and Jacob Zallel Lauterbach. "Psalms, Midrash to (Midrash Tehillim)." In *Jewish Encyclopedia*, edited by Isidore Singer and Isaac K. Fund. New York: Funk and Wagnalls, 1906.

Baldwin, Andrew. "The Political Theologies of Climate Change-Induced Migration." *Critical Studies on Security* 2, no. 2 (2014): 210–222.

Baldwin, Andrew, and Giovanni Bettini, eds. *Life Adrift: Climate Change, Migration, Critique*. London: Rowman and Littlefield, 2017.

Ballif, Michelle. "Regarding the Dead." *Philosophy & Rhetoric* 47, no. 4 (2014): 455–471.

Barnard, John Levi. "The Bison and the Cow: Food, Empire, Extinction." *American Quarterly* 72, no. 2 (June 2020): 377–401.

Barnosky, Anothony D., Elizabeth A. Hadly, Jordi Bascompte, Eric L. Berlow, James H. Brown, Mikael Fortelius, Wayne M. Getz et al. "Approaching a State Shift in Earth's Biosphere." *Nature*, 486 (2012): 52–58.

Barrow, Mark V. *Nature's Ghosts: Confronting Extinction from the Age of Jefferson to the Age of Ecology*. Chicago: University of Chicago Press, 2009.

Baskin, Cindy. *Strong Helpers' Teachings: The Value of Indigenous Knowledges in the Helping Professions*. Toronto: Canadian Scholars' Press, 2011.

Bastian, Michelle. "Encountering Leatherbacks in Multispecies Knots of Time." In *Extinction Studies: Stories of Time, Death and Generations*, edited by Deborah Bird Rose, Thom van Dooren, and Matthew Chrulew, 149–185. New York: Columbia University Press, 2017.

Bauman, Whitney A. *Religion and Ecology: Developing a Planetary Ethic*. New York: Columbia University Press, 2014.

Bayard, Trina S., and Chris S. Elphick. "Planning for Sea-Level Rise: Quantifying Patterns of Saltmarsh Sparrow (*Ammodramus Caudacutus*)

Nest Flooding Under Current Sea-Level Conditions." *The Auk* 128, no. 2 (April 2011): 393–403.

Bednarsek, N., G. A. Tarling, D. C. E. Bakker, S. Fielding, E. M. Jones, H. J. Venables, P. Ward et al. "Extensive Dissolution of Live Pteropods in the Southern Ocean." *Nature Geoscience* 5 (2012): 881–885. https://www.nature.com/articles/ngeo1635.

Behringer, Wolfgang. *Witches and Witch-Hunts: A Global History.* Cambridge, UK: Polity, 2004.

Bell, Catherine. *Ritual Theory, Ritual Practice.* Oxford: Oxford University Press, 1992.

Bendell, Jem. "Deep Adaptation: A Map for Navigating Climate Tragedy." Rev. 2nd ed. Initiative for Leadership and Sustainability paper, July 27, 2020. https://www.lifeworth.com/deepadaptation.pdf.

Benton-Benai, Edward. *The Mishomis Book: The Voice of the Ojibway.* Minneapolis: University of Minnesota Press, 2010.

Berger, Martin. "Is Farmed Salmon Really Salmon?" *Nautilus* 30 (November 26, 2015). https://nautil.us/is-farmed-salmon-really-salmon-235688/.

Berger, Peter. "A Bleak Outlook Is Seen for Religion." *New York Times*, February 25, 1968.

———. *The Desecularization of the World: An Overview.* Grand Rapids: Eerdmans, 1999.

Bergmann, Sigurd. "Places of Encounter with the Eschata: Accelerating the Spatial Turn in Eschatology." In *Embracing the Ivory Tower and Stained Glass Windows*, edited by Jennifer Baldwin. New York: Springer, 2016.

———. *Religion, Space, and the Environment.* London: Routledge, 2017.

Bergmann, Sigurd, et al., eds. *Nature, Space and the Sacred: Transdisciplinary Perspectives.* Aldershot: Ashgate, 2009.

Berman, Marshall. *All That Is Solid Melts into Air: The Experience of Modernity.* London: Verso, 1988.

Bernstein, Ellen. *The Splendor of Creation: A Biblical Ecology.* Cleveland: Pilgrim, 2005.

Berry, Thomas. *The Dream of the Earth.* San Francisco: Sierra Club, 1988.

———. *The Great Work: Our Way into the Future.* New York: Bell Tower, 1999.

Berry, Wendell. "Faustian Economics." *Harper's Magazine*, May 2008. https://harpers.org/archive/2008/05/faustian-economics/.

———. *Life Is a Miracle: An Essay Against Modern Superstition.* Washington, DC: Counterpoint, 2000.

———. "The Long-Legged House." In *The Long-Legged House*, 123–191. Berkeley: Counterpoint, 2012.

———. "The Pleasures of Eating." In *The World-Ending Fire: The Essential Wendell Berry*, edited by Paul Kingsnorth. Berkeley: Counterpoint, 2018.

Bielo, David. "Will We Kill Off Today's Animals If We Revive Extinct Ones?" *Scientific American*, March 19, 2013. https://www.scientificamerican.com/article/de-extinction-to-bring-back-extinct-species-but-challenges-conservation/.

Bird-David, Nurit. "Animism Revisited: Personhood, Environment, and Relational Epistemology." *Current Anthropology* 40 (1999): 67–79.

———. "Beyond the Original Affluent Society: A Culturalist Reformulation." *Current Anthropology* 33, no. 1 (1992): 25–47.

Blackburn, Carole. *Harvest of Souls: The Jesuit Missions and Colonialism in North America, 1632–1650*. Montreal: McGill–Queen's University Press, 2000.

Blackstock, Cindy. "The Occasional Evil of Angels: Learning from the Experiences of Aboriginal Peoples and Social Work." *International Indigenous Journal of Entrepreneurship, Advancement, Strategy, and Education* 1, no. 1 (2009): 1–24.

Blumenberg, Hans. *The Legitimacy of the Modern Age*. Translated by Robert M. Wallace. Cambridge, MA: MIT Press, 1985.

Bloch, Ernst. *The Principle of Hope*, vol. 2. Translated by Neville Plaice, Paul Knight, and Stephen Plaice. Cambridge, MA: Harvard University Press, 1995.

Boff, Leonardo. "Alternate Earth Charter," *Petropolis*, November 13, 1998. https://cartadelatierra.org/wp-content/assets/virtual-library2/images/uploads/Alternate%20Earth%20Charter%20Proposal.pdf.

Bonneuil, Christophe. "The Geological Turn: The Anthropocene and Its Narratives." In *The Anthropocene and the Global Environmental Crisis: Rethinking Modernity in a New Epoch*, edited by Clive Hamilton, Christophe Bonneuil, and Francois Gemmene, 17–31. New York: Routledge, 2015.

Bowker, John, and Jean Holm, eds. *Rites of Passage*. London: Pinder, 1994.

Bowman, Marion. "Ancient Avalon, New Jerusalem, Heart Chakra of Planet Earth: The Local and the Global in Glastonbury." *Numen International Review for the History of Religions* 52, no. 2 (2005): 157–190.

———. "Belief, Legends and Perceptions of the Sacred in Contemporary Bath." *Folklore* 109 (1998): 24–31.

———. "'The Need for Healing': A Case Study in Bath." In *Healing and Religion*, edited by Marion Bowman, 96–97. Enfield Lock: Hisarlik, 2009.

———. "A Tale of Two Celticities: Sacred Springs, Legendary Landscapes and Celtic Revival in Bath." *Journal for the Academic Study of Religion* 20, no. 1 (2007): 95–117.

———. "Vernacular Religion, Contemporary Spirituality and Emergent Identities: Lessons from Lauri Honko." *Approaching Religion* 4, no. 1 (2014): 101–113.

Bowman, Marion, and Tiina Sepp. "Caminoisation and Cathedrals: Replication and the Heritagisation of Religion." *Religion* 49, no. 1 (2019).

Brace, Catherine, and Hilary Geoghegan. "Human Geographies of Climate Change: Landscape, Temporality, and Lay Knowledges." *Progress in Human Geography* 35, no. 3 (2010).

Brand, Stewart. "Rethinking Extinction." *Aeon Magazine*, accessed August 6, 2022. https://aeon.co/essays/we-are-not-edging-up-to-a-mass-extinction.

———. *Whole Earth Discipline*. New York: Viking, 2009.

Brantlinger, Patrick. *Dark Vanishings: Discourse on the Extinction of Primitive Races, 1800–1930*. Ithaca, NY: Cornell University Press, 2003.

Braude, William, trans. *The Midrash on Psalms*. New Haven, CT: Yale University Press, 1959.

"Britain's Original Natural Thermal Spa." Thermae Bath Spa, accessed June 1, 2019. https://web.archive.org/web/20211027123629/https://www.thermaebathspa.com/news-info/about-the-spa/spa-history/.

Brockman, John. "Constructive Biology: George Church." Edge.org, June 26, 2006. http://www.edge.org/3rd_culture/church06/church06_index.html.

———. "We Are as Gods and Have to Get Good at It." Edge.org, August 18, 2009. https://www.edge.org/conversation/stewart_brand-we-are-as-gods-and-have-to-get-good-at-it.

Browning, Heather. "Won't Somebody Please Think of the Mammoths? De-extinction and Animal Welfare." *Journal of Agricultural and Environmental Ethics* 31 (2018): 785–803.

Bugbee, Henry. "A Way of Reading the Book of Job." In *Wilderness in America: Philosophical Writings*, edited by David Rodick. New York: Fordham University Press, 2017.

Bullen, Jamie. "Extinction Rebellion: Shell HQ Windows Smashed as Climate Protest Blocks London Roads." *The Telegraph*, April 16, 2019. https://www.telegraph.co.uk/news/2019/04/15/extinction-rebellion-activists-threaten-bring-london-standstill/.

Burrus, Virginia. *Ancient Christian Ecopoetics: Cosmologies, Saints, Things*. Philadelphia: Pennsylvania University Press, 2019.

Cafaro, Philip. "Three Ways to Think About the Sixth Mass Extinction." *Biological Conservation* 192 (December 2015): 387–393.
Campbell, Douglas Ian, and Patrick Michael Whittle. *Resurrecting Extinct Species: Ethics and Authenticity*. Cham, CH: Palgrave Macmillan, 2017.
Capaldi, Colin A., Holli-Anne Passmore, Elizabeth K. Nisbet, John M. Zelenski, and Raelyne L. Dopko. "Flourishing in Nature: A Review of the Benefits of Connecting with Nature and Its Application as a Wellbeing Intervention." *International Journal of Wellbeing* 5, no. 4 (2015): 1–16.
Carlson, Colin J., Kevin R. Burgio, Eric R. Dougherty, Anna J. Phillips, Veronica M. Bueno, Christopher F. Clements, Giovanni Castaldo et al. "Parasite Biodiversity Faces Extinction and Redistribution in a Changing Climate." *Science Advances* 3, no. 9 (September 2017). https://doi.org/10.1126/sciadv.1602422.
Carrington, Damian. "Humanity Is 'Cutting Down the Tree of Life,' Warn Scientists." *The Guardian*, October 15, 2018.
———. "Plastic Pollution Discovered at Deepest Point of Ocean." *The Guardian*, December 20, 2018. https://www.theguardian.com/environment/2018/dec/20/plastic-pollution-mariana-trench-deepest-point-ocean.
Ceballos, Gerardo, Paul Ehrlich, and Rodolfo Dirzo. "Biological Annihilation via the Ongoing Sixth Mass Extinction Signaled by Vertebrate Population Losses and Declines." *Proceedings of the National Academy of Sciences* 114, no. 30 (July 10, 2017): E6089–E6096.
Chalier, Catherine. *La nuit, le jour: au diapason de la creation*. Paris: Editions de Sueil, 2009.
Chen, Angela. "Will Bringing Back the Woolly Mammoth Save Humanity from Itself? A Chat with Author Ben Mezrich about Bringing Back Long-Extinct Animals." *The Verge*, July 27, 2017.
Christie, Douglas E. *The Blue Sapphire of the Mind: Notes for a Contemplative Ecology*. Oxford: Oxford University Press, 2013.
———. "The Night Office: Loss, Darkness, and the Practice of Solidarity." *Anglican Theological Review* 99, no. 2 (Spring 2017): 211–232.
Chrulew, Matthew. "Saving the Golden Lion Tamarin." In *Extinction Studies: Stories of Time, Death, and Generations*, edited by Deborah Bird Rose, Thom van Dooren, and Matthew Chrulew, 49–88. New York: Columbia University Press, 2017.
Chryssides, George D., and Benjamin E. Zeller, eds. *Bloomsbury Companion to New Religious Movements*. New York: Bloomsbury, 2014.
Church, George, and Ed Regis. *Regenesis: How Synthethic Biology Will Reinvent Nature and Ourselves*. New York: Basic Books, 2012.

Clark, Nigel. "Strangers on a Strange Planet: On Hospitality and Holocene Climate Change," in *Life Adrift: Climate Change, Migration, Critique*, edited by Andrew Baldwin and Giovanni Bettini, 134. London: Rowman and Littlefield, 2017.

Cohen, Shlomo. "The Ethics of De-Extinction." *Nanoethics* 8 (2014): 165–178.

Colebrook, Claire. "Transcendental Migration: Taking Refuge from Climate Change." In *Life Adrift: Climate Change, Migration, Critique*, edited by Andrew Baldwin and Giovanni Bettini, 115–130. London: Rowman and Littlefield, 2017.

Coleman, Simon, and Marion Bowman, eds. "Religion in Cathedrals: Pilgrimage, Place, Heritage, and the Politics of Replication." Special issue, *Religion* 49 (1): 74–98.

Cone, James H. "Whose Earth Is It Anyway?" *CrossCurrents* 50, no. 1/2 (Spring/Summer 2000): 36–46.

Connolly, William E. *Facing the Planetary: Entangled Humanism and the Politics of Swarming*. Durham, NC: Duke University Press, 2017.

Conradie, Ernst. *An Ecological Christian Apology*. London: Routledge, 2016.

Correll, Maureen D., Whitney A. Wiest, Thomas P. Hodgman, W. Gregory Shriver, Chris S. Elphick, Brian J. McGill, Kathleen M. O'Brien, and Brian J. Olsen. "Predictors of Specialist Avifaunal Decline in Coastal Marshes." *Conservation Biology* 31, no. 1 (February 2017): 172–182.

Crist, Eileen. "Cloning in Restorative Perspective." In *Restoration and History: The Search for a Usable Environmental Past*, edited by Marcus Hall, 284–292. New York: Routledge, 2009.

———. "On the Poverty of Our Nomenclature." *Environmental Humanities* 3 (2013): 129–147.

Crockford, Susannah. "Thank God for the Greatest Country on Earth: White Supremacy, Vigilantes, and Survivalists in the Struggle to Define the American Nation." *Religion, State and Society* 46, no. 3 (2018): 224–242.

Cronon, William. "The Trouble with Wilderness: Or, Getting Back to the Wrong Nature." *Environmental History* 1, no. 1 (January 1996): 7–28.

Czajka, Agnes, and Aine O'Brien, eds. *Art, Migration and the Production of Radical Democratic Citizenship*. London: Rowman and Littlefield International, 2021.

Danowski, Déborah, and Eduardo Viveiros Castro. *The Ends of the World*. Cambridge, UK: Polity Press, 2017.

Darwin, Erasmus. *The Temple of Nature; or, The Origin of Society*. Canto 1, "The Production of Life," lines 295–302. London: T. Bentley, 1803.

Produced for Project Gutenberg by Stephen Gibbs and Christine P. Travers, October 9, 2008. http://www.gutenberg.org/files/26861/26861-h/26861-h.htm.

Davidsen, Markus A. "The Spiritual Milieu Based on J. R. R. Tolkien's Literary Mythology." In *Handbook of Hyper-real Religions*, edited by Adam Possamai. Leiden: Brill, 2012.

Davie, Grace. *Religion in Britain: A Persistent Paradox*. Malden, MA: Wiley-Blackwell, 1994.

Davies, Douglas. *Emotion, Identity, and Religion: Hope, Reciprocity, and Otherness*. Oxford: Oxford University Press, 2011.

Dawson, Ashley. *Extinction: A Radical History*. New York: OR Books, 2016.

Deane-Drummond, Celia. *Eco-Theology*. London: Darton, Longman and Todd, 2008.

Delahaye, Pauline. "Ritual Mimicry: A Path to Concept Comprehension." *Biosemiotics* 12, no. 1 (2019): 175–188.

Deloria, Vine, Jr. *C. G. Jung and the Sioux Traditions: Dreams, Visions, Nature, and the Primitive*. New Orleans: Spring Journal, 2016.

———. *God Is Red: A Native View of Religion*. Golden, CO: Fulcrum, 1994.

DeMello, Margo, ed. *Mourning Animals: Rituals and Practices Surrounding Animal Death*. East Lansing: Michigan State University Press, 2016.

Denyer, Simon, and Chris Mooney. "The Climate Chain Reaction that Threatens the Heart of the Pacific." *Washington Post*, November 12, 2019. https://web.archive.org/web/20230328011649/https://www.washingtonpost.com/graphics/2019/world/climate-environment/climate-change-japan-pacific-sea-salmon-ice-loss/.

Derrida, Jacques. "Fors: Les Mots Anglés De Nicolas Abraham Et Maria Torok." In *The Wolf Man's Magic Word: A Cryptonymy*. Minneapolis: University of Minnesota Press, 1986.

Desforges, Jean-Pierre, Ailsa Hall, Bernie McConnell, Aqqalu Rosing-Asvid, Jonathan L. Barber, Andrew Brownlow, Sylvain De Guise et al. "Predicting Global Killer Whale Population Collapse from PCB Pollution." *Science* 361, no. 6409 (2018): 1373–1376. https://science.sciencemag.org/content/361/6409/1373.

Despret, Vinciante. "It Is an Entire World That Has Disappeared." Translated by Matt Chrulew. In *Extinctions Studies: Stories of Time, Death, and Generations*, edited by Deborah Bird Rose, Thom van Dooren, and Matt Chrulew. New York: Columbia University Press, 2017.

Díaz, Sandra, Josef Settele, Eduardo Brondízio, Hien T. Ngo, Maximilien Guèze, John Agard, Almut Arneth et al. "Summary for Policymakers of the Global Assessment Report on Biodiversity and Ecosystem Services of the Intergovernmental Science-Policy Platform on Biodiversity and Ecosystem Services." Intergovernmental Science-Policy Platform on Biodiversity and Ecosystem Services (May 2019), accessed September 17, 2019. https://www.ipbes.net/news/Media-Release-Global-Assessment.

Dickason, Olive P. *The Myth of the Savage: And the Beginnings of French Colonialism in the Americas.* Edmonton: University of Alberta Press, 1984.

Dillard, Annie. *Teaching a Stone to Talk: Expeditions and Encounters.* New York: Harper Collins, 2009.

Dirzo, Rodolfo, Hillary S. Young, Mauro Galetti, Gerardo Ceballos, Nick J. B. Isaac, and Ben Collen. "Defaunation in the Anthropocene." *Science* 345, no. 6195 (July 2014): 401–406.

Doherty, Ben. "'Disaster Alley': Australia Could Be Set to Receive New Wave of Climate Refugees." *The Guardian,* April 4, 2017.

Dumont, Jim. "Onaubinisay at the 2018 World Parliament of Religions." YouTube video, posted November 26, 2018, accessed April 1, 2023. https://www.youtube.com/watch?v=AB-Fi31klTs.

Durkheim, Emile. *The Elementary Forms of the Religious Life.* Translated by Karen Fields. New York: Simon & Schuster, 1995.

Edgerton, W. Dow. "Asking About Who We Are." *Theology Today,* January 1, 1994.

Edwards, Denis. "Every Sparrow that Falls to the Ground: The Cost of Evolution and the Christ-Event." *Ecotheology: Journal of Religion, Nature & the Environment* 11, no. 1 (March 2006): 103–123.

Eliade, Mircea. *The Myth of the Eternal Return: Cosmos and History.* Princeton, NJ: Princeton University Press, 2005.

———. *The Sacred and the Profane: The Nature of Religion.* Translated by W. R. Trask. New York: Harcourt, Brace & World, 1959.

Elphick, Chris S., Susan Meiman, and Margaret A. Rubega. "Tidal-Flow Restoration Provides Little Nesting Habitat for a Globally Vulnerable Saltmarsh Bird." *Restoration Ecology* 23, no. 4 (July 2015): 439–446. https://doi.org/10.1111/rec.12194.

Environment Canada. "Bald Eagle Populations in the Great Lakes Region: Back from the Brink," 2001, accessed May 24, 2022. http://publications.gc.ca/collections/Collection/En40-222-13-2001E.pdf.

Estes, Nick. "Fighting for Our Lives: #NoDAPL in Historical Context." *Wicazo Sa Review* 32, no. 2 (2017): 115–122.

———. *Our History Is the Future: Standing Rock Versus the Dakota Access Pipeline, and the Long Tradition of Indigenous Resistance.* New York: Verso, 2019.

Estes, Nick, and Jaskiran Dhillon, eds. *Standing with Standing Rock*. Minneapolis: University of Minnesota Press, 2019.

Evans, Brad, and Julian Reid. *Resilient Life*. London: Polity, 2014.

Fagan, Brian. *The Little Ice Age: How Climate Change Made History, 1300–1850*. New York: Basic Books, 2001.

Faires, Nicole. "Can De-extinction Save Our Planet? An Interview with Brit Wray." Eartheasy, October 13, 2017. https://learn.eartheasy.com/articles/can-de-extinction-save-our-planet-an-interview-with-britt-wray/.

Farina, Almo, and Andrea Belgrano. "The Eco-field Hypothesis: Toward a Cognitive Landscape." *Landscape Ecology* 21, no. 1 (2006): 5–17.

Field, Christopher R., Trina S. Bayard, Carina Gjerdrum, Jason M. Hill, Susan Meiman, and Chris S. Elphick. "High-Resolution Tide Projections Reveal Extinction Threshold in Response to Sea-Level Rise." *Global Change Biology* 23, no. 5 (May 2017): 2058–2070. https://doi.org/10.1111/gcb.13519.

Figueres, Christiana. "Faith Leaders Need to Find Their Voice on Climate Change." *The Guardian*, May 7, 2014.

Fleischfresser, Stephen. "What Is De-extinction and How Do You Do It?" *Cosmos Magazine*, March 7, 2017. https://cosmosmagazine.com/nature/woolly-mammoth-what-is-de-extinction-and-how-do-you-do-it/.

Fletcher, Amy. "Genuine Fakes: Cloning Extinct Species as Science and Spectacle." *Politics and the Life Sciences* 29, no. 1 (March 2010): 48–60.

Francis I. *Laudato Si': On Care for Our Common Home*. Vatican City: Vatican Publications, 2015.

Francovich, Eli. "Salmon Spawning in Upper Columbia River for First Time in More Than Eighty Years." *The Wenatchee World: The Spokesman Review*, December 17, 2020. https://www.wenatcheeworld.com/news/salmon-spawning-in-upper-columbia-river-for-first-time-in-more-than-80-years/article_fbba53a4-4155-11eb-808d-6bc4189e0971.html.

Frazer, James George. *The Golden Bough: A Study in Magic and Religion*. London: Macmillan, 1960.

Freud, Sigmund. "Mourning and Melancholia." In *The Standard Edition of the Complete Psychological Works of Sigmund Freud*. Translated by James Strachey. London: Hogarth, 1966.

Friedlander, Gerald. Translated by Pirkei de Rabbi Eliezer. Skokie, IL: Varda, 2004.

Galbraith, R. J. "Quebec's Bald Eagles Return from Verge of Extinction." *Montreal Gazette*, 2014. https://web.archive.org/web/20210126014003

/http://www.robertgalbraith.com/quebecs-bald-eagles-return-from-verge-of-extinction/.

Gebara, Ivone. *Out of the Depths: Women's Experience of Evil and Salvation*. Translated by Ann Patrick Ware. Minneapolis: Fortress, 2002.

Gemie, Sharif, and Brian Ireland. *The Hippie Trail: A History*. Manchester: Manchester University Press, 2017.

Gennep, Arnold van. *The Rites of Passage*. Chicago: University of Chicago Press, 1960.

Ghosh, Amitav. *The Great Derangement*. Chicago: Chicago University Press, 2017.

Giblett, Rod. *Postmodern Wetlands: Culture, History, Ecology*. Edinburgh: Edinburgh University Press, 1996.

Girard, René. *Violence and the Sacred*. London: Continuum, 2005. First published 1988.

Gittings, John A., Dionysios E. Raitsos, George Krokos, and Ibrahim Hoteit. "Impacts of Warming on Phytoplankton Abundance and Phenology in a Typical Marine Ecosystem." *Scientific Reports* 8, 2240 (2018). https://www.nature.com/articles/s41598-018-20560-5.

Glissant, Édouard. *Caribbean Discourse*. Charlottesville: University of Virginia Press, 1989.

Goethe. *Faust, Part One*. Translated by David Luke. Oxford: Oxford University Press, 1987.

———. *Faust, Part Two*. Translated by David Luke. Oxford: Oxford University Press, 1994.

Goldfarb, Ben. *Eager: The Surprising, Secret Life of Beavers, and Why They Matter*. White River Junction, VT: Chelsea Green, 2018.

Goodin, David K. "Abrahamic Religions and Climate Change: Tradition and Political (In)action." *Journal of the Council of Research for Religion* 2, no. 1 (2020): 92–107.

Graves, Jenny. "Saving DNA: The Frozen Ark Project." Australian Academy of Science, accessed August 6, 2022. https://www.science.org.au/curious/earth-environment/frozen-ark-project.

Grecequet, Martina, Jack DeWaard, Jessica J. Hellmann, and Guy J. Abel. "Climate Vulnerability and Human Migration in Global Perspective." *Sustainability* 9, no. 5 (2017): 720.

Greely, Henry T. "Is De-extinction Special?" *Hastings Center Report* (July/August 2017): 30–36.

Greenlaw, Jon S., Chris S. Elphick, William Post, and James D. Rising. "Saltmarsh Sparrow (*Ammospiza caudacuta*), Version 2.1." In *Birds of

North America, edited by Paul G. Rodewald. Ithaca, NY: Cornell Lab of Ornithology, 2018.

Greer, Allan, ed. *The Jesuit Relations: Natives and Missionaries in Seventeenth-Century North America*. Boston: Bedford/St. Martin's, 2000.

Greely, Henry T. "De-Extinction: Hubris or Hope?" YouTube, April 1, 2013, accessed August 6, 2022. https://www.youtube.com/watch?v=HuRkoV2LoMY.

Greer, Allan. *Mohawk Saint: Catherine Tekakwitha and the Jesuits*. Oxford: Oxford University Press, 2006.

Gregersen, Niels Henrik. "The Cross of Christ in an Evolutionary World." *Dialog* 40, no. 3 (Fall 2001): 192–207.

———. "The Extended Body of Christ: Three Dimensions of Deep Incarnation." In *Incarnation: On the Scope and Depth of Christology*, edited by Niels Henrik Gregersen, 225–251. Minneapolis: Fortress, 2015.

Griggs, Mary Beth. "No, the Woolly Mammoth Won't Actually Be Resurrected by 2019." *Popular Science*, February 17, 2017. https://www.popsci.com/wooly-mammoth-will-not-be-resurrected-in-two-years/.

Grunwald, Michael. "Will Your Next Salmon Come from a Massive Land Tank in Florida?" *Politico*, July 16, 2020. https://www.politico.com/news/agenda/2020/07/14/florida-bluehouse-fish-farm-352495.

Gudynas, Eduardo. "Religion and Cosmovisions Within Environmental Conflicts and the Challenge of Ontological Openings." In *Church, Cosmovision and the Environment*, edited by Evan Berry and Robert Albro, 225–247. New York: Routledge, 2018.

Guha, Ramachandra. "Radical American Environmentalism: A Third World Critique." *Environmental Ethics* 11 (1989): 71–89.

Gunkel, Hermann. *Creation and Chaos in the Primeval Era and the Eschaton: A Religio-historical Study of Genesis 1 and Revelation*. Translated by K. William Whitney Jr. Grand Rapids: Eerdmans, 2007.

Habermas, Jürgen. "Religion in the Public Sphere." Paper presented at the Fourth Annual Kyoto Laureate Symposium, University of San Diego, CA, March 4, 2005.

Hallmann, Caspar A., Martin Sorg, Eelke Jongejans, Henk Siepel, Nick Hofland, Heinz Schwan, Werner Stenmans et al. "More Than 75 Percent Decline Over 27 Years in Total Flying Insect Biomass in Protected Areas." *PLOS One* 12, no. 10 (October 2017). https://doi.org/10.1371/journal.pone.0185809.

Halter, Abbie. "Australia Could Face Waves of 'Climate Refugees.'" *Canberra Weekly*, October 25, 2021.

Haraway, Donna. *Staying with the Trouble: Making Kin in the Chthulucene.* Durham, NC: Duke University Press, 2016.
Harvey, Graham. *Animism: Respecting the Living World.* New York: Columbia University Press, 2006.
———. *Listening People, Speaking Earth: Contemporary Paganism.* London: Hurst, 1997.
Hatley, James. "Blood Intimacies and Biodicy: Keeping Faith with Ticks." In *Unloved Others: Death of the Disregarded in a Time of Extinction,* edited by Deborah Bird Rose and Thom van Dooren. *Australian Humanities Review* 50 (2011): 63–75.
———. "Telling Stories in the Company of Buffalo." *Environmental Philosophy* 13, no. 1 (Spring 2016): 105–122.
———. "Walking with Ōkami, the Large-Mouthed Pure God." In *Extinction Studies: Stories of Time, Death, and Generations,* edited by Deborah Bird Rose, Thom van Dooren, and Matthew Chrulew, 19–48. New York: Columbia University Press, 2017.
Havard, Gilles. *The Great Peace of Montreal of 1701: French-Native Diplomacy in the Seventeenth Century.* Montreal: McGill–Queen's University Press, 2001.
Heise, Ursula K. *Imagining Extinction: The Cultural Meanings of Endangered Species.* Chicago: University of Chicago Press, 2016.
Helleiner, Eric. "Think Globally, Transact Locally: Green Political Economy and the Local Currency Movement." *Global Society: Journal of Interdisciplinary International Relations* 14, no. 1 (2000): 35–51.
Hepburn, R. W. "Wonder." In *"Wonder" and Other Essays: Eight Studies in Aesthetics and Neighbouring Fields,* 131–154. Edinburgh: University of Edinburgh Press, 1984.
Herczeg, Rabbi Yisrael Isser Zvi, Yaakov Petroff, and Yoseph Kamenetsky, ed. and trans. *Rashi: Sepher Berishit (The Torah with Rashi's Commentary Translated, Annotated, and Elucidated),* ArtScroll Series. Brooklyn: Mesorah, 1995.
Herlihy, David. *The Black Death, and the Transformation of the West.* Cambridge, MA: Harvard University Press, 1997.
Hill, Susan M. *The Clay We Are Made of: Haudenosaunee Land Tenure on the Grand River.* Winnipeg: University of Manitoba Press, 2017.
Hine, Dougald, and Paul Kingsnorth, "Uncivilisation: The Dark Mountain Manifesto." Dark Mountain Project, accessed May 24, 2022. https://dark-mountain.net/about/manifesto/.
Hobbs, R. J., Eric Higgs, and Carol M. Hall, eds. *Novel Ecosystems: Intervening in the New Ecological World Order.* Oxford: Wiley-Blackwell, 2013.

Hollenbach, David. "Religion and Forced Migration." In *The Oxford Handbook of Refugee and Forced Migration Studies*, edited by Elena Fiddian-Qasmiyeh, Gil Loescher, Katy Long, and Nando Sigona. Oxford: Oxford University Press, 2014.

Holmes, Rolston, III. "Values Gone Wlld." *Inquiry* 26 (1983): 181–207.

Horwitz, Nathaniel. "Heath Hen's Boom Could Echo Again on Martha's Vineyard." *MV Times*, July 16, 2014. http://www.mvtimes.com/2014/07/16/heath-hens-boom-echo-marthas-vineyard/.

"How Religion Has Changed in England and Wales." Office for National Statistics, June 4, 2015. https://www.ons.gov.uk/peoplepopulationandcommunity/culturalidentity/religion/articles/howreligionhaschangedinenglandandwales/2015-06-04.

Hubbell, J. Andrew. "A Question of Nature: Byron and Wordsworth." *The Wordsworth Circle* 41, no. 1 (2010): 14–18.

Hutton, Ronald. *Pagan Britain*. Oxford: Oxford University Press, 2013.

———. *The Triumph of the Moon: a History of Modern Pagan Witchcraft*. Oxford: Oxford University Press, 1999.

Ingold, Tim. "On the Social Relations of the Hunter-Gatherer Band." In *The Cambridge Encyclopedia of Hunters and Gatherers*, edited by R. B. Lee and R. Daly, 399–410. New York: Cambridge University Press, 1999.

Innis, Harold A. *The Fur Trade in Canada: An Introduction to Canadian Economic History*. Toronto: University of Toronto Press, 1999. First published 1930.

Interfaith Oceans. "About Us." Interfaith Oceans, accessed May 22, 2018. https://www.interfaithoceans.org/about-us.

Intergovernmental Panel on Climate Change. "Summary for Policymakers." October 8, 2018. https://www.ipcc.ch/2018/10/08/summary-for-policymakers-of-ipcc-special-report-on-global-warming-of-1-5c-approved-by-governments/.

Intergovernmental Science-Policy Platform on Biodiversity and Ecosystem Services. *Global Assessment Report on Biodiversity and Ecosystem Services of the Intergovernmental Science-Policy Platform on Biodiversity and Ecosystem Services*. Bonn: IPBES Secretariat, 2019.

International Union for Conservation of Nature. "Almost a Third of Lemurs and North Atlantic Right Whale now Critically Endangered—IUCN Red List." IUCN, July 9, 2020. https://www.iucn.org/news/species/202007/almost-a-third-lemurs-and-north-atlantic-right-whale-now-critically-endangered-iucn-red-list.

Ives, Chris, and Jeremy H. Kidwell. "Religion and Social Values for Sustainability." *Sustainability Science* 14 (February 19, 2019). https://doi.org/10.1007/s11625-019-00657-0.

Jackson, Zakiyyah Iman. *Becoming Human: Matter and Meaning in an Antiblack World*. New York: New York University Press, 2020.

Jacobs, Gae Ho Hwako Norma. *Q da gaho de:s: Reflecting on Our Journeys*. Edited by Timothy B. Leduc. Montreal: McGill–Queen's University Press, 2022.

Jenkins, Willis. "'Enemies of Humanity': Political Theology from the Pipelines." *Political Theology Network*, June 11, 2020. https://politicaltheology.com/enemies-of-humanity-political-theology-from-the-pipelines/.

———. "The Mysterious Silence of Mother Earth in Laudato Si'." *Journal of Religious Ethics* 46, no. 3 (September 2018): 441–462.

———. "Whose Religion? Which Ecology? Religious Studies in the Environmental Humanities." In *Routledge Handbook of Religion and Ecology*, edited by Willis Jenkins, Mary Evelyn Tucker, and John Grim, 44–54. New York: Routledge, 2016.

Jennings, Bruce. "The Moral Imagination of De-extinction." *Hastings Center Report* (July/August 2017): 54–59.

———. "Unnatural Selection." Center for Humans and Nature, June 21, 2017.

Jennings, Willie James. *The Christian Imagination: Theology and the Origins of Race*. New Haven, CT: Yale University Press, 2010.

Johnson, Elizabeth A. *Ask the Beasts: Darwin and the God of Love*. New York: Bloomsbury, 2014.

Jørgensen, Dolly. "Endling: The Power of the Last in an Extinction-Prone World." *Environmental Philosophy* 14, no. 1 (2017): 119–138.

Kanagy, C. L., and F. K. Willits. "A 'Greening' of Religion? Some Evidence from a Pennsylvania Sample." *Social Science Quarterly* 74, no. 3 (1993): 674–683.

Kane, Pandurang Vaman. *History of Dharmasastra: Ancient and Mediaeval Religious and Civil Law in India*, vol. I. Pune: Bhandarkar Oriental Research Institute, 2016. First published 1930.

Kearns, Laurel. "Noah's Ark Goes to Washington: A Profile of Evangelical Environmentalism." *Social Compass* 44, no. 3 (September 1997): 349–366.

Keller, Catherine. *Apocalypse Now and Then: A Feminist Guide to the End of the World*. Minneapolis: Augsburg Fortress, 2004.

———. *Face of the Deep: A Theology of Becoming*. London: Routledge, 2003.

———. *Facing Apocalypse: Climate, Democracy and other Last Chances.* New York: Orbis, 2021.

———. *On the Mystery: Discerning Divinity in Process.* Minneapolis: Fortress, 2008.

Keller, Catherine, and Mary-Jane Rubenstein, eds. *Entangled Worlds: Religion, Science, and New Materialisms.* New York: Fordham University Press, 2017.

Kennedy-Kish (Bell), Banakonda, Raven Sinclair, Ben Carniol, and Donna Baines. *Case Critical: Social Services and Social Justice in Canada*, 7th ed. Toronto: Between the Lines, 2017.

Ker-Lindsay, James. "Climate Change and State Death." *Survival: Global Politics and Strategy* 58, no. 4 (2016).

Khattab, Mustafa, trans. *The Clear Quran: A Thematic English Translation.* Bolingbrook, IL: Book of Signs Foundation, 2017.

Kibiten, Gaston. "Laudato Si's Call for Dialogue with Indigenous Peoples: A Cultural Insider's Response from the Christianized Indigenous Communities of the Philippines." *Solidarity: The Journal of Catholic Social Thought and Secular Ethics* 8, no. 1 (2019). https://researchonline.nd.edu.au/solidarity/vol8/iss1/4.

Kidwell, Jeremy H. "Mapping the Field of Religious Environmental Politics." *International Affairs* 96, no. 2 (March 2020). https://doi.org/10.1093/ia/iiz255.

———. "Re-enchanting Political Theology." *Religions* 10, no. 10 (September 2019): 550–564.

Kimmerer, Robin Wall. *Braiding Sweetgrass: Indigenous Wisdom, Scientific Knowledge and the Teachings of Plants.* Minneapolis: Milkweed, 2013.

Kingsnorth, Paul. "The Myth of Progress: An Interview with Paul Kingsnorth." *Emergence Magazine*, August 22, 2018. https://emergencemagazine.org/interview/the-myth-of-progress/.

Klein, Naomi, *The Shock Doctrine: The Rise of Disaster Capitalism.* Toronto: Random House of Canada, 2007.

Kotva, Simone. "Cosmopolitical Spiritualities of Deep Time: J. G. Ballard's Mystical Impulse." *Worldviews* 26, no. 3 (2022): 228–241.

Krantz, David. "Tehillat HaYam: A Psalm of the Sea." AYTZIM: Ecological Judaism, Resources, accessed September 13, 2019. https://web.archive.org/web/20220520045122/http://aytzim.org/resources/hayam/284.

Kuperus, Gerard. "Listening to Salmon: Latour's Gaia, Aboriginal Thinking and the Earth Community." *Environmental Philosophy* 16, no. 2 (2019): 379–395.

Ladurie, Emmanuel Le Roy. *Times of Feast, Times of Famine: A History of Climate Since the Year 1000*. Garden City, NY: Farrar Straus & Giroux, 1988.

LaPier, Rosalyn R. *Invisible Reality: Storytellers, Storytakers, and the Supernatural World of the Blackfeet*. Lincoln: University of Nebraska Press, 2017.

Lassander, Mika. "From Security to Self-Expression, the Emergent Value Pattern and the Changing Role of Religion." Unpublished PhD thesis, Milton Keynes, Open University, 2010.

Latour, Bruno. "Agency at the Time of the Anthropocene." *New Literary History* 45, no. 1 (Winter 2014): 1–18.

———. *Down to Earth: Politics in the New Climatic Regime*. Hoboken: John Wiley & Sons, 2018.

———. *Facing Gaia: Eight Lectures on the New Climatic Regime*. Hoboken: John Wiley & Sons, 2017.

Lawrence, Bonita. "Gender, Race, and the Regulation of Native Identity in Canada and the United States: An Overview." *Hypatia* 18, no. 2 (2003): 3–31.

Leduc, Timothy B. *A Canadian Climate of Mind: Passages from Fur to Energy and Beyond*. Montreal: McGill-Queen's University Press, 2016.

———. "Falling with Heron: Kaswen:ta Teachings on Our Roughening Waters." *Social and Cultural Geography* 21, no. 7 (2020): 925–939.

Lee, Martha F. *Earth First! Environmental Apocalypse*. Syracuse, NY: Syracuse University Press, 1995.

Lees, Alexander C., Simon Attwood, Jos Barlow, and Ben Phalan. "Biodiversity Scientists Must Fight the Creeping Rise of Extinction Denial." *Nature: Ecology and Evolution*, August 18, 2020. https://www.nature.com/articles/s41559-020-01285-z.pdf.

Legge, Marilyn. "Negotiating Mission: A Canadian Stance." *International Review of Mission* 93, no. 368 (2004): 119–130.

Leopold, Aldo. *Round River: From the Journals of Aldo Leopold*. Edited by Luna B. Leopold. Oxford: Oxford University Press, 1972.

Letcher, Andy. "'Gaia Told Me to Do It': Resistance and the Idea of Nature within Contemporary British Eco-Paganism." *Ecotheology: Journal of Religion, Nature and the Environment* 8, no. 1 (2003): 61–84.

———. "'If You Go Down to the Woods Today . . .': Spirituality and the Eco-Protest Lifestyle." *Ecotheology: Journal of Religion, Nature and the Environment* 7, no. 1 (2002): 81–87.

LeVasseur, Todd, and Anna Pearson, eds. *Religion and Ecological Crisis: The "Lynn White Thesis" at 50*. London: Routledge, 2016.

Levinas, Emmanuel. *Otherwise than Being, or Beyond Essence*. Translated by Alphonso Lingis. Pittsburgh: Duquesne University Press, 1998.
———. "To the Other." In *Nine Talmudic Readings*, edited by Annette Aronowicz. Bloomington: Indiana University Press, 1991.
Lien, Marianne Elisabeth. "Unruly Appetites: Salmon Domestication 'All the Way Down.'" In *Arts of Living on a Damaged Planet: Monsters of the Anthropocene*, edited by Anna Tsing, Heather Swanson, Elaine Gan, and Nils Bubandt. Minneapolis: University of Minnesota Press, 2017.
Lindström, Kati, Kalevi Kull, and Hannes Palang. "Landscape Semiotics: Contribution to Culture Theory." In *Estonian Approaches to Culture Theory*, edited by Valter Lang and Kalevi Kull, 110–132. Tartu: University of Tartu Press, 2014.
Logan, William Bryant. *Oak: The Frame of Civilization*. New York: Norton, 2005.
Lopes, Helena, and Teresa Calapez. "The Relational Dimension of Identity—Theoretical and Empirical Exploration." *Review of Social Economy* 70, no. 1 (2012): 81.
Lorbiecki, Marybeth. *A Fierce Green Fire: Aldo Leopold's Life and Legacy*, 2nd ed. Oxford: Oxford University Press, 2016.
Lorimer, Jamie. "Hookworms Make Us Human: The Microbiome, Ecoimmunology, and a Probiotic Turn in Western Health Care." *Medical Anthropology Quarterly* 33, no. 1 (March 2019): 60–79.
———. *Wildlife in the Anthropocene*. Minneapolis: University of Minnesota Press, 2015.
Luibhéid, Colm, and Paul Rorem, eds. *Pseudo-Dionysius: The Complete Works*, Classics of Western Spirituality, vol. 54. New York: Paulist, 1987.
Lysaght, Patricia., *The Banshee: The Irish Supernatural Messenger*. Dublin: O'Brian, 1986.
Marder, Elissa. "Mourning, Magic and Telepathy." *Oxford Literary Review* 30, no. 2 (December 2008): 181–200.
Marian, Simion Florea. *Înmormântarea la Romani*. Bucharest: Grai și Suflet, 1995.
Marris, Emma. "Moving on Assisted Migration." *Nature Climate Change* 1 (2008): 112–113.
"Mars & Beyond." SpaceX.com, accessed January 10, 2019.
Martinelli, Lucia, Markku Oksanen, and Helena Siipi. "De-extinction: A Novel and Remarkable Case of Bio-objectification." *Croatian Medical Journal* 55, no. 4 (August 2014): 423–427.
Matthews, Freya. "When the Media Won't Report the Environment, It's Time to Rethink the News." *The Conversation*, August 19, 2012. https://

theconversation.com/when-the-media-wont-report-the-environment-its-time-to-rethink-news-8862.

McDowall, R. M. "The Origin of Salmonid Fishes: Marine, Freshwater ... or Neither?" *Reviews in Fish Biology and Fisheries* 11 (2002): 171–179.

McFague, Sallie. *The Body of God: An Ecological Theology.* Minneapolis: Augsberg Fortress, 2006.

McFarland Taylor, Sarah. "No Planet B v. Disposable Planet: Self-Fulfilling Technocratic Apocalyptic Prophecies in the Marketing of Mars Colonization." International Society for the Study of Religion, Nature, and Culture conference, Cork, Ireland, June 2019.

McGilchrist, Ian. *The Master and His Emissary: The Divided Brain and the Making of the Western World*, new expanded ed. New Haven, CT: Yale University Press, 2019.

McKay, George. *Senseless Acts of Beauty: Cultures of Resistance since the Sixties*. London: Verso, 1996.

Medin, Douglas L., and Scott Atran, eds. *Folkbiology*. Cambridge, MA: MIT Press, 2000.

Medred, Craig. "Losing Salmon." CraigMedred.news, January 7, 2021. https://craigmedred.news/2021/01/07/losing-Salmon/.

Merchant, Carolyn. *The Death of Nature: Women, Ecology, and the Scientific Revolution*. San Francisco: Harper and Row, 1980.

Miao, Hannah, and Michael Sheetz. "Jeff Bezos Says First Spaceflight Was "Tiny Little Step" in Blue Origin's Plan to Build a Road to Space." *CNBC*, July 20, 2021. https://www.cnbc.com/2021/07/20/jeff-bezos-says-this-is-a-tiny-little-step-toward-blue-origins-plan-to-build-a-road-to-space.html.

Miller, Peter. "George Church: The Future Without Limits." *National Geographic*, June 2, 2014. https://www.nationalgeographic.com/science/article/140602-george-church-innovation-biology-science-genetics-de-extinction.

Miller, Timothy. *The 60s Communes: Hippies and Beyond*. Syracuse, NY: Syracuse University Press, 1999.

Mills, Charles W. *The Racial Contract*. Ithaca, NY: Cornell University Press, 1997.

Milman, Oliver. "Pizzly or Grolar Bear: Grizzly-Polar Hybrid Is a New Result of Climate Change." *The Guardian*, May 18, 2016.

Minteer, Ben. *The Fall of the Wild: Extinction, De-extinction, and the Ethics of Conservation*. New York: Columbia University Press, 2018.

Mirzoeff, Nicholas. "It's Not the Anthropocene, It's the White Supremacy Scene; or, the Geological Color Line." In *After Extinction*, edited by

Richard Grusin, 123–149. Minneapolis: University of Minnesota Press, 2018.

Mitchell, Audra. "Beyond Biodiversity and Species: Problematizing Extinction." *Theory, Culture and Society* 33, no. 5 (September 2016): 23–42.

———. "Decolonizing Against Extinction Part II: Extinction Is Not a Metaphor—It Is Literally Genocide." *Worldly*, September 27, 2017. https://worldlyir.wordpress.com/category/extinction/.

———. "Is IR Going Extinct?" *European Journal of International Relations* 23, no. 1 (2017): 3–25.

Mohawk, John. *Utopian Legacies: A History of Conquest and Oppression in the Western World*. Santa Fe, NM: Clear Light, 1999.

Morgan, Jan, and Graeme Garrett. *On the Edge: A-Way with the Ocean*. Reservoir: Morning Star, 2018.

Morton, Timothy. "Guest Column: Queer Ecology." *Proceedings of the Modern Language Association* 125, no. 2 (2010).

Mueller, Martin Lee. *Being Salmon Being Human: Encountering the Wild in Us and Us in the Wild*. White River Junction, VT: Chelsea Green, 2017

Naeem, Shahid. "Ecosystem Consequences of Biodiversity Loss: The Evolution Of A Paradigm." *Ecology* 83, no. 6: 2002.

Nash, James A. *Loving Nature: Ecological Integrity and Christian Responsibility*. Nashville: Abingdon, 1991.

———. "The Bible vs. Biodiversity: The Case Against Moral Argument from Scripture." *Journal for the Study of Religion, Nature & Culture* 3, no. 2 (2009): 213–237.

Nassar, Dalia. *The Romantic Absolute: Being and Knowing in Early German Romanticism: 1795–1804*. Chicago: Chicago University Press, 2014.

National Inquiry into Missing and Murdered Indigenous Women and Girls. "Reclaiming Power and Place: The Final Report," 2019, accessed May 24, 2022. https://www.mmiwg-ffada.ca/wp-content/uploads/2019/06/Final_Report_Vol_1a-1.pdf.

Newport, John. P. *The New Age Movement and the Biblical Worldview: Conflict and Dialogue*. Grand Rapids, MI: William B. Eerdmans, 1998.

Neyrat, Frédéric. *The Unconstructable Earth: An Ecology of Separation*. New York: Fordham University Press, 2019.

Nicholsen, Shelley. *Love of Nature and the End of the World*. Cambridge, MA: MIT Press, 2001.

Nita, Maria. "'An Altar inside a Circle': A Relational Model for Investigating Green Christians' Experiments with Sacred Space." In *Material Religion: The Stuff of the Sacred*, edited by Timothy Hutchings and Jo McKenzie, 133–151. London: Routledge, 2018.

———. "Balneoterapia în Europa." *Techirghiol* 4, no. 12 (October 2018). https://sbtghiol.ro/wp-content/uploads/2018/10/techirghiol12-site.pdf.

———. "Christian Discourses and Cultural Change: The Greenbelt Art and Performance Festival as an Alternative Community for Green and Liberal Christians." *Implicit Religion* 21, no. 1 (2018): 44–69.

———. "Humour, Concealment and Death Mindfulness in Romanian Funerals." *Contemporary Religion in Historical Perspective* (blog). Open University, 2018, accessed May 24, 2022. http://www.open.ac.uk/blogs/religious-studies/?p=676.

———. "'Inside Story': Participatory Storytelling and Imagination in Eco-pedagogical Contexts." In *Storytelling for Sustainability in Higher Education: An Educator's Handbook*, edited by Petra Molthan-Hill, Heather Luna, Tony Wall, Helen Puntha, and Denise Baden, 154–167. London: Routledge, 2020.

———. *Praying and Campaigning with Environmental Christians: Green Religion and the Climate Movement*. New York: Palgrave Macmillan, 2016.

———. "Spirituality in Health Studies: Competing Spiritualities and the Elevated Status of Mindfulness." *Religion and Health* 58, no. 1 (2019): 1605–1618. https://link.springer.com/article/10.1007/s10943-019-00773-2.

———. "Sky vs. Earthly Empowerment: From Angels and Superheroes to Humans and Community in the Marvel Universe and Green Christian Cosmology." *Journal of Religion and Popular Culture* 31, no. 3 (2019): 236–249.

———. "Where Are Extinction Rebellion's Cultural Roots?" *Contemporary Religion in Historical Perspective* (blog). Open University, 2019, accessed May 24, 2022. http://www.open.ac.uk/blogs/religious-studies/?p=980.

Nita, Maria, and Gemie Sharif. "Counterculture, Local Authorities and British Christianity at the Windsor and Watchfield Free Festivals (1972–5)." *Twentieth Century British History* 31, no. 1 (2020): 51–78.

Nongbri, Brent. *Before Religion: A History of a Modern Concept*. New Haven, CT: Yale University Press, 2013.

Northcott, Michael. *An Angel Directs the Storm*. London: Bloomsbury, 2004.

Northcott, Michael S. *Place, Ecology and the Sacred: The Moral Geography of Sustainable Communities*. New York: Bloomsbury, 2015.

Novak, Ben J. "Flights of Fancy." Project Passenger Pigeon, accessed August 6, 2022. http://passengerpigeon.org/Flights-Stories/Novak.html.

O'Brien, Kevin J. *An Ethics of Biodiversity: Christianity, Ecology, and the Variety of Life.* Washington, DC: Georgetown University Press, 2010.

O'Dell-Chaib, Courtney. "The Shape of This Wonder? Consecrated Science and New Cosmology Affects." *Zygon* 54, no. 2 (2019).

O'Hara, David. "Ash Wednesday, All Saints' Day, and the Bodies of Salmon, Given for You." Presented at the annual meeting of the Society for Nature, Philosophy, and Religion, Pittsburgh, PA, November 1, 2019.

Ontario Climate Consortium. "State of Climate Change Science in the Great Lakes Basin," 2014, accessed May 24, 2022. https://climate connections.ca/app/uploads/2014/07/OCC_GreatLakes_Report _Full_Final.pdf.

Oppermann, Serpil. "From Ecological Postmodernism to Material Ecocriticism: Creative Materiality and Narrative Agency." In *Material Ecocriticism,* edited by Serenella Iovino and Serpil Oppermann, 21–37. Bloomington: Indiana University Press, 2014

Osborn, Peter. *Politics of Time: Modernity and Avant-Garde.* London: Verso, 2011.

Otto, Rudolf. *Mysticism East and West: A Comparative Analysis of the Nature of Mysticism.* New York: Macmillan, 1932.

Parker, Laura. "6 Ways the Border Wall Could Disrupt the Environment." *National Geographic,* January 10, 2019.

Patton, Kimberley. *The Sea Can Wash Away All Evils: Modern Marine Pollution and the Ancient Cathartic Ocean.* New York: Columbia University Press, 2006.

Perret, Megan. "Extinction in Public." Presentation at online symposium hosted by University of Leeds, July 2020.

Phan, Peter C. "Embracing, Protecting, and Loving the Stranger: A Roman Catholic Theology of Migration." In *Theology of Migration in the Abrahamic Religions,* edited by Elaine Padilla and Peter C. Phan, 77–110. London: Palgrave Macmillan, 2014.

Pihkala, Panu. *Early Ecotheology and Joseph Sittler.* The Studies in Religion and the Environment series, vol. 12. Berlin: LIT Verlag Münster, 2017.

Pike, Sarah M. *For the Wild: Ritual and Commitment in Radical Eco-Activism.* Oakland: University of California Press, 2017.

Pirkei d'Rabbi Eliezer. Translated by Rabbi Gerald Friedlander. London: Keegan Paul, Trench, Turner & Co., 1916.

Plumwood, Val. *Feminism and the Mastery of Nature.* New York: Routledge, 1993.

Poveda, Oriol. "Religion in the Anthropocene: Nonhuman Agencies, (Re)enchantment and the Emergence of a New Sensibility." In *Routledge*

International Handbook of Religion in Global Society, edited by Jayeel Cornelio, François Guathier, Tuomas Martikainen, and Linda Woodhead, 469–477. New York: Routledge, 2020.

Powell, Miles A. *Vanishing America*. Cambridge, MA: Harvard University Press, 2016.

Preston, Christopher. "De-extinction: A Tale of Two Visions." *Humans and Nature*, September 9, 2015.

Primavesi, Anne. *Gaia's Gift*. London: Routledge, 2003.

Quill, Elizabeth. "These Are the Extinct Animals We Can, and Should, Resurrect." *Smithsonian Magazine*, May 2015. https://www.smithsonianmag.com/science-nature/these-are-extinct-animals-we-can-should-resurrect-180954955/.

Rappaport, Roy A. *Ritual and Religion in the Making of Humanity*. Cambridge, UK: Cambridge University Press, 1999.

Ray, Celeste. *The Origins of Ireland's Holy Wells*. Oxford, UK: Archaeopress, 2014.

Ray, Gene. "Resisting Extinction: Standing Rock, Eco-Genocide, and Survival." Accessed May 24, 2022. https://www.documenta14.de/en/south/25218_resisting_extinction_standing_rock_eco_genocide_and_survival.

Record, Nicholas R., Jeffrey A. Runge, Daniel E. Pendleton, William M. Balch, Kimberley T. A. Davies, Andrew J. Pershing, Catherine L. Johnson et al. "Rapid Climate-Driven Circulation Changes Threaten Conservation of Threatened Atlantic Right Whales." *Oceanography* (June 2019): 163–169.

Régnier, Claire, Guillaume Achaz, Amaury Lambert, Robert H. Cowie, Phillipe Bouchet, and Benoît Fontaine. "Mass Extinction in Poorly Known Taxa." *Proceedings of the National Academy of Sciences* 112, no. 25 (June 2015): 7761–7766.

Reid, Julian. "Climate, Migration, and Sex: The Biopolitics of Climate-Induced Migration." *Critical Studies on Security* 2, no. 2 (2004): 196–209.

Reid, Sîan. "Renovating the Broom Closet: Factors Contributing to the Growth of Contemporary Paganism in Canada." *The Pomegranate* 7, no. 2 (2005): 128–140.

Renner, Susanne S., and Constantin M. Zohner. "Climate Change and Phenological Mismatch in Trophic Interactions Among Plants, Insects, and Vertebrates." *Annual Review of Ecology, Evolution, and Systematics* 49 (November 2018): 165–182.

Renser, Berit, and Katrin Tiidenberg. "Witches on Facebook: Mediatization of Neo-Paganism." *Social media + society* 6, no. 3 (2020): 1–11.

Rice, Brian. *The Rotinonshonni: A Traditional Iroquoian History through the Eyes of Teharonhia:wako and Sawiskera*. New York: Syracuse University Press, 2013.

Rich, Nathaniel. "The Mammoth Cometh." *New York Times Magazine*, February 27, 2014. https://www.nytimes.com/2014/03/02/magazine/the-mammoth-cometh.html.

Richards, Robert J. *The Romantic Conception of Life: Science and Philosophy in the Age of Goethe*. Chicago: University of Chicago Press, 2002.

Riederer, Rachel. "The Woolly Mammoth Lumbers Back Into View." *The New Yorker*, December 27, 2018.

Rigby, Kate. "Animal Calls." In *Divinanimality: Animal Theory, Creaturely Theology*, edited by Stephen D. Moore, 116–133. New York: Fordham, 2014.

———. "Of Mice and Men and Surging Seas: Discerning Distributed Agency in Storm's *Der Schimmelreiter*." In ecocritical special issue, edited by Heather Sullivan and Bernhard Malkmus, *New German Critique* 128 (2016): 153–176.

———. *Reclaiming Romanticism: Towards an Ecopoetics of Decolonization*. London: Bloomsbury, 2020.

———. *Topographies of the Sacred: The Poetics of Place in European Romanticism*. Charlottesville: University of Virginia Press, 2014.

Roach, John. "Source of Half the World's Oxygen Gets Little Credit." *National Geographic*, June 7, 2004. https://www.nationalgeographic.com/news/2004/6/source-of-half-earth-s-oxygen-gets-little-credit/.

Rogers, S. A. "The Tree that Sparked the Revolutionary War: Eastern White Pine's Colonial History." 2013, accessed May 24, 2022. https://web.archive.org/web/20210411174223/https://easternwhitepine.org/the-tree-that-sparked-the-revolutionary-war-eastern-white-pines-colonial-history//.

Rose, Deborah Bird. "Double Death." Accessed March 1, 2019. https://web.archive.org/web/20190408065055/https://deborahbirdrose.com/144-2/.

———. *Reports from a Wild Country: Ethics for Decolonisation*. Sydney: University of New South Wales Press, 2004.

———. "Shimmer: When All You Love Is Being Trashed." In *Arts of Living on Damaged Planet: Ghosts and Monsters of the Anthropocene*, edited by Anna Tsing, 51–63. Minneapolis: University of Minnesota Press, 2017.

———. "Val Plumwood's Philosophical Animism: Attentive Interactions in the Sentient World." *Environmental Humanities* 3, no. 1 (May 2013): 93–109.

———. *Wild Dog Dreaming: Love and Extinction*. Charlottesville: University of Virginia Press, 2013.
Rose, Deborah Bird, Thom van Dooren, and Matthew Chrulew. *Extinction Studies: Stories of Time, Death, and Generations*. New York: Columbia University Press, 2017.
Rose, Deborah Bird, Thom van Dooren, Matthew Chrulew, Stuart Cooke, Matthew Kearnes, and Emily O'Gorman. "Thinking Through the Environment, Unsettling the Humanities." *Environmental Humanities* 1, no. 1 (May 2012): 1–5.
Rosenberg, Kenneth V., Adriaan M. Dokter, Peter J. Blancher, John R. Sauer, Adam C. Smith, Paul A. Smith, Jessica C. Stanton et al. "Decline of the North American Avifauna." *Science* 366, no. 6461 (October 2019): 120–124.
Rowlands, Anna. "The Suffering of Creation: Human and Nonhuman Migration." Panel at Radical Ecological Conversion after Laudato Si': Discovering the Intrinsic Value of All Creatures conference, Pontifical Gregorian University, Rome, March 8, 2018.
Rubenstein, Mary-Jane. *Strange Wonder: The Closing of Metaphysics and the Opening of Awe*. New York: Columbia University Press, 2008.
Ruggerone, Greg, and James Irvine. "Numbers and Biomass of Natural- and Hatchery-Origin Pink Salmon, Chum Salmon, and Sockeye Salmon in the North Pacific Ocean, 1925–2015." *Marine and Costal Fisheries: Dynamics, Management, and Ecosystem Science* 10 (2018): 152–168.
Sánchez-Bayo, Francisco, and Kris A. G. Wyckhuys. "Worldwide Decline of the Entomofauna: A Review of Its Drivers." *Biological Conservation* 232 (April 2019): 8–27.
Sandilands, Catriona, ed. *Rising Tide: Reflections for Climate Changing Times*. Halfway Moon Bay, BC: Caitlin, 2019.
Sandler, Ronald. "The Ethics of Reviving Long Extinct Species." *Conservation Biology* 28, no. 2 (2013): 354–360.
Schaefer, Donovan. *Religious Affects: Animality, Evolution, and Power*. Durham, NC: Duke University Press, 2015.
"The Scientist Trying to Reverse Extinctions (Think 'Jurassic Park')." FiveThirtyEight, November 25, 2015. https://fivethirtyeight.com/features/the-scientist-trying-to-reverse-extinctions-think-jurassic-park/.
Scott, Peter. "The Re-homing of the Human? A Theological Enquiry into whether Human Beings Are at Home on Earth." In *Christian Faith and the Earth: Current Paths and Emerging Horizons in Ecotheology*, edited by Ernst M. Conradie, 115–135. London: T&T Clark, 2014.

Seddon, Philip J. "The Ecology of De-extinction." *Functional Ecology* 31 (May 8, 2017): 992–995.

Serres, Michel, and Philippa Hurd. *Angels, a Modern Myth*. Paris: Flammarion, 1995.

Shapiro, Beth. "Pathways to De-extinction: How Close Can We Get to Resurrection of an Extinct Species?" *Functional Ecology* 31, no. 5 (2016): 996–1002.

Shapiro, Daniel L. "Relational Identity Theory: A Systematic Approach for Transforming the Emotional Dimension of Conflict." *American Psychologist* 65, no. 7 (2010): 634–645.

Shepard, Paul. *The Only World We've Got: A Paul Shepard Reader*. San Francisco: Sierra Club, 1996.

Sheridan, Joseph, and Daniel Longboat. "The Haudenosaunee Imagination and the Ecology of the Sacred." *Space and Culture* 9, no. 4 (2003): 375.

Sherkow, Jacob S., and Henry T. Greely. "What If Extinction Is Not Forever?" *Science Magazine* 340 (April 5, 2013): 32–33.

Shiva, Vandana. *Monocultures of the Mind*. London: Zed, 1993.

Shriver, W. Gregory, Kathleen M. O'Brien, Mark J. Ducey, and Thomas P. Hodgman. "Population Abundance and Trends of Saltmarsh (Ammodramus caudacutus) and Nelson's (A. nelsoni) Sparrows: Influence of Sea Levels and Precipitation." *Journal of Ornithology* 157, no. 1 (January 2016): 189–200.

Sideris, Lisa H. *Consecrating Science: Wonder, Knowledge, and the Natural World*. Oakland: University of California Press, 2017.

———. "Grave Reminders: Grief and Vulnerability in the Anthropocene." *Religions* 11, no. 6 (June 2020): 293–309.

———. "The Human as World-Maker: An Anthropocene Dogma." In *Christian Theology and the Modern Sciences*, T&T Clark Companion Series, edited by John Slattery. London: T&T Clark, 2020.

Silliman, Brian R., Brent B. Hughes, Lindsay C. Gaskins, Qiang He, M. Tim Tinker, Andrew Read, James Nifong, and Rick Stepp. "Are the Ghosts of Nature's Past Haunting Ecology Today?" *Current Biology* 28, no. 9 (2018): R533–534.

Sioui, Georges. *Histories of Kanatha: Seen and Told*. Ottawa: University of Ottawa Press, 2008.

———. *Huron-Wendat: The Heritage of the Circle*. Vancouver: University of British Columbia Press, 1999.

Skrimshire, Stefan. "Activism for End Times: Millenarian Belief in an Age of Climate Emergency." *Political Theology* 20, no. 6 (2019): 518–536.

———. "Climate Change and Apocalyptic Faith." *WIREs Climate Change* (2013).

———. "Extinction Rebellion and the New Visibility of Religious Protest." Open Democracy, May 12, 2019.

———. "Rewriting Mortality: A Theological Critique of Geoengineering and De-extinction." In *Calming the Storm: Theological and Ethical Perspectives on Climate Engineering*, edited by Forrest Clingerman and Kevin J. O'Brien, 103–126. London: Lexington, 2016.

Skrokosz, Meric, and Rebecca S. Watson. *Blue Planet, Blue God: The Bible and the Sea*. London: SCM, 2017.

Smith, Jonathan Z. "Religion, Religions, Religious." In *Critical Terms for Religious Studies*, edited by Mark C. Taylor, 269–284. Chicago: University of Chicago Press, 1998.

Sodikoff, Genese Marie, ed. *The Anthropology of Extinction*. Bloomington: Indiana University Press, 2012.

Solnit, Rebecca. "On Letting Go of Certainty in a Story that Never Ends." Literary Hub, April 23, 2020. https://lithub.com/rebecca-solnit-life-inside-this-strange-new-fairytale-doesnt-have-to-be-lonely/.

Soskice, Janet. "Creation and the Glory of Creatures." In *Being-in-Creation: Human Responsibility in an Endangered World*, edited by Brian Treanor, Bruce Ellis Benson, and Norman Wirzba, 143–158. New York: Fordham University Press, 2015.

———. "Why *Creatio ex nihilo* Today?" In *Creation ex nihilo: Origin, Development, Contemporary Challenges*, edited by Gary Anderson and Marcus Bockmuehl. South Bend: University of Notre Dame Press, 2018.

Southgate, Christopher. *The Groaning of Creation: God, Evolution, and the Problem of Evil*. Louisville, KY: Westminster John Knox, 2008.

———. "The New Days of Noah?" In *Creaturely Theology: On Gods, Humans, and Other Animals*, edited by Celia Deane-Drummond and David Clough. London: SCM, 2009.

Southgate, Christopher, Cheryl Hunt, and David Horrell. "Ascesis and Assisted Migration: Responses to the Effects of Climate Change on Animal Species." *European Journal of Science and Theology* 4 (2008): 99–111.

Starhawk, *Webs of Power: Notes from the Global Uprising*. Gabriola Island, BC: New Society, 2003.

St. John, Graham. "Protestival: Global Days of Action and Carnivalized Politics in the Present." *Social Movement Studies Journal* 7, no. 2 (2008): 167–190.

Stock, Timothy. "A Broken Fast in Advance: 'The Bread from My Mouth' as Ethical Transcendence and Ontological Drama." *Levinas Studies* 12 (2016): 165–184.

Stokes, Dale. *The Fish in the Forest: Salmon and the Web of Life*. Berkeley: University of California Press, 2014.

Stout, Adam. *Glastonbury Holy Thorn: Story of a Legend*. Glastonbury: Green & Pleasant, 2020.

Swart, Sandra. "Frankenzebra: Dangerous Knowledge and the Narrative Construction of Monsters." *Journal of Literary Studies* 30, no. 4 (December 2014): 45–70.

Szerszynski, Bronislaw. "Gods of the Anthropocene: Geo-Spiritual Formations in the Earth's New Epoch." *Theory, Culture & Society* 34, no. 2–3 (Spring 2017): 253–275.

Tanner, Kathryn. "Eschatology and Ethics." In *The Oxford Handbook of Theological Ethics*, edited by G. Meilaender and W. Werpehowski, 41–56. Oxford: Oxford University Press, 2010.

Taylor, Bron. *Dark Green Religion: Nature Spirituality and the Planetary Future*. Oakland: University of California Press, 2010.

Taylor, Bron, Gretel Van Wieren, and Bernard Daly Zaleha. "The Greening of Religion Hypothesis (Part Two): Assessing the Data from Lynn White, Jr., to Pope Francis." *Journal for the Study of Religion, Nature and Culture* 10, no. 3 (2016): 306–378.

Taylor, Charles. *A Secular Age*. Cambridge, MA: Harvard University Press, 2009.

Teresa of Avila. *The Life of Teresa of Jesus*. Translated and edited by E. A. Peers. New York: Image Books, 1960. First published in 1565.

Theriault, Noah, Timothy Leduc, Audra Mitchell, June Mary Rubis, and Norma Jacobs Gaehowako. "Living Protocols: Remaking Worlds in the Face of Extinction." *Social and Cultural Geography* 21, no. 7 (2020): 893–908.

Thomas, Jacob. *Teachings from the Longhouse*. Toronto: Stoddart, 1994.

Thomas, Keith. *Religion and the Decline of Magic: Studies in Popular Beliefs in Sixteenth and Seventeenth Century England*. Harmondsworth, UK: Penguin, 1973.

Thomas, Robert J., James O. Vafidis, and Renata J. Medeiros. "Climatic Impacts on Invertebrates as Food For Vertebrates." In *Global Climate Change and Terrestrial Invertebrates*, edited by Scott Johnson and T. Hefin Jones, 295–316. Oxford: Wiley Blackwell, 2017.

Thomas, Scott M. *The Global Resurgence of Religion and the Transformation of International Relations*. London: Palgrave Macmillan, 2005.

Thurman, Howard. *Jesus and the Disinherited*. Boston: Beacon Press, 1976. First published 1949.

Tinker, George E "Tink." *American Indian Liberation: A Theology of Sovereignty*. New York: Orbis, 2008.

Todd, Zoe. "Fish, Kin and Hope: Tending to Water Violations in Amiskwaciwâskahikan and Treaty Six Territory." *Afterall: A Journal of Art, Context and Enquiry* 43, no. 1 (Spring/Summer 2017): 102–107.

———. "Fish Pluralities: Human-Animal Relations and Sites of Engagement in Paulatuuq, Arctic Canada." *Études/Inuit/Studies* 38, no. 1–2 (2014): 217–238.

Townes, Emilie M. *Womanist Ethics and the Cultural Production of Evil*. New York: Springer, 2006.

Truth & Reconciliation Commission of Canada. "Executive Summary Report," 2015, accessed May 24, 2022. http://www.trc.ca/websites/trcinstitution/File/2015/Exec_Summary_2015_06_25_web_0.pdf.

Tsing, Anna Lowenhaupt, Heather Anne Swanson, Elaine Gan, and Nils Bubandt, eds. *Arts of Living on a Damaged Planet: Ghosts of the Anthropocene*. Minneapolis: University of Minnesota Press, 2017.

Tuan, Yi-fu. *Space and Place: The Perspective of Experience*. Minneapolis: University of Minnesota Press, 2005

Turner, Victor. *Ritual Process: Structure and Anti-Structure*. London: Aldin Transaction, 1969.

Tweed, Thomas A. *Crossing and Dwelling: A Theory of Religion*. Cambridge, MA: Harvard University Press, 2009.

UK Government. Joint Nature Conservation Committee, Special Areas of Conservation, River Avon, accessed May 14, 2019. http://jncc.defra.gov.uk/protectedsites/sacselection/sac.asp?EUCode=UK0013016.

University of California–Santa Cruz. "Alaska's Salmon Are Getting Smaller, Affecting People and Ecosystems." Phys.org, August 19, 2020. https://phys.org/news/2020-08-alaska-Salmon-smaller-affecting-people.html.

———. "Two Laws: Steps toward Decolonisation in the Shadow of the Anthropocene." For Global Ecologies—Local Impacts, 6th Biennial Conference of the Association for Study of Literature, Environment and Culture, Australia and New Zealand, Sydney, AU, November 23, 2014.

United Nations Environment Programme's Stockholm Convention. "Overview." Stockholm Convention, accessed December 12, 2020. http://chm.pops.int/implementation/industrialpops/pcbs/overview/tabid/273/default.aspx.

Valiente-Banuet, Alfonso, Marcelo A. Aizen, Julio M. Alcántara, Juan Arroyo, Andrea Cocucci, Mauro Galetti, María B. García et al. "Beyond Species Loss: The Extinction of Ecological Interactions in a Changing World." *Functional Ecology* 29, no. 3 (March 2015): 299–307.

Van Dooren, Thom. *Flight Ways: Life and Loss at the Edge of Extinction*. New York: Columbia University Press, 2014.

Van Dooren, Thom, Eben Kirksey, and Ursula Münster. "Multispecies Studies: Cultivating Arts of Attentiveness." *Environmental Humanities* 8, no. 1 (May 2016): 1–23.

Vatican News. "Pope's September Prayer Intention: For Protecting the Oceans." *Vatican News*, August 31, 2019. https://www.vaticannews.va/en/pope/news/2019-08/pope-francis-september-2019-prayer-intention-oceans.html.

Vondey, Wolfgang. "Religion as Play: Pentecostalism as a Theological Type." *Religions* 9, no. 3 (2018). https://doi:10.3390/rel9030080.

Von Schnurbein, Stefanie. *Norse Revival: Transformations of Germanic Neopaganism*. Leiden: Brill, 2016.

Wallace, Mark I. *When God Was a Bird: Christianity, Animism, and the Re-enchantment of the World*. New York: Fordham University Press, 2018.

Walzer, Michael. "Islamism and the Left." *Dissent* 62, no. 1 (Winter 2015).

Waples, Robin S., George R. Pess, and Tim Beechie. "Evolutionary History of Pacific Salmon in Dynamic Environments." *Evolutionary Applications* 1, no. 2 (May 2008): 189–206.

Weaver, Alain Epp, "On Exile: Yoder, Said, and a Theology of Land and Return." *Cross Currents* 52, no. 4 (2003): 3.

Welch, Craig. "Half of All Species Is on the Move." *National Geographic*, April 27, 2017. https://www.nationalgeographic.com/science/article/climate-change-species-migration-disease.

Westhelle, Vitor. *Eschatology and Space*. London: Palgrave, 2016.

Weston, Anthony. *Back to Earth: Tomorrow's Environmentalism*. Philadelphia: Temple University Press, 1994.

Weston, Kath. *Animate Planet: Making Visceral Sense of Living in a High-Tech Ecologically Damaged World*. Durham, NC: Duke University Press, 2017.

Whale, Helen, and Franklin Ginn. "In the Absence of Sparrows." *Mourning Nature: Hope at the Heart of Ecological Loss and Grief*, edited by Ashlee Consulo Willox and Karen Landman, 92–116. Montreal: McGill–Queen's University Press, 2017.

Wheatley, Patrick V., Hoyt Peckham, Seth D. Newsome, and Paul L. Koch. "Estimating Marine Resource Use by the American Crocodile *Crocodylus Acutus* in Southern Florida." *Marine Ecology Progress Series* 447 (2012): 211–229. https://doi.org/10.3354/meps09503.
White, Lynn, Jr. "The Historical Roots of our Ecological Crisis." *Science* 155 (1967): 1203–1207.
Whyte, Kyle Powys. "Indigenous Environmental Movements and the Function of Governance Institutions." In *Oxford Handbook of Environmental Political Theory*, edited by Teena Gabrielson, Cheryl Hall, John M. Meyer, and David Schlosberg, 563–580. Oxford: Oxford University Press, 2016.
———. "The Dakota Access Pipeline, Environmental Injustice, and US Colonialism." *Red Ink: An International Journal of Indigenous Literature, Arts, & Humanities* 19, no. 1 (Spring 2017).
Wilkins, John S. *Species: A History of the Idea*. The Species and Systematics series, vol. 1. Oakland: University of California Press, 2009.
Williams, Florence. "This Is Your Brain on Nature." *National Geographic Magazine*, January 2016. http://www.nationalgeographic.com/magazine/article/call-to-wild.
Williams, Linda. "Deep Time and Myriad Ecosystems: Urban Imaginaries and Unstable Planetary Aesthetics." In *The Aesthetics of the Undersea*, edited by Margaret Cohen and Killian Quigley, 167–179. London: Routledge, 2019.
Williams, Rowan. "Creation, Creatureliness, Creativity: The Wisdom of a Finite Existence." In *Being-in-Creation*, edited by Brian Treanor, Bruce Ellis Benson, and Norman Wirzba. New York: Fordham University Press, 2015.
———. "On Being Creatures." Eric Symes Memorial Lecture, delivered at Westminster Abbey, May 15, 1989.
Wilson, Edward O. "Beware the Age of Loneliness." *The Economist*, November 18, 2013.
World Wildlife Fund. Accessed May 14, 2019, https://www.worldwildlife.org/species/whale.
Wuerthner, George, Eileen Crist, and Tom Butler, eds. *Keeping the Wild: Against the Domestication of Earth*. Washington, DC: Island Press, 2014.
WWF-Canada. "Watershed Report: The St. Lawrence River," 2015, accessed May 24, 2022. http://watershedreports.wwf.ca/#sws-020/by/threat-overall/threat.

Yong, Ed. "The Last of Its Kind." *The Atlantic*, July 2019.
Yusoff, Katherine. "Biopolitical Economies and the Political Aesthetics of Climate Change." *Theory, Culture & Society* 27, no. 2–3 (2010): 73–99.
Zornberg, Avivah Gottlieb. *The Beginnings of Desire: Reflections on Genesis*. New York: Doubleday, 1995.

INDEX

Page numbers in italics denote figures.

the abject, 21, 93, 223, 257, 259
Abraham, Nicolas, 76
Abrahamic faiths: displacement, 198; Earth conceptualized as home, 178–79; fleeing persecution, 198; founding narratives, 198; "in exile," 181; making home for the stranger, 198; sojourning, 181, 191–93; willful extinction as a sin, 267. *See also* Christianity; Islam; Judaism
Abram, David, 252–53, 259–60, 262, 263, 264, 266–67, 278, 280, 290n37
Ackerman, Diane, 311–12, 322
activism: Christian environmental, 69, 90; constructing rituals of mourning, 77; private religion and, 63; the protestival, 113; Tolkienesque, 113. *See also* environmental activism; extinction activism; Standing Rock Sioux reservation uprising
Adorno, Theodor, 221
affect theory, 40
African peoples, 26
Agamben, Giorgio, 190
agriculture, 157, 194, 213, 216, 273–74
Akiva ben Yosef, 252, 254, 259
alligators, freshwater, 82

Amazon rainforest, 201
ambiguity, 5, 10, 321, 322
American Indian theologies, 31
anarchic differentiation, 288n15
animism, 47, 149
Antarctica, 184, 186, 203
Anthropocene: anti-racist criticism, 31; new era of solitude, 144; reimagination of a future nature, 311; science and godlike creation, 313; storytelling about, 294–95; unhousing plankton, 217; vulnerability, 270
Anthropocene boosterism, 293–94, 322–23
Anthropocene discourse, 48
anthropocentrism, 23, 28, 110, 223, 295, 309, 325
anthropogenic extinctions: benign acceptance, 89; as cataclysmic, 268; fetishization, 270; human complicity, 299–300; incarnation, 30; *Loving Nature* (Nash), 28; North Atlantic Christian theology and, 28; posing questions, 250–51; religious institutions and, 9, 202; responsibility for survival of other

366 INDEX

anthropogenic extinctions (*cont.*)
  species, 20; rights of all species to exist, 28
anthropogenic species metacide, 278–79
anthropological optimism, 73
anthropology, 47, 66, 72, 149, 153; extinction as issue of, 4. *See also* theological anthropology
anticipatory absence, 74–75
anti-racism, 22, 31
apocalypticism, 194, 270
apocalyptic narratives, 11, 105, 191, 193
Archer, Michael, 306, 318–19
arts of attentiveness, 51–52
Attenborough, David, 213–14
autonomy: being human, 259; creatureliness and, 256–58, 261–62; eating other creatures, 265–66, 274; of nature, 317; values, 258

Babylonian polytheism, 226
Bailey, Liberty Hyde, 28
Bath: Aquae Sulis, 103–4, 118; Extinction Rebellion protest ritual, 103, 124, 127, 131; heritization of religion, 118–19, 123–24, 127; sacred waters, 12, 120–22, 127, 215–16; Sulis, 214–15, 238–39; unhealthy waters, 215
Bauman, Whitney, A., 48
beavers, 150, 216
Bendell, Jem, 6
Berger, Peter, 65–66
Bernstein, Ellen, 251–52
Berry, Thomas, 152, 153, 154, 156, 157, 159
Berry, Wendell, 273–74, 323, 326
Bhaba, Homi, 205
biodiversity: ecological novelties, 83; effect of expansion of modern systems, 162; extinction discourses, 179; loss of, 232–33; in Noah's Ark, 29; novel ecosystems, 86, 185; things that affect, 181–82

biodiversity conservation, 183
bioethics, 299–300, 322
biopolitics, 20, 30, 185–6, 206, 309
biosemiotics, 101, 102, 122, 124
Bird-David, Nurit, 149, 153, 156
bison, 21, 22, 43
black collective trauma, 79
Black environmental imaginaries, 79
Black liberation theology, 22
Black Lives Matter movement, 25
Bloch, Ernest, 238
Blumenberg, Hans, 87
Boff, Leonardo, 201
Bowman, Marion, 240n1
Brand, Stewart, 296–97, 300, 306, 312, 316–17, 319
Brantlinger, Patrick, 74
Brébeuf, Jean de, 152, 153
brown bears, 249. *See also* polar bears
Burrus, Virginia, 236, 242–43n17

Cafaro, Philip, 41
Callière, Louis-Hector de, 140, 141, 147–48, 149
Campbell, Douglas Ian, 314–15
Canada: endangered species, 158; inaction on environmental issues, 155–56; National Inquiry into Murdered and Missing Indigenous Women and Girls (2019), 157; residential school system, 155, 157, 161, 162; Treaty of Niagara, 168–69
capitalism, 23–24, 217, 228, 309
care and connect rules, 44–45, 49
Casas, Bartolome de las, 72
cataclysm, 267–68, 275
Catholicism, 69, 152, 159
ceremonies: of death and grief, 169; Haudenosaunee Condolence, 169; looking at death, 170. *See also* rituals
cetaceans, 237. *See also* whales
chaos monster, 223, 228–29, 230. *See also* sea monsters

Charlevoix, Pierre-François-Xavier de, 146, 148, 152
Christian environmental ethics, 19–20
Christian ethics, 17, 18–19, 28, 32, 239
Christianity: Contemporary Paganism and, 131; conversion and colonialism, 161; creatio ex nihilo, 163–64, 242–43n17; creation as the abode for creaturely existence, 179; the Early Church, 114, 115; Eco-Paganism and, 116, 117–24; exceptionalism, 284; Extinction Rebellion (XR) and, 132; forced migration, 198; tehomophobia, 219–21; virginal origin stories, 152, 153. *See also* Abrahamic faiths; Catholicism
Christian theology: Christ as zero point, 87; mass extinction and, 19; the sparrow and white supremacy, 21, 22
Christie, Douglas E., 46–47
Chrulew, Matthew, 35, 36–37
Church, George, 302–3, 305, 312, 319, 325, 311 6
climate change: 2015 Paris Climate Accords, 99; affecting marine species, 216–17; anxiety over losing home, 179; desecularization of climate policy, 67; disappearance of Okjökull (glacier), 61; effects of, 142–43, 153–54; grolar bears, 83, 184; indicator of trouble with humanity: religious response required, 16; Indigenous forms of natural science, 70; in *Laudato Si'*, 32; migration due to, 182–83; mitigation of, 329n39; need to phase out fossil fuels, 143; neighbor love, 239; rehoming, 200; re-inhabitations and recolonization of ecosystems by creatures, 82–83; religious communities responsibilities, 206
climate movement, 127. *See also* Extinction Rebellion (XR)

cloning (SCNT). *See under* de-extinction
cobecoming, 164, 230–35, 239, 244n34. *See also* relational living
Colebrook, Claire, 187, 188, 189
colonial expansion: compared to creation, 228; reason for extinction, 143, 144; slavery, 154–55, 223; "time of Goethe" (Goethezeit), 221
colonialism: apologies for, 161; human as head of household, 186; proleptic elegies and, 74; relationship to extinction in Christian thought, 19–20; religion as driver of extinction, 12; Saltmarsh Sparrow and, 23–24; undermining agreement to live relationally, 151; weaponizing of creation narratives, 284; white exceptionalism, 30–31; white supremacy, 74. *See also* human exceptionalism; Indigenous peoples
colonial relations, 140–41, 142
colonial violence, 154; relationship to extinction, 158
colonization: disappearances as consequence of, 72; of Earth, 228; migration and, 187–88; of planets, 6–7, 193, 194
Cone, James, 22
Connolly, William, 44–45, 46, 49, 66
Conservation: assisted migration strategy, 180; on bio-sentinel species, 158; Brand on, 312, 316; connection to de-extinction, 304–5; de-extinction and, 307, 308, 315, 328n22; ecological novelties, 81–82, 84; marine mammals, 213, 216–17, 242n11; polar bear relocation, 184; of species based on loss, 193; synthetic biology's opposition to, 311. *See also* biodiversity conservation; environmental conservation; new conservationism

conservation biology, 81, 87–88
conservation science, 91–92, 143
consumerism, 152, 154, 156, 157
Contemporary Paganism: acceptance of death and decay, 100; Christianity and, 131; compared with Eco-Paganism, 116, 117, 122; Forest Church movement, 99; Gaia and the Spirit of Activism, 122, 123; Glastonbury, 115, 119, 121; identity narratives, 111–12, 115; as post-Christian movement, 98; resistance against secularization, 118–19; sacred springs, 101; view of death, 104–5
cosmopolitics, 42–43, 45, 46, 51–52
counterculture: humorous tone of protest rituals, 127–28; influence on Extinction Rebellion (XR), 99–100, 113–14, 130; relationship with Christianity, 116
covenant with creatures: approach to emergencies, 275–76; creaturely discernment, 275; eating and, 274; transhuman etiquette, 275
COVID-19 pandemic, 124–25, 129
cranes, 36–37, 150
creatio ex profundis, 163–64, 230–35
creation narratives: ambiguity in, 322; the believer as pilgrim on Earth, 191–92, 197; creatio ex nihilo, 163–64, 219–20, 242–43n17; Eco-Paganism origin story, 114–16; emergence of fish, 251; Hebrew, 225–28; of humans (Adam), 259–60; Indigenous, 234, 284; Jesuits origin story of Indigenous peoples, 153; made in the image of God, 227–28, 231; mimicked by de-extinction rhetoric, 321; oceanic origins of life, 231–35; privileging of permanence over transience, 220; Sky Woman's fall, 150, 152, 167–68; Sumerian, 226; *tohu va bohu*, 226, 234–35, 239, 289–90n32; virginal origin stories, 152, 153

creatureliness: autonomy and, 256–58, 261–62; *con-venire*, 265; de-extinction and, 318; as fact, 320; *in-venire*, 265; limited vs limitless, 323–24; moral imagination and, 322; wonder and, 324–25
the creaturely, 11, 283, 285
creaturely discernment, 260–63, 266, 275, 276–86
creaturely praise, 258
Crist, Eileen, 294–95, 308, 314

dark ecology, 78–79
dark green religion, 46
Darwin, Charles, 4, 233–34, 302–3
Darwin, Erasmus, 234
Davie, Grace, 85
death: as an offering to allow others to flourish, 253; in Christian tradition, 105–6; denial of, 323; fear and loss of control, 154; intertwined to place on earth, 252; of languages and culture, 3; as last enemy to be destroyed, 318; role in reconciliation and renewal, 161–62; salmon migrations, 170
decolonization, 161, 163, 226, 227–28
Deep Adaptation Movement, 6
deep de-extinction, 303–4, 305, 306–7, 309
Deep Ecology, 129
de-extinction: argument from coolness, 314–15; breeding, 300–301; case for, 306–10; coolness of, 313–15, 324; as disguised religion, 318–24; extinction denial, 296–300; as future oriented, 312–18; genetic engineering, 232–33, 300–301; good vibes argument, 310–12; mythic narrativization of, 294–95; obstacles to, 313; potential medical benefits, 314, 318–19; propriety (fittingness), 326; reintroduction of the revived, 304–5, 307–8; restoration of value, 308–9; Revive & Restore,

306, 312; risks and downsides, 303–6; as ritual of atonement, 317–18; salvation narrative as justification, 194; scientists as divine figures, 313, 319, 320; SCNT (somatic cell nuclear transfer), 300–302; self-deification, 317; synthetic biology, 300, 311, 319; technologies, 299–306; what does it mean to be human, 321–22; wonder and, 162. *See also* deep de-extinction; wonder; woolly mammoths

Deloria, Vine, Jr., 149, 165

Derrida, Jacques, 65, 76–77

Dillard, Annie, 196–97

dispensionalism, 195

displacement, 26, 42, 186–87, 198, 204, 206

domination: of humankind over nature, 22, 228; of the ocean, 223, 238; social relations of, 220

eagles: bald, 21, 158, 162, 166; feeding on salmon, 170, 249; role in mysticism, 162–63; in Wendat culture, 145–46, 148

Earth as home: Beheimatung, 211n46; *Body of God* (McFague), 195; definitions of home, 180–81; Eden-Exile-Return model, 199–200; home as fortress, 180–81, 183, 186, 200, 207; homelessness, 191–96; household, 178–79, 186, 197; as impermanent, 204; rehoming vs being at home, 200; technological salvation, 193; threat to terrestrial security, 182–83; uninhabitable, 188–89; unworlding, 204, 206

ecocide, 4, 214, 284–85

ecological catastrophes, 194

ecological novelties, 81–85; adaptation to fresh/saltwater, 82, 279–80; "being with," 90; confluence of mass death and novel life, 85–94; conservation, 81–82, 84; ecosystems, 86, 185; forms of ritual action, 62; human introduced, 299; religious reactions to, 63; scale of, 83; species settling into, 82–83

ecomelancholia, 88

ecomodernism, 293–94, 310–11. *See also* modernism

Eco-Paganism: antiroad movement, 99–100, 113–14, 120; Christianity and, 116, 117–24; compared with Contemporary Paganism, 116, 117, 122; counterculture (1960s), 113; as distinct from other Contemporary Paganism, 113, 131; Gaia, 120; nonviolent direct action (NVDA), 99, 113; origin story for, 114–16; protest camps, 16–17; relationship with sacred water, 117–24; subculture of Contemporary Paganism, 99, 113

ecopragmatism, 293, 296

eco-protest culture, 119

ecospirituality, 121, 238

ecotheology, 22, 23, 181, 182, 193, 196, 199, 202–3

Edgerton, W. Dow, 322

Edwards, Denis, 29

elephants, 107, 301, 302, 303

Eliade, Mircea, 89

endangered species: Asian elephants, 303; cost of media attention on, 179–80; eagle (shöndahkwa'), 158; Endangered Species Act, 29; environmentalism, 23; "ghost species," 3; modernism's relationship to, 19–20, 23; mourning the lesser known, 2–3; in River Avon, 216; showing up in material life, 25; survival tales of individual animals, 36–37; whales, 216–17; Wilson's half Earth thesis, 183. *See also* Saltmarsh Sparrow

the Enlightenment, 72, 258, 260–61
environmental activism, 8, 69, 113
environmental conservation: private religion and, 63
environmental ethics, 10, 19–20, 296, 299
environmental humanities, 47–48
environmentalism: and Christian belief in a world to come, 197; dark idiom of destruction, 293–94, 295; endangered species, 23; folk religion, 70–71; lament and grief, 73; new conservationism and, 293–94; postsecular presence of religion in, 75; relationship with Earth as home concept, 180. *See also* radical environmentalism
environmental science, 71, 83
epidemics, 146, 153–54
escapist eschatology, 194–95, 197–98, 204
eschatological imagination, 206–7
eschatological narratives, 11
eschatological salvation, 192–93
ethnobotany, 70
evolutionary biology, 233, 234–35
exclusive humanism, 31
exile: Abrahamic faiths, 181, 198, 204–5; creation narrative, 226; ecotheology and, 196–97; estrangement and, 201–2; religious perspective on, 202; return from, 201–2; stewardship, 202–3
exilic ecotheology, 202–3
exilic religion, 196–206
exilic theology, 194, 201
extinction: alternative hopes, 6; as antiseptic and distant, 165; appearance and, 63; attached to species, 306; capitalism, 12; as capitalistic opportunity, 309; as catalyst for reflection, 6; as concept, 9–10; death rituals and, 104–11;

defining, 2–4, 143, 158, 298–99; denial of, 296–300; as emptying of life, 191; endlings, 297–99; expectation of pure absence, 62; as form of world breaking, 202; habitat destruction, 217–18; as a hyperobject, 10; imagined (Tasmanian peoples), 74; migration and, 180, 181–91; as productive, 4; racism as driver of, 12; reactions to, 88; relationship with forced migration, 180; religion missing from discussion, 5; requires change in human through reflection, 324; species differentiation, 270–71; as symptom of human-centered worldview, 316; value and, 307–8; as work of providence, 28. *See also* Abrahamic faiths; anthropogenic extinctions; human exceptionalism; mass extinction; religion; rituals
extinction activism: demographics of, 7; engagement with death and mourning, 6; protest rituals in, 98. *See also* Extinction Rebellion (XR)
extinction discourses, focuses of, 179
Extinction Rebellion (XR): agenda, 236; Christianity and, 98–99, 117, 132; Contemporary Paganism and, 98–99, 100, 111–12; counterculture (1960s), 99–100, 113–14, 130; defining of extinction, 2; description as global, 7–8; die-ins, 105–6, 109–10, 125–26, 131; do not talk of Earth with reverence, 129–30; earth as home, 178; emphasis on human extinction, 126–27; empowerment through vulnerability, 130–31; "Faith Bridge" in demonstrations, 63; forms of protest, 5; history of, 99–100, 102; protest actions, 113, 119–20; protest death rituals, 98, 105–6, 110; protest ritual at Bath, 103, 124, 127, 131; Red

Brigade, 126, 126–27; roots of, 99–101. See also XR Christians
extinction studies, 12, 90–91, 92
Extinction Studies Working Group, 3–4

fascism, 74
Faust (Goethe), 221–24, 231–32, 294
Faust (Marlowe), 323
fear: Age of Loneliness, 182; death and loss of control, 154; habitat loss, 190; of hybridity, 185; and the potentially lost, 73; threats and, 185–86
feminism, 195, 200
fetishization, 92, 270, 298
Figueres, Christiana, 67
Fisher, Mark, 65
flight ways: ecological novelties and, 83; as expansive species, 96n36; living dead species, 80; mass extinction, 35, 36, 80, 83; religions, 48, 52
flood narrative, 225, 267–69. See also Noah and the flood
folk religion, 88
folk science, 88
forbidden knowledge, 319
Forest Church movement, 99, 129
fossil fuel extraction, 181
fragility, 72–73, 92, 130, 131, 219
Francis I, Pope, 178, 180, 239
Frankenstein myth, 294, 319
Freud, Sigmund, 75, 93
frogs, 2, 295, 318–19
Frozen Zoo (San Diego), 302, 304, 309

Gae Ho Hwako (Norma Jacobs), 142, 143, 165, 171
Gaia, 45, 122, 288n15
Gebara, Ivone, 192–93
Gemie, Sharif, 115, 116
genetic engineering, 232–33, 300–301
genocide, 27, 155, 278
geo-spiritual formations, 48
Germany, 38, 221

Ghosh, Amitav, 179
ghosts, 83, 90, 92, 143
glaciers, 60, 61. See also Okjökull (glacier)
Glastonbury: Chalice Well spring, 119, 120; the Early Church, 114–15; festival growth, 112–13; heritization of religion, 123–24; rivalry with Bath, 121; symbolic of shared territory between Christian and Pagan discourses, 114–15
Glissant, Édouard, 88–89, 93
globalization, 188
globalization movements: local-global dynamic, 120
Goddess Spirituality, 113, 114, 121
Goethe, William von, 221, 224, 233–34
Greely, Henry T., 313–14
Green Christianity, 114, 120, 124, 128–29, 130
greening of religion, 7, 246n49
Green movement, 102, 120, 127
Gregerson, Niels, 30
grief: as a crypt, 77; Haudenosaunee Condolence ceremony, 146–47, 158–59; of North American Indigenous peoples: Haudenosaunee Condolence, 169; opening up affects relations, 93; as quintessential part of ecological concern, 78
grolar bears, 83, 184
Grunwald, Michael, 282
Gudynas, Eduardo, 42
guilt, 92, 222, 310

Habermas, Jürgen, 66
habitat loss, 84, 142–43, 307
Haraway, Donna, 80, 90, 190
Hatley, James, 40–41, 165, 170
Havard, Gillies, 148, 160
hawk, 145, 145, 148–49, 158, 261
heath hen, 21–22, 305

Hebrew Bible, 38–39; the cathartic ocean, 219–20; creation as temporary, 191–92; Noach and the flood, 267–69, 274, 276, 285; praise, 254–56
Heise, Ursula, 17, 23, 36–37, 310
Hepburn, R. W., 324
Herlihy, David, 154
Hervieu-Léger, Danièle, 68
heteroprocity, 285
Hine, Dougald, 5
Hobsbawm, Eric, 88
Hollenbach, David, 206
Holmes, Rolston, III, 271
the Holocene, 48, 187–88
homelessness. *See* Earth as home
Horkheimer, Max, 221
hospitality, 186, 203, 205–6
Hughes, Ted, 238
human creatureliness, 324–25. *See also* creatureliness
human dominion, 228
human exceptionalism: creaturely discernment, 260–61; denial of mass extinction, 325; Endangered Species Act claimed as Noah's Ark, 29; faithlessness, 262; humans as creators, 297; modernism, 262; in religious ethics, 296; settler colonialism and, 32, 284; the sparrow as, 21–23; white exceptionalism, 30–31. *See also* humans
human extinction, 7
humanism, 31. *See also* posthumanism
humans: as creator, 319, 320, 322; as drivers of planetary change, 315; as feared species, 185–86; as gods, 319; as limited creatures, 323; as a living kind, 257; as nature's saviors, 296, 297; place in ordering of creatures, 256; as planetary managers, 294, 295; relationship to animals, 260; upright posture, 259–60. *See also* human exceptionalism

humility: absence of, 266; anarchical, 262–63, 285; radical, 262–63; wonder and, 324

identity: Canadian, 155; Contemporary Paganism, 111–12, 115; death rituals and, 109; guaranteed homeland, 189; heritagization and, 119; imperial logic, 199; national, 190; relational identity theory, 101–4, 124; resilience, 207; strangers in a strange land, 205; white, 182, 189
Imitatio Dei, 267
imperialism, 199, 219
incarnation discourse, 30–31
Indigenous peoples: cosmovisions, 42–43; creation narratives, 234, 284; displacement, 26, 201; extinction as form of world breaking, 202; interpretations of extinction, 42–43; Standing Rock Sioux reservation uprising, 7–8, 45, 46; storytelling practices, 285
Indigenous sovereignty, 31–32, 42
industrialism, 19–20, 143, 155, 217
industrialization, 155, 215, 216, 221, 281
infanticide, 221–22
Innis, Harold, 155
Intergovernmental Science-Policy Platform on Biodiversity and Ecosystem Services, 35, 63, 242n11, 297
International Union for Conservation of Nature and Natural Resources Red List of Threatened Species, 2, 18, 25
Islam, 179, 204, 220. *See also* Abrahamic faiths

James, Jennifer, 79
Jantzen, Grace, 192
Japan, 253, 277
Jenkins, Willis, 65, 180, 296

Jennings, Bruce, 322
Jennings, Willie, 25–26, 27, 31
Jesuits: conversion of Indigenous peoples, 146, 153, 155, 157; mission to convert, 146; origin story of Indigenous peoples, 153; translators, 142, 148–49. *See also* Charlevoix, Pierre-François-Xavier de
Johnson, Elizabeth, 30
Judaism: creatio ex nihilo, 219–20, 242–43n17; creation as the abode for creaturely existence, 179; forced displacement, 204; midrashic, 250, 285; the prophet in exile, 203–4; tehomophobia, 219–21, 225; transcendence, 284–85. *See also* Abrahamic faiths
Jurassic Park (film), 294, 301
justice, xi, 28, 42, 94, 195, 202, 266, 314; injustice, 4, 12, 41, 169–170, 197, 205–206; reparative justice, 307, 310; restorative justice, 306; species justice, 295

Kanagy, Conrad L., 7
Kant, Immanuel, 256–57, 258
Keller, Catherine, 10, 164, 219, 225–26, 230, 231
Kent, 111, 127
Kidwell, Jeremy H., 185, 208
Kimmerer, Robin Wall, 156, 160, 161, 162, 167–68
kingdom of ends, 256–60
Kingsnorth, Paul, 5
Kondiaronk: Condolence ceremonies, 146–47, 158–59; death ceremony, 147, 167; death of, 153, 160; life, 146–47; Tree of Peace on the highest mountain, 139, 140; vision of relational living, 156, 161. *See also* Wendat
Kosselek, Reinhart, 87
Krantz, David, 237

lament: death rituals as, 110; function of, 92; response to mass death, 83–84
landscapes/landforms, facing extinction, 3
LaPier, Roslyn R., 43
Latour, Bruno, 45, 188, 189, 190, 200n13
Laudato Si' (Francis I), 32, 246n48
the Lazarus Project, 318
Lazarus story, 125, 294
Leduc, Timothy B., 8; ethnobotany, 70
Legge, Marilyn, 161
Letcher, Andy, 113, 116–17
Leuba, James H., 66
Levinas, Emmanuel, 250, 287n2, 288–89n16, 291n40, 292n50
liberationism, 23, 200
Lichterman, Paul, 66
Lien, Marianne Elisabeth, 280–81
Little Ice Age, 153–54
living dead species, 80
Lonesome George, 298
Luckmann, Thomas, 68

Macy, Joanne, 129
mammophant, 303, 308
mammoths. *See* woolly mammoths
Marder, Elissa, 75, 76
marginalization: hierarchical violence and, 157; movements and class, 102; sacred space, 128; of the sparrow, 27–28; via secularism, 48
Marian, Simion Florea, 106
Marx, Karl, 87
Marxism, 87–88
mass extinction: 2019 Global Assessment Report from the Intergovernmental Science-Policy Platform on Biodiversity and Ecosystem Services, 35; anthropogenic drivers of, 19; asymmetry between moral agency and planetary stress, 44; blissonance, 40; bound to the land, 25–26;

mass extinction (*cont.*)
  care for oppressed people, 21, 22;
  classification of species and, 33–34;
  creaturely wonder complicates, 325;
  cultural production in everyday life,
  24–25; declensionist framework, 182;
  as declensionist, 296; the disposable
  life, 20–21, 296; endangered species,
  25, 36–37; endlings, 297–98;
  Extinction Studies (van Dooren,
  Bird, Chrulew), 35; *Facing the
  Planetary* (Connolly), 44; fantastic
  hegemonic ignorance, 23–27; flight
  ways, 35, 36, 80, 83; as fulfillment of
  end-time prophecy, 195; ghosts, 92;
  human exceptionalism, 21–23, 32;
  Imagining Extinction (Heise), 17;
  Indigenous cosmovisions, 42–43;
  Indigenous interpretations, 42–43;
  Indigenous sovereignty, 32; insect
  decline, 16–17, 22, 38, 39, 40, 51; *Jesus
  and the Disinherited* (Thurman), 27;
  lament, 92; love, 23, 51; marginality
  as significant, 27–33; Noach and the
  flood, 267–69; redemption, 29, 31;
  relationship to ecological relations,
  26–27; religious narratives and,
  41–42; rights of all species to exist,
  28, 34; sign of corruption of the
  modern industrial order, 19–20,
  23; sixth mass extinction, 1, 41, 142,
  183, 187; species loss, 33–34, 35–36;
  spirituality of freedom, 44–45;
  stories of extinction as part of human
  identity, 17, 32; theology of, 11;
  white supremacy, 22, 25–26. *See also*
  extinction; International Union for
  Conservation of Nature and Natural
  Resources Red List of Threatened
  Species; Saltmarsh Sparrow; the
  sparrow; swarms
McFague, Sallie, 195, 197
McFarland Taylor, Sarah, 69, 193

Medred, Craig, 277
melancholia, 75, 79, 80, 93
memorialization, 62, 124–25, 130
Mezrich, Ben, 312–13, 315
Midgley, Mary, 196
migration: in Abrahamic faiths,
  204–5; assistance to animals, 180,
  186, 203; assisted, 203, 205; climate
  refugees, 182, 186, 187; defined, 180;
  due to climate change, 182–83; end
  of refuge, 190; exodus as concept to
  build community, 190; forced, 198,
  203, 205–6; founding narratives of
  Abrahamic faiths, 195; hazard and,
  184–85; hybridity and, 184, 185;
  immobility through detention, 189;
  in Jewish and Muslim histories, 204;
  loss of lifestyle, 187–89; migratory
  crisis, 188–90; narratives, 185,
  198–99; problem of mass movement,
  183–84; as resilience, 205; security
  and, 182–83, 185–86, 207; as surplus
  of life, 191
millenarianism, 113–14, 116
millennialist eschatology, 194
Mills, Charles, 31
Minteer, Ben, 316–17
Mitchell, Audra, 27, 34, 51
modernism: expansion, 143; fragility,
  72; human exceptionalism, 262;
  The Legitimacy of the Modern Age
  (Blumenberg), 87; linear orientation
  of time, 87–88; mastery of nature, 221;
  nature as resource, 165; relationship
  to endangerment and extinctions,
  19–20, 23. *See also* ecomodernism
modernity: Eco-Pagans, 120;
  entzauberung, 118; expectations
  of purity, 62; Green Christianity,
  114; millinarian, 113; protest
  camps, 117; tehomophobia, 224–25;
  Tolkienesque, 113. *See also* Faust
  (Goethe)

Mohawk, John, 157
Moody, Dwight L., 195
Morton, Timothy, 47, 78–79; hyperobjects: ambiguity, 10; need to adopt new forms of care and collaboration, 86
mourning: the crypt, 76–77; "don't mourn, organize," 300; ecological grief, 75, 77; in extinction discussions, 4, 5; hauntology, 65; losses not yet absent, 64–65, 92; Okjökull (glacier), 61–62, 64, 71, 91; proleptic elegies, 74, 77–78, 92; proleptic grieving (anticipatory), 73; proleptic mourning, 77; protest death rituals, 110–11; psychoanalytical approaches to, 75–76, 79; ritual as boundary between life and death, 107; rituals of, 73, 77, 80, 92. *See also* Okjökull (glacier)
Mueller, Martin Lee, 279, 281, 283, 284
murmuration, 17, 43–49, 52
Musk, Elon, 193, 195

Nash, Jim, 28–29, 34
nationalism, 206
neoliberalism, 6–7, 183
new animism, 47
new conservationism, 293–94, 310–11
new religious movements, 5, 90
Neyrat, Frédéric, 311
Nicholsen, Shierry, 178
Nita, Maria, 73, 90, 92–93
Noah and the flood, 267–69, 274, 276, 285, 321
Nongbri, Brent, 66, 67, 68, 71, 176n84
nonhistory, 88–89, 93
North Cascades, 60–61, 93–94
Northcott, Michael, 23–24, 194
Norway, 279, 280
nostalgia, 22, 72, 93
Novak, Ben, 312, 315

oak trees, 151, 154, 157, 160
the ocean: the cathartic ocean, 219–20, 225; creatio ex profundis and cobecoming, 230–35; cry of the earth, 239; domination, 223, 238; fish stocks, 213, 218, 236, 237, 276–77, 279; goodness of the ocean, 228–29; hydrological terrorism, 224; Leviathan, 225, 228–29, 269; as life giving, 232–34; life originated in, 233–35; PCBs in marine environments, 217; "Psalm of the Sea" (Krantz), 237–38; role in heat distribution, 235; sea monsters, 255; tehomophobia, 220–21, 225; *Temple of Nature; or, The Origin of Society* (Darwin), 234; the Wisdom tradition, 229; a world of wounds, 116; wounds inflicted upon (list), 218, 236. *See also* salmon
O'Dell-Chaib, Courtney, 79
O'Hara, David, 249
Okjökull (glacier), 61–62, 64, 71, 91
Onaubinisay, Jim Dumont, 176n84
onerahtase'ko:wa (white pine), 139, 140, 144, 148–49, 150; about, 139, 140; geographical location, 139; oak sapling and, 151, 157, 160; offering gratitude, 144; role as clan signature, 148–49, 150; use in European shipbuilding, 154
optimism, 72, 73, 84, 294, 297, 310–11, 312–13, 320
Orsi, Robert, 69
otherness, 79, 160, 161, 164

Pacific Islanders, 182
Patton, Kimberly, 218–19
paranoiesis, 272–73, 285
passenger pigeons, 21, 27, 73, 294, 295, 302, 312
Pentecostal Christianity, 69, 81
plankton, 217–18

Pleistocene megafauna, 295, 306–7. *See also* woolly mammoths
Pleistocene Park, 329n39
Plumwood, Val, 157
Pluto, 105
polar bears, 184, 185, 186, 202
political theology, 74–75, 194, 198
political theory, 20, 23, 25–26, 32, 45–46
postcolonial critical theory, 66–69, 205
post-denial, 6
posthumanism, 46–47. *See also* humanism
postsecularism, 7, 62, 64, 65, 66, 75, 121
postsecular religion, 84–85
poststructuralism, 231
Poveda, Oriol, 47–48
praise: by all of creation, 254–55; the creaturely, 258–59; creaturely discernment, 260–63, 266; for eating other creatures, 263–67, 273–76; hallelujah as, 254–55; midrashic, 250–51, 255–56; reciprocity, 262–63, 264–65; *Tehlillim*, 287–88n13. *See also* creaturely praise; vultures
presence and absence, 80–81
Preston, Christopher, 317
private religion and public religion, 63–64
privilege: climate movement and, 102; displacement and, 187; elegized in activism, 77; human migration and, 181, 188; rituals of mourning, 80, 92; solidarity, 78; space, 188–89; white, 79
process philosophy, 87, 93, 97n47
process theology, 231
protest death rituals: antinuclear protests, 99–100; die-in rituals, 109–10; die-ins, 105–6, 109–10, 125–26, 131; extinction and, 124–25, 130; in Extinction Rebellion (XR), 98, 105–6; Green Christian movement, 99; Green Christian protest, *105*, 106; humor, 127–28; relational analysis of, 101–4; symbolism in, 98, 100, 102, 106, 111, 128
public religion and private religion, 63–64
Pyrenean ibex, 301, 303–4

Queer ecology, 86–87
Qur'an, 39, 192

radical disempowerment, 228
radical environmentalism, 113
Radical Presence, 124, 129
Ranger, Terence, 88
Rashi, 289
redemption, 29, 31, 224, 225, 317, 318
red-tailed hawk, 150
red-tailed hawk feather, 145, *145*
Regis, Ed, 319
Reid, Julian, 183, 185
relational epistemology, 149, 156–57, 158, 160
relational identity theory, 101, 124
relational living: adoptive intention, 160–61; appropriating otherness to eradicate it, 148, 160, 164; benefits of, 166; broken cultural protocols, 143–44; Canadian control over Indigenous land and resources, 155; colonizers' desire to transcend, 152, 154; double death, 144–45, 158, 159, 164, 168–69, 170; the Ganǫhǫnyǫhk (Thanksgiving Address), 142, 145, 149, 156–57, 166; Haudenosaunee condolence ceremony, 146–48, 166; hawk (yändehsonhk), 145, *145*, 148–49, 158, 163; multifaith ceremonies, 147, 149; sun representing divinity, 153; via naturaliza, 163–65; via negativa, 163–64; windigo, 156, 157, 159, 170. *See also* cobecoming; Kondiaronk; onerahtase'ko:wa (white pine); Tree of Peace

relationships. *See* relational identity theory
relativism, 3
religion: believing without belonging, 85; bias in book, 11–12; call by United Nations (UN) Framework Convention on Climate Change, 67; Dark Mountain Project, 5; deep green religion, 90; environmental injustice and, 12; environmental science and, 71; facing a threat of extinction, 84–85; flight ways, 48, 52; fostering living relationally, 144–45; fragility in public, 63–64; illness and healing, 125; missing from extinction discussion, 5, 296; as murmuration, 17; negative impact on ecological awareness, 191–92; power of, 13; privatization of, 65; reactions to novelty, 63; Religion vs, 161–62; as response to extinction, 7; resurgence in, 9; study of ultimate things, 10–11
religion, defining: as a category, 12; folk, 69–71, 85, 86; *The Invisible Religion* (Luckman), 68; lack of homogeneity, 69–70; postcolonial critical theory, 66–69; *Psychological Study of Religion* (Leuba), 66; sociology of religion, 90–91; Tweed's summary, 50–51
religious ethics: attention to extinction, 16, 193, 296; of hospitality, 205–6;
Saltmarsh Sparrow, 19, 296
resurrection biology, 294. *See also* de-extinction
Rigby, Kate, 121, 163–64
rituals: activism and, 77; as boundary between life and death, 107; death rituals, 106, 109–10, 124–25, 126; Deep Ecology, 129; of loss and lament, 92; of mourning, 73, 77, 80, 92; mourning Okjökull (glacier), 61–62, 64, 71, 91; proleptic grieving (anticipatory), 73; relational analysis of, 101–4;

in response to ecological crisis, 5; response to mass death, 83–84; Romanian funerals, 106, 107–9. *See also* protest death rituals
Romania, 103, 104, 106, 107–9, 115, 138n91
Rose, Deborah Bird, 13, 52, 288n14; collaborative life and death, 167; double death, 144, 158, 164; Indigenous teachers from Australia: teaching about extinction, 144; need to respond to collective death, 35
The Routledge Handbook of Religion and Ecology, 9
Rowlands, Anna, 189, 205

the sacred: in everyday lives, 143; illness and, 130; Intergovernmental Science-Policy Platform on Biodiversity and Ecosystem Services, 63; mourning, 75; mud in Wendat origin stories, 150; need to reconceptualize, 131–32; religious traditions and, 196; the sea as, 219
sacred waters: in Bath, 12, 120–22, 127, 215–16; Chalice Well spring, 103, 119, 120, 121, 123; Contemporary Paganism, 101, 121; as healing, 103, 118, 119, 121; Romania, 103, 104, 138n91; secularism and, 123–24
Said, Edward, 205
salmon: anthropogenic species metacide, 278–79; cataclysmic treatment of, 268; changes in population, 276–77; deaths allow others to flourish, 253, 263–64; farmed, 277–78, 279–82; as food for others, 249, 263–64, 266; luminous embodiment of, 284; as a mechanism, 283; place in ordering of creatures, 256; reciprocity, 262–63, 264–65; relationship to habitat, 251–52; restoring historic runs, 277–78;

salmon (*cont.*)
  spawning, 247–50, 252–53, 257, 266–67; species differentiation, 270–71
Saltmarsh Sparrow: about, 18–19, 33; capitalism and, 23–24; colonialism and, 23–24; creaturely peril, 27; diet, 37–38; eternal life and, 29; as God's incarnation, 30; Indigenous caretakers of territory, 31–32; love and, 51; need for mobility, 37; North Atlantic Christianity, 16; on Red List, 18, 25; species loss, 33–34. *See also* the sparrow
salvation, 193–94, 199–200, 318
Sandler, Ronald, 22, 306, 307, 309–10, 328, 328n20
Schaefer, Donovan, 39–40
scientific practice, 70
Scott, Duncan Campbell, 155
Scott, Paul, 199
sea monsters, 255. *See also* chaos monster
secularism, 6–7, 9, 48, 65–66, 123–24
settler colonialism. *See* colonialism
Shapiro, Beth, 313, 315
Shephard, Paul, 157
Sherkow, Jacob, 313–14
Shiva, Vandana, 157
shöndahkwa' (eagles). *See* eagles
Sideris, Lisa, 79, 162, 194, 232–33
Silliman, Brian R., 82
Sioui, Georges, 141, 148, 151, 152, 160, 167, 169
Skrimshire, Stefan, 83, 84, 217, 294
Smith, Jonathan Z., 66
social movements. *See* activism; extinction activism; Extinction Rebellion (XR)
sojourn, 195–97, 204
solastalgia, 40, 73, 81
solidarity: exile and, 201; migration, 181; new forms of, 78; result of mass extinctions, 74, 76, 94; sparrow as icon of, 22; through exile, 203
Solnit, Rebecca, 325
Soskice, Janet, 220
soteriology, 30, 31
Southgate, Christopher, 29, 186, 203, 205
sovereignty: Indigenous, 31–32, 42; national, 186, 199; over the ocean, 224–25; place based, 42, 205; place of birth, 190
the sparrow: as a disposable life, 20–21, 296; "His Eye Is on the Sparrow" (hymn), 22–23; marginality as significant, 27–33; rescue and redemption, 29; as sign of love, 23. *See also* Saltmarsh Sparrow
species: decline, 38; defining, 271; effect of extinctions on migration, 182–83; endlings, 297–98, 299; loss of specific, 73–74; personal names, 297–98; as specimen, 299
species metacide, 283, 284–85
Srokosz, Meric, 219
Standing Rock Sioux reservation uprising, 7–8, 45, 46
Starhawk, 113–14
stem cells, 302
Stewart, Margaret Marion, 121, 238
Strine, Casey, 198–99
the sublime, 6, 315–16
suicide, 98–99, 110, 111
swarming: of people, 182, 207, 263; politics of, 44; in the sea, 251, 252, 263
swarms, 37–43, 49–52; allelomimesis, 43, 44, 50, 52; bird migration, 49–50; blissonance, 40; conveys disaster across religions, 39; as divine judgment, 39; feeding salmon, 282; in Hebrew Bible, 38–39; insect, 22, 51; locusts, 44; militant pluralist assemblage, 44–45, 50, 52; murmuration, 17, 43–49, 52; religious,

22; salmon spawning, 253; spirituality of freedom, 44–45
Swart, Sandra, 319
sympatry, 271–72
Szerszynski, Broniclaw, 18

Tasmanian tiger (thylacine), 295
Taylor, Bron Raymond, 46, 90
Taylor, Charles, 47
techniques of cosmopolitical care, 51–52
technology, 4, 6, 72, 89, 154, 162, 193–4, 206, 218–223, 232, 236–8, 294–326; biotechnology, 299, 308, 325
tehom, 219, 225–27, 231
tehomophobia, 219, 221, 224–25, 243n27
temporality: disruption, 83; freedom and ghosts, 90; history, 88–89; linear orientation of time, 87–88; pluralizing history, 88–89; temporal reorientation, 86–87; of "traditional" societies, 89
theological anthropology, 294
theological ethics, 11, 20
theological imaginaries, 191
theological scholarship, 11
theology of creation, 214
theopolitical imaginary, 80
Theriault, Noah, 202
Thomas, Jacob, 140, 145
Thurman, Howard, 27
Tillich, Paul, 28
Tinker, Tink, 31–32
Todd, Zoe, 43
Tolkien, J. R. R., 113, 116–17
Torok, Maria, 76
Townes, Emilie, 24–25
Tree of Peace: clarifies responsibility for relational living, 150–51; fallen in windstorm, 142, 151–52, 157, 158–60; Ganǫhǫnyǫhk (Thanksgiving Address), 142, 143, 145; Gayensra'go:wa (Great Law or Tree of Peace), 139–40; guardian birds of prey, 145–46, 148–49, 158; importance of Haudenosaunee condolence ceremony, 146–47; Jesuit translators, 142, 148–49; negotiations in Montreal, 140–41, 147–48; opening of space for spirits, 149; raising of, 139, 140; relational living, 142, 156, 167–68; replanting of, 170–71; Sewatokwa'tshera't (Dish with One Spoon), 141, 151, 156, 159, 159, 160, 164, 166, 168–69; treaty signed with pictographs for clans, 149–50, 151, 160, 164; via naturaliza, 165; violation of values through colonial practices, 154, 164
Tsing, Anna, 89–90, 190
Tweed, Thomas A., 50–51

United Church of Canada, 161
United Kingdom: asylum seekers, 189; Church of England, 238–39; Contemporary Paganism, 111, 112, 114–15; the Early Church, 114, 115; Eco-Paganism in, 114–16, 117; Extinction Rebellion (XR) in, 5, 7–8, 99; River Avon, 215–16; sacred springs, 103–4, 118–22
United Nations: 2018 global assessment report on biodiversity, 178; Christiana Figueres, 67
United States: declining freshwater alligators, 82; Frozen Zoo (San Diego), 302, 304, 309; Interfaith Oceans campaign, 236–37; as postsecular society, 66; premillennialist apocalypticism, 194; Whole Earth festival, 122
US Endangered Species Act, 29

van Dooren, Thom, 35, 36–37, 48, 51–52, 96n36, 299
vertebrate extinctions, 179–80

vertebrate species decline, 38
via naturaliza, 163–65
via negativa, 163–64, 170, 231
virtue theory, 40
Vondey, Wolfgang, 69
vulnerability: and community, 207; creatureliness, 320; and Extinction Rebellion (XR), 98, 117, 130–31; Saltmarsh Sparrow, 18, 25, 30, 37; though empowerment, 130–31; wondering and, 324–25
vultures, 261, 263, 269

Wallace, Mark, 27, 28
Wallace-Wells, David, 179
Walzer, Michael, 66
Watson, Rebecca, 219
Weber, Max, 118
Wendat: guardian clan, 148; Sky Woman's fall, 150, 152, 167–68. *See also* Kondiaronk
Weston, Anthony, 275
Weston, Kath, 47
whales, 216–17, 230
whaling, 216, 236
White, Lynn, Jr., 191–92
Whitehead, Alfred North, 97n47, 231, 232
white supremacy: Christian theology, 21, 22; cultural production in everyday life, 24–25; linked to ecological destruction, 22; role in theological coproduction of ignorance, 25–26
Whittle, Patrick Michael, 314–15
Whyte, Kyle Powys, 43
Willits, Fern K., 7
Williams, Rowan, 323–24
Wilson, Edward O., 182
wolves, 306
wonder: alignment with anthropocentric values, 309; coolness as, 313–14; creatureliness and, 324–25; as driving de-extinction, 310–12; fittingness, 326; goad to innovation, 300; as interrogative impulse, 322; as motivation for de-extinction, 295, 305–6, 310; as product of de-extinction, 295; a questioning mode, 321; shallow claims to, 300, 313–14; the sublime, 316; turned inward vs outward, 316–17
woolly mammoths, 295, 302–3, 308, 312, 313, 314, 315, 319, 329n39, 330n61
Wray, Britt, 320
Wuthnow, Robert, 68

XR Christians, 106. *See also* Extinction Rebellion (XR)

yändehsonhk. *See* hawk
Yi Fu Tuan, 197–98

Zornberg, Avivah Gottlieb, 259

For Indiana University Press
Emily Baugh, Editorial Assistant
Brian Carroll, Rights Manager
Gary Dunham, Acquisitions Editor and Director
Anna Francis, Assistant Acquisitions Editor
Brenna Hosman, Production Coordinator
Katie Huggins, Production Manager
David Miller, Lead Project Manager/Editor
Dan Pyle, Online Publishing Manager
Stephen Williams, Marketing and Publicity Manager
Jennifer Witzke, Senior Artist and Book Designer

www.ingramcontent.com/pod-product-compliance
Lightning Source LLC
Chambersburg PA
CBHW021815300426
44114CB00009BA/184